Supervision and the Improvement of Instruction

Supervision and the improvement of instruction

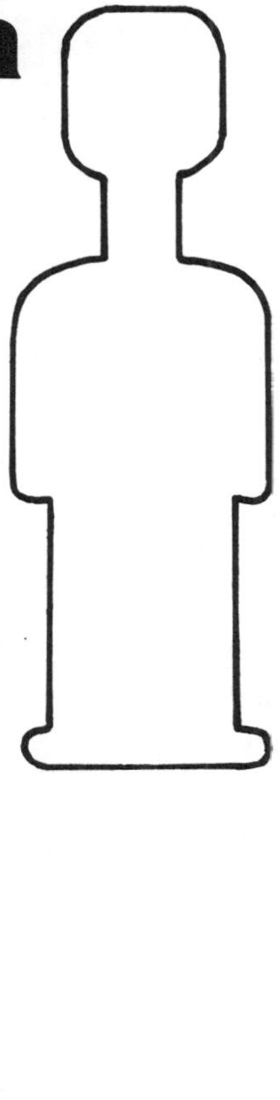

NATHAN STOLLER
HUNTER COLLEGE,
CITY UNIVERSITY OF NEW YORK

EDUCATIONAL TECHNOLOGY PUBLICATIONS
ENGLEWOOD CLIFFS, NEW JERSEY 07632

Library of Congress Cataloging in Publication Data

Stoller, Nathan.
Supervision and the improvement of instruction.

Bibliography: p.
Includes index.
1. School supervision. I. Title.
LB2822.S75 371.1'02 77-26097
ISBN 0-87778-103-6

Printed in the United States of America.

Library of Congress Catalog Card Number:
77-26097.

International Standard Book Number:
0-87778-103-6.

First Printing: February, 1978.

To Dr. May Violet Seagoe

Professor Emeritus

University of California
Los Angeles

Preface

Dear ZA,

I began this work after making two decisions:

- that although supervision in education is not an established academic discipline, there are many supervisors who could make productive use of a guide to their conduct; and
- that such a guide would be hampered by the usual third-person impersonal textbook format.

So I began to write a first-person manuscript, of direct communication between you and me, ZA, you being all the pre-service and in-service supervision students I have had, with first and last names ranging from Z to A.

But as I wrote and as I imagined you reading, I also began to hear what many of those ZA's had said in class in response to the ideas I was presenting here. So what began as one-way communication from NS to ZA turned into a discourse between the collective you, ZA, and the single me.

Before we hear the "overture" in Chapter I, please listen to a *most important caution*:

There are complete transcriptions of four lessons and five post-observation conferences in this discourse. All four lessons plus the first four conferences include teachers who must be classified as "traditional," no matter how you define the term. (The last conference has an open-classroom teacher as its protagonist.) *This does NOT mean that I stand eight-to-one in favor of traditional instruction.* When you've read the full discourse and studied the Empirical Grid and the Primitive Assessment Tool, you'll see that I'm anything but a traditionalist.

The distribution is what it is because I believe that the ratio of traditional to all other "more open" forms of instruction is surely at least 8-to-1 and very likely nearer 99-to-1. Since I believe in beginning "where the learner is," and since I see him doing mainly traditional teaching, I include so many such lessons and conferences.

What I *advocate* is consonance with Principles of Learning. Since I don't see any *labelled* form of instruction as substantially in consonance with Principles of Learning, I refuse to assign a label to my point of view. But if you insist on giving me one, ZA, why then call me a Seagoe-ist, after Prof. May V. Seagoe, to whom this book is dedicated and who wrote my two educational bibles: *A Teacher's Guide to the Learning Process*, and *The Learning Process and School Practice.*

N.S.

Acknowledgments

To: Susan Bertelmann, Barbara Binghi, Joan Campbell, Cynthia Cashman, Dennis Franco, Evelyn Fulton, Paul Morris, Barbara Murray, Rafaella Pandolfo, Stanley Pogrow, Stephen Radin, Milton Shapiro, Carole Sklerov, Michael Skodnick, Willard Smith, Linda Waldman, John Wittekind

This list includes teachers whose videotaped teaching I have used in my supervision classes, teachers who permitted me to record my post-observation conferences with them for my personal study, and one teacher who facilitated my efforts to do videotaping in a particular school.

Six of the above, who must remain hidden among their colleagues, are the true protagonists here. Without their professional dedication and their willingness to be quoted verbatim, this volume could not have been written. My gratitude to them is infinite.

Prof. May V. Seagoe read portions of the manuscript and made valuable suggestions about its contents. Mrs. Dorothy H. Johnson gave me considerable personal and professional support, in addition to reading portions of the manuscript. And my wife, Selma, who proofread all the typing, patiently bore all the usual burdens of an author's spouse. I am most grateful to each and all of them for their help and support.

The discourse contained in this volume could not have been

produced without the memories of the many supervision students who took such an interest in my views as to give me the full benefit of their diverse opinions.

Table of Contents

Supervision and the Improvement of Instruction

I.

Overture

Before we raise the curtain on the substance of this book, ZA, let's look at its several themes. My major theses are:

A. That researchers and writers in the field of learning have begun to codify their data into what some of them call "Principles of Learning." One strand of my ideas about supervision deals with the translation of such principles into observable classroom behavior of teachers and students. I will be presenting you with material to explain and illustrate how one can apply such a translation to the analysis of that observable behavior. My premise is this: if there are valid statements that describe instructional conditions which optimize learning, then we should be looking for instructional behavior which is consonant with those principles of learning.

B. That no teacher gets as much as 10 percent supervision, because the principals, assistant principals, and department chairpersons wear two hats, one of which (administrator) is worn much more often than the other (supervisor). All the in-service ZA's in my classes have always agreed that whether they teach 900 hours per year (five hours per day for 180 days) or some smaller total, none has had his instruction under study by another professional for 90 hours or 10 percent of the time. Schools have not seen it necessary to devote that much professional time to such intimate and concentrated observation of teaching practices. But even if they did (or do), teachers are still alone with their students 90 percent of the time.

My premise is this: if teachers are alone with their students 90 percent of the time, then a major objective of supervision should be to help teachers to master a means of self-supervision. After we have worked our way through the analysis strand in this book, I will present material to explain, rationalize, and illustrate a supervisory cycle with just that objective in mind.

As of this writing, ZA, there are two supervisory cycles available for study, one by Cogan[1] and another by Goldhammer.[2] I consider both books "must" readings in the field, and urge you to study both of them. However, I have decided not to compare them with each other nor to contrast my supervisory cycle with theirs. Supervision is a long way from being a discipline. It has no generally accepted set of parameters, and even lacks a precise and universal definition. In the absence of such definitions, and lacking yardsticks against which to measure any given supervisory cycle, any comparisons I might make would hardly serve as definitive evaluations. What we need is a massive effort to test a variety of cycles so as to accumulate data for study and analysis.

Now, I am well aware that Amidon, Bellack, Flanders, Medley, and others[3] have developed a host of classroom interaction analysis instruments. You should also examine and study these instruments, ZA, at the very least to the extent of a careful review of *Mirrors for Behavior*. But many of these are research tools, and not particularly practical for day-to-day supervision. I shall also not compare my PAT ("Primitive Assessment Tool") (see Chapter VIII) with any of theirs. That too would require a massive study based on most defensible definitions and criteria.

Instead, I propose to set before you a rationale for each of my two strands. If you are currently an administrator/supervisor, you will be able to weigh the rationales and their implementation against your daily experiences. If you are a classroom teacher, you will at least be in a position to see whether my PAT provides you with useful data and whether my supervisory cycle has merit when used with you by supervisors and fellow teachers. Since the largest majority of my supervision students are classroom teachers, I can vouch for the practicality and value of my suggestions. I require my students to apply both strands.

Notes

1. Cogan, Morris L. *Clinical Supervision*. Boston: Houghton Miflin Company, 1973.

2. Goldhammer, Robert. *Clinical Supervision: Special Methods for the Supervision of Teachers*. New York: Holt, Rinehart, and Winston, 1969.

3. Simon, Anita, and Boyer, E. Gil. *Mirrors for Behavior III. An Anthology of Observation Instruments*. Wyncote, Pa.: Communications Materials Center, Inc., 1974.

II.

Definitions and Questions

Since I see supervision as the title for a process whose unique content is the improvement of instruction, and since you already know me to be a stickler for definitions, ZA, let's define terms. I would like to proceed backwards, defining INSTRUCTION and IMPROVEMENT before SUPERVISION, because the latter is, after all, our main focus.

My dictionary[1] says that *instruction* means "education; knowledge, information, etc. given or taught; any teaching; lesson." Since the curricula of schools and colleges do not now and may never include all the knowledge and information in the world (like walking the tight rope, being a juggler, becoming an astronaut, etc.), the meaning of instruction seems to contribute little to understanding supervision.

On the surface, *improvement* seems clear enough: "an increase in value or in excellence of quality or condition"; etc. The major issue is the yardstick which tells us the present quality and condition of instruction and which helps us determine whether and when there has been an increase.

Supervision is "direction; management"–which takes on a clearer meaning when we look up *supervise:* "to oversee or direct (work, workers, a project, etc.); superintend." From *oversee* we get "to survey; watch." From *direct* we get "to manage the affairs of; guide; conduct; regulate; control; give authoritative instructions to; ordain (that a thing be done); order; command; to move, turn or point (a person or thing) toward a place, object or goal; aim; head."

Therefore, supervision as the improvement of instruction seems to be concerned with

–overseeing, directing, guiding, conducting, regulating, controlling, moving toward a goal, etc.

–workers (teachers), who give or teach knowledge or information

–in such a manner that there is a resulting "increase in value or in excellence of quality or condition."

Which, in turn, raises a series of questions:

I. Which "knowledge, information, etc." is to be "given or taught"? Who decides? How? Why?

II. Who gives "education" or teaches "knowledge, information, etc."? Who is *a* (*the*) teacher? What is teaching?

III. Since "an increase in value or in excellence of quality or condition" implies criteria or goals: Are there goals for instruction? Who defined them? How? What are these goals? How is movement toward them detected and measured?

IV. Is it possible to define manners of teaching which result in movement toward goals and in an "increase in value . . ."?

V. By means of what techniques does one oversee, direct, guide, etc., the teachers? Who uses these techniques? Why?

I don't really intend to deal with each of these questions in detail, ZA. It's just that my ideas about the first three form a necessary context for the last two. So bear with me.

Note

1. *Webster's New World Dictionary of the American Language* (College Edition). New York: The World Publishing Company, 1962. (*N.B.*–All further dictionary references will be to this publication.)

III.

Knowledge and Information

I expect that you and your colleagues, ZA, have already been exposed to readings, lectures, and discussions on "Which knowledge, information, etc. is to be given or taught? Who decides? Why? How?" Here is my view.

There is no single "who" that decides on the knowledge and information to be taught. But no matter who that is, he is (they are) bound by an obvious restriction: there is encyclopedic knowledge and information available in this world, in quantity beyond the capacity of any single human brain. Thus, each statement about what should be taught is some selection from this enormous storehouse.

Secondly, the notion that certain things should be taught to certain learners at certain times is just that: a notion. It is *not* a scientific fact, principle, or concept. It *is* an expression of that person's view of what the goals of schooling are. As such it is fallible; its premises are moot. Supervisors of instruction should be as concerned about these premises as they are about the actual knowledge proposed for study.

Thirdly, even if there were an official, single, authoritative, definitive source of what should be studied, and even if that source communicated its dicta in prescriptive documents, these prescriptions could not, in actual reality, be regarded as *design*, because they would affect students only through the actions of teachers, who cannot be programed like computers.

I define *design* as the combination of those activities and experiences planned, executed, and controlled by the teacher (or teachers) on behalf of students.

Which you are to interpret as meaning: (1) that even the most competent teacher takes the course-of-study and the curriculum bulletins and adapts them to his own capabilities and to his expectations of what he can accomplish with his particular students at a particular time; (2) that activities and experiences which do not turn out as the teacher planned them, or which escape his full control, are nonetheless still *design*; (3) but that experiences in and around the school which the teacher does not and can not plan for, much as they may affect the child, are not *design*, because they are not part of a plan for reaching the goals of the teacher.

I regard *design* as a planned program for achieving particular goals. Since human circumstances are beyond absolute and total control, I expect that students will have accidents (i.e., unplanned experiences) in the school, and that such events will have an impact of some duration, during which the students' normal approach to learning will be affected. The competent teacher(s) will plan activities to minimize the possible occurrence of such events, but since one cannot anticipate them nor include them in plans for reaching goals, they cannot rationally be included under *design*.

Fourthly, how and why certain knowledge and information are suggested for study are of great importance to both teacher and supervisor. If the curriculum or course-of-study promulgated by school authorities suggests or mandates the inclusion of certain particulars in a teacher's *design*, then an understanding of how and why such selections were made will help to determine plans for teaching such material to students. Since I consider this a statement for context, ZA, I won't get into a long discussion on this issue. Suffice it to say that knowing why certain things are to be studied, what objectives such study is meant to achieve, and how these things came to be selected in place of others (which could also lead to the same objectives) helps sharpen perceptions for dealing with the material.

I'd like to break in here, NS. May I?

Please do.

I agree with your first point, the one about encyclopedic knowledge. The second point is not as clear. Isn't it true that it's easier to begin learning certain things, like foreign languages, playing the violin, ballet dancing, at an earlier age? Instead of it being a notion that certain things should be taught to certain learners at certain times, can't there be a somewhat scientific criterion such as maturation? There are studies that do indicate some patterns of development in children.

Yes, there are such studies, but their results don't say to learn a foreign language, the violin, or ballet. Also, just because children *can* learn such skills as these at an early age is not in itself a reason for *having* them do so. The choice of what to learn is therefore a notion.

Let's leave it at that. You did say that you were only pursuing these points to create a context for your main points, so I'll accept the first two on that basis. But number three does not go down as easily. Yes, I do remember your saying, rather forcefully at a number of our sessions, that what's important is not the name or handle one assigns to a phenomenon, but what the phenomenon really *is*. A rose is a rose, etc. So if you want to assign *design* to what a teacher plans, executes, and controls, I can't quarrel with you. Yet how meaningful an entity have you identified? Maybe in traditional classrooms, with students in symmetrical rows, teacher up front, etc., one could talk about *design* as you define it. But that was yesterday. Today we're into open classrooms and corridors, individually prescribed instruction, projects—you know the picture. Can you really afford to still talk of teachers planning, executing, and controlling?

If the public were ever to decide that schools were merely custodial institutions, to keep unemployed children and youth off everybody's neck until they were old enough to go to work, and if successful schools were those that did this job with the least amount of friction at the lowest possible cost, then we'd be into another ball game. Even here, friction and cost could be criteria of effectiveness. But that's not the picture. The public very vociferously wants the schools to accomplish certain objectives. There are arguments over reading, over liberal vs. vocational education, etc., but there's no trend towards a purely custodial institution.

Once the school is to be held responsible for achieving certain objectives, then those very objectives become the yardsticks against which we measure teacher preparation, teacher performance, materials, methods, physical structures, grouping and interaction patterns, etc. So if you're a teacher who's being held accountable, you create a *design.*

I want to be honest: as of this date I've read more about open classrooms than I've seen, and I'm not terribly impressed with either. Which certainly does *not* mean that I'm impressed with traditional patterns of instruction. But if the people advocating such patterns of organization view them to be as effective as or more effective than traditional ways of having students learn, then there must be *planning* to see that such patterns are as or more effective than the old ways. They, too, need *design.*

> I see the point. Just one more objection. I also want to be honest and say that I've taken a couple of courses in supervision at another institution. Their experts seem to insist that the handle is *curriculum,* which is to include all the experiences students have at a school, maybe even those on the way between home and school. You yourself said that students do have "accidents" which have an impact on their normal approach to learning. Why do you substitute *design* for curriculum and define the former as you do?

What it boils down to, ZA, is this: if you can *plan* a curriculum, course-of-study, syllabus, or design, to achieve certain objectives, *before* teachers and students engage in the activities marked out by those plans, how do you include "accidents" without being a seer? You minimize their possible occurrence, take them into account once they have occurred, but they can't be part of an *a priori* plan.

> You can't tell that I've done so, NS, but there's a long pause after the words "*a priori* plan." I put the book down and have been mulling over what you said. You've aroused my suspicions. On more than one occasion in class you would get someone going this way, laying out a logical progression for him to follow, convincing him that rationality dictated his taking every step, and then he'd find himself far removed from where his original position had been and he'd be in a conflict. He'd been

> comfortable where he was. Being where you now had him seemed right, but the old ambience was missing. It didn't feel right. . . . That's how I feel. I tell myself that I have one advantage: I'm not in your class now, I'm only reading a book, and you won't ever know when I put it down. Still I'm curious where all this will lead to. I've just looked back at the fourth point you were making, about "how and why certain knowledge and information are suggested for study" being "of great importance." Would you go on with that one, please?

Yes, thank you. I have an example to cite and a final point in this list. The example is this:

A common objective is to have pupils learn how to read. Some school systems select basal readers, which are neither mathematics, science, or social studies books, nor books on the arts, though they make some effort to be literature. There is nothing sacred about the content. We could have books in science, arithmetic, history, geography, etc., each controlled for levels of decoding, where the emphasis would be on learning the content, not on decoding per se. That at least some educators choose to teach reading as though it were a subject, and that they try to do so via basal readers, must be viewed as a how-and-why issue. Other choices are possible.

Finally, there is continuous flux in what is regarded as true and factual. Not only does the absolute quantity increase, but new concepts and new facts replace older ones at some indefinite, but rapid, pace. In fact, a major question in education today is what to do about the knowledge explosion. The problem of selection, which I've already discussed, has become severe and can be projected to become ever more severe. One suggested solution is to identify the structure of each discipline and to focus on the major elements of that structure, which are likely to change at a slower pace than specific facts and general concepts. A corollary proposal is to focus on "process" rather than "content," that is, on the modes of inquiry and problem-solving in the various disciplines, with content as something to chew on and process as the thing to master. Choosing either structure or process or both does not solve everything at once. Even if the structure of each discipline were already known and generally accepted, and even if the processes peculiar to each discipline were equally known and accepted, no discipline is that simple that all of its structures and/or processes could be studied at once. Gradations would have to be made in relation to the maturity of the students and to the complexity of the structural elements and/or processes. Furthermore, there are a good many disciplines. Do we begin on all of them simultaneously in the first grade? Do we delay others to later grades? Are there some, or parts of some, we won't get to even by the end of high school? How does one decide?

Certainly, I'm making no attempt here to suggest answers, ZA. I raise these points to alert teachers and supervisors to the lack of agreement on who is to decide what is to be taught, in what manner, for which reasons. Our discourse is ultimately concerned with questions IV and V raised in Chapter II (manners of teaching and techniques of supervision), which I am now saying, ZA, are quite independent of what is to be taught. Since quite is not absolutely, since manners of teaching are related to what is taught, and since supervision is related to both, it is essential for supervisors to give thought to this first question. The five points I make about it don't even begin to exhaust the dimensions of the issue; they are, however, related to my approach to the other four questions.

IV.

What Is Teaching?

We come now to question II, which arose from an elaboration of the definitions of supervision, improvement, and instruction: Who gives "education" or teaches "knowledge, information, etc."? Who is *a* (*the*) teacher? What is teaching?

Since it's easy enough to duck the first two parts by saying that the teacher is the one who teaches, the real question becomes: what is teaching?

If there is encyclopedic knowledge to choose from, if that choice is a notion, if design is unique to the particular teacher who creates it, and if there is continuous flux in what is regarded as true and factual, then one can't be scientific about teaching by varying its definition according to the combination of the variables one happens to be examining. So I take a different tack:

Teaching can be defined without immediate reference to who does it, with whom it is done, in what structures, under which conditions, and for what purposes.

One child can teach another to ride a bicycle, parents can teach children how to cook, or work in the garden, and, of course, school teachers teach a whole range of concepts and skills to their pupils.

I define *teaching* as *the creation and control of conditions under which learners take on new patterns of responses to either old or new stimuli.*

This means that the teacher must be able to:

A. define both the stimuli and the responses;
B. determine whether the particular learners are ready to understand and deal with the particular stimuli and to make the necessary responses;

C. stimulate the learners to want to take on the new response patterns;
D. select and use materials and activities which will lead the learners to acquire the new responses and/or to practice existing responses;
E. control the process so that this acquisition or practice is efficient and effective; and to
F. determine to what degree each learner did, in fact, take on the new response patterns or affirm the existing ones.

A. Defining stimuli and responses

Let's begin with a simple case: child A wants to learn to ride a bike. The motivation is not an issue; the "teacher" doesn't need to be concerned about stimulating the learner to take on the new response pattern. Child A either has a bike or hopes to get one, and wants to learn to ride.

However, clear as the stimuli are, the responses are not nearly so. In the case of child A, to ride a bike probably means no more than being able to get on and stay on while going up and down the sidewalk or going around in some relatively safe area such as a playground or schoolyard. His parents will not immediately consent to his riding in the gutter, expecially in urban areas congested with automobile traffic. They will want to be convinced that he has technical control of the bike and prudent regard for his safety before giving permission for that kind of a ride. If we jump suddenly to the adult who rides to work on his bike, or to the (now probably passé) six-day bike racer, we see that each of these people also "rides" a bike, though very obviously the level of performance is quite removed from that of child A. It's like saying that Vladimir Horowitz and Van Cliburn "play" the piano and little Suzy from grade two will "play" the piano in the assembly program. Our language lacks individual verbs which in themselves express the level of performance.

If we now move to a school task—learning to read—we can easily see that "read" is not very precise. A first-grader reads a primer; you, ZA, can read another author's book on supervision; and a research biologist reads the reports of colleagues on the latest work in cancer research. Again, the verb "read" does not indicate the level of performance.

Therefore, when the definition says that the teacher must be able to define the responses, I'm not talking about the aim of a lesson being "to read . . ." or "to learn to read . . ."; I'm talking about a much more precise and definitive description of the responses sought. It's not even enough to add "to read the first story in the primer." Those who have tried to teach young children to read are well aware that a child can sound out the words and yet not comprehend what he sounded. Since primers are supposed to use words which are in the meaning and speaking vocabularies of young students, the first response ought to be an oral one: do the pupils understand the words in their spoken form? If they don't, then being able to sound them out from the book will not lead to comprehension. And surely the real business of reading is to comprehend what an author has written.

In like fashion, defining stimuli is more than handing a child a bike or a primer. The teacher needs to specify which words, in what context, the child is both to sound out and comprehend. If the teacher does not do so, then he will not be able to "determine to what degree each learner did, in fact, take on the new response pattern . . . ." He will not know "where the learners are," as the old axiom had it, and so will not be able to take the next step with the children.

"Defining stimuli and responses" means that the teacher must be able to set up discrete stimuli, in terms easily comprehended by the students, and must have identified, in advance, those behaviors which are acceptable responses to the particular stimuli. In skill areas the major complication is that of specifying the level of performance. A music teacher can specify the sounds to be produced on a particular instrument, with qualifications about pitch, timbre, tempo, volume, etc. He cannot as easily ask that the student "make music" on the instrument, because this involves aesthetic judgments beyond merely being in tune and in tempo. There is no precise "right answer" or definable response, because musical taste cannot be measured by a tuning fork and a metronome.

This issue becomes even more complex in concept learning. The teacher who focuses on the concept that initial and medial vowels in monosyllables are generally short can at least begin with one-syllable words the students have already learned to decode, can lead them to make the generalization, and can then provide each learner with a list of words to check, only some of which obey the generalization. But, if the object is to understand the checks and balances system among our three branches of federal government, what are the stimuli and what are the acceptable responses? Can one ask: Explain the system of checks and balances among the three branches of government. Even a cursory search of the relevant literature will reveal a large number of volumes devoted to the issue in general and to its specific elaborations at various times in our history. Certainly, the teacher doesn't equate the response sought with the contents of such a volume. So what does the teacher really expect in the way of a response?

The usual expectation is that the students can state (in either oral or written form) those highlights of the concept upon which the teacher has focused attention. This is generally regarded as "understanding" the concept. Some go further and ask for analogous institutional relationships which are governed by checks and balances. Or, at a higher level, one may pose for the students the problem of structuring a social order where seizure of absolute power can be precluded by the kinds of controls under which various functionaries must operate.

The implications for Supervision as the Improvement of Instruction (S.I.I.) are that if two ingredients of instruction are, indeed, being able to define stimuli and responses, then surely supervisors must have skills in these areas in order to be able to assess teacher performance and to help teachers who are not fully competent.

> This time you've really done it, NS; you've delivered a lecture; actually one-sixth of a lecture, if I kept an accurate count of the sub-heads under your definition of teaching. So let's pause a moment. I'm not going to make such global comments as that the approach sounds mechanistic and Pavlovian. A, you have five-sixths to cover, and B, you're probably ready for me. I'll save those until after the whole Gestalt is revealed. But assuming what you've said so far re teaching, how about this: are you saying that anyone can be a teacher, so long as he can define stimuli and responses in your fashion and follow through with your other five steps?

Yes, I'm saying that anyone who does what my definition and its six elaborations require is teaching. *But*, to call everyone who teaches *a teacher* would so dilute the specificity of the responsibilities of school teachers and their supervisors that, illogical as it may seem to deny the title teacher to anyone who teaches, I am doing so. In our discourse I want to reserve that title for those people who attend to what I consider to be their prime function: the intellectual development of the learner. I will use the title instructor for all others who teach.

Please don't press me at this point to explain why I make the distinction between teacher and instructor, and just what I mean by intellectual development. They make up one large issue, which I want to postpone until, at least, we've gone all the way through teaching and its sub-heads.

> O.K. But here's a more immediate problem, NS. I think you've painted yourself into a paradox. You made it very evident in any number of our classroom discussions that you want teachers to teach students to make decisions. How can they, when designs are planned *a priori* by teachers, when teaching means creation and control by teachers, and when stimuli and responses are defined by teachers?

There are two things to be said here, ZA. First, the less mature the student, or the further away he is from mastery in a given field, the less able he is to decide the specifics of a learning program. Second, even when people decide to become auto drivers, golf players, lawyers, teachers, etc., they've made only global decisions. They can't decide precisely which concepts and skills they must master and which attitudes they should develop. Those decisions already exist before an individual opts for those fields. Obviously, the more unitary or the less complex the task (for example, playing solitaire, riding a bike), the more the choice is congruent with the specifics to be learned.

> I think I follow you, NS. How does what you say apply to such non-"book larnin' " objectives as becoming independent, developing a mind of one's own, discovering one's strengths and weaknesses, working effectively with other people, and so on?

Each of the terms you use, ZA, requires definition. One can't really aim at independence, self-knowledge, etc., without some conception of what it looks like and feels like to be that way. There must be proximate, intermediate, and terminal goals, so as to be able to note progress and total mastery. Since only some experiences aid one to move towards independence, the instructor/teacher, who really knows what independence is, must also know the proximate, intermediate, and terminal goals so as to be able to create and control conditions . . . . As the learner begins to progress, he can share in the teaching, as I define it, so as to become more and more his own teacher.

What I'm saying, ZA, is that the real pro in teaching knows what it takes to be or to do whatever society or the student wants done, and is able to guide the learner along a direct path to mastery. Whether there are formal classes, in serried rows, with lecterns and note-taking, or whether there is Individually Prescribed Instruction, freedom to move and experiment, and so on, really makes little difference. *IF, and that's the single most significant IF in this business*, if schools and colleges *do have* goals for students–goals translated into curricula and courses-of-study–then teachers must have designs for teaching, or else anything goes. One of the reasons I'm not so impressed by open education in its various forms is that either the essential goals of education are the same as those of other modes of instruction–and what we need is to determine, scientifically, whether this form of organization is more effective than other forms–or that the constellation of goals is truly different, but that this form of organization is effective in achieving those goals, which must also be determined scientifically.

I regard classroom organization as FORM. What interests me is SUBSTANCE. FORM is a medium, like oil painting, water colors, symphony, sonata, essay, novel, etc. That a practitioner handles FORM as form is craft; that it communicates is art. Just because a teacher can direct a traditional or an open structure is no indication that learning is taking place. Of course, one can't begin with disorder. But order by itself is just order. Whether changes are taking place in the minds of learners is the real question. To get such changes to take place, with a given direction in mind, requires curricula, courses-of-study, and design.

Again, I've paused, NS. One problem, that must be

even more severe for those who have not discoursed with you in person and who are yet to accustom themselves to your emphasis on precision in language, is that you press us to use words in particular ways in a field which is hardly noted for its precision. Be patient.

I'll try. But we should go on to the second sub-head.

B. Pupil readiness for stimuli and responses

I see teachers as having some concept of terminal goals for their pupils over the span of a school semester or year, as being somewhat analogous to physicians with concepts of "normal" bodily functioning. Therefore, teachers need to be able to diagnose whether students are ready to deal with particular stimuli and to learn appropriate responses. One does not ask a student of first-year Russian to tackle Dostoevski in the original, or ask a music student to play the Mendelssohn violin concerto after just ten lessons. One has to answer at least two questions:

- What mastery over which skills and/or concepts will it take to comprehend and respond to the new stimuli? and
- How does the teacher diagnose the learners' capabilities to determine whether they have that mastery?

The teacher may have clearly defined the new stimuli and the appropriate responses, but, unless he has diagnosed pupil readiness, he may have either over-estimated or under-estimated the outcomes. If there is a gap between "where the learners are now" and the task at hand, he will be dooming his students to failure. And if they already know what he wants them to learn, the lesson will be over as soon as it has begun. If he persists, the students will either tell him "we had that last year" or may go along with the teacher, who will then take credit for teaching what the students already knew. This is to say nothing about the boredom such an underestimation can induce.

Another way of putting it is that instructional sessions should have a past, a present, and a future. The past is the "apperceptive base," the background of experiences, skill-mastery, fact-knowledge, and concept-comprehension each pupil brings to the learning process. The present includes the new stimuli and responses and the conditions under which these will be faced. The future is the relationship between present responses and the next step in the learning sequence, as well as the application of such learning to relevant phenomena and problems in life outside the school.

C. Stimulating the learners

Child A is not likely to be as self-motivated about learning to read as he is about learning to ride a bike. There's hardly a school teacher alive who isn't concerned about the "motivation" in each lesson. (And, with him, the supervisor.) The reality is that altogether too many children are not intrinsically interested in the things schools and teachers want them to learn. It's fashionable today to ask that education be "relevant" and "meaningful," both because this is what students seem to be demanding, and because, at least in theory, the learner will be more easily stimulated by relevant and meaningful studies. In the "old days" we used to say that people only really learn what they want and need to learn, not what we think we're teaching them. The meaning is the same: learners need to be stimulated to see that what we are trying to teach them is related to who they are, what they are, how they see life, and how the new learning will contribute to their growth and personal satisfaction. It's not that the teacher gives over to his students full control over the design, and teaches them what they want to learn (although the more mature the student, the weightier his judgment in this area); it is that the teacher must be able to relate his instruction to the life-experiences of his students in order for them to take on the new response patterns.

I need to interrupt your presentation again, NS. What you say about readiness sounds very familiar. Nor is the material on motivation so different, if you don't mind my saying so. But when you combine the two, a question arises. And I may have to develop a prelude before I can ask it. May I?

Please do, ZA.

In discussing readiness, you say that a teacher has to answer two questions, one dealing with prior mastery of skills and concepts, the other with techniques to diagnose that mastery—which seems to imply that one doesn't have to make a study of the so-called "whole child" who is ready for the stimulus. Yet, in discussing motivation, you want us to relate the learning "to who

> they are, what they are, how they see life, and how the new learning will contribute to their growth and personal satisfaction." I won't accuse you again of being in a painted paradox, but surely an explanation is in order. No?

Yes, ZA, an explanation is in order. My elaboration of sub-heads "A. define both the stimuli and the responses" and "C. stimulate the learners to want to take on the new response patterns" suggests that I have them in inverse order. Maybe one should get the larger picture of the learner before getting down to the small details of particular stimuli and responses. I made the order what it is because it seemed logical to decide on stimuli and responses before checking on readiness and deciding on motivation. Another reason is that I'm defining teaching without regard to who does it, with whom, etc. Not all such teaching is done by those I'm going to call *teachers*, whereas the elaboration you refer to is meant to apply only to *teachers*. I'm again going to ask you to wait for a full development of that concept, but I do want to make the explanation you request.

If you go to a driving school, the instructor doesn't need to know much about you, except that you're so motivated, seem to be able to see and hear, have the necessary muscular coordination, have a learner's permit, and money for the lessons. Similarly, if you're teaching a youngster penmanship, you need to check on muscular coordination, some ability to follow instructions, a desire to make organized marks on paper, and so on. You *don't* need to know where he lives, whether his parents love him, when he got his first teeth—in other words, you need to see whether he's ready to make the responses to the stimuli. Instead, I've seen teachers going all out investigating the "whole child" without much of an attempt to analyze what they're being asked to do: that is, to identify stimuli and responses and to determine readiness.

What sounds like a paradox is that I expect teachers (my kind) to have a very firm grasp of relationships between what students are to learn and what such students *are.* For example, I once saw a rather humane, witty, knowledgeable teacher working with a group of high school students on various forms of fossil formation. He used fairly effective materials, his board illustrations and notes were clear and communicative, his manner invited participation, and the students were with him. But the only points of contact between students and fossil formation were: there are fossils in a museum in town, you might find some in the park or at an excavation, and one can make a good living being a paleontologist (the meaning of which he explained in terms of searching for oil). But these were urban students, far removed from both fossils and paleontology, and the material was basically not relevant to them.

I'm not saying that this material belonged neither in the course-of-study nor in the teacher's design. I *am* saying that the motivation was based largely on the teacher's ability to interest the students in *himself* and to have them follow *him* because he was who he was; it was *not* based on their need or desire to deal with the material. Had he sought a solution to the latter problem, he would not (repeat: would *not*) have had to know each "whole child" in the class. But he would have had to ask himself: just because this material is in the course-of-study, does it belong in my design for this particular group of adolescents? What connection do such young people have with this material? What light does it shed on the world they see and on themselves and the people around them?

I reject the "whole child" concept because even psychiatrists can't always master that problem, on a one-to-one basis. Why should I expect this of teachers? I expect *teachers* to understand the relationship of academic material to real living and to know a fair amount about the learners as individuals and as a group. On the other hand, when you have checked on readiness, when the learner has "passed muster" and still can't respond, then the teacher looks beyond the immediate, along the lines, however, of what it takes to make the response. One doesn't leap to the conclusion that the learner isn't responding because he's deprived, disadvantaged, unloved, the product of a broken home, black, Puerto Rican, Chicano, etc. To begin with, the teacher can't undo any of this. Neither can the school. What is more significant: blaming a learning problem on such symbols makes it possible for teachers to avoid facing the real problem: what responses *is* the learner ready to make to *which* stimuli along *what* road of study? Of course there are learners who represent insurmountable learning problems to many teachers. Then we do what doctors do:

we create intensive care units, manned by specialists who can provide the best available therapy.

Now look, ZA, you set me going and I climbed on a soap box to preach. I'm sorry. Did I answer your question?

> If I understand you correctly, NS, you're saying that readiness is keyed to the response the learner is to make. Presumably, if one could prove that being unloved blocks a learner from making a particular response, then you would approve an investigation of that cause-and-effect relationship. Until then you're only going to study the learner to the extent needed to prepare and motivate him to the response he's to make.

Yes, ZA, that's my present position. Now, let me present the remaining sub-heads, so we can look at the total statement.

D. Selecting materials and activities

There are, in my way of looking at it, two "hearts" to the matter of teaching: the selection of materials and activities and the control of the actual learning process (item E).

Suppose, for example, that the teacher has determined that his students are ready to deal with the individual's right to privacy, an issue raised by the questionable legality of wire-tapping, the confidentiality of personnel files, the legislation of "no knock" laws for use in criminal investigations, etc. We will even assume that the teacher has solved the problems of defining stimuli and responses, student readiness, and student motivation. The next question is: what will teacher and students do, using what materials?

A typical gambit is to discuss a previously assigned reading on privacy or, in the absence of such readings, to ask the students what they think privacy is and to begin with student perceptions. The major problem with these tactics is that the burden of instruction is borne by the most abstract medium of communication: symbols (words). And if there is a real qualitative difference between bright and other students, it is in their ability to handle abstractions. Supervisors ought to impress teachers with one injunction regarding this element of teaching: Always select and use materials and activities that are as concrete, as real as the classroom (and its extensions into the community) will permit.

Rather than simply talking about privacy, wire-tapping, confidential files, etc., teacher and students could at least develop some roleplays to illustrate both the facts and the feelings engendered in the minds of those who are the victims of such situations. It would obviously be even more realistic to obtain the participation of members of the community who have a recent or current involvement in such matters.

I once had to teach an eighth-grade class of boys the meaning of the Bill of Rights. A novice myself at the time, fortune favored me because my boys were more interested in whether police had a right to frisk them for a ball with which they had been playing stick-ball, a New York City street version of baseball, played in the gutter in the days before parked cars were a problem, using a rubber ball and an old broomstick. This often resulted in the ball going into someone's yard or in breaking a window. The police would be called by the irate home owner or apartment dweller. Hiding the stick was easy: you lowered it down a manhole cover through one of its holes, for easy retrieval. Even its loss was not permanent; in those days sticks were easy to acquire. But a ball cost money, and money (usually ten cents) was not easily obtained. So the boys pocketed the ball. Ergo, the police, having probably played stick-ball themselves, would try to frisk the boys.

So the students wanted to know why the police could frisk them as they engaged in masked innocent chatter when the cops arrived.

This was a far better "motivation" for the study of the Bill of Rights than any I could then have devised on my own. You can well imagine, ZA, how one could lead into the need for rules in society from so intrinsic an issue. Yes, we talked; but we talked about events that were real to the boys and to me, I being just past my own stick-ball-playing days.

E. Controlling the learning process

This is certainly the most complex element in teaching. The well-prepared teacher understands the concept to be mastered; however, even such a teacher generally cannot retrace the steps he went through, from absolute ignorance to present degree of mastery. He may even be able to demonstrate the level of performance of the skills his students are to master, though this is not true for skills which require continuous practice plus youthful agility. (Surely, the football coach can no longer run, block, throw, and catch the ball the way his young athletes are supposed to.)

Readers whose mothers inducted them into the mysteries of cooking before the days of cookbooks, can probably remember the informal proportions indicated by mother. You put in a pinch of salt, shake in a handful of flour, etc. But, Ma, how much exactly? I tried following your recipe and look what came out!

Or: the impatient husband-instructor unwillingly teaching his wife to drive the car. Just turn on the ignition, put the car in gear and step on the gas. No! No! Give it more gas or she'll stall! What's so hard?!

The effective teacher can define ground zero, keep the learning steps small and in sequential order, use unambiguous instructions, keep in mind that what is so very clear to him is an absolute fog for the learner, and provide for success at each level of understanding or performance.

This is where the supervisor can be of greatest help, when he reflects back to the teacher the impact on the students of the process the teacher is using, a topic which I will later treat in great detail under manners of teaching.

F. Determining what was learned

It needs little elaboration to demonstrate that the teacher cannot re-engage his students in the learning process unless he and they know precisely how far they have come. Not only must the students know how much progress they have made, but the teacher cannot re-enter the teaching cycle with his students unless he knows where the students are now.

V.

Who Is the Teacher?

NS, I'm only partially clear as to why you define teaching as you do, why you want to deal with it as a process apart from who does it, with whom, where, under which conditions, and for what purposes. I assume that "purposes" must include what is to be learned, that is, the subject matter. The breakdown into six sub-heads is logical, though not far removed from other analyses I've encountered. I'll presume you'll put the definition and breakdown to use later on, judging by the effort devoted to explaining it. My immediate interest, however, is in the distinction you make between teacher and instructor, and in the intellectual development you assign the teacher. Would you go into these matters now, please?

ZA, I said a little while ago that, for me, the biggest IF in education was whether schools and colleges had goals for students. At least twice now I've indicated that my kind of teacher works to achieve particular goals. And the third question I derived from the definition of Supervision as the Improvement of Instruction (S.I.I.) is: Since "an increase in value or in excellence of quality or condition" implies criteria or goals: Are there goals for instruction? Who defined them? How? What are these goals? How is movement towards them detected and measured?

So we'll discuss goals, the distinction between teacher and instructor hinging on the goals each is to accomplish.

A community may assign to its schools any goals it chooses. It may keep the buildings open every hour of every day and night in the whole year to render a multitude of services to children, youth, and adults. To do so it would have to employ, in addition to what we generally call teachers, a great many other functionaries. Even though schools are not open all the time now, there already exist some rather clear divisions of labor on the staff of a school. Custodians, doctors, nurses, psychiatrists, psychologists, social workers, guidance counselors, cafeteria personnel, secretaries, and clerks perform functions other than teaching, and are either required to have official certification to practice or are prevented by law or regulations from practicing outside their prescribed fields.

My argument is that if teachers are to be held accountable for their performance, if teacher education programs are to be held accountable for identifying and preparing such people, then, as a teacher educator, I must know the functions of teachers (and supervisors) before I even begin to identify likely candidates. The rub is that there is no universal agreement on what teachers are to do and on what the goals of education are. Here's a summary of a summary by Taba* who states that there are at least three broad divisions among writers in this field.

One group sees "education as preserver and transmitter of the cultural heritage." "This group argues that since all cultural traditions have roots, cultural continuity is possible only if education preserves this heritage by passing on the truths worked out in the past to the new generation, thus developing a common cultural background and loyalties."

A second group sees "education as an instrument for transforming culture," maintaining "in effect, that education can and does play a creative role in modifying and even reshaping the culture in which it functions, that education and public policy are intimately related, and that progress in one is limited without progress in the other. They maintain that education must deal with the needs of current culture and even help to shape the future."

A third group emphasizes "education for individual development." "One theme of this conception is that education, among other things, is a gateway to mobility, an arm of equalization society uses in democratizing its inevitably hierarchical structure

*Taba, Hilda. *Curriculum Development: Theory and Practice*. Harcourt, Brace, and World, Inc., 1962, pp. 16-30.

of economic, social, and intellectual opportunity. One function of the school, therefore, is to fill the gaps and correct the deficiencies in socialization which occur because of limitations imposed on opportunities by social structure. It is the task of the school to select and nurture ability that may be stultified by the limitations imposed by social background."

It is possible to argue not only that other classifications can be made, but also that these three are not very discrete. Those who favor preservation and transmission place great emphasis on "intellectual development as the distinctive function of the public school." If the public schools performed this function successfully, would this not lead to individual development? And would not such individuals thus be better equipped to effect changes in society?

The relevant dictionary definition of "culture" is "the concepts, habits, skills, arts, instruments, institutions, etc. of a given people in a given period; civilization." Therefore, to modify and reshape the culture must mean to so affect "given people in a given period" that they modify and reshape their "concepts, habits, . . . institutions, etc." Modifying and reshaping require the ability to develop criteria against which changes are first projected and then made. To do this requires not only intellectual development, but also an understanding of what has been transmitted and preserved from the past, which will serve both as a summary and as a starting point for modification and reshaping. In addition, concepts, habits, etc., are not entities outside of human beings; they are characteristics and properties of *people*. Modifying and reshaping must be done on people, which seems to be another way of stating the idea of individual development. Finally, individuals are not developed in a vacuum. If the schools were indeed able "to fill the gaps and correct the deficiencies in socialization which occur because of the limitations imposed on opportunities by the social structure," this would obviously modify and reshape the culture. It seems impossible to conceive that correcting such deficiencies can exclude developing intellectual powers.

Therefore, you might say that these are just three facets of the same stone. Polishing one facet affects the other two. However, it is also true that if you read carefully the individual expositions of each philosophy, you will note differences I've glossed over in my argumentation, differences which are both apparent and real in terms of the kind of schooling each suggests and implies.

All of which sounds like another lecture, ZA, plus a hint that you might want to read Taba's statement in full. I wanted to alert both of us to the arguments on this subject as a prelude to stating my views.

I see no way of achieving consensus on what education should seek to achieve. As I have said, the people can have their schools do whatever they want done. And just as they want government to do and give them more and more, so they make ever greater demands of schools. That may well be progress. Whatever you call it, I'm not about to get in its way.

But I am deeply concerned with the impact of these demands on what you presently call teachers, ZA. Though the school may be held accountable for rendering many services, *the roles of teachers are not congruent with the roles of schools.* I italicized that phrase, ZA, because that's the real issue. We not only don't ask teachers to render medical services; we forbid them to do so. We insist that only licensed psychologists and psychiatrists render their unique services to students. I'm sure you can extend the list without me, ZA. What I want is a special province for teachers.

Then I say to myself: doctors don't treat the whole child; they don't attend to social, emotional, psychological, aesthetic, intellectual, political, economic, moral, spiritual (have I left anything out?) development beyond the physical, so why should teachers think that they can? Their education is shorter and less rigorous; they deal primarily with groups, not individuals; they don't specialize anywhere near to the extent that doctors do; so why? I don't really care how we arrived at this stage; all I want is out. No single human being can be that totally responsible for any other *even single* human being, let alone a group of them.

The next step is to limit the teacher's responsibility—and I have. I say that *the person I call TEACHER is the one who devotes himself to the intellectual (for me that includes aesthetic) development of students.* All others who teach I call *instructors.* Nor do I mean that to sound hierarchical. Teacher and instructor simply do different kinds of teaching; neither is more valuable to society than the other. We need both.

We need automobile mechanics just as surely as we need theoretical physicists. The latter can't fix cars and the former can't design new means of non-polluting propulsion. An instructor can teach you the elements of auto mechanics; a teacher educates new physicists.

> Just a minute, NS. If I'm not being too bold, haven't you built us up to high expectations, then presented us with the same old ideas? You put us off for some time, saving your definition of teacher for special consideration; you outline Taba's three schools of thought, seemingly rejecting each of them as being no more than a facet instead of a whole stone; and now you say that your kind of teacher is solely concerned with intellectual and aesthetic development. Though I will likely take the hint and read Taba's statement, till then I can only go by your summary. Except for your inclusion of aesthetic development, don't you really just belong in Taba's first group? And if you do, then the distinction between instructor and teacher is hierarchical, isn't it, NS?

You're missing my major point, ZA. I don't equate "education" with what a teacher does. Keep in mind that all this is a prelude to dealing with teaching and supervision, both of which are sub-heads to schooling, which is itself a sub-head of education. Also keep in mind that I have defined teaching neutrally: no matter who does it, where, etc. Which means that the system I will soon elaborate for analyzing teaching can as well be applied to learning French or Hindustani, business arithmetic or calculus, the North's view of the Civil War, or the South's view of the War Between the States; to learning to become subservient or independent, tolerant or bigoted, humane or cruel, democrat or communist, progressive or reactionary.

I believe that what we already know about how people learn, and the great deal we have yet to learn, is all neutral with respect to both culture and subject matter. The principles of learning to which I will later refer apply with equal force whether the learners are in the U.S. or in China, and whether the subject matter is liberal or vocational. Therefore, I analyze teaching on two levels: one I call instructional technology, meaning the whole array of efforts subsumed under the six sub-heads of the definition of teaching; the other has no special name, but is concerned with the long-range objectives the teacher is aiming at (or isn't).

I can conceive of walking into a classroom where a teacher of history is using instructional technology superbly to teach students to feel superior to members of particular minority groups. And by superbly I mean that he has done precisely what the six sub-heads (and their later elaborations) demand of him. I can admire the technology, but will most definitely ask what mandate we have from the Board of Education to inculcate the attitude on which he's focusing.

Another point is this: even if I were to equate schooling with education, and even if I were to grant to schools an influence equal to the sum total of the "education" that emanates from the home, the mass media, the peer group, one's place of employment, and the church/synagogue, I have no such grand illusions about the impact of the small number of teachers you or your colleagues will ever supervise, ZA. Their work must be viewed on a smaller scale, not in terms of the whole child and the entire culture.

Let's pause a moment to reflect on some matters, ZA. I began by putting words in your mouth, but now you're seemingly speaking for yourself. I hear you in my head. Since you know that I love heated, sharp, pointed discussions, where matters are at issue on an imaginary round table, and where the concern is with substance not personalities, be most bold in questioning my ideas.

Secondly, you might have been even bolder and asked: What's the point of all this long overture to the opening curtain? Why don't you just deal with your definition of teaching, with what you call manners of teaching, and with how to supervise? In the boldest terms, aren't you simply using this as an opportunity to give us your views on almost every educational issue on which you have a view?

Well, let's see what I would have answered.

I began with a short overture on the two strands and the premises that undergird them.

Then I defined supervision (as the improvement of instruction), and extracted a series of questions, which we are now discoursing. The material on "Knowledge and Information" plus most of what I've been saying about "Who Is the Teacher?" is meant to press you into developing a philosophic position of your own. Schooling is a value-based enterprise. It assumes that human beings can be improved, for their own sake and for that of society. But there is very little agreement at the level of specifics on what we're to improve and on how to do so.

If I hadn't begun with the premise that both teaching and supervision can be defined and treated as neutral technology, if I had conceived of schools and teachers as aiming for certain definite goals, then I would have stated the goals, described the kinds of teaching implied, and your role in moving towards those goals.

I said that supervision is not a discipline. But if it is ever to be one, we must decide what its parameters are, how it differs from related fields, what terminology it uses, what those terms mean, and how that subject matter can be treated in non-judgmental, non-valued, neutral terms. However, since supervision operates within a value-based context, since those values are in flux and in question, I added material to describe that context.

Finally, as to my using this as a free-speech soap box: there are many, many more issues in our field (about which I have views of varying intensity) than I've touched upon. Those that I have discussed are all part of my total view of supervision. I could not have stated the case in full without them.

> Alright, NS. You precis is a "medial summary," I guess. It tells us where we've been and what we're up to. You seem to be saying, by the material you discussed just before the summary, that teachers have a limited sphere of activity, that their focus is on intellectual and aesthetic development, and that this presumably also narrows the supervisor's responsibilities. But you really haven't said how you differ from Taba's first group, nor responded to the matter of hierarchy between teacher and instructor.

The major difference, ZA, is that the material from Taba deals with what education and schooling are to accomplish, whereas I'm discussing the spheres of teachers and instructors. Suppose a community were to base its schools on Taba's third group, on the theme that education "is a gateway to mobility, an arm of equalization society uses in democratizing its inevitably hierarchical structure of economic, social, and intellectual opportunity . . . . It is the task of the school to select and nurture ability that may be stultified by the limitations imposed by social background . . . the school must not only introduce the students to the skills and powers necessary for survival or for self-realization in our culture; it must also act as an integrating force in shaping beliefs and attitudes to make them coherent with the requirements of the democratic way of life."* If it meant to implement this commitment, the community might well have to provide instruction in the graphic arts, in music, in dance, in various handicrafts, in sailing, driver education, and so on, which would nurture abilities "stultified by the limitations imposed by social background," meaning that your family couldn't subsidize your pursuit of such interests. In addition, the school would have to shape beliefs and attitudes supportive of a democratic way of life.

From my point of view, all these commitments could not be discharged by what I call teachers. And I speak as a one-time music teacher and currently practicing musician. Just because someone is giving you piano lessons doesn't mean that he's necessarily developing your musical intellect or your aesthetic sensibilities. The kind of person I would call *a music teacher* could do both of these without teaching you to perform on any instrument. To assume otherwise would mean that only those who had learned to perform had developed musical intelligence and aesthetics. Of course, under ordinary tutelage, one can (not must) develop a heightened appreciation of great performance when one experiences it, but it doesn't follow as a matter of course. You must have a *teacher* who aims for you to develop such sensitivity.

The matter of shaping attitudes and beliefs is a lot more complicated. First of all, it sounds like indoctrination, not teaching, and I don't think indoctrination is part of intellectual development. Secondly, it assumes that democracy, even in its purest form, is necessarily the absolute ultimate in human self-government. There are people who look upon socialism, communism, and other "isms" as equally worthy if not better solutions. To close the book on so vital an issue is anti-intellectual.

*Taba, *ibid*., p. 29.

It also implies that if our society can shape its people to support a present form of government, why can't other societies do likewise? This would shut the book really tight.

In actual practice, of course, we don't live in a textbook democracy. For public schools to have the right to shape attitudes in keeping with the authorities' (the school boards') views of "the requirements of the democratic way of life" would be positively disastrous. Ergo, I accept the need for instructors to teach skills, but I insist upon teachers who handle intellectual and aesthetic development.

Of greater consequence is this: I distinguish between instructor and teacher because I've seen too many instructors and too few teachers in our schools. I've seen "teachers" who focus on rote skill teaching, with little or no attempt at intellectual and aesthetic development.

Now, as to the question of my position being in Taba's first group. If I understand the rational humanists and classicists, then I'm with them in emphasizing intellect, reason, rationality, solid grounding in forms of communication; in short, what is generally subsumed under the liberal arts. The difference I perceive (and the vision may only be in the eye of the beholder) is that methodologically I won't begin by creating a curriculum and courses-of-study based on the accumulated wisdom of mankind. I begin with the problems and decisions facing students and help them see that other humans, at other times, in other places, have faced the same (or similar) problems and have come up with certain insights and conclusions. Do these "wisdoms" shed light on current versions of age-old issues, or are the issues so new that we need to develop new wisdoms?

But I have absolute faith in the light that the great minds of humanity can shed on today's problems, when their wisdom is brought to bear on current problems by real *teachers*, who both know the historic wisdom and understand how their students perceive problems and decision-making points.

If all this means that I, too, am a classicist, a rational humanist: Amen, So Be It!

One absolutely final point: The effective teacher is the one who has helped you learn to be your own teacher and imbued you with the desire *and* the willpower to pursue your development independently. Those who teach you to perform particular skills smoothly, efficiently, and even with personal satisfaction, are instructors. They become teachers as they set you on the road to further independent learning by helping you develop insight into why certain operations are performed as they are, what decisions one must make when altering operations relative to circumstances, and how one can create new operations in the face of new circumstances.

You're right, ZA; in this sense I really value teachers more than instructors!

VI.

Manners of Teaching: The Empirical Grid (EG)

Were our discourse taking place in class, ZA, I would have come to this session with a stack of duplicated papers. Before distributing them, I would say something like the following.

The papers I will shortly give you contain something I call an empirical grid, based on the six sub-heads of my definition of teaching. Each sub-head is further subdivided into varying numbers of units. The units have titles, questions to indicate their thrust, plus principles of learning to undergird that thrust. In order for you to grasp a structure containing six sub-heads, 33 units, and 222 principles, I need to make some explanatory remarks.

First—One philosophical base for my approach to supervision is that we must begin with what is known about how people learn. What we know about learning has already been codified by a few writers into statements I will refer to as principles, though only two of the authors use this term for their statements. To teach effectively, I reason, is to set up learning conditions which are consonant with, obedient to, these principles. To supervise effectively is to help teachers set up and function under such learning conditions.

Second—We have really just barely begun to develop firm generalizations about conditions favorable to learning. Though the papers I will give you contain 222 statements, some areas are untouched, and few if any have total coverage. Therefore, the principles are set into an empirical grid, meaning a structure based on what I think is known from practical experience.

Third—The grid, the six sub-heads of teaching, and the questions in each unit are all based on the idea that teaching is to be studied as it occurs in the interaction between those who teach and those who learn, excluding, *deliberately*, what those who teach do before and after each interaction by way of preplanning and postanalysis. Learners are affected by what happens during the interaction; the impacts of preplanning and postanalysis enter only through what takes place in the interaction. As in football, the game is won or lost on the field, not in practice sessions and in the study of re-plays of the game. This does not mean that preplanning and postanalysis are any less significant for teaching than practice and re-plays are for football. Nor does it mean that supervision is any less concerned with these elements of teaching than coaching is with its comparable elements. The payoff in both cases is in the interaction between the protagonists, not in how each prepares himself before and after. It's one thing to know what should be done or what should have been done; it's quite something else to have had the control to do so during the interaction.

Fourth—Despite the deliberate omission of preplanning and postanalysis, the grid is meant to be equally useful to teachers/instructors and to supervisors. Though the entire supervisory cycle I will later describe and illustrate is a postanalysis, it is also a kind of preplanning. The major thrust of this cycle is to teach the teacher to be his own supervisor, with the grid as the major tool for doing so.

Finally—The grid, the sub-heads, etc., are confined to the interaction because I think we can derive from them a method for assessing the effectiveness of instruction. After we have discussed and understood the empirical grid in these papers, I will show you how far I have come in converting its elements into a primitive version of an assessment device.

So here are the papers. Try to grasp the structure of sub-heads and units first, then read the questions under each unit, and, finally, read the principles under the questions.

AN EMPIRICAL GRID WITH SUPPORTING PRINCIPLES

Prelude: The teacher should be equipped with working techniques which jibe with psychological principles. A teacher should be an expert in the technology of learning, but as is true of other technologists, must continually appraise techniques in terms of new discoveries and research. It is literally true that many of today's principles may be outmoded or changed in a few years. It is thus imperative that teachers retain an open-mindedness which allows revision of their teaching methods as new discoveries are made. (BJB, p. 257)*

Teaching: The creation and control of conditions under which learners take on new responses to either old or new stimuli.

This means that the teacher must be able:

A. to define both the stimuli and the responses;

1. *Stimuli*
   a. Does teacher seem to have prepared either a

*1. BJS – Blair, Glenn N., Jones, R. Stewart, and Simpson, Ray H. *Educational Psychology* (Third Edition). New York: The Macmillan Company, 1968.
2. B – Bugelski, B.R. *The Psychology of Learning Applied to Teaching*. Indianapolis: The Bobbs-Merrill Company, Inc., 1971.
3. HB – Hilgard, Ernest R., and Bower, Gordon H. *Theories of Learning*. New York: Appleton-Century-Crofts, 1966.
4. K – Kuethe, James L. *The Teaching-Learning Process*. Glenview, Illinois: Scott, Foresman and Company, 1968.
5. S – Seagoe, May V. *A Teacher's Guide to the Learning Process*. Dubuque, Iowa: Wm. C. Brown Company, 1961.
6. Sc – Seagoe, May V. *The Learning Process and School Practice*. Scranton, Pennsylvania: Chandler Publishing Company, 1970.

definitive stimulus situation or a precise set of stimuli or a definite single stimulus to which students are to respond?

b. Does the situation (or the set, or the single stimulus) seem to be related to other recent learning activities?

c. Is the stimulus (in whatever of the forms above) the same for all the learners in the group or is it varied for different students?

d. Has teacher foreseen the possible negative consequences of the stimulus?

P1.* The elimination of potentially competing stimuli from learned responses or from responses yet to be learned can facilitate accurate responding to today's stimuli. (B, p. 206)**

2. *Responses*

a. Does teacher propose purposes and aims which state what the teacher will do (e.g., to present, to teach, to review), or which state what the learners will do (e.g., to write, draw, construct, speak)?

b. Where on a continuum (long-range, medium-range, short-range) is (are) the purpose(s)?

c. Is what students are to do now (short-range) related to some medium or long-range purpose(s) which teacher has projected for an area of study larger than can be encompassed in a single lesson?

d. Are there guidelines or parameters which mark out the area of responses?

e. Did earlier student responses play some obvious (to the students) role in the selection of today's material?

f. Does teacher check first to see what students know about today's material before adding new information and/or directing students to search for new information?

*Principle #1.

**Henceforth, the page number citation will appear without the letter "p."

g. Does teacher use what students say or can do to correct misinformation, misinterpretation, superstitions, prejudice?

h. Has teacher foreseen the consequences that might ensue from the required responses?

P2. Eliciting, parading, and extinguishing partially erroneous responses will facilitate learning. (B-207)

P3. A common purpose for all the participating learners will point the learning towards a common end. (S-16)

P4. The statement of goals in terms of learner behavior is one prerequisite for producing effective transfer. (BJS-288)

3. *Communication*

a. Are the stimuli clearly communicated?

b. Are the responses learners are to make clearly delineated and communicated?

c. At what point(s) in the learning activity does the communication of stimuli and responses take place?

d. Does teacher ensure that students know exactly what they're to do? How?

e. If students call for a second explanation of stimuli and responses, does teacher make one? Using the original words? Using new words?

f. Does teacher change or re-define instructions mid-stream?

g. Has teacher foreseen the consequences of the mode of communication?

h. Does teacher use the most concrete means of communication (via real materials, visuals, AV media) or does teacher rely on words alone?

P5. The responses the learners are to take on should be made clear at the beginning of the learning process. (S-16)

P6. Learning presented in a familiar, partially learned context is more rapid than learning presented in an unusual context. (S-133)

P7. A given stimulus situation may be assigned different meanings by different individuals, resulting in different responses. (S-42, HS-565)

B. to determine whether the particular learners are ready to understand and deal with the particular stimuli and to make the necessary responses;

1. *Potential*
   a. Does teacher seem to know pupils' potentials?
   b. Are the stimuli and responses geared to the potentials of the learners?
   c. Are stimuli and responses varied with respect to individual differences in potential?

P8. Because the abilities of learners are important, provision should be made for the varying potentials they bring to the learning situation. (HB-564)

P9. Rapid learners achieve higher mastery and longer retention of learned materials. The slow learner is not the more thorough learner. (S-55)

P10. What the individual expects is tied to the reality of his earlier success in that experience; what he hopes for or aspires to is related to his self-image. As the task increases in difficulty and as he fails to reach his goals, the difference between expectation and aspiration increases. (S-43)

P11. Learners make inaccurate estimates of their own potential and achievement, underestimating past and overestimating future accomplishments. (S-43)

2. *Achievement*
   a. Has teacher determined that learners have sufficiently mastered prior skills and concepts so as to be ready for today's stimuli and responses?

P12. Goals should be within the achievement range of individual participating learners. (K-54)

C. to stimulate the learners to want to take on the new response patterns;

1. *General*
   a. Does teacher seem to understand what motivation is?

P13. An individual can be said to be motivated when he evidences some desire to attain some specified goal. Therefore, a teacher can be said to be motivating a student when such a desire is recognized and increased/

intensified by the teacher, or when the teacher imbues the student with a desire the student has not previously evidenced. (K-99)

P14. The potential learner must be motivated to perceive the environment, or else he will neither understand, nor react, nor learn. (S-166)

P15. The more alert the learner is to the learning task and the more precisely he is instructed, the more effective will be his learning. (S-167)

P16. However, some learning will occur even without external motivation, as long as the individual is attending to the stimuli in some attempt to understand. (S-166)

P17. In the absence of instructions as to what to learn, the individual's incidental learning is different in different situations, depending in part on prior practice in those situations and in part on age. (S-169)

P18. Attitudes are typically acquired as incidental by-products of involvement in an activity. (K-49)

2. *Physical Plant*
    a. Are room temperature, light, and ventilation conducive to student interest and application?
    b. Is the room so decorated as to make for a pleasant learning atmosphere?
    c. Are there plants, aquaria, centers of interest, or other items, relevant either to the nature of the relevant materials?
    d. Are there plants, alquaria, centers of interest, or other items, relevant either to the nature of the learning activities and/or to simple comfort and attractiveness?
    e. Is the seating arranged for maximum audibility and visibility, with special attention to students handicapped in one way or another?
    f. Is the seating flexible, and then arranged to suit the needs of the learning situations?

P(none)

3. *Focus*
    a. Is the motivation focused on specific acts?
    b. Is the focus on the learning or on paying attention to the teacher?

c. Is the motivation more than "Put away your homework, take out your math books, and turn to page 57?"

P19. Motivation (both positive and negative) is most effective when focused on the specific response pattern at issue. (S-77)

4. *Form*

a. Is the motivation situational or symbolic?

P20. The learner's personal experience of either success or failure in a given task is superior to verbal feedback from the teacher. (S-77)

5. *Origin*

a. Is the motivation intrinsic (i.e., based on an inherent interest in the material, concepts, skills to be dealt with), or is it extrinsic (i.e., based on rewards or punishments which teacher, school, parents, or community can mete out)?

P21. The impact of any form of motivation is limited by the difference between a learner's potential in a given area and his past achievement in that area. (S-24)

P22. Extrinsic motivation causes the learner to increase his effort over a given period of time, thus temporarily increasing his output, whereas intrinsic motivation has the effect of facilitating learning over longer periods of work-time. (S-24)

P23. Though both extrinsic and intrinsic forms of motivation eventuate in more learning, the amount is greater for intrinsic forms. The more relevant the incentive is to the goal, the more effective and rapid is the learning. (S-24)

P24. The emotionally less stable student responds more to extrinsic motivation than the highly stable one. (S-25)

6. *Proximity*

a. Does teacher seem to know students' interests?

b. Are student interests exploited to motivate them to take active part in the learning?

c. Does teacher try to elicit students' interests?

d. Is the motivation based on student familiarity with the elements to be dealt with?

e. Is it related to pupils' levels of aspiration?

f. Is the motivation related to what will follow, or does teacher use something that captures attention (Let's play a game!), but then turns it into something unrelated (Let's see who can come to attention first!)?

P25. Children's interests are not native, but result from repeated exposure to new experiences and materials. (S-29)

P26. The same interest may be aroused by different forces in different individuals. (S-30)

P27. Interest is aroused when learners are given opportunities for overt bodily activity, investigation, adventure, contact with others, and for use in real life. (S-30)

P28. Long-term interests in activities and materials are the outcome of success in such experiences. (S-30)

P29. The learner can be motivated by the desire to improve over his previous performance. (K-118)

7. *Polarity*

a. Is the motivation bland (dull), or is it characterized by some feeling tone?

b. Is the motivation positive or negative?

P30. Learning and recall are facilitated when the learner's efforts result in some emotion-bearing responses, whether pleasant or unpleasant, from the situation or from the teacher. (S-75)

P31. Praise and success are generally more effective in facilitating learning than reprimand and failure. (S-76)

P32. Varying learner responses to forms of motivation:

- *Bright* respond more constructively to negative than *Slow*, who respond more strongly to positive.
- *Boys* respond more constructively to negative than *Girls.*
- *Older students* respond more strongly to both forms than *Younger students,* who prefer positive forms.
- *Well-adjusted students'* histories have a predominance of positive, while *Poorly-adjusted students'* histories have negative predominance.

- *Introverts* respond best to continued praise; *Extroverts* can use reprimand constructively. (S-78)

8. *Strength*
   a. Is the motivation weak, moderate, strong, excessive?
   b. Is it strong enough to overcome distraction from other sources?

P33. To learn, one must be aroused, awake, under some tension. Individuals differ as to optimal levels of tension. (B-166)

P34. The distance between a learner and his goal is a most important factor in reduced motivation. (K-124)

P35. Strong motivation raises the learner's level of activity but lowers the quality of his output. Weak motivation allows for distraction by non-relevant factors. (S-39)

P36. Learning is maximized when the degree of motivation is moderate. (S-38)

P37. The stronger the motivation becomes, the more variable are the responses of the participating learners. (S-38)

P38. The learning process is disrupted when motivational tension exceeds some optimal level. The learner may become satiated by the motivation; he may freeze or become rigid; or he may, in extreme cases, resort to aggression as a release for the motivational tension. (S-38)

P39. The impact on the learner of being encouraged to learn is based in part on his level of anxiety. (HB-564)

P40. A given activity will be experienced as success or failure depending on ego involvement. High ego involvement produces high levels of motivation, of pressure to fulfill one's aspiration on penalty of loss of self-esteem. (S-44)

9. *Variety*
   a. Is one kind of motivation used to arouse all the learners, or is there variety, based on some obvious knowledge of what might arouse individual students?

P41. Repeated use of any given motivation diminishes its value. Whether the polarity is positive or negative, the strength should be moderate, with a balance in favor of positive forms. (S-77)

10. *Timing*
    a. Where in the lesson is the motivation injected?
    b. Is it re-injected (for all students, for individuals) at points where efforts seem to flag?

P(none)

D. to select and use materials which will lead the learners to acquire the new responses and/or to practice existing responses;

1. *Scholarship*
    a. Does teacher know the subject matter?
    b. Does teacher know the modes of inquiry in the subject?
    c. Is what is marked out for learning significant within itself, both in terms of the discipline from which it comes and in terms of the students?

P(none)

2. *Materials*
    a. Are the materials appropriate to the stimuli and responses?
    b. Is their use and care effectively demonstrated/explained?
    c. Are materials distributed at the optimal time for their use?
    d. Does the manipulation hinder or help learning?
    e. Does each learner have his own, or is the sharing inhibitive or productive?

P(none)

3. *Meaningfulness*
    a. Are stimuli, responses, and subject matter meaningful to students? What evidence is there?

P42. If any single factor can be said to determine the course of a learning situation, it is the nature of the material to be learned. (K-50)

P43. Material meaningful to the learner is learned more quickly and retained longer than nonsense material. (S-132)

P44. Making that material meaningful to the learner is a

matter of relating it to what he has already learned. (K-75)

P45. Logical learning (that is, learning of essential ideas) involves the organization of material into concepts and principles. Verbatim learning involves the exact reproduction of details. The former is faster and more permanent than the latter. There is more transfer from logical to verbatim than from verbatim to logical. This suggests that understanding given material should precede attempts to memorize it. (S-132)

P46. Logical learning and sense material are at one end of a single continuum whose other end includes rote learning and nonsense material. Thus, both types of learning differ in degree rather than in kind. (S-133)

P47. Individuals differ markedly in their ability to use rote and logical learning. These differences can be related to such learner characteristics as intelligence, age, sex, and scholarship, and to such learning-process factors as the type of material, sensory mode of presentation, serial position, etc. Specifically, learners high in potential and low in achievement do better with logical learning, while those low in potential and relatively high in achievement gain more from drill or rote learning. (S-135)

4. *Structure*
   a. Is the subject matter organized in some logical way?
   b. Is the content structured in such a way as to make it challenging, but not too difficult to grasp?
   c. Does the segment of learning come from a larger unit of study to which it will be, or is now, related?
   d. Are specialized vocabulary and terminology isolated for study?
   e. Does teacher break down units into smaller elements where necessary?

P48. Learning is facilitated when the material to be learned is closely related rather than loosely related, and when the learner is allowed to select his own structure for the material rather than having a structure imposed upon him. (S-133)

P49. Instructional units need to be structured clearly and simply because difficulty in learning depends partly on how much the material needs to be structured in order to be meaningful to the learner. Though learning is a matter of understanding whole-qualities, the concept of a whole is relative rather than absolute. What is a whole for any individual depends on such factors as his learning purposes, his maturity, how meaningful the material is to him, how closely structured the material within a given unit is, and the situation in which the learner will later apply what he has learned. (S-142)

P50. In presenting new material to students, the teacher should begin with some outline or systematic arrangement before going into the details. (K-74)

P51. When a structured unit is too complex for the learners, the procedure to follow is to present the major outline first, to focus on one part, and to relate that part to the whole unit, all within a single learning situation. (S-142)

P52. The learner prefers some form of part method because he can master a smaller unit with less initial effort, because he experiences a new success with each part he masters, and because the sum total of such part successes exceeds the gratification derived from the single-success of working with the totality of the material. (S-141)

P53. Learnings unrelated to each other should be taught separately. (S-142)

P54. Older, brighter, more mature, and more stable learners generally do better with whole learning than learners who lack these attributes. (S-143)

5. *Summaries*
   a. Does teacher provide for medial and/or terminal summaries?
   b. Does teacher elicit summaries or make them himself?

P(none)

E. to control the process so that this acquisition or practice is efficient and effective;

1. *Attention-Distraction*

a. Are recurring or repetitive activities handled by well-rehearsed routines which minimize interference with substantive learning activities?
b. Is the attention of the learners focused on the stimuli and responses?
c. Are controllable distractions under control?
d. Are non-controllable distractions (street noises, sounds from other parts of the school) minimized in influence?

P55. The distractability of a stimulus depends on its novelty to the particular individual. (S-20)

P56. The more meaningful the stimulus is to the individual, the more attention he gives. (S-20)

P57. When two or more stimuli compete for the learner's attention, he turns to the strongest stimulus, to the stimulus most meaningful to him. (S-21)

P58. A stimulus extraneous to a learner's task causes a loss of full attention to that task. (S-21)

P59. When the level of distraction is high, the learner must expend more energy to maintain focus on his task. The side effects of this effort result in a decrease in accuracy at the task. (S-21)

P60. Learners need to become accustomed to the usual distractions which are part of their learning situations, so that these stimuli diminish in novelty and appeal. (S-21)

P61. A learner's area of attention has a central focus (in which all elements related to a task are clearly perceived), and a peripheral area (in which those elements related to the task and others uniquely attractive to the individual are perceived). (S-167)

P62. A response pattern to be reproduced under varied conditions should be learned under varied conditions. (B-199)

2. *Discipline*

a. Is the management of students, spaces, equipment, etc., such that activities move without interference?
b. Are there apparent standards of behavior?

c. Are there apparent standards of work?
d. Do students seem to be trained in self-control?
e. Does teacher handle "discipline problems" with minimal negative impact on the learning program?

P63. Praise and reprimand are most effective when used within the time-space of a learning experience or immediately thereafter. (S-77)

P64. As new memories overlay old ones, the pleasant/unpleasant feeling tones associated with the latter recede to a neutral value. This suggests the advisability of putting off a response to highly charged behavior until such a recession has occurred. (S-77)

P65. Negative reinforcement for a specific undesirable response helps the learner to extinguish that response. (S-76)

P66. The non-recurrence of non-habitual behavior is facilitated when such behavior is ignored by the teacher. (S-76)

3. *Media*

a. Does teacher perceive self as a medium of instruction and use appearance, voice, posture, movement, and gestures to enhance effectiveness?
b. Does teacher attempt to be cheerful, courteous, tactful, self-controlled, sympathetic, patient, poised, dignified?
c. Is teacher a good listener?
d. Do teacher actions indicate respect, fairness, and an absence of prejudice towards students, parents, and others?
e. Does teacher evidence confidence, leadership, initiative, firmness, and enthusiasm about the learning process, yet is touched with both humility and humor?
f. Does teacher appeal to a number of senses, via a variety of audio-visual materials?
g. Does teacher make effective use of the blackboard and other projection devices?
h. Does teacher use role-play and/or dramatic play to advantage?

P67. Learning is facilitated by the use of all the sensory modalities which are appropriate to a given learning situation. (S-162)

P68. No one sense is superior to the others as a learning modality. However, in a particular situation, one sense may be superior, given the nature of the material and the senses relevant to it. (S-162)

P69. Individuals differ in respect to which sensory modality will have a greater appeal. (S-163)

P70. Learning is facilitated when the material is patterned. Textual material supplemented by pictures, graphs, or maps is easier to understand than sheer text. (S-162)

P71. A given piece of material attracts attention when it varies in relative size to the other material in a learning situation, but the effect quickly fades after the initial presentation. (S-156)

P72. Items in a color that differentiates them from the rest of the material claim attention. (S-156)

P73. Learning is facilitated by a stimulus pattern involving the factor of movement. (S-156)

P74. It is the unusual, the novel (in size, color, movement, or change) that attracts the learner's attention. (S-156)

P75. The time required for drill is reduced as vividness is increased by the exploitation of such factors as size, color, movement, novelty, and sensory appeal. (S-157)

P76. Superior learning is achieved by the presentation of a given content in a variety of contextual situations. Thus, extensive reading increases the learner's interest in the content, his desire to read about it voluntarily, plus his grasp and retention of the content. (S-148)

P77. By contrast, intensive study is most useful for the exact reproduction of the specific facts involved. (S-148)

4. *Interaction Pattern*
   a. If one learns by doing, who does the "doing": teacher, some students, all students?
   b. Is teacher able to spread student participation?
   c. Is teacher an effective group leader?
   d. Do student contributions, when relevant, have an impact on the direction and substance of the learning?

e. Do students make real decisions about the direction, parameters, pacing, etc., of the learning process?

P78. The nature of the learning task determines the degree of required activity, with some tasks requiring only internal emotional responses. (B-166)

P79. The learner should be active during the learning situation, although the activity may be as limited as looking at or listening to the stimuli. (B-281)

P80. However, learning involving overt learner movement is superior to such purely ideational learning. (B-281)

P81. The more the learner actively participates in the learning process, the more he learns. One order of superiority is: laboratory experimentation, lecture-demonstration, lecture-discussion, and lecture, with reading last. Note-taking (in summary rather than verbatim form), asking questions, test-taking, and self-grading are all superior to passive listening. Learners recall responses rather than stimuli. (S-172)

P82. The more time the learner spends in making responses, the more he learns. Early and frequent attempts at recall should be introduced as soon as the totality of a piece of material has been presented and the learner has had time to read and comprehend the material. (S-173)

P83. Although older and brighter learners can learn more than younger and less apt students from working with symbols (via lectures and reading), all learners gain more from being active rather than passive in the learning process. (S-173)

P84. Learners involved in solving problems need time to explore a problem and to manipulate its elements in order to achieve clarity. (S-180)

P85. In problem-solving, the learner's discovery of a directional cue leads him to a meaningful reorganization of the elements of that problem. Although the teacher may use a question for cueing the learner, that question should not provide so much guidance that the learner loses the psychological initiative. (S-180)

P86. When the learner has achieved a meaningful reorganization of the field so that its elements fall into place, then it can be said that insight has occurred. (S-181)

P87. The initial effect (which soon wears off) of working in the presence of classmates is an increase in the learner's activity level and intensity of work. (S-98)

P88. The quality of a learner's work remains the same or sometimes deteriorates when done in the presence of other learners. Learning and retention are superior when both occur in the absence of an audience. (S-98)

P89. Performance is disturbed when the audience is either unknown or unanticipated, with large or attentive audiences being more disturbing than small or inattentive ones. (S-99)

P90. The learner is disturbed when attending to a playback of his own recorded performance. (S-99)

P91. A member of an audience learns by watching someone else's performance before that audience. (Sc-84)

P92. A child's emotion is heightened when he's spoken to by the teacher in the presence of his classmates. (S-99)

5. *Questioning*
    a. Does teacher ask questions in forms that require no restatement?
    b. Does teacher give students time to respond, or does teacher fill waiting time with rephrasings of questions?
    c. Does teacher ask questions calling for different kinds of comprehension and retention?
    d. Do teacher questions elicit critical thinking?
    e. Does teacher encourage and teach students to ask questions?
    f. Does teacher act as though each student question must be one on which the teacher is fully briefed?
    g. Does teacher admit to honest ignorance?
    h. Does teacher regard every question as deserving of immediate response?

P(none)

6. *Competition-Cooperation*
    a. Does teacher handle grouping patterns in ways that facilitate learning?

b. Does teacher stress competition with student's prior efforts?
c. Does teacher foster cooperation?
d. Is the privacy of the individual guarded where it does not interfere with the group?

P93. The learner competing with others does more work, but its quality remains the same or deteriorates. (S-105)

P94. Competition with one's own work or that of a single other individual is more effective than competition against a group. (S-105)

P95. A learner is motivated by competition when he thinks there is a chance he will succeed. Allowing him a handicap based on past achievement will increase his active participation. (S-105)

P96. Older learners are more responsive to competition than younger ones. (S-105)

P97. The response to competition by average or slow learners, who take longer to develop internalized standards, is more favorable than that of bright students. (S-105)

P98. The relative effectiveness of cooperation and competition seems to depend on the nature of the task or the goal being sought. (S-110)

P99. Competition is marked by negative personal interrelations, cooperation by positive ones. (S-110)

P100. For effective functioning, groups should contain a relatively small number of students, who know and like each other, and who choose to work together on the basis of some common interest. (S-110)

P101. Because our culture fosters competition, training is required to achieve cooperation which, therefore, occurs more in older than in younger students. (S-111)

P102. The learner working in a group, with or without interaction with other learners, tends to increase the tempo of his work, although the quality is the same as that he achieves when working alone. (S-96)

P103. The learner working with others on a task will stay with that task longer than if he worked on it alone. (S-96)

P104. Whereas the child under three is little affected by the presence of other children, the six-to-twelve-year-old of average mental ability is more affected than the bright child, who does his best work alone, especially on difficult tasks. (S-96)

P105. Group action results in a higher quality, not quantity, of work, especially in the solution of difficult problems. It has little impact on routine tasks. (S-116)

P106. As the group increases in size, the superiority of group work over individual work increases, but at a decelarating rate, depending on the size of the original group. (S-115)

P107. A group working on a task, clearly-structured and comprehensible to its membership, is more influenced by its better-informed members than by those with less information. When the task is either too difficult or ambiguous, the group is likely to assume that its enthusiastic members are also the better-informed ones. (S-115)

P108. With ability held constant, students learn more in group work than in individual work. The most able student in the group gains little or nothing. (S-116)

P109. The quality of a group's output is as good as the individual work of the best member and considerably better than the individual work of the average member. (S-113)

P110. The benefits of group work are available only when the members support each other as the group moves towards goals consensually defined. (S-116)

7. *Practice*
   a. Is practice provided after comprehension, or in an effort to achieve comprehension?
   b. Is practice individualized according to need?

P111. Practice alone doesn't help the student to learn more; it helps him to improve the retention of what he has already learned, provided his rehearsal is accurate and done under full attention. (S-193)

P112. Repeated reproduction of the same response results in some reorganization and change in that response. (S-196)

P113. The repeated response is modified to fit the learner's perception of its meaning, in vocabulary familiar to him; incongruities are made congruent; complexities are simplified; and gaps are filled in, resulting in a symmetrical, complete structure. (S-196)

P114. Forced repeated reproduction beyond the stage of modification (as in P113) results in disorganization, in learner refusal to continue making the response, in distorted recall, and finally in destruction of the learned response. (S-197)

P115. Bright students are more accurate in repeated reproduction, but tire soon. Slower students modify the response more. (S-197)

P116. Since over-reproduction of a response can weaken or destroy it, one can extinguish an habitual wrong response by conscious and deliberate over-reproduction of it. (S-199)

P117. The extinction of wrong habitual responses through negative practice does not result in the establishment of correct responses. (S-199)

P118. Given a fixed amount of practice time, spacing or distributing that time yields more effective learning and retention than concentrating or massing that time. (K-62, S-204)

P119. The optimal schedule includes practice periods of decreasing length and rest periods of equal or increasing length. (K-62, S-205)

P120. The length of practice periods, the duration of rest periods, and their frequency depend on the learner and on the nature of the material. The less able the learner and the more tedious and difficult the material, the more effective is spaced practice. (K-62, S-205)

P121. The gain from spaced practice is greatest in delayed recall. (S-206)

8. *Pacing*
   a. Is the learning process adjusted to the pace of the individual learners?
   b. Are there time limits for tasks?
   c. Are there work limits for tasks?

P122. Individual motivation is a central factor. This dictates the need for individual pacing. (BJS-239)

P123. With high-level teaching, bright students accelerate while slow ones lose touch with the learning situation. With low-level teaching, bright students learn less while slow ones learn more than they would otherwise. (K-75)

P124. To learn to make the new responses required in a given learning situation takes time, the length varying with the learner's past experience and abilities and with the difficulty of the task. (B-282)

P125. Learning will not occur if the learner is asked to acquire more responses in a given period of time than he has the capacity to acquire. (B-282)

P126. Learners organize their work more effectively and increase their rate of learning when time or work limits are set for learning tasks. (S-55)

P127. Each learner seems to have a consistent rate of work for problems of a similar character. If urged to exceed this rate for any but brief periods of time, he will be frustrated. (S-55)

P128. Moderate changes in timing, which make demands the learner is able to meet, facilitate learning. Repeated or intensified changes in timing impede learning. (S-56)

P129. Learners tend to recall material in the order in which it is learned. If elements in a series are to be recalled apart from the whole series, then the context in which these elements are learned must be varied. (S-123)

P130. The initial and terminal positions in a series are more favorable for learning than the weak medial position, although these differences decrease over time. (S-123)

P131. Emphasizing the medial position decreases its weakness. Demands for recall in the order of original learning bring out the initial position. Free recall tends to elicit the material in terminal position. (S-124)

P132. An individual's memory span, his ability to reproduce some number of items immediately after just one exposure, is relatively fixed, but its dimensions are dependent on a large array of factors, such as the nature of the material and its presentation, his familiarity with the material, his intelligence, age, maturity, etc. (S-126)

P133. As items are added to a series and thus exceed an individual's memory span, his difficulty in learning the material increases geometrically. (S-126)

P134. An increase in the complexity of the material is coupled with a disproportionately greater increase in the difficulty of mastering it. (S-127)

P135. Grouping and patterning the material in a long and complex series facilitates its mastery. (S-127)

P136. Learners, carried along by the momentum of a task in process, have a strong tendency to carry that task through to completion. (S-201)

P137. Immediate retention of material is improved and his motivation to resume that learning is increased if the learner is interrupted when he is near the completion of the task. (S-201)

P138. Reminiscence, the improvement in recall of material after an interruption in the learning process, is temporary, and decreases in impact in inverse proportion to the length of the interruption (or rest period). (S-201)

P139. The learner gains from the interruption only if he suffers no loss of self-esteem—if he does not view the interruption as an indication of failure. (S-201)

P140. The impact of reminiscence is greater when the learner's interest is high, when the learning is meaningful to him, and when he's been practicing for a long period on difficult material at a fast pace. (S-202)

P141. The impact of the reminiscence phenomenon is somewhat greater on the learning of young children, slow learners, and those in initial achievement gain. (S-202)

9. *Accuracy-Speed*

   a. Is accuracy stressed before speed of response?

   b. Are rates adjusted to individual capacities?

P142. In teaching for speed of response one should include instruction on accuracy. (S-55)

P143. The first response in learning should be accurate because it's much more difficult to extinguish an incorrect initial response and to have the learner take on the correct response than to make sure that the initial response is accurate. (S-167)

P144. The more capable learner's intelligence, purpose, and motivation, his opportunity to use unlimited resources, plus the difficulty of the material, its logical character, and the continuity of the context, all affect the extent to which he can speed up his learning. (S-55)

F. to determine to what degree each learner did, in fact, take on the new response patterns or affirm the existing ones.

1. *Feedback-Reinforcement*
    a. Does teacher arrange for students to know the results of their efforts?
    b. Does the feedback provide specific cues for mastery of accurate responses?
    c. Does teacher treat incorrect responses as evidence of a need for re-teaching?
    d. Do students play a role in on-going monitoring of their efforts?

P145. The learner will make little or no progress unless he gets feedback on the adequacy of his responses. (S-60)

P146. The learner's feedback on the adequacy of his responses can come from demonstrations and experiments as well as in verbal form from the teacher. (K-53)

P147. Reinforcement from individuals esteemed by the learner facilitates his learning. (K-55)

P148. When the learner is given feedback on the results of his efforts, there is a marked improvement in his performance. (S-60)

P149. Students are likely to repeat activities which originally raised their self-esteem. (K-51)

P150. Positive reinforcement for a response increases the probability of its recurrence. (K-50)

P151. The more the learner is told, specifically and in detail, about the results of his efforts, the more he progresses. (S-60)

P152. Informing the learner that a given response is correct results in greater progress than telling him that a response is wrong. (S-61)

P153. The learner profits more from immediate feedback on his learning efforts than from delayed feedback. (S-61)

P154. Positive reinforcement reduces the learner's anxiety and facilitates his learning. (K-51)

P155. As the frequency of positive reinforcement for a given response is increased, so the probability of its recurrence is increased. (K-50)

P156. The learner loses interest when reinforcement is commonplace and remains constant in form. (K-55)

P157. The learner can become overly dependent on a particular reinforcement or on a singular form of reinforcement. (K-55)

P158. Learning to monitor his own responses and to reward himself are important steps forward for the student. (K-51, 54)

P159. It is possible to keep a learner at work on a learning activity by use of social reinforcement until the learner achieves the level of self-reinforcement through an increase in self-esteem and the development of an intrinsic interest in the activity. (K-55)

P160. Positive reinforcement should be given for both the quality and the quantity of learner output. (K-60)

P161. Quality output criteria should be increased in steps distinguishable by the learner, but not in increments which discourage him from further efforts. (K-60)

P162. When students believe that they will receive positive reinforcement regardless of the quality of their efforts, they diminish their application to the task. (K-61)

P163. The frequency of a given response diminishes when positive reinforcement is withdrawn. (K-64)

P164. Any given reinforcement may have a different impact on different learners because their needs vary. (BJS-175)

P165. Knowledge of results of their efforts has the greatest impact on better students, a greater impact on younger than on older students, and the least impact on poor students. (S-61)

P166. Learner behavior can be modified by rewards for responses that are partially correct. This is particularly useful in working with slow learners. (K-54)

P167. Responses which had only partial reinforcement are more resistant to extinction than those given either continuous or 100 percent reinforcement. (K-64)

P168. However, continuous reinforcement, particularly of the learner's early efforts, facilitates the more rapid acquisition of new skills. (K-65)

P169. A given student response may not be reinforced positively once and negatively another time. (BJS-176)

P170. The absence of expected positive reinforcement is seen by the learner as at least a sign of disapproval or possibly a form of punishment. (K-52)

P171. Punishments do not necessarily weaken response patterns in the way that rewards strengthen them. (BJS-176)

P172. Guidance (that is, the assistance rendered to a learner in the discovery of solutions to problems) is best given in small amounts, so that the learner either makes his own discoveries or at least believes that he does. (S-176)

P173. Guidance is best given in the early stages of skill development, after the learner has been given time to explore the new task, and in response to the learner's feeling of a need for assistance. (S-177)

P174. The most effective form of guidance is that which permits the learner to retain the initiative to act. If teacher demonstrates, then learner tells her what to do, later doing it himself. If learner does something, then teacher tells him what to do, but the learner translates the words into acts. The guidance is in symbolic form. (S-177)

P175. Guidance should stress correct rather than incorrect responses. (S-178)

2. *Success-Failure*
    a. Did students learn to make the new responses?
    b. Was failure by students mitigated?
    c. Does teacher provide opportunities for each pupil to succeed more often than he fails?

P176. The average individual defines his goals on the bases of the expectations of parents and social groups. (S-44)

P177. The learner who experiences success in a task is able to make a more realistic estimate of his next goal and to exert the effort to achieve it. (S-44)

P178. The learner should not feel that he has been guaranteed success in a learning task, but that he has a good chance of being successful. (K-93)

P179. The learner who experiences failure in a task greatly overestimates (or occasionally grossly underestimates) his future achievement. (S-44)

P180. The effect of failure is to decrease the level of muscular action which normally accompanies attempted solutions of problems, although the learner may at times speed up his efforts just to reduce tension. (S-86)

P181. The effect of failure is to slow down the learning process. The learner uses more time to arrive at correct responses and makes fewer of them. (S-86)

P182. The learner who is failing retreats from reality into daydreams, quitting the task, and regression. (S-86)

P183. The effect of failing to make the correct response is to give emphasis to and fix the wrong one, and leads to non-adjustive behavior by the learner. (S-87)

P184. Different learners respond differently to failure: some evidence aggression, some regress, others panic. (S-87)

P185. Failure and its attendant unproductive behavior can be offset by providing the learner with tasks of increasing difficulty in which he can be successful. (S-87)

P186.

Learner succeeding	*Learner failing*
–time seems short	–time seems long
–task seems easy	–task seems difficult
–enjoys the activity	–dislikes the activity
–more likely to resume task after interruption	–less likely to resume task after interruption
–increased activity level	–becomes passive
–greater effectiveness of work	–lesser effectiveness of work
–more recall of related material	–forgets related material
–more language expression	–less language expression
–longer period devoted to initial effort	–tires quickly

(S–76)

3. *Retention-Forgetting*

   a. Did teacher take steps to insure maximum retention of new response patterns?

b. Were students told how their retention would be checked, and when?

c. Were assignments made to firm up the response pattern?

P187. Learning generally follows an S-shaped pattern, characterized by an accelerating initial rise and a slow leveling off. Plateaus in that curve may indicate that the learner's motivation has flagged, that his learning situation has been altered, or that his progress needs to be measured in smaller units. (S-188)

P188. Forgetting is characterized by a proportionately larger loss immediately after learning and a smaller loss later on. (S-188)

P189. There is neither permanent learning nor total forgetting. Material is retained in memory in relation to its functional use. (S-188)

P190. Recall may be accurate but selective, as in the tendencies to recall facts with which one agrees, to have difficulty recalling those with which one disagrees, and to recall interrupted more effectively than completed tasks. (K-70)

P191. The learner's memory may be skewed in a direction dictated by his value system. (K-68)

P192. Relating new material to material already mastered facilitates recall of new material. (K-70)

P193. Learners tend to recall material to which the teacher has directed their attention. (K-70)

P194. Though the learner's initial perception of a situation may be accurate, if the plan he uses to organize his recall differs from the reality of the situation, then the recall will differ to the same extent. (K-69)

P195. High level performance, achieved with the aid of continuous reinforcement, can be made less susceptible to extinction by the use of partial reinforcement. (K-65)

P196. Practice or drill on skills, facts, or concept-applications already learned to the point of mastery is called overlearning. Retention is more permanent with overlearning than with mastery alone. (S-193)

P197. Overlearned material is less susceptible to interference from other learning than material studied with lesser intensity. (B-195)

P198. Practicing half again as long as it took to reach mastery (i.e., 50 percent overlearning) seems to facilitate retention; additional practice beyond this point results in diminishing returns for the effort expended. (S-193)

P199. Retention may be measured by recall, recognition, or relearning. Of the three, the ability to recall demonstrates the greatest amount of retention, relearning the least. (S-190)

P200. Material forgotten beyond recall or recognition can be relearned with extreme efficiency. (B-206)

P201. The amount of learning forgotten over a summer vacation (i.e., summer loss) is greater in such specific skill areas as spelling and arithmetic fundamentals than in such content fields as literature and science. (S-211)

P202. The amount of summer loss varies inversely with the extent of mastery of the skills or materals. (S-211)

P203. The amount of summer loss varies inversely with the transferability of such learning to non-school activities. (S-211)

P204. Since the activities of individual learners vary over a summer, there is a high degree of variability in summer loss among individuals. (S-211)

P205. Overlearning in spring can help retard summer loss. (S-212)

P206. The student who attends summer school gains little or nothing in achievement, but his skills in such subjects as spelling and arithmetic are kept from deteriorating. (S-212)

P207. The student can be helped to regain what he lost over the summer by means of a review in the early weeks of school. (S-212)

4. *Transfer*

   a. Does teacher aim at the transfer of concepts and skills?

   b. Does teacher guide students to see how transfer can and does occur?

P208. Transfer (the impact of one learning upon the acquisition of a second) does occur. (S-219)

P209. When performance is facilitated by prior learning we have positive transfer. When that performance is interfered with by prior learning we have negative transfer. (K-81)

P210. Positive and negative transfer are a single mental process of reinforcement and interference and part of a larger process in which any given learning experience merges with past learnings, which, in turn, affect future learning experiences. (S-236)

P211. When learning situations A and B are similar and the appropriate responses to both are the same, positive transfer occurs. (K-83)

P212. When learning situations A and B are similar, but B calls for responses other than those that were appropriate to A, then negative transfer occurs. (K-83)

P213. As the similarity in meaning between A and B increases, so does the potential for negative transfer. (S-230)

P214. As the similarity in external circumstances between A and B increases, so does the potential for negative transfer. (S-230)

P215. Positive transfer is fostered when the learning in A is complete and accurate, when the materials in both A and B are meaningful and structured, when the learner's attitudes in both A and B are favorable, and when the elapsed time between A and B is relatively short. (S-224)

P216. Positive transfer is fostered by that learning situation which focuses the learner's attention on classifying entities, making generalizations about them, establishing relationships between them, and organizing them within a logical structure. (S-224)

P217. The learner who evidences active behavior in a learning situation is likely to do better on transfer tasks than the one who is passive. (BJS-288)

P218. The learner who is actively involved in the discovery of principles and rules and the strategies for employing them is likely to transfer their application to other situations. (BJS-288)

P219. Though individuals differ in their ability to transfer, the brighter, more mature, and more widely experienced learners evidence a greater ability to transfer than those with the opposite characteristics. (K-87, S-225)

P220. A learner impacted by negative transfer evidences confused and erratic behavior and even a total cessation of activity. (S-231)

P221. To lessen the impact of negative transfer between two situations, overlearning in the first one will decrease the negative impact on the second one. (S-231)

P222. A period of learning followed by a comparatively inactive one of rest and/or sleep decreases the possibility of negative transfer. (S-230)

> Before we discuss your quite lengthy empirical grid, NS, I'd like to say a few things: Somewhere in your discussion of the six sub-heads you said we could react to that total scheme after you had fully presented it. Since it seemed logical to see how you would move from that exposition into your EG, I decided to wait. Now I can combine my responses to both the sub-heads and the EG into a single set of statements and questions. I can see how defining supervision as the improvement of instruction led you to further define each term, and to extract the six questions which became the foundations for your sub-heads. What I would like you to elaborate on first is the notion of units, especially the names you assigned them.

What our discourse represents, ZA, is the current status of my thinking on the subject of supervision. My ideas about it have undergone many changes and will probably be changing again even as you read these words.

I began by asking such questions as are in the Empirical Grid (EG) some years ago, without immediate concern for an overall structure. When I came across Seagoe's book, I began to organize her statements and my questions into groupings, which I then used as a grid for looking at live and recorded instructional sessions. ZA's in my supervision classes tested my ideas against their experiences, used portions of the various drafts of the EG to look at recorded lessons, and asked searching questions. The EG you now have is the culmination of an attempt to marry principles of learning to empirical questions. Unit titles are really appellations for each of the 33 marriages (units); they're not the names of the question-partners alone.

I am not permanently wedded to the units, questions, and principles in the EG, although I don't foresee any chance of a divorce from the concept of an empirical grid.

> Then you have asked every question you can think of?

Yes, up to the point of putting the words down on paper. Not only have I no doubt that more questions can be asked and that you, ZA, can suggest many more, but I'm equally certain that others will want to organize the grid (assuming they even agree on such a structure) in different ways. It would be gratifying to see this happen.

What I most want you to understand is this: The grid is my attempt to systematize the scholarly examination of the teaching-learning process from a supervisor's point of view. The grid is meant to supply a framework for this examination. If others pick up the idea, keep refining the grid, and more research is done to bolster or refute the empirical evidence, yielding newer and more accurate principles, then I will have achieved my objective. I expect that other questions will be asked; I expect that some, maybe many, principles will be challenged. But if the framework remains, and if at least some principles are fully accepted, then we'll have made a start on codifying what we know and what we need to know about this whole matter.

What about the principles, NS? Is there some significance to your use of only five sources? And why these particular five sources?

Once Seagoe's work opened the door for me, I began to look for other kindred collections. Though I found no comparable compendium of statements, the four additional sources I quote do take positions comparable to hers on various issues in learning. That is, they try to reduce learning research data to general statements which suggest or imply conditions under which learning does or does not take place. I did search through other volumes, but the returns diminished to the point where further searching seemed unprofitable. So I stopped.

I notice that your principles contain no quotation marks. Are they totally paraphrased?

Yes, ZA. I began with some 330 quotations. They contained a substantial amount of duplication, plus the unique "voices" of different authors. It all made for a very cumbersome EG. The present form eliminates all duplications and reduces the voices to mine alone.

One thing you most impressed me with in your class is to avoid an immediate challenge to words and phraseology, but to test a person's substantive ideas against reality. In that way I could see whether differences were semantic or real. So would you show us, NS, how you would apply this to an actual school situation?

Fine, ZA. Were we still in a college classroom, I would show you one of the recorded lessons in our collection. As a substitute, I have made a verbatim transcript of such a lesson, which is the substance of the next chapter.

But keep the following in mind, ZA. First, our concern will be with the meaning and applicability of the EG. Though we will be analyzing a lesson, our purpose is not to analyze, but to see whether the EG yields a set of judgments which seem acceptable. Since there is no standard yardstick for measuring instructional quality, I'm going to ask you to state your views of the lesson before we use the EG. Of course, you're not here to answer me; but I have shown this tape to a goodly number of students and can reconstruct their responses.

Second, as artificial as my construction of your presumed judgments may be, ZA, it is much less artificial than the whole procedure of working from a verbatim transcript. As a functioning supervisor in a school, you will probably never have such a transcript. In addition, though video equipment is becoming available in more and more schools, the odds are that you will most often observe teachers in person, with no playback on a TV screen.

> Then why don't you give us as text the notes a supervisor might have made in direct observation of this lesson, NS, instead of handing us the transcript?

There is surely no likelihood, ZA, that you and I would have made the same notes, because we would be sifting the events through different human filters. Even with a verbatim transcript we don't begin at the same starting point: in recording this lesson I came away with non-verbal memories of what occurred, memories reinforced by the many playbacks I have viewed of it. As we discuss the lesson, it may seem appropriate to inject some of these memories into our discourse.

Finally, the EG is too cumbersome a device to apply under normal supervisory conditions. As I said earlier, after we have analyzed some transcripts to get the full measure of what I've included in the EG, I will show you my derived primitive version of an assessment tool and tie it into the supervisory cycle I will later explain and demonstrate in great detail.

VII.

High School Science Lesson

Picture for yourself a science room in a large urban high school. The central portion of the room contains movable chairs, occupied by some 25-30 students. There are a number of lab tables encircling this central portion, plus a large demonstration table up front, behind which is the blackboard.

Because we were recording this lesson on videotape, and occupying the right side (as the teacher sees it when standing with blackboard at his back), the teacher, who moved a great deal, used the aisle between his demonstration table and blackboard, and especially the left side, occasionally putting one haunch up on a lab table on that side of the room. He never really sat down.

The students were somewhere in the middle of their high school career, taking the required year-course in science, which had been stretched to three semesters for some students. This was the second of the three for these particular students, many of whom spoke with accents indicating that English was not their first language.

I have masked the identity of the school by omitting some of the teacher's remarks, which would easily identify it and, therefore, him.

The transcript begins with a copy of the material the teacher put on the board after erasing the homework assignment. That assignment read:

Review Book

Read p. ..... to .....

Answer questions ..... to .....

Since we did not check on the nature of that book, since no reference was ever made to it in the lesson, I've omitted the page and question numbers, though the teacher did specify them.

Of course, all the blackboard material does not appear at once. As you read the transcript, you'll be able to gather at what point each item is added.

The transcript contains three columns. The first is a record of time passing, using four numerals to denote minutes and seconds. It will help us to make specific references. The second column identifies speakers: T (teacher); K ("kid," that is, student, because I use "S" for stimulus).

The third column is the verbatim transcript. I missed a few words here and there, and have identified the places. But very little is missing except, of course, the feelings engendered in a listener (to the tape) by the shades and nuances in the words, and in a viewer (of the videotape) of the whole process. Nonetheless, you'll find much virtue in the transcript.

We did not try to keep a record of how many different students actually spoke. My guess is around ten. One spoke a great deal; his statements begin thus: (K).

Blackboard Material

Aim: How Fossils Form?

IGNEOUS
PALEONTOLOGY

1. *Fossil*–Remains of impressions of ancient life

2. *Fossil Formation*

   A. Formed by sedimentation
      1. Fish dies, falls to bottom
      2. Covered by sediment* QUICK BURIAL
      3. More sediment is deposited–sedimentary rock

   B. *By Refrigeration*
      1. Wooly mammoth

   C. *By Petrifaction*
      1. Petrified wood

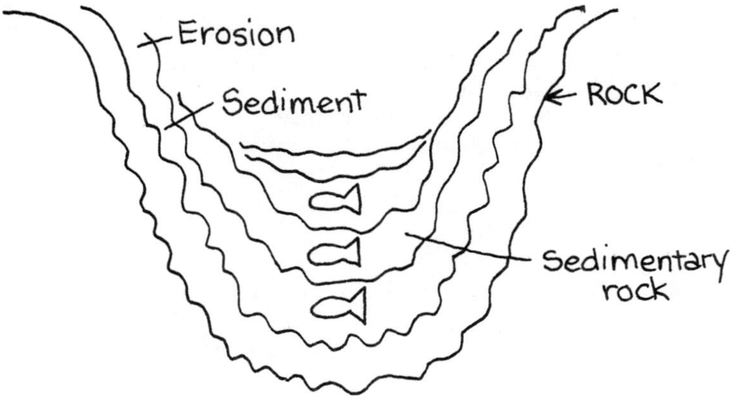

TRANSCRIPT

High School Science Lesson

0000 T We're having a very short period. (Some noise as students enter.) Would you kindly sit down? While you're getting yourselves settled, will you please copy tomorrow's homework assignment? I won't collect the homework today, just to save a few moments of time. (Begins taking attendance, calling each K by name.) (Ks copy HW.)

0140 T Has everybody copied the assignment for tomorrow? Please get your notebooks out. (T circulates–moves around the room.)

0222 T You know, one of the big things that happens in this country is the building of roads. People are always building highways. Why are they so busy building new roads and new highways across this country?

0235 (K) To go from different towns and cities. Like that, transportation.

0242 T Yes, very nice. Of course, they knock down a few trees and dig up the countryside, and so on. Now, I happen to live in a very far away place called . . . (omitted from transcript). You must have heard of . . . . We get a lot of publicity in the newspapers, you know. In any event, they were digging up not too far from my house and I was walking around there one day and I found a rock. And I want to show this to you, but you're not to say a word. Just look at it, OK? I'll walk around with this. My kind of rock.

0325 T Take a quick look. (More such comments as he walks around the room, holding the rock for each K to see.)

0353	T	I would pass it around, but I'm afraid we might drop it by mistake, and then I'd be heartbroken because this is my rock. (Two Ks each say: Fossil, fossil.) Now, you've seen rocks in the past. No big deal about a rock. Why might this attract somebody's attention if they were walking along the road there and found this thing?
0417	K	It's a fossil, a fossil.
0420	K	It has an imprint in it.
0423	T	Don't all rocks have imprints? It seems to me I see them all the time.
0428	K	It takes age, it takes time for an imprint on a rock. (K spoke softly.)
	T	I have a bad cold. I can't hear you. C'mon, you're doing good.
	K	No, forget it.
0444	T	No, I'm not going to forget it. (Pause) Alright, I'll forget it (pause) for a minute.
0450	K	(different K) You know, when you see an imprint on it, that catches your attention.
	T	Very good. Somebody used a word here to describe what we found on this rock. Would somebody please raise your hand and tell us what the word was.
0505	(K)	Fossil.
	T	Good. What question might come to mind about the fossil on the rock? Angelo*?
0517	K	When was the imprint? How did it get there?
	T	That's it. Or, how was this fossil formed? And that's what we're trying to find out today. Let's start out then with our aim. (0533) (Writes on blackboard.)
0558	T	Now, what is the first thing we must define at this point? Jack?
	K	A fossil.
	T	Good, OK, you're on. I know one of my aunts is usually called . . .—well, anyway. (Writes on bb.) Anybody?
0628	(K)	The skeleton of some primitive animal that was, you know, preserved, like, it was in rock, or something. It still remains.
0639	T	Good, good. Anything else that you may say about a fossil? (no response) You used the words, primitive animal. Suppose you find the skeleton of an elephant, in Africa. Why would that not be a fossil?
0658	K	It's not primitive. It's not primitive.
	T	Uh-hm. Alright. Anything else? C'mon, somebody else. (Refering to (K)) . . . is all by himself today. Carmen?

*The real names of all teachers and students in the entire book have been replaced by appropriate pseudonyms.

K (Carmen's response inaudible on tape.)

T I can't hear you, honey.

K It doesn't mean there was any change.

0725 T That's a very good word. Instead of primitive, which might be a term that isn't appropriate here, what might be a better word that we might use instead of primitive?

K Extinct.

0738 T That's a good word. Though it may not be absolutely so. (Writes on bb.) Don't write this yet. What does the word extinct mean?

(K) (starts to reply.) T: Sh, sh, sh.

K It means no longer existent.

0800 T Exactly. So let's put all of those things together to see if we can come up with a definition of the word fossil. It's a remain, a part, perhaps, an impression . . . some words that were used . . .

(K) It was usually stone.

0813 T Wait, wait. Let's see if we can get this definition down. (pause) Hm, alright, it's a remain. (Writes on bb.) What did we say about these living things, as far as their existing today on earth? Jack?

K They're not living.

0841 T OK, let's say ancient life, or life that is no longer in existence. So, fossils are remains or impressions (talks as he writes on bb). OK. Now, any questions on this so far? (none) Why then would an elephant not be considered a fossil?

(K) Because it's still around.

0907 T Exactly. You just go out into . . . Park or walk along . . . You can go . . . , you may see them. Yes?

K How come the animal has to be extinct?

0920 T Good question. Anybody? Very good question.

K What's the question?

T Alright, once more.

K How come the animal has to be estinct? (mispronunciation)

T EXtinct! K: OK (T corrects the K's pronunciation in a way which elicits class laughter at the play on words.)

0940 K Because the way the word fossil is defined. It would have to be extinct for it to remain to have the same meaning.

0948 T Actually, that's a very good point. In fact, we were discussing it inside (referring to the departmental office on the same floor) a few days ago. It may not have to be extinct. In fact, I remember reading, you might have seen it, they found, quote, a living fossil. If it's extinct, how is it living? But I think we got around it by using the term here (underscores *ancient* on bb). Very, very old. Alright, we got our definition of a fossil.

1016 T Let's get back to our friend here. What does this tell us about how the earth might have looked a long, long time ago in . . .? Let's use our time machine. Remember how we used it? OK, we'll just project ourselves back, back, back, thousands and millions, tens of millions, hundreds of millions. Yes?

K You know, I think the earth must have been covered by water at some time.

1050 T Very good. Very proper question. Why do you think . . . was covered with water? Easy now, don't strain yourself.

K (makes inaudible statement which includes:) water.

1121 T Ah, you said the magic word water. How do you know? (Shows rock to K.) What's this supposed to be?

K A fish.

T Aaahhhh. Very good.

K I didn't notice . . .

T I guess I went too fast. (Asks K to speak louder for the videotaping.) Can you tell that once more? Loud and clear!

K It must have been covered with water, because there's a fish on the rock.

1153 T Excellent. Now let's see if we can make a picture of this. (Goes to bb.) First of all, let's put down our next thing (the outline). I'm going to leave out something in A. Just leave a little space about over here.

1218 T And let's see if we can sort of put a camera, way back, a hundred million years ago, two hundred million years ago, in . . . , and it might look perhaps something like this. (draws) You're supposed to admire this beautiful picture. How do we know from the work that we discussed yesterday and the day before that the earth's surface might have had cracks and ridges and big holes in it, way, way back?

1258 K Earthquakes and volcanoes.

T Well, that's a possibility, yes.

1303 K Ice and snow. Glaciers.

T Good. Anything else?

(K) When the earth was created it was hot. You know, it was mostly lava. As it started cooling off, it started contracting. As it started contracting, rocks started sprouting up.

T (points to drawing) OK, this is rock (labels drawing) and this is a crack or a crevice or a huge basin in the earth. Now, let's assume water began to form and the water began to run down this rock. By what process might this rock have been worn away?

K Erosion?

1347 T Very good. So we have erosion. How would you describe the pieces of rock that might be carried down into this basin? Jack?

K –

T Yes, in size, that is.

K Oh, yes, big.

T Suppose the water is pouring down in torrents, century after century after century. Redeem yourself.

K Small.

1413 T Good. Tiny pieces. Not necessarily, but all different sizes, but mostly small pieces. What name might we give to the pieces that are constantly falling down into this opening or hole?

K Sand?

1429 T Yes, it might eventually form sand. But there's another word and they call it (a barely audible K's voice saying sentiment) sediment. And let's say the water keeps rushing down. And by the way, you know, this rock would have different minerals in it, and just to make it easier, we'll use different colors (of chalk). For example, the sediment might be carried down and then sort of coat the bottom of this pond, and then, as the rains keep falling, let's try another color. This is being done in living color. And you might find another layer of sediment. And then, of course, the waters keep pouring down and this thing might sort of fill in with water, and then we have our little friend here. Let's put him over here (draws fish). This picture will not be hanging in the Louvre, I promise you (a catching of breath by some K or Ks). Well, in any event, there he is swimming around, having a good time. But eventually, as it must to all fish, what's going to happen to him?

K Perish.

1542 T Amanda? In about 35, 40, 50 years? Getting tired and old of living.

K He's going to die.

T The Herring Maven [reference to a then-current local television commercial] gets him. No, what happens to him? (One K chuckles.)

K He dies.

T Good. Not good that he dies, but it happens.

K He gets covered with sediment.

1600 T Wait, wait, wait. Let's get him dead first. (Class laughs.) There he is. He finally dies. When he dies, what might occur to the body? Instead of it floating, let's say it falls down here (draws). Who said that? Juan? Now tell us.

K In about a thousand years the fish will be covered with sediment.

T As this continues, yes go ahead, let's get another layer of rock, another layer (draws more layers). What we now have is sort of a shallow sea. Carmen?

K You have a little valley.

1655 T Yah. What happens to the valley as it keeps going on millions and millions and millions of years?

K (inaudible) T: Can't hear you. K: –

T What'll it be?

K A lake.

T Might be.

(K) Might be a flat shore.

1717 T Yes, it would be land here. How would we compare the pressure at the bottom of this particular ancient lake that's no longer a lake or a sea, let's say in this spot. Let's keep filling it up (draws). How would you compare the pressure of that in the middle with that on top? How about somebody else, huh? (pause)

K On top it would be less.

1748 T Very good. Let's say you save up a whole pile of newspapers. Ever save newspapers? (K: Yeah.) Don't. Big mess, but we save 'em, for about a week anyway. Let's say for two or three weeks you keep piling them up and you want to get one that's three weeks old. Why might you have a harder time pulling it out than one that's two or three days old?

K There's plenty of papers over it.

T Yes, then how would you compare the pressure then?

K It's harder.

1822 T Yes, what else? The pressure is greater. You can't yank the thing out. So if you have these little pieces of rock and you took a sample of that rock as I went back in my time machine. I happen to have a sample. It's not rock yet. (Shows class a core of soil in a tall glass container.) Sand, mud, and so on. What do you notice about this particular type of arrangement here? Jack?

K Different colors.

T Good, what else? (Adds to the drawing on the bb, making some inaudible comments.)

K It looks like just the opposite of what the earth looked like before the erosion.

1908 T Ummmmmmmmmm. No.

(K) The more dirt fall on top of it, it causes more pressure. The rock in the bottom gets more concentrated. See, here it's mud. It would be like packed tight together and all the water evaporates. It would just become solid rock where it used to be just mud.

1928 T Good. And what type of rock would finally form after millions of years of this tremendous pressure being built up? Not an inch or a foot, but a thousand feet, two thousand feet, ten thousand feet? What would be the name of this type of rock?

K Fossil

T (explodes) NO!!! (Class laughs, because the explosion was

meant to be humorous.) Not yet anyway. The name of the type of rock?

(K) Sedimentary rock?

1957 T Ahhh, ohhh (pleasurable). How did you figure that out? (Class laughs.) Remind me to pass that fellow. (Writes on bb.) So therefore, if we ask the question: In what type of rock would you expect to find fossils? How would we answer that question?

K Sedimentary.

T Yes. Why wouldn't you find it in the rock that originally formed when the earth was very hot and then it cooled?

K Because you told us yesterday that everything . . .

T (interrupting) Don't say that! (Class laughs.)

K . . . whatever was caught up in the rock would burn up and melt, you know.

2039 T Exactly. In fact, there's a name for that type of rock, the rock that is formed from the cooling of the earth after the earth was born. (Writes on bb.) Anybody know what this word means, from your background in other languages perhaps? Igneous? Well, it means fire rock. It would be pretty hard to find the remains or a trace of an ancient animal. So, getting back to our little friend, we can see perhaps how, in our time machine, how this particular animal might have left a trace or a remain. (2119) Now we call this method of fossil formation, we call it, let's say, formed by sedimentation. One type of fossil formation. (2140) Let's see if we can just indicate the steps that took place now. Let's see if we can put it together. First thing, what happened to my fish after a while? No calling out please. (Pause) How about Dick? (Pause) He's swimming around. Eventually what's going to happen to him?

K The fish? He'll die.

2205 T OK. Very good. (Writes on bb.) Of course, nobody has asked me this question; maybe you thought of it: How did the fish get there in the first place?

Ks Yeah, yeah.

T I'm not going to tell you. I will not tell you. But later on we might talk about it. But anyway, there he is minding his own business. Plop! What's the next thing that happens? Amanda?

K He's covered by a layer of sediment, –

2246 T Sediment is fine. I'm going to add something to this and I want you to think and perhaps figure out why this is so important. In fact, we can even put a star here. (Writes on bb.) Quick burial. Why do you think it's so important for this animal to be buried quickly, in these circumstances? Dick, I can't hear you.

K If he's not, he won't be preserved.

T Why not? Very good.

K He'll rot away; his bones will be eaten up.

2337 T Good. What happens to most living things after they stop living?

K They die. (Laughter) Their bodies decay and their bones become separated.

T And the bones can also rot away. So you have to have a quick burial. That might indicate why, out of all the millions and billions of living things that were on earth for the last . . . well, since life has been on earth . . . only very few have remained to be found in this form or other forms of fossils. So, the idea of quick burial. Why might a very dry hot place preserve the remains of ancient forms of life?

(K) No moisture in the air.

T So?

(K) It's water that like spoils it, you know. Then the moisture in the air . . .

2428 T I don't mean to interrupt you. What actually causes decay? Let's see if we can go back to Bio I. I know it's against the rules, but let's do it anyway.

K The oxygen, the moisture?

T You mean the moisture itself? No.

K I think it's caused by germs, like bacteria.

T Then why won't bacteria make a living if there's no water around?

K Because they have to live in moist places, you know.

2454 T They need water like all forms of life need water. It's like raisins and grapes. You put a bowl of grapes on the table and a bowl of raisins on the table. Why would the raisins perhaps not spoil and the grapes will, eventually, after about a year or two or three? In my refrigerator I always find them stuck in a corner somewhere. Yes? Can't hear you, Carmen.

K The raisins are already dry.

2522 T Good. So therefore, when we have extreme dryness, it might help to preserve living things. You know, there's a desert in China called the Gobi Desert, and there they have found the bones of dinosaurs, in very good condition. Because of the fact that they had some sort of quick burial. We'll go back to that later on. And, the next step, after it's buried quickly, what's going to start piling on on top, on top, on top of this?

K Sediment.

2558 T OK. (Writes on bb.) More sediment is deposited and eventually you get the formation of (writes sedimentary rock on bb). Now, question, suppose this occurred a thousand feet below the surface, and it could very well happen that way, how did I possibly find this rock ten or fifteen feet below the surface when they were digging up this road? (Pause)

K In the first place, part of the earth is being pushed up, and you know, earthquakes causing the earth to change its regular course. It could be pushed up to the top by erosion.

2656 T That's beautiful. Tell 'em that again. That's perfect.

K I said earthquakes cause a change in the regular level of the earth, forcing it upward, and erosion washing away the rock and soil on top, finally causing it to come near the top of the earth.

2715 T Remember how we were discussing that the earth is constantly changing, that things happen. Now, of course an earthquake is a dramatic change, but there are smaller, subtle changes that are going on all the time; if we go back in our time machine, we saw just now that the earth has changed. (Pause) Now, I hate to say how long ago this was. About . . . years ago I was out in Colorado. Anybody know where Colorado is?

(K) West in the United States.

2743 T Yeah, in the western part, just on our side of the Rocky Mountains. And not very far from the university where I happened to be taking a course. Very nice. People took tennis in the morning, fishing in the afternoon. Nice place to go. And there was a place called Fossil Ridge Road, where we walked along. We found these round rocks. With a sledge hammer we'd just take it and crash it on another rock and split it open, and we found impressions of clams and different types of sea life. What does that indicate about how the earth's surface had changed from that time till now, obviously?

(K) There used to be a sea where you people were walking.

K (Amanda says something.)

T Can't hear you, Amanda.

K First it was covered by the water and then it might be earthquakes or something like that.

2843 T Yes. Why would scientists who study fossils, why would they be interested in looking through these layers of rock to find the remains, if possible, of ancient forms of life? Why bother?

K To see whether there was water there before.

2905 T Who cares? Look, we're having our own problems now. Why worry about what went on a million or a billion years ago? Jack?

K To see the way the animals and different things were in ancient times, compared to the way they are now.

T What do we call this particular change in plants and animals from ancient times to now? What name do we give to this whole process?

K Evolution.

2930 T Yes. Here are men spending all of their lives digging up fossils. You know we have a name for this science of digging of fossils. (Writes on bb.)

K (Reading it from bb.) Paleontology.

T Paleontology. Do you know that oil companies have paleontologists on their payroll? Why would an oil company pay some guy to perhaps dig up, looking for fossils?

K Because by the position of the earth they could probably tell where they would most likely find oil.

3007 T Of course. How do we think oil was formed?

K By the decaying of plants and animals which are trapped under the earth.

T Right. So if you guys want to get a nice career in the Iranian oil fields or something, become a paleontologist, make a lot of money.

K (Under T's voice) How long does it take? (Class laughs at T.)

3025 T So, this is one type of fossil formation. These steps which we think take place. One question before we go to a couple of other examples. Suppose we found a fish fossil here and another one here (draws on bb) . . . don't draw this . . . and another one here. Why would a person trying to understand evolution be very interested in this particular sequence of events?

3053 (K) How it changed fishes, evolution. If they've gotten stronger, weaker. How the environment may have changed the fishes.

T I don't think you can tell from a fossil whether it's a strong or weak animal. But it might be.

(K) You can tell by the bone structure. If it has heavy bones . . .

3110 T Alright, suppose you did a census and you wanted to find the age of these particular fish, what might we know from this particular business here? Carmen, you have a gleam in your eye. Sure you do.

K (Carmen) He says the fossils were formed when the rocks were formed.

T Yeah, so?

K So we can find how old the rocks were.

T And . . .

K And how old the fishes might be.

T Who would like to make a prediction, to give a comparison in age, within a few million years or so, the age of these rocks, how might you be able to do it? Something we said yesterday. How might we find out the age of a rock?

K Look the furthest down.

3218 T Yes, that's true, but I mean to actually say this thing is 158 million years old, this one is 80 million years old, this one is 20 million years old. Yes?

K Check the amount of lead in the rocks and the amount of . . .

T The ratio . . . what would be the other end of the ratio?

K Uranium.

3240 T Alright, very good. Now let's see if we can get some other types of fossil formation. We have it by sedimentation. Has everyone finished copying this? (Meaning the HW assignment) (Kiddingly) I would erase it anyway, you know, but . . . (Does so.) Now if you were running around perhaps in a certain part of Russia. Pretty cold up there. And if we had nothing else to do, you might be getting very hungry. And you might have found an animal intact in the ice. (Pause) They actually found . . . I had a picture of it but I couldn't dig it up . . . an entire huge animal, at least 30,000 years old, in ice, and you know the food was still edible. (Pause) And it isn't true that it was shipped to our cafeteria. (Laughter) The dogs ate it. The dogs did eat it.

3342 (K) It was a mammoth.

T Very good. Hold it. Now we have by sedimentation. (Writes on bb.) An example of this would be (writes). Perhaps someone can describe or give some sort of a relationship of a wooly mammoth to an animal that's in existence today.

K Elephant.

T Why is the wooly mammoth not an elephant? That's a grim question. Because it isn't, of course. Yes?

3422 K 'Cause it's not wooly.

T Exactly. It's a relative. So if we find the remains of a wooly mammoth, we would call it a fossil, isn't that so? But it is a relative of the animal. They actually found the whole thing intact, trunk and everything. How is that possible for this thing to have been preserved for 20,000 years?

3443 (K) The ice. Like it froze. All the cells in the mammoth's body were kept from corroding. Like the ice, it closed off the oxygen that was in there and any water that was in that mammal was frozen solid so it couldn't corrode.

T Alright. Why would it have to be very, very quickly? The theory is that it actually fell into the ice crevice and there was a tremendous amount of ice and snow falling over it immediately. Why would quick burial again have to be essential for this animal to be preserved?

K Because, like you say, it would start decaying.

3527 T In fact, they even found the food in his stomach. It was eating, minding his own business, having a little lunch, and TTCCHH, there he goes. So you never know what's going to hit you. (Pause) Now, in other parts of the United States, by the way, you could find an area where ancient trees, the remains of ancient trees, can be found rather intact, trees that might have grown a million, two, three million years ago. How might they have been preserved? (Pause) In fact, there's a name for this, as you would suspect. A type of forest. In fact, there's a very good play by that . . . Yes?

3610 K Petrified.

T Yes, and the method is by (writes on bb) petrifaction. What's petrified mean? If I say: God, I'm petrified. HM? Yes?

K In a solid state.

T Yeah, rock-like. I happen to have a piece of petrified wood here. (Holds it up for class to see.) In fact, I know it is (snickering, shows label). What does it say here, Scott?

K Petrified rock.

T Very good. (Bangs it on lab table.) The living material is replaced by minerals. How do we know this was once wood? Tell us. (Has K look at it.)

3711 K By the bark.

T It isn't bark. It looks like bark. Very good. Here's an animal that was buried in the mud and the minerals replaced it. (Holds up snail shell). What does it look like?

(K) A snail.

T Yeah. (Bangs it on lab table.) Suppose I know how old the rock layer was where this was found, what might I know about the age when this thing was swimming around having a grand old time in ancient seas?

3754 (K) Because, well, if the rock is about 50,000 years old and you found a fossil in there, the only way the fossil could have gotten in there is that it died at that time.

3801 T Very good. So there are other methods of fossil formation we'll try to pick up tomorrow. Now you don't have to go to . . . , you don't have to go to Colorado, you don't have to go to Russia. You can . . . from this school and be a paleontologist and see some of the most marvelous, exciting remains of ancient life . . . Where you can find these beautiful samples of the greatest . . .

K . . . (Class laughs)

T No, you're very close. (General talking, no clear voice.)

(K) . . .

3850 T . . . We're going to plan a trip, not actually a trip (Bell sounds.) . . . trail you take to look through all those beautiful fossils. Thank you. OK, kids, you did beautifully. (3920)

I presume you now want my views of the lesson, NS, so here goes: The teacher was obviously prepared. The homework assignment was on the board; he had his materials ready; he knew what he wanted to accomplish; and he was ready to deal with as much or as little as the students could absorb under the circumstances.

He had a rock and a story for starting off the discussion, both of which led rather quickly (by 0533) to an aim, which he largely elicited from some of the students.

Though he could have written the aim on the board and lectured his way through the material, he chose to involve the students in stating the aim, in defining the technical terms (fossil, extinct, etc.), in using previously learned material for dealing with the new topic, in tracing through fossil formation by sedimentation, and so on. In general, he took what students knew and led them to new knowledge without being the sole source of data himself. Though he did talk more than the students, he never lectured. There was much student participation, but the transcript doesn't tell us how many individual students participated.

He had a medial summary. This took the form of asking the class to reconstruct the steps in formation by sedimentation. (Again, he might have done the summary himself, but did not.)

As best as I can gather from your copy of the boardwork, NS, he seemed to have used the board as an effective aid, both in terms of his drawings and in terms of the verbal outline the students could copy.

The students required very few instructions on what to do. Aside from being told to copy the homework, they seemed to know what to do, probably from previous practice.

He had good rapport, he injected humor into the discussion, he provided much latitude for student contributions, he encouraged some reticent students, and he seemed to be enjoying it all, although he's probably been through this material before.

Finally, though I can't say which students learned how much about fossil formation, I would say that they followed him carefully, and that he will be able to tell from homework assignments and tests who learned what. All in all, it was a successful effort: he had an aim and he moved in the direction of achieving it in this and some succeeding lessons. (I don't know whether it's germane, but he taught what some call a "developmental lesson.")

That's a good start, ZA. Have you any suggestions on what he might do, if anything, to improve his instruction?

I would be in a better position had I seen the tape or the lesson itself. Maybe the student contributions came from too few students. Maybe those who spoke were more facile in English than those who didn't and he didn't allow enough time or create enough opportunities for them to get involved. Maybe he only called on students he knew to have done well in the past. After all, you were putting his work on a fairly long-life tape. I see now what you mean by your non-verbal memories.

Alright, ZA, let's leave it at that. I didn't put into your mouth such comments as students have made after seeing the tape, because that wouldn't be logical. Now let's see what happens when we apply the EG to this lesson.

NS, I know you would like to go on with the analysis, but I can't help being curious. Isn't this the very teacher about whom you've already made some decisions, back in Chapter IV, a couple of pages into your discussion of item C?

You're very observant, ZA; it is the same teacher, and obviously his second appearance is not an accident. However, restrain yourself awhile, till we've made the analysis and we'll then go back to the global judgment I rendered earlier.

Since it would take up much space to restate each question in each unit, let alone all the principles, I suggest we deal with units as total items.

A. to define both the stimuli and the responses;

1. *Stimuli*

The stimuli included the rock-fossil, how he came to find it, the outline and drawing on the board, the two samples of petrified fossils, the core of soil, the information injected by the teacher, and the questions he asked. The teacher was so clear on the stimulus situation he wanted to create that, apart from telling students to sit down, copy the homework, and take out their notebooks, he gave them no other instructions. The exhibit of the rock and the questions that followed provided most of the stimulus structure. In addition, he was ready with the other fossils and the core, and with other means of fossil formation. Whether he had prepared specific questions for this session, or whether he had taught such lessons at other times, is only speculation.

There were a number of references to prior learning. Here are a few:

0428–K knew it took time to form an imprint on a rock.
0505–K knew the rock was a fossil.
0628–(K) defined a fossil.
1045–K inferred that the earth was covered by water.
1218–T referred to "the work we discussed yesterday."
1346–K referred to erosion.

Whether what students knew came from prior study with this teacher is discernible in some of the references only, not in all of them. What isn't clear is exactly how and why fossil formation followed immediately preceding lessons. The teacher had no obligation to establish this connection in this lesson; he might well have done so in "yesterday's" lesson, whenever that had been.

The stimuli were generally the same for all students, except where he called on particular Ks to respond to particular situations.

The only obviously negative consequence he foresaw was the handling of the rock fossil. He exhibited it to each K for fear of its being dropped. In general, one can credit him with having foreseen the possible consequences of a lecture-type procedure, because he followed a different instructional pattern. We can only speculate on the impact of our camera on the behavior of the students.

2. *Responses*

The responses included copying the boardwork (plus whatever was said that individual students wanted to record) into their notebooks, listening to the teacher and to each other, recalling data from previous learning, and, in general, knowing and understanding how fossils are formed via three major processes. Since the teacher's only evaluation of new learning was the involvement of the class in retracing the steps on formation by sedimentation, and since a majority (my non-verbal memory) were not vocal participants, we must assume that oral reviews of this material, homework assignments, and tests will tell the teacher how effective the process was. He cued the students at various points as to which items were significant. For example:

1957–So, therefore, if we ask the question: In what type of rock would you expect to find a fossil? How would we answer that question?

2140–Let's see if we can just indicate the steps that took place now. First thing, what happened to my fish after a while?

The subject matter seemed to have been drawn from a continuum of material, although the teacher never said that what they had done so far led naturally into fossil formation. But a number of connections were established with the past. He also indicated that they would continue with fossils the next time. So one can conclude that fossil formation is part of a larger block of subject matter.

One might also say that the students' responses were repetitive, though not part of a continuum. That is, listening, taking notes, perceiving cues, answering questions, and being responsible for knowing, understanding, and remembering were probably required responses at each session, thus repetitive. That they were part of a continuum, from simple to complex, or from superficial to profound, we cannot say. My guess is that unless each new piece of science made ever greater response-demands, then the responses would be repetitive on a process level, though different as the subject matter changed.

The aim (How Fossils Form) was neither a statement of what T would do nor an indication of what Ks would do. It was a question to which both would direct their attention. It implied that Ks would come to understand the process involved, but without indicating what Ks would do to achieve that understanding and to demonstrate their achievement.

Are you suggesting, NS, that you have some reservations here?

It's not a question of reservations, ZA. In her expansion of P5, Seagoe says that questions can help set the objectives of classwork, they can focus K attention on the major points of the content, and they can help Ks to organize their ideas around these major points. (S-16)

He did follow this dictum, and well. He even elicited, mildly paraded, and sought to extinguish some erroneous responses. (P2) What disturbs me in such lessons as this one, where the general objective seems to be "to understand" something, is that students make few overt responses right then and there as feedback to the teacher on whether they are grasping a concept. Even under the best of circumstances, teachers tend to assume that the vocal students (no one of whom is vocal on every issue to which any single K is responding) somehow are representative of the whole group. Teachers don't, and very likely can't, parade each individual's potentially erroneous responses for immediate correction. They wait, and maybe they have to wait (in such an instructional format), for homework assignments and tests to see who understood how much. But, if we learn by doing, what do attentive listeners and note-takers do except to listen (an act we cannot monitor) and take notes (which teachers can't or don't read as the Ks make them)?—All of which opens up a large issue we might better postpone till later in the analysis, ZA.

3. *Communication*

If purpose (P3) can be equated with topic and note-taking, then his consonance with the principle was high: at 0140 they were told to take out their notebooks, and at 0533 he was already writing "our aim" on the board.

Since no students ever asked what they were or were not to take note of and remember, we must assume that the pattern had been laid down some time ago. In addition to the boardwork, there were the cues I mentioned earlier. So, although the students were not told exactly what to do, there was effective communication.

B. to determine whether the particular learners are ready to understand and deal with the particular stimuli and to make the necessary responses;

1. *Potential*

The teacher made no obvious effort to determine student potential. Since the interaction did not call for each student to respond to major segments of the topic, we don't know how well prepared each was for fossil formation. The teacher perhaps knows from earlier association with this class how effectively each student listens, takes notes, knows, understands, etc., and pitched this lesson accordingly. Though any class surely has some range of potential, there seemed to be no attempt to adjust the lesson to individual differences.

2. *Achievement*

Always keep in mind, ZA, that both the EG and the primitive assessment device I will later show you are directed at an analysis of classroom interaction, not at pre-planning or post-analysis. A supervisor cannot (or least does not) observe every lesson in a chain of instructional sessions. If teacher and students have forged such a chain, there's no need to demonstrate the links in any given lesson just to bring an observer up to date. So, in this lesson, we have only minimal evidence of prior student mastery of related concepts and skills, except that taking out notebooks, copying the boardwork, and maintaining contact with teacher and content all seemed to be well-rehearsed. There's even some evidence that at least some vocal students could recall related material from other learning. The single question under "Achievement" suggests the need to know what students have already learned, but since a lesson bent on "understanding" often calls for no immediate overt responses by each and every student, we can tell neither whether they had sufficiently mastered prior skills and concepts nor whether they are understanding this day's concepts. Though the teacher may have evidence of prior mastery, he won't be able to tell how effective a preparation this was for today's work until he checks homework and marks tests.

C. to stimuluate the learners to want to take on the new response patterns;

1. *General*

If we accept as a starting point the opening words of P13 under this heading, that an individual can be said to be motivated when he evidences some desire to attain some specified goal, and when the teacher recognizes and increases/intensifies such a desire, etc., then I would find it very difficult to say that this teacher motivated the students. Yes, he attracted their attention to his fossil, he held them with his wit and humor and humaneness, but the only goals I can infer for the students were the usual ones of following what the teacher said and did, so they could (very likely) reproduce it when called upon, and thus pass the course.

2. *Physical Plant*

This is an item one has to score in the live situation. All I can remember is that when I videotaped this lesson, the items subsumed by the six questions under this heading seemed to have neither a positive nor a negative bearing on the proceedings. I do remember that the rows were so spaced that the teacher could work his way through them, showing the fossil to each student.

3. *Focus*

The focus was not on specific acts the students were to engage in. Other than "take out your notebooks," and "don't draw this," there were no instructions re specific acts. Apparently the students knew what this teacher expected of them. But the focus was definitely on paying attention to the teacher and to the proceedings.

> I can't contain myself any longer, NS. Even without having seen and heard this man, his transcript is most interesting. He captures and holds the attention of a group of adolescents who surely could not have had an intrinsic interest in fossils; he gets them to help him reconstruct a process they were surely not familiar with; he sets up the data for clear conceptualization via his boardwork; he moves around, adds humor to a rather dry (unintentional pun) topic, has a medial summary, etc., etc., etc. Why are you so down on the man?

I'm not down on the man as a man, ZA. He's a gentleman of the first rank, with the courage to put his teaching on tape; a successful teacher, by his standards and yours, and probably those of most of his students. I'm not even down on the conception of teaching he exemplified in this lesson, though I'm certain that he could as successfully pursue the kind of teaching I'm talking about. You must not confuse my analysis of some 40 minutes of instruction with a judgment on either the total teacher or his definition of teaching. In addition to taking into account the obvious but unfathomable impact of a TV camera and crew on both teacher and students, you must keep in mind that my grid is a tool for looking at the interaction between those who teach and those who learn; no single application of it can give you a total score for a teacher, any more than participation in one game tells you the total score on a ball player. You can get a conception of how the player approaches the game or the teacher his teaching; you can't make a total judgment.

But since I've just begun my analysis, ZA, please let me finish it. Its outline format and the time markers on the lesson transcript will make it very easy for us to go back to any points you want to discuss.

4. *Form*

Although this item appears in the empirical grid, I, at least, came upon it via the Seagoe principle that undergirds it. It was the principle that caused me to create an item in the grid.

The teacher rates very high on this item, because the stimuli he projects to the class, whether in material form (fossils) or via his questions, made the kind of demands that these students (at least the ones who spoke) could meet. Only one response is a failure (1908), in that the teacher mildly rejects it. The few others that miss on the first try are given a second chance ("Redeem yourself."). So that, on the whole, this teacher created a situation that flowed, less because of his approving remarks and more because he made success possible for students who started out knowing very little about fossil formation.

5. *Origin*

I didn't want to confound the structure of the grid with explanations about the meaning of each unit. Most of the units can be understood simply by the cues inherent in the questions and the principles. "Origin" and "Proximity" are probably less clear, are interrelated, and need elaboration.

Viewing extrinsic and intrinsic as the north and south poles of a motivation continuum, Seagoe (Sc-20) makes two distinctions between these poles: (1) A motivation may be relevant to real life and so be intrinsic; or it may be irrelevant to real life and so be extrinsic. (2) A motivation may originate with a given individual learner and so be intrinsic to that learner; or it may originate with someone else and so be extrinsic to that learner.

"Origin" deals with questions and principles probing and governing the source of motivations and is an outgrowth of the first of Seagoe's distinctions.

She elaborates her second distinction by saying that learners may have interests, that these should be identified by teachers and should be built into the learning process. However, the motivation may also be extrinsic: teachers have a responsibility to create new interests. (Sc-25)

"Proximity" deals with questions and principles probing and governing intrinsic student interests plus teacher efforts to create new ones.

With that as a prelude, here are my comments re Origin: He reawakened in some students and probably awakened in others an interest in fossils and their formation. The only relationship to real life came in the brief treatment of paleontology, though I don't think this is what Seagoe means by her first distinction between intrinsic and extrinsic. He maintained attention largely because of the way he presented himself, his materials, and his role in the situation.

6. *Proximity*

I don't see that the teacher was aware of and exploited prior student interest in fossil formation. It was a topic in the course-of-study, nothing more. He stimulated interest by providing opportunities for a kind of investigation and adventure in a socially stimulating situation. So he was expanding horizons, without an intrinsic student interest as a starting point.

7. *Polarity*

The teacher scores high here, for reasons too obvious to detail.

8. *Strength*

The same must be said here. Much as he talked about his personal experiences, his ego was not involved. He protected the most contributing student by trying to limit him when others could fill a gap and by accepting his other statments. Only at 2428 does he interrupt him, says he doesn't mean to interrupt, yet succeeds in moving that student out of the discussion for a time (until about 2742). The transcript seems to read as though the teacher didn't want the class to be misdirected by this student's statement concerning moisture, but if you could hear the audiotape you'd catch an ego flavor to the interruption. For the rest, both before and after, the touch was light and pressed no egos.

9. *Variety and Timing*

Since I never admitted that he really motivated the students, then I can't say that he varied the motivational situation. But he did keep to a lively pace, was ready with quips and word-plays, and moved the topic along.

D. to select and use materials and activities which will lead the learners to acquire the new responses and/or to practice existing responses;

1. *Scholarship*

This is where a former-teacher-of-science supervisor would be at an advantage. My limited knowledge says that he knew more than he needed to know for what was not, after all, a treatment in depth. However, any one of you, ZA, who has a background in science instruction is in a better position to evaluate the teacher on this unit of questions. (Parenthetically, this is an appropriate place to say that the EG and the primitive assessment device might well need two kinds of assessors, or at least one assessor with two kinds of expertise: one knowledgeable in subject matter; the other well-versed in the remaining units of both instruments.)

2. *Materials and Activities*

There were no materials for students to manipulate. The teacher showed the rock-fossil to each student; he had one student look at it carefully to spot the fish on it; and one student actually held the petrified wood sample. I'm listing these actions simply to catalogue what occurred, ZA, not to imply that it was minimal. Since the goal seemed to be to learn how fossils are formed, with the amount learned to be surely checked via verbal responses, I can't fault the teacher on this score despite a variety of principles that emphasize student activity.

3. *Meaningfulness*

Meaningfulness and *Structure*, which are really extensions of *Scholarship*, are probably the most crucial units in the entire grid. This is because all of my experience as a teacher, administrator, and supervisor have convinced me that if I had to name one factor as being most responsible for lack of success in teaching I would not hesitate before saying: ignorance of subject matter. Which hardly sounds as though it merits an introduction by blaring trumpets. Nor am I implying that you must give special attention to it because I'm an educationist, who would be expected to point his finger at teacher lack of proper training in methodology. No, ZA. I'm stating what I regard to be a matter of simple truth: elementary school teachers in particular, and middle school, junior high school, and high school teachers each to a lesser degree, have simply not mastered the subject matter they're supposed to be teaching in the classroom. Since I can't "prove" all this with solid research data, you surely have the option of totally disregarding my view. The only piece of factual support I can offer is what my experience in student-teaching supervision has taught me: that the best majors in an academic subject are rarely advised, by their major professors, to go into teaching; and that even in liberal arts colleges which train teachers, let alone in what were formerly teacher education colleges, it is assumed that prospective elementary teachers have already mastered the subject matter they will later teach and so need no college-level study in those areas.

I didn't mention this when discussing *Scholarship* because the focus of those questions is on what a teacher can tell himself and what an expert in the discipline involved might be able to discern from the learning situation. The questions under *Meaningfulness* and *Structure* are more subject to examination by an observer, even one who is not an expert in the particular discipline. My major disappointment is that the principles I've located offer such little help to the teacher. Of the six under *Meaningfulness*, only the third (P44) does more than laud this factor: to make material meaningful you relate it to what students already know. But what does relate really mean in terms of teacher behavior? No clues. The seven principles under *Structure* do point to the distinction one should make between the whole and its parts, but what's a whole? Is fossil formation a whole? Is by sedimentation a part? By what criteria: those of the experts who have imposed order on data, or those of the ignorant students whose perception of the data we can't appreciate until after we've tried to have them learn the material?—No, ZA, this is not a digression to the discussion I've asked you to postpone. Treat it as a prelude to my comments on the units involved.

If the best one can do about *Meaningfulness* is to relate new learning to what students already know, then this teacher is only partially successful. Yes, he uses bits and pieces that no more than a third of the students contribute:

0417—It's a fossil, a fossil.
0420—It has an imprint in it.
0428—(It takes time for an imprint to be formed.)
0628—(K) The skeleton of some primitive animal that was . . . preserved . . . in rock . . .

0757–(re extinct) It means no longer existent.

0812–(K) It was usually stone.

0917–How come the animal has to be extinct?

1045–. . . I think the earth must have been covered by water . . .

1346–Erosion? (re process by which rock might have been worn away)

1715–(K) Might be a flat shore.

1912–(K) The more dirt fall on top of it, it causes more pressure.

2325–If he's not (buried quickly) he won't be preserved.

2445–I think it's caused by germs, like bacteria.

2642–In the first place, part of the earth is being pushed up . . .

2826–(K) There used to be a sea where you people were walking.

2929–Evolution.

3010–(Oil was formed) by the decaying of plants and animals which are trapped under the earth.

3205–(The oldest is at the bottom.) Look the furthest down.

3230–Check the amount of lead in the rocks . . .

3238–Uranium.

3443–(K) The ice. Like it froze . . . etc.

3610–(The) Petrified (Forest).

3631–In a solid state.

3754–(K) Because, well, if the rock is about 50,000 years old . . . etc.

Of course, ZA, you may be impressed with this list. It may even be a longer list than one could abstract from most lessons. But if to be meaningful is to relate new material to material known by students, and if learning is a personal process (with no one being in a position to learn for anyone but himself), then what did this teacher know about each student's present knowledge? Can he assume that the vocal minority represent what the silent majority might have contributed? What evidence does he have as to how meaningful the material was?

We can answer for him: he'll be able to tell from homework assignments (when, of course, he can't tell who helped whom with what) and tests (where he may learn who is able to respond to teacher cues to remember certain things in certain forms, *not* to whom the material is necessarily meaningful).

But, but . . .

OK, ZA, I relent. Talk, please.

Thank you. I really couldn't wait. You haven't finished this subhead and have two more to go. As Seagoe says, I have a relatively fixed normal memory span and you're taxing it to the limit, even in writing I can reread. And I don't even know where to begin, except for that principle on serial order where first and last positions are the strongest. So let's take this last point.

What do you *want* from teachers? Are you looking for some ideal situation, which only some few of us in this whole business might be able to produce for you? Why do you deliberately choose to apply your grid for the first time (for us, at any rate) to someone who has done as well as this man did? Isn't it enough that he creates a whole structure, in so humane and witty a fashion, not by lecturing, but by eliciting so much from his students? That he gives them a system for recording and retaining the information? That the class fully accepts him and he them? That he absolutely accentuates the positive? That he's personal and self-revealing without a trace of egotism? And that he probably knows exactly how to find out who learned what and how much of it?

You raise a number of important issues, ZA. Let me begin by listing the negative points I made since my first judgment (p. 24) and we'll see what that adds up to:

24 But the only points of contact between students and fossil formation were: there are fossils in a museum in town, you might find some in the park or at an excavation, and one can make a good living being a paleontologist (the meaning of which he explained in terms of searching for oil). But these were urban students, far removed from both fossils and paleontology, so that the material was basically not relevant to them . . . the motivation was based largely on the teacher's ability to interest the students in *himself* and to have them follow *him* because he was who he was; it

was *not* based on their need or desire to deal with the material.

91 What isn't clear is exactly how and why fossil formation followed immediately preceding lessons.

92 . . . the students' responses were repetitive . . .

93 What disturbs me in such lessons as this one, where the general objective seems to be "to understand" something, is that students make few overt responses right then and there as feedback to the teacher on whether they are grasping a concept.

94 Though any class surely has some range of potential, there seemed to be no attempt to adjust the lesson to individual differences.

94 So, in this lesson, we have only minimal evidence of prior student mastery of related concepts and skills . . .

94 . . . I would find it very difficult to say that this teacher motivated the students . . . but the only goals I can infer for the students were the usual ones of following what the teacher said and did, so they could (very likely) reproduce it when called upon, and thus pass the course.

97 The only relationship to real life came in the brief treatment of paleontology . . .

97 I don't see that the teacher was aware of and exploited prior student interest in fossil formation.

97 Since I never admitted that he really motivated the students, then I can't say that he varied the motivational situation.

99 If the best one can do about *Meaningfulness* is to relate new learning to what students already know, then this teacher is only partially successful.

When you boil all this down, I'm saying that, despite the many positive features in the situation, he established no essential contact between students and subject matter. He didn't relate it to what they knew, not about the earlier material to which he had exposed them, but about the social and personal usefulness of such knowledge to the world at large and to these students in particular. To put it in current terminology, he was irrelevant.

Had I chosen a teacher and lesson that could have been faulted on many other units in the grid, I would not have been pressed to deal with my essential criticism of so much school instruction. So I chose a very capable man, whose lesson has impressed many of the ZA's who've seen it on videotape, a lesson the man himself viewed with some pride on the playback. And if one accepts its unstated definition and goals of school instruction, it was a very highly laudable performance.

That's the problem: it was a performance. No, ZA, you didn't supply the epithet; I did. And if I now knock it down, then I'm guilty of having raised a straw man to suit my purposes. Unfortunately, I have no choice. This is not the transcription of an actual discourse, though the words I'm putting in your mouth, ZA, are generally the words I've heard ZA's say in my classes.

I believe that a "teacher" is that individual who aims at getting you to stand on your own two feet, "to be a man" (as we used to say and mean, in the best sense, before Women's Lib), but who limits himself to intellectual and aesthetic independence. I leave it to other professionals and non-professionals to add their contributions in other areas of development.

Making one's way through life, with a maximum of fulfillment, is obviously a broad process. No single academic discipline provides all the guidance one needs. Each discipline can contribute data, concepts, and modes of thinking which help one in life. But life's problems are never purely biology-cal, physics-cal, chemistry-cal, mathematics-cal, etc. Ergo, I believe in what some call "process education," as opposed to content education. To guide an individual's intellectual and aesthetic development is to help him define what he wants and needs, why he wants and needs it, what obstacles are in the way of getting it, what resources he can command to help him get it, what the consequences of success and/or failure might be, and how to face these consequences.

Therefore, though I want my "teachers" to be totally prepared in content, they must be experts on process; they must be able to elicit from students and/or to perceive for themselves what students need and want to know, so as to lead students to see that man's wisdom is codified in the humanities, the arts, the social sciences, the physical sciences, and mathematics, and that proper study of the data, concepts, and modes of thinking in these disciplines will help them to achieve independence in intellectuality and aesthetics.

So you begin by knowing "who they are, what they are, how they see life, and how the new learning will contribute to their growth and personal satisfaction." Notice, ZA, that the verbs in the quotation are in either the present or the future tense, and not by accident. How students got to be the way they now are may be of importance to those who find merit in trying to undo the past. My "teachers" have to begin with the present and project into the future. I can't undo a child's handicaps, created by his race, religion, family environment, etc. But I can begin to help him decide what he wants to do about the social box he's now in and how to go about doing it. My "teachers" will help him find company and solace in the arts, plus guidance from the humanities, social and physical sciences, and mathematics. Thus, when they relate the subject matter to the obstacles students face in developing intellectually and aesthetically, they and their material will then be meaningful, by my definition.

Since I'm constructing your responses, ZA, let me suggest your next one: Then tell us, NS, how you would have gone about teaching the topic fossil formation to these students.

The answer is simple, ZA: I wouldn't.

> But what if the topic really is in the curriculum, and in the course of study? How can you keep it out of your design, NS?

You're using my terminology, ZA, so let's review what design is. I defined it "as the combination of those activities and experiences planned, executed, and controlled by the teacher (or teachers) on behalf of pupils." When you combine that definition with what I just said "teachers" are to begin by knowing about pupils, you should be able to see why I can't tell how I would teach fossil formation to the students. I don't know who these students are, what they are, etc. Therefore, I can't tell you how I would make it relevant to them. Instead, let me tell you a true story about some experiences I had as a junior high school music teacher in New York City.

If you're now in a secondary school, ZA, your curriculum may well still include "required general music" courses for your students. If not, you very likely were a student in such a course in your student days. Anyway, for a number of years I had as many as ten different sections of such a course each term. And I began by teaching as I had been taught (which is what so many novices do for openers), not as my teachers-college professors had instructed me to do.

For music appreciation I brought in my own records, because the school had nothing usable. It went over like the typical lead balloon. Because I told the kids that these were my records, they wanted to bring in theirs. I had to agree to their logic. Their records turned out to be the popular tunes of that day, on discs badly scratched and worn, but whose sounds turned on lights in the students' eyes.

I don't really remember why, maybe because I had recently taken a very good course on musical form, but I asked the students why they liked to listen to their records. The melodies were short, and even on the ten-inch 78's we were playing the whole performance consisted of some three statements of the theme.

To make a long story short, my students began to hear that their records had forms (what is called ABA in music), and that their interest was held by the instrumentation in each statement, and (much later) by the mode of statement. They began to be able to spot each A and B, to hear the instrumentation, and to enjoy doing so. We moved on to simple marches, which now added CDC, EFE, ABA, CDC, etc., configurations.

Then arguments (mild ones) arose as to whether they were hearing this instrument or that one. So I brought in brass and wood-wind instruments (from our band room), plus extra mouth-pieces and cotton swabs and alcohol to clean them with, and let anyone who wanted "to play" have a turn. I still relish (after over twenty-five years) the fruitless exertions most of them made and the cheers for those who got any sound at all out of an instrument. The major result, that I could observe in school, was that my students began really "to appreciate" what it meant to make music, even to showing their appreciation at the performances of our bands in the auditorium and of individual performers in our talent shows.

And as I gradually polished my techniques for dealing with form and instrumentation, I began to realize that my overarching aim in the entire music program (required general music, chorus, bands, talent shows, etc.) should be to create an intelligent fandom for music, much as The Knothole Gang in those old Brooklyn Dodger days sought to create baseball fans.

> That's very interesting, NS, but since music teachers make up only a small fraction of the teaching sorority-fraternity, and since I know what I can construct and approve of where I am now (philosophically and methodologically), can't you try to do something in any discipline in which you may have some expertise?

Alright, ZA, let's take fossil formation, science teacher that I'm not. But I can't, logically, give you a design for such instruction, since I use that term to designate the particular learning program which a single particular teacher (or maybe a small team of teachers) will create for his particular students during a particular span of time in a particular school under particular conditions. Nor do I know the science course of study from which this topic is drawn. I can only give you a general idea of how I might respond to the situation, given all the limitations I've now enumerated. My main reason for even attempting a response is this: though you will find my "lesson" neither new nor revolutionary, it will serve to demonstrate a most major aspect of my views about teaching.—So here it is:

No matter when you're reading this, ZA, assume that it would not be difficult to locate a news item on some electric utility: seeking a rate increase, advertising pleas to "save a watt," appearing at hearings dealing with some conservationists' effort to curtail strip mining of coal or to stop the pollution of some river or lake, announcing that all service had now been restored after the last brown-out, etc.

Without my producing a typical lesson plan, you may be able to see how I would use one or more such events to stimulate students to tell whether and how they had been or are then affected. Maybe the family's full refrigerator load was lost through a protracted brown-out; maybe a voltage reduction had an impact on their TV reception; maybe they've heard parents cuss out the utility because of the latest rate increase; etc. If I really knew the science involved, I would lead my students around to an examination of the technical aspects. But we could either go to visit the utility, see its operations, learn what fuels it uses to produce electricity, ask why brown-outs are occurring and why they want an increase for such poor service, etc., or have a representative come to us.

In due time we'd get around to learning how coal and oil are used to produce electricity, and work our way back to fossil formation. At this point, our treatment of the topic would be highly relevant and meaningful, because it's in the context of a social box my students are surely in, one way or another.

(And I don't know what words to put in your mouth, ZA. I like both of my examples, this one and the musical one, but I don't want to construct an approving response from you. Except . . .)

> Are you saying, NS, that each topic in a teacher's design is to be set into a social (broadly defined) context?

It would be a kind of intellectual arrogance, ZA, for me to say YES, because I can't possibly have given consideration to every topic, in every discipline, from kindergarten through high school graduation. And yet the answer is YES. Look at it this way:

"Know then thyself, presume not God to scan;
The proper study of mankind is man."

says Alexander Pope in "An Essay on Man." I'm convinced that his is the advice to follow. No matter what the topic is, the reality of it is the one man's senses tell him it is. Surely, if man heard and saw other wavelengths than he does, reality would have a different appearance. If man lived only in climates which he could tolerate while nude, he would no more need heaters and air conditioners than all other animals do. In fact, he covers and uncovers his body more for social than for physical reasons.

For me the prime subject matter, especially at least below the college level, is that encompassed by the social sciences, which can be transmuted into contexts for the effective study of all other subject matter. Both of my examples are embedded in a social context.

> I begin to sense the spirit of your approach, NS; the print is still too small for me to decipher the letters. Why don't you complete your analysis, give us a chance to talk about it, and then maybe "show" us another taped lesson?

Thank you, ZA. We were just past *Meaningfulness*, but hadn't begun on:

4. *Structure*

In discussing both of these units parenthetically, I said that the principles under this one provided a little more, but not much more direction to the teacher and observer than those under the preceding heading. The principles don't provide criteria for distinguishing part from whole, simple from complex, essential features from their contrasting ones, etc. But let's see what the questions in this unit can help us decide.

Certainly, the material on fossil formation had a logical structure. Though he didn't begin with an overview of all methods of fossil formation before beginning on sedimentation, the omission seemed not to affect the clarity of the presentation. At least the students said nothing to indicate the impact of such an omission. He did deal with each type of fossil formation separately, though keeping them under one umbrella. And specialized vocabulary was given due attention.

5. *Summaries*

There was (as you said, ZA) a medial summary, in the form of a retracing of the steps in by-sedimentation. And he involved the students in its construction. There was no terminal summary. Instead he directed students to where they could see fossils, a section I have censored in spots, to avoid identification of the teacher and school.

E. to control the process so that this acquisition or practice is efficient and effective;

1. *Attention-Distraction*

The only recurring or repetitive activities involved having the students take their seats, get out their notebooks, copy the homework, and respond to the roll-call, all of which he handled very easily and smoothly. When he was ready to begin on the material for the day (at 0222), he opened with a statement and a question. From there on, despite the TV equipment and crew, he held their attention. My transcript doesn't show it, but there were street noises, sounds from traffic in the school's hallways and from athletic events in the schoolyard below, none of which distracted the students. He focused their attention with great success.

2. *Discipline*

He had no problems here.

3. *Media*

Back on page 103, in the midst of our long digression, I said, "That's the problem: it was a performance." You may well ask me: if that's the case, why is the first question in this unit, "Does teacher perceive self as a medium of instruction and use appearance, voice, posture, movement, and gestures to enhance effectiveness?" Well, it seems to me that no matter how you structure a learning situation, the teacher is bound to be a central figure. Even in open classrooms where teachers are meant to be guides, resource people, etc., instead of authority figures centrally located at their prominent desks or lecterns, learners are both interested in and affected by their teachers' appearance, voice, etc. Therefore, it seems logical for teachers to have self-awareness and to control the features I list in the first question for maximum pupil growth.

Our science teacher seemed to have this self-awareness, which only the videotape itself can reveal in full. In addition, he must be rated high on each of the other questions. I would only fault him for not using films or filmstrips of fossil formation. He might say that his school has none, has no funds for renting or buying them, or that he would be using them in subsequent lessons. That he used what he had to advantage is undeniable.

4. *Interaction Pattern*

If one does learn by doing, what did the students do? I repeat what I've already said more than once: they came in, sat down, responded to the roll-call, took out notebooks, listened, observed the boardwork, copied down what each was moved to copy, spoke, presumably tried to grasp the ideas about sedimentation, and went to their next class.

> We seem to have reached another bone of contention, NS. What would you have wanted the students to do, beyond what you say they did? This was not a skill lesson. The aim was "How Fossils Form." Since that process takes millenia to occur, they obviously couldn't have replicated it by doing something in 40 minutes. Besides, look back at the principles under this unit. P78 says that some learning tasks require only internal emotional responses. P79 says that a learner can learn by looking and listening. P80 says that learning involving overt movement by the learner is superior to such

purely ideational learning, but implies that ideational learning is possible. Of course, if I had seen the tape, and if the tape has frequent closeups of student faces, I might be better able to prove that they were active listeners, making internal responses.

If your approach to teaching is going to rule out the validity and value of instruction aimed at the development of student understanding of various concepts, then aren't you knocking the props out from under this whole discourse? Yes, you'll say that a book is not a teacher, by your definition, but surely you've learned many things by reading books. Furthermore, in most subjects much time must be spent on the development of student understanding, where large segments of material cannot be treated on a learning-by-doing basis, especially in what seems to be your favorite subject, social studies. One can be "doing" in math, bio, chemistry, physics, earth sciences (to a degree), music, art, physical education; one can even "do" in studying literature, especially drama. But what do you "do" in history, political science, etc.?

You raise a very potent set of arguments, ZA, and I seem to have no answers. Obviously, a good deal of pre-service and in-service teacher education takes place away from real children in real schools. Even you, ZA, sat with me in college classrooms, at night, where I tried to lead you to understand and apply supervision concepts with altogether much too little "doing" on your part as feedback to my efforts at teaching. Maybe it's because I have such misgivings about how we tend to educate teachers and supervisors that I'm overly sensitive on this issue.

I say that before one sets out to have students learn to make responses to stimuli, one must know, in advance, which responses will be acceptable. Put simply, you can't give a spelling or a math test without prior agreement on what the right answers are. In the same way, if my goal is to have students understand, after instruction, what they didn't understand prior to instruction, how do I tell (after instruction) who understood, how much? I reject homework (as feedback) because I sometimes help my daughter with hers, without telling her teachers that I do. The same is true in studying for exams. What a teacher gets back on tests, papers, and projects is a quite unreliable reflection of the effect of his input.

But, if the teacher is to be largely his own supervisor (a thesis that undergirds my material on supervision in later chapters), it seems to me he needs immediate feedback on whether and what the students understand, along with a pre-measure of what they understood before instruction, or else the teacher takes credit (on the post-measure) for what students might already have known on a pre-measure.

As I said, ZA, I have no answers. Maybe teachers ought to set up units of concepts, devise pre-measures for evaluating how much students understand, guide each one to learn what he doesn't, and use the same test or a comparable one as a post-measure. And it could be detailed enough to be administered in parts, before and after an instructional session. Then we might be able to correlate teacher input with student output.

> Maybe, NS. But one final comment before I, at least, lose the real thread of our discussion. Your attempt at precision in defining terms, in circumscribing conditions conducive to learning, your general pattern of disputation, and now your pre- post-measure idea all seem to be leading to a systematizing of teacher-pupil relationships which squeezes out the warmth and humanity, the pleasure of watching kids grow and develop, which keeps so many of us in the profession. To use a favorite example of yours, novice cooks measure every ingredient. Real pros, at least the ones who teach or demonstrate cooking on TV, seem to be able to tell how much is just right without measuring spoons, etc. Why do you insist on treating us like novices, NS?

The only nice thing about having your own pie thrown in your face, ZA, is that the licking is tasty and sweet. As the current ad says, "I needed that!" But, with my face clean enough for speech, I'll say this: We are nowhere near the stage in teaching where even the real pros can discard measuring spoons, etc., and rely on "feel" for the proper quantities of ingredients. And even so, there may well be as few TV stars among teachers as there are among cooks.

I must admit to being less impressed with the other issue you raise. Being a musician, I use musical analogies (maybe too much). The soloist and/or the orchestra or chorus that communicate, with warmth and sincerity, the composer's message, sacrifice none of the technical elements of performance: pitch, tempo, dynamics, attacks, releases, etc. Conductors stress these as tools, but as tools to be submerged to the main thrust: communication. Being only approximately accurate in pitch, tempo, etc., would make hash of the attempt to communicate.–I think that teachers fall back on "the pleasure of watching kids grow and develop" precisely because they can't take pride in the effectiveness with which they have marshalled the elements required to have pupils acquire new responses to either old or new stimuli. They fall back on symbolic rewards, not on concrete successes in precise tasks. They even take credit for changes that would occur in any case, or at least for changes to which their contribution is undefined. If I'm to learn to be a better teacher, I must have the same feedback that pupils must have as they learn. Or else how do I adjust my responses to the stimuli?

5. *Questioning*

I've just reread the transcript, ZA, and made a tally of all the questions it contains. You may be as surprised by the count as I am. There are just four student questions, one of which the teacher elicits. But the teacher asks *sixty* questions. Unfortunately, if you will look on page 56, you'll find no principles of learning undergirding my questions in this unit. Which meant that I have been unable to find research support for any position I might take. But at least we can try to answer the unit questions.

Though he surely didn't memorize or program himself to ask sixty questions, he does not have to restate them; they're clear to the students in their initial statement. Only once (at about 3420) does his inventiveness fail him: "Why is the wooly mammoth not an elephant? That's a grim question. Because it isn't, of course."

He gives students time to respond, in the sense of not filling empty time (while students are considering their responses) with words. So many teachers are so often guilty of impatience that his technique seems almost flawless by comparison. What the transcript doesn't show is how many potential respondents there are for each question. My memory says that he never had more than a few to choose from. Maybe if he had waited a little longer more hands would have gone up. Maybe. Both of us will probably agree that experienced teachers are able to tell when the law of diminishing returns takes effect. In addition, a teacher can legitimately be concerned with maintaining a certain rhythm in this kind of instructional pattern, a rhythm which calls for rather immediate responses to teacher questions.

His questions do call for some different kinds of comprehension and retention, but the range is limited and the thinking is not particularly critical. Though he cautions one student not to strain himself in attempting a response, my subjective view is that the vocal students gave little evidence of strain. At 0423-0450 there's an interchange with a student who makes a good beginning on a response but who becomes discouraged on being asked to speak louder. And at 3110 he pulls Carmen into the pattern by telling her: "Carmen, you have a gleam in your eye. Sure you do."

The one question he elicits comes just past 0505: "What question might come to mind . . .?" The best unsolicited question comes at about 0910, when a student asks: "How come the animal has to be extinct?" Since students ask only two more questions, one can hardly say that, in this lesson, he encourages students to ask; which makes my remaining unit questions inapplicable.

Just what does all this mean, ZA? In the absence of learning principles, your view, any view, my view are all admissible. Even the issue of 60-to-4 questions is only an issue if you refuse to accept the premises for what you so rightly called a developmental lesson, ZA. And finally, if one regards questions as "Stimuli," there's only one principle in that unit; it offers no useful guidance in evaluating the teacher on "Questioning."

6. *Competition-Cooperation*

Neither the unit questions nor the principles here seem particularly applicable to this lesson. He taught the class as a whole. Students were not involved in "doing" activities which would make "competition with student's prior efforts" an observable phenomenon. He fostered cooperation only in the sense of maintaining student focus on a common problem (How Fossils Form); what took place did not offer students a choice between competition and cooperation. The only individual (with a privacy to be guarded) was the (K) student to whom I've already made some earlier references.

The real issue is something we've already discussed, ZA. If the aim is to understand something, can there be, need there be, any "doing" by students? If yes, were they grouped in such a way that the "doing" facilitated the learning?

> Well, NS, since you can't rule out the aim "to understand" despite the seeming impossibility of translating it into observable behavior, and since two of your own principles admit the possibility of being an active listener, the question is (or so it seems to me): did his grouping patterns and his questioning techniques make it possible for students to do this? Though I find myself more and more hampered by having to read a transcript instead of seeing the lesson in person or on tape, I would have to come down on his side.
>
> You say he moved around a great deal, he showed the fish fossil to each student individually, he presumably made it easy to view each of the other items he demonstrated, his boardwork was equally visible to all, there was no evidence of competitive strain among students—therefore the grouping pattern is at the very least neutral if not positive with regard to facilitating learning.

Maybe, ZA. Let's go on and see.

7. *Practice*

Since no skill was involved, one might say there was nothing to practice, which makes the entire unit inapplicable to the lesson.

8. *Pacing*

Pacing, on the other hand, brings us back to the bone we've gnawed at a number of times, ZA. We might have renewed the gnawing with the first question of the preceding unit: "Is practice provided after comprehension, or in an effort to achieve comprehension?" When you add to it the first Pacing question ("Is the learning process adjusted to the pace of the individual learners?"), and the emphasis on individually-adjusted pacing in P122, P124, P127, and P128, on not pressing the learner to acquire responses beyond his capacity in a given length of time in P125, and on serial order and recall in a number of the other principles in this unit, the bone seems to acquire a larger set of dimensions.

You're right, of course, ZA, to say that neither of us can

relinquish student understanding of concepts (and of the rationales undergirding skills) as legitimate objectives of instruction. But if "understanding" *is* a student response (which it has to be or we may as well join Alice and the Queen of Hearts), then students should practice because it helps them retain what they have already learned. All of this vacillation between the two units isn't helping you, ZA, so let's see if I can lay out a clear path between the units.

I have seen teachers (and occasionally been one of them) tell students to practice a response they didn't understand, though the response was "right." I once taught junior high school math and did what my college calculus professor used to have me do: follow the model example, do exactly what it says, make sure you compute accurately, and you'll get the right answer. Maybe after you've done a few examples "the light will dawn."

I have also seen teachers assign homework to students which they were to do though it was obvious they had little or no understanding of what was involved.

So I ask: "Is practice provided after comprehension, or in an effort to achieve comprehension?"

Then we come to Pacing. If individual motivation dictates the need for individual pacing (P122), if the time it takes a learner to acquire new responses varies with some of his personal attributes as well as with the difficulty of the task (P124), and if learners have given capacities to learn just so much in a given period of time (P125), then can't we say that our teacher was not consonant with these principles?

Can't we in fact say: if "I do understand" and "I don't understand" are both legitimate responses to a stimulus situation created by a teacher, and if no one learns for anyone but himself, can't we say that the combined impacts of the following principles at least challenge the very validity of trying to achieve the aim "I understand how fossils form" via a developmental lesson?

P78. (partial quote) . . . with some tasks requiring only internal emotional responses.

P79. The learner should be active during the learning situation, though the activity may be as limited as looking at or listening to the stimulus.

P80. However, learning involving overt movement by

the learner is superior to such purely ideational learning.

P81. (partial) The more the learner actively participates in the learning process, the more he learns.

P82. (partial) The more time the learner spends in making responses, the more he learns.

P83. (partial) . . . all learners gain more from being active rather than passive in the learning process.

P122. (partial) Individual motivation . . . dictates the need for individual pacing.

P124. To learn to make the new responses required in a given learning situation takes time, the length varying with the learner's past experiences and abilities and with the difficulty of the task.

P125. Learning will not occur if the learner is asked to acquire more responses in a given period of time than he has the capacity to acquire.

Let me tackle that one, NS. Whereas the principles you quote do seem to favor the learner's making active responses, at his own pace, in a time-span proportionate to material-difficulty and learner-background, the principles also admit the possibility: of purely ideational learning; of making only internal emotional responses; and of learning via looking and listening. Furthermore, it seems to me that only the Practice unit principles distinguish between learning skills and learning concepts.

I maintain that learning to understand how fossils form is in a different class of objectives than learning how numbers behave, how elements can be combined into compounds, how groups of written letters are translated into spoken words, how levers and pulleys multiply human energy, etc. Each of these objectives can be met by actual manipulations of objects or symbols, and that manipulation is, of course, observable. But we can't replicate fossil formation, the Civil War, the rise of nationalism, the emergence of new African nations, etc. Surely you're not going to say that teachers can't aim at student understanding of such matters, NS!

No, I'm not, ZA. My concern is of a different order: what does a student do which permits a teacher to conclude that a student understands? And how does a teacher create situations which allow each and every individual student the time to achieve and demonstrate understanding? Even if I were to drop my insistence on some observable evidence of understanding, *right there in the classroom,* doesn't whole-class instruction implicitly violate the requirement of individual pacing?

> Well, now, NS, this time I will be as bold as you earlier challenged me to be! For a person who argues for knowing "who *they* are, what *they* are, how *they* see life," etc. (my *italics,* NS); who argues against knowing the whole *child;* and who says he's addressing himself, in pragmatic terms, to practicing performers; for a person, in short, who seems to accep the practical necessity of group instruction, are you now saying that whole-class instruction is out where "to understand" such concepts as fossil formation is concerned?

No, ZA, I'm not outlawing large-group instruction. In a given "laboratory" in the physical sciences, math, reading, art, music, dance, driver education, woodworking, etc., one can have both large-group and whole-class instruction (when tasks are outlined, samples of student effort are discussed, conclusions compared, etc.) without giving up either individual pacing or the teacher's ability to check on each student's response to the stimuli. The limitations lie in the student-teacher ratio. In X amount of time one gets around to just so many students. What I'm trying to answer, to myself even more than to you, ZA, is how do you set up a non-laboratory situation (that is, a practically non-"doing" situation) where you do aim at student understanding, and where you maintain a pace which takes into account each student's apperceptive base, the "bag" of background he brings to the situation? Maybe the answer does lie in open education, in individually prescribed instruction, in organizational patterns minus a teacher-at-a-desk-up-front, etc.

> Then why do you speak so unfavorably about open education, NS, or make no case thus far for IPI?

I do both, ZA, for different reasons, just as I find it hard to accept our science lesson, a lesson I've both praised and faulted on many grounds, with more to come. I think Individually Prescribed Instruction (IPI) assumes that the same package will suit many learners in the absence of a live teacher who will sense a given learner's unique reactions to items within a package and who has time, options, and materials for exploiting those unique reactions as they occur. What is even more critical to me is that:

P105. (partial quote) Group action results in a higher quality, not quantity, of work, especially in the solution of difficult problems.

P106. (partial) As the group increases in size, the superiority of group work over individual work increases . . .

P107. (partial) A group working on a task, . . . is more influenced by its better-informed members than by those with less information.

P108. (partial) With ability held constant, students learn more in group work than in individual work.

P109. The quality of a group's output is as good as the individual work of the best member and considerably better than the individual work of the average member.

P110. The benefits of group work are available only when the members support each other as the group moves towards goals consensually defined.

Learning is an individual process which seems to function most effectively in a social setting. If schooling is to be any sort of preparation for living, then it has to provide for both privacy and togetherness. We need to be alone and with others.

But isn't that what open education provides, NS?

Yes, ZA, but what *I've seen* it lack, not what its rationale may account for nor its stellar practitioners include, is an organized confrontation either with selected human problems or with some selected subject matter, as foci for the learning situation. Keep the "beauty-is-in-the-eye-of-the-beholder" advice in mind as you read the following:

In an open classroom (and I've only seen them in the lower half of elementary school) there are many stimuli. My first reaction to them was that they were over-stuffed with materials. (My eyes prize order, organization, design; I *am* that way.) But even as I came to sense the very orientation of OE, I also saw that what there was, was again a selection from the enormous storehouse of knowledge I began with so long ago in our discourse. No matter how large the room or rooms involved, someone or ones had selected some comparatively few stimuli from the huge available stock. The process rationale was that students could interact with stimuli alone or jointly in an effort to discover ideas for themselves. And whereas there was a general commitment for this discovery to lead to progress in such communication arts as reading, writing, listening, speaking, computing, drawing, painting, constructing, etc., there was a much weaker commitment to some such organizing curricular focus as the structure of a given discipline or the processes in that discipline.

ZA, you would be wrong to jump to the conclusion that I wanted the teachers to have something "to cover." No, I'm concerned with "Meaningfulness" and "Structure," which we discussed at such length. I'm concerned with accountability, with being loyal to my definition of "teacher," and with a set of units we have yet to face that should tell us how we know how much each learner did in fact learn.

> Just one last point, NS, before we take your hint to move on with the rest of the EG. You've said that you believe in process education, in subject matter to chew on, and in process to master. So if OE does focus on processes (at least you admit to "communication arts"), and since you might even concede that students improve in such skills because of their involvement in them each day, and that they do so each at his own pace, why the negativism towards OE?

I thought I made that clear. The development of intellectuality and aesthetics is not a chance by-product of some other effort. It requires curricula, courses of study, and designs expertly focused on these objectives. Given what I've seen and read about OE, I find no solid evidence of such a focus.

I say that subject matter, like food, is something to chew on. But though we are all practiced chewers on what may generally be classified as food, we are much, much less practiced on the process of selecting nourishment of the kind best suited to good health. Our choices do not reflect what is known about health; our choices are, therefore, less than totally rational.

The same can be said about schooling. Just because students in open classrooms (and elsewhere) do engage, with enthusiasm, in such processes as reading, writing, drawing, constructing, discussing, etc., doesn't necessarily mean that what they're chewing on is intellectually nourishing. I don't mean that they're chewing on air, ZA. Of course, they chew on subject matter segments. But I don't see that these are selected by teachers on the basis of some definitive curricular focus. Ergo, I question the contributions of such organizational patterns to intellectual and aesthetic development.

I'm not saying that OE, IPI, etc., *can not* have such a focus. I *am* saying that the focus ought to be explicit, and that we ought to weigh the effectiveness of these organizational patterns against their progress towards this focus. Or, as I said earlier, OE may have a different set of objectives; in which case we must also see how well it moves learners towards those objectives.

9. *Accuracy-Speed*

The two questions in this unit appear to be inapplicable to the lesson, as do all three principles. The second principle (P143) brings us back to the bone again, ZA, but I'll restrict myself to a nibble. The first response in learning should be accurate, it says, because it's much more difficult to extinguish an incorrect initial response and to have the learner take on the correct response than to make sure the initial response is accurate. In our lesson the teacher had no way of telling whether each individual student did understand how fossils form. If the homework assignment is on the same issue, he will know at the next session who did it and what each one decided was the proper set of responses. He won't know whether any given student had any assistance in doing the HW. When he gives his test on fossil formation, he will come closer to knowing who understood how much, provided all the students are equally good test-takers, and provided that it's not more a test of English than of science for his particular students.

F. to determine to what degree each learner did, in fact, take on the new response patterns or affirm the existing ones.

1. *Feedback-Reinforcement*

And we're right back to the "doing" again, ZA. The students made no responses to which the teacher might have provided feedback-reinforcement. And again you might expect me to say that the unit questions are inapplicable to this lesson. After all, you might say, we can't really expect every lesson to contain every ingredient in the EG. And I would have to agree with you.

Except that my whole definition of teaching is rooted in the learners making new responses to old or new stimuli. And except that, for the few vocal students who responded to the teacher's questions, no one was afforded the opportunity to do something which might be equated with "Yes, I understand how fossils form." So there was: no feedback, no knowledge of results, no student "role in on-going monitoring of their efforts."

2. *Success-Failure*

"Did the students learn to make the new responses?" is the first unit question. At a little past 0517 the teacher says: ". . . Or, how was this fossil formed? And that's what we're trying to find out today. Let's start then with our aim." If teaching is "the creation and control of conditions under which learners take on new responses to either old or new stimuli," then the stimulus was: How Fossils Form. And the response would presumably be the ability to explain and perhaps illustrate (diagram) how fossils form. But there's only limited evidence that the students learned to make this response. At 2140 he begins the "medial summary" which is a review of fossil formation by sedimentation. Now, even if the tape could tell us how many different students took part in this summary; in fact, even if each student in the whole class made at least one contribution to the summary, the teacher could still not be sure who really understood the total process. Therefore, we don't know who did "take on new responses" nor whether (unit question #2) failure was mitigated. I did indicate some time back, ZA, that he asked questions which students could answer, so that he was mitigating failure and he was providing opportunities for success where questions were concerned, but not in regard to the total response.

The principles stress the importance of being successful. However, since the students were not making the seemingly-called-for response, the issue of success-failure can not be resolved.

Back a long ways in our discourse, NS, I said that you have a way of leading us away from a comfortable old ambience to a strange though logical new one. Persuasive as your points are, and much as I hate to give up my position, I am swaying; but I'm also resisting.

Since you've already agreed that every unit and principle in the EG can't necessarily be applied to each lesson or segment of instruction, why can't we postulate the following?

a. The teacher led the students through an introductory lesson on fossil formation. He treated only one process in detail (by sedimentation) and will treat the others (by refrigeration and petrifaction) in succeeding lessons.
b. The aim in all the lessons on this topic will still be "How Fossils Form."
c. Quick burial, extinct species, the steps in each process will be common elements in all forms of fossil formation.
d. The teacher will remember to involve more and different students in succeeding lessons, especially those who were camera-shy or about whom the teacher was camera-shy.
e. He will be checking homework, reviewing previous material, and involving students in both efforts, as a way of determining what students are learning.
f. He will give quizzes along the way and a definitive test at the end.

Now, NS, you surely can't argue against any of these assumptions. Teachers do engage in precisely just such activities. If you refuse to measure a whole teacher by one lesson, why do you insist on measuring what students learned about fossil formation on the basis of only the first of a number of lessons, an abbreviated and recorded one at that?

It's my turn to compliment you, ZA, on your disputation. All you say is certainly possible. But since we only saw what you call "an introductory lesson," let's discuss that.

I've heard teachers use that term, but I've not heard what such a lesson is or how it differs from succeeding lessons. My dictionary says that introductory means "use as an introduction"; that introduction (among other things) means "3. anything that introduces, or prepares the way for; specifically, a) the preliminary section of a book, speech, etc. usually explaining or defining the subject matter;" and, in a special note: "introduction, in strict usage, refers to the preliminary section of a book, etc. that explains and leads into the subject proper; . . ." So let's say that an introductory lesson would explain or define the area or unit of study and lead "into the subject proper." And, if you agree with that definition, then we did not see and are not discussing a so-called introductory lesson.

Because what might an introductory lesson consist of? Well, we can get some guidance from the principles under *Structure*, beginning on p. 50, speaks of presenting new material to students by beginning with some outline or systematic arrangement before going into the details. P49 asks that instructional units be structured clearly and simply, but sets up a variety of factors which together determine what is a "whole" for any given student. P48 suggests that the learner be allowed to impose his own structure on material to be learned. And P51 says: When a structured unit is too complex for the learners, the procedure to follow is to present the major outline first, to focus on one part, and to relate that part to the whole unit, all within a single learning situation.

You're suggesting that the unit of study is "How Fossils Form" and that the parts are by sedimentation, refrigeration, and petrifaction. Not being a science teacher, ZA, I can't say whether your suggestion is acceptable. But assuming that you're right, what might an introductory lesson contain? The principles seem to say that the whole should have preceded a study of the parts, that a general schema or plan should have preceded dealing with specifics, etc. Surely, that's not quite what this lesson was about.

And even if I were to grant you that his was an introductory lesson, that would not ipso facto excuse the teacher for failing to obey all the principles I say he violated. Since we're still discussing the Success-Failure unit questions, introductory lesson or not, we don't know what new responses such a lesson would call for nor have we any evidence that they learned to make them.

To go back to the principles in this unit and the preceding one for a moment: the Feedback-Reinforcement principles generally address themselves to responses learners make and the feedback-reinforcement they need in order to learn. They all indicate that the learner must make some response to which he gets feedback, feedback which should be immediate (P153), positive (P152), and specific (P151). Even if the teacher later administers the quizzes you mention, and even if the feedback to them meets the criteria inherent in this unit's principles, no such quizzes were part of this lesson.

The Success-Failure principles, by emphasizing the grave and destructive effects of failure, strongly imply that learners should be successful at learning tasks. All we have, as any kind of solid evidence, is that the minority of vocal students were individually able to answer a few questions each. I don't see how that can be equated with understanding how fossils form, even by sedimentation alone.

3. *Retention-Forgetting*

The teacher took some steps to insure retention of the material he was presenting. He gave them a plan for organizing recall (P194) in the form of the outline and drawing on the board. He followed at least a large part of some advice by Kuethe that learners are often able to recall material which captured their attention by being dramatic or humorous or having some other attractive quality. (K-70) He obeyed P193. (Learners tend to recall material to which the teacher has directed their attention.) And there was a review of formation by sedimentation.

There was no announcement of how and when their retention would be checked, but that was probably a routine procedure which needed no announcement. Nor could I tell whether the homework assignment on the board was related to fossil formation. Very likely it was. The absence of instructions re what to copy into their notebooks and re testing and homework all indicate the probable existence of well-defined procedures which do not require daily rehearsal.

4. *Transfer*

Presumably, when teacher and students develop fossil formation by refrigeration and petrifaction they will be able to carry over the pattern from formation by sedimentation. That would be a kind of transfer. The teacher didn't say, in so many words, that the students were to think of the sedimentation analysis as a basic framework for the other two, but the outline on the board could be interpreted in this manner.

One might also say that the discussion of the age of various fish fossils and the reference to a ratio were a transfer from earlier learning, which can be projected for additional use in other lessons. Neither of these is very striking evidence of teaching for transfer, but they did require mention.

* * *

That's it, ZA, a quiet, undramatic conclusion to an analysis that included some rather high peaks, an analysis much longer than any you've probably ever been part of, and surely many times longer than any you will have time to conduct as a supervisor. Since I didn't mean it as a model for practical use, there are no apologies.

Back on p. 73, before handing you the EG, I said that our first "concern will be with the meaning and applicability of the EG." I suspect that each unit of it is now an understandable entity; the entire EG is probably too long to grasp at one sitting. As to applicability: as we discoursed the EG I began to have second thoughts about applying it to another lesson. So I will bring in my PAT (Primitive Assessment Tool) in the next chapter, show you how and why it differs from the EG; then we'll apply it to a couple of lessons.

Back on p. 73 I also said that "our purpose is not to analyze, but to see whether the EG yields a set of judgments which seem applicable." On p. 88 you made a set of judgments, prior to my analysis, because we have "no standard yardstick for measuring instructional quality." (p. 73) Let's just take a few minutes to compare judgments.

Your first one was: ". . . he knew what he wanted to accomplish; . . ." Yes, we can assume that in a general sense he knew that he wanted his students to understand how fossils form.

> Why "in a general sense," NS? Didn't he lead the students through a full-length development of fossil formation by sedimentation? Weren't all terms defined? Didn't he outline and illustrate the ideas on the board? Shouldn't you really be saying "in a specific sense?"

We're both of us guessing, ZA, because neither of us knows what the students will be responsible for knowing and understanding on whatever measures the teacher uses to check on learning. If we project that the measures will include every technical term, each step in formation by sedimentation, plus the review of items recalled from earlier learning, plus the lesser material on refrigeration and petrifaction, then, if we equate high scores on such measures with "understanding," he will have to be credited with "in a specific sense." My experience leads me to say that a test covers less territory than a lesson, on the presumption that high student performance on selected highlights is a safe base for projecting comparable competence on the rest of the learning. However, whether a total test or a partial test is equivalent to "understanding" is a separate issue.

Do you remember what I said a long time ago about Van Cliburn "playing" the piano and little second-grade Suzy also "playing" the piano? No matter how lengthy a test our teacher gives, could even a 100 percent student be said "to understand" fossil formation as the teacher understands it? Of course, at some point in the past our teacher understood no more than his current students; and at some point in the future some current student of his, then majoring in paleontology at a college, will likely understand more than our teacher does now. But even though those two statements seem clear on the surface, the differences in "understanding" are masked by the absence of verbs which in themselves denote quality of performance.

In other words, I believe that "understanding" can be translated into behavioral terms. Let's go back to my drawing board, my dictionary:

> *understand, v.t.,* 1. to get or perceive the meaning of; know or grasp what is meant by. 2. to take or interpret as the meaning or implication; infer; assume. 3. to take as meant or meaning; interpret. 4. to take as a fact; accept as a condition. 5. to supply mentally (an idea, word, answer, etc.). 6. to get as information; learn. 7. to know thoroughly; grasp or perceive clearly and fully the nature, character, functioning, etc. of.

Perhaps you'll agree with me, ZA, that there's a qualitative difference between the first and the seventh meanings of the verb. Where fossil formation is concerned, a practicing paleontologist should be expected "7. to know thoroughly; grasp or perceive clearly and fully the nature, character, functioning, etc. of." An average high school student would do no better than "perceive the meaning of; know or grasp what is meant by."

So a teacher can decide that his average high school students need to know no more than

- what a fossil is,
- the names of the processes by which fossils are formed, and
- the general conditions characteristic of each process.

Only the first of these can be checked by non-verbal techniques. The other two would require written or oral responses.

That same teacher, serving as an adjunct professor at a local college, would obviously expect his paleontology majors to "understand" much more, for which he would have to devise appropriate measures.

To assume that we cannot distinguish the novice from the expert by various techniques would be absurd. Nor do we have to rely on their credentials. So I say that it *is* possible to translate "understand" into observable behavior, provided that the teachers themselves "know thoroughly; grasp or perceive clearly and fully the nature, character, functioning, etc. of." Oh, I'm not asking your high school general science colleagues to be paleontologists, chemists, biologists, etc., etc., all rolled into one. But I do expect a degree of expertise which has prepared them to create learning as well as evaluative situations for their students.

So our teacher could have devised a pre-measure to diagnose current student knowledge and understanding. It could have included blind leads, superstitions, old folks' tales, as well as truth. He could have summarized the responses for the whole class to see. There could have been a time allotment for studying materials, looking at displays, going to that museum, etc., before a return to the classroom for a largely verbal treatment of the material, followed by some measures of evaluation. Then, who understood, that is, who grasped and knew the meaning of what the teacher had marked off in advance as the parameters of this learning experience, that would then be quite clear.

So, ZA, the deserved phrase is "in a general sense."

> Alright, NS, I see the point . . . I think. But instead of ending this chapter by looking at the other judgments I may have made on p. 88, let me see whether I can think my way through to your position.
>
> You're saying that concepts can be grasped, under-

stood at different levels of intensity, presumably in the same way that skills can be used to different degrees of mastery. Skill performance can be observed; so even though we lack verbs which in themselves indicate levels of performance, we aren't handicapped at ball games, Olympic meets, etc.

You're also saying that teachers can set the parameters for different intensities of understanding, and that these can be tested for by both verbal and non-verbal means. To which you add that such testing can precede instruction to determine both what students know as truth and what they accept as truth which is not true.

That's very good, ZA.

Then just one absolutely final question, NS: you want teachers to aim at both intellectual and aesthetic development. Appreciation would come under aesthetics, wouldn't it?

Yes, it would, ZA; so . . .

So, how would your kind of teacher set parameters for appreciation?

We need the dictionary again, ZA. After defining "understand," my dictionary includes the following very useful statement:

> SYN.–*understand* and *comprehend* are used interchangeably to imply clear perception of the meaning of something, but, more precisely, *understand* stresses the full awareness or knowledge arrived at, and *comprehend*, the process of grasping something mentally (a foreigner may comprehend the words in an American idiom without understanding at all what is meant); *appreciate* implies sensitive, discriminating perception of the exact worth or value of something (to appreciate the difficulties of a situation).

Now, to discriminate is to "tell the difference between, distinguish." To perceive is "to grasp mentally; . . . to become aware (of) through sight, hearing, touch, taste, or smell." And the relevant meaning of sensitive is "responding or feeling readily and acutely; very keenly susceptible to stimuli: as, a sensitive ear; . . ." Therefore, someone who appreciates has the particular sense(s) so well honed, so razor-sharp, that he/she can distinguish the exact worth or value of something. Of course, ZA, worth and value are culturally determined.

I see the teacher's role as helping learners to develop a value system, not as pressing them to accept a particular one. What people ultimately choose to value should and must be their own business, or else we violate my parameters on intellectual development. The teacher's role in aesthetics (put most briefly) is to focus on sensitive, discriminating perception, on sharpening the operative sense(s) so that learners can "tell the difference between; distinguish." The "worth or value of something" is their personal decision. Teachers have a duty to expose learners to variations in taste over time, space, and culture. I, at least, won't grant them the right to indoctrinate.

VIII.

Primitive Assessment Tool (PAT)

Before we examine the Primitive Assessment Tool (PAT), let's take a few minutes to see how it is derived from the Empirical Grid (EG). I can best clarify the derivation by using the "1. Feedback-Reinforcement" unit (p. 62) as an example.

To save turning pages back and forth, ZA, here's a restatement of the first five principles in that unit:

- P145. The learner will make little or no progress unless he gets feedback on the adequacy of his responses.
- P146. The learner's feedback on the adequacy of his responses can come from demonstrations and experiments as well as in verbal form from the teacher.
- P147. Reinforcement from individuals esteemed by the learner facilitates his learning.
- P148. When the learner is given feedback on the results of his efforts, there is a marked improvement in his performance.
- P149. Students are likely to repeat activities which originally raised their self-esteem.

I chose this unit because it has the largest number of principles (31) and because their translations probably exemplify most if not all the issues one can raise in this area.

If you will now focus on these five principles, you may be ready to agree that the first four can be translated into observable behavior, but that the fifth one cannot. P145 suggests that learners be given feedback on the results of their efforts. P146 says that such feedback can be both non-verbal (demonstrations and experiments) and verbal. P147 suggests the use of persons esteemed by the students. And P148 overlaps P145, but indicates an outcome of feedback. In each case we can see the teacher creating and controlling "conditions under which . . . etc."

P149 tells us that students will likely return to activities which had previously escalated their self-esteem. That implies that if the teacher wants the students to repeat certain activities, he must have arranged for such escalation to take place at the prior interaction between students and activities. As a supervisor using the PAT, you may not have been present at that prior interaction, so you can't know that the students are "today" (when you are observing) repeating activities that had originally raised their self-esteem. Or, if "today" you see the teacher providing positive reinforcement for certain student activities, you can't be sure that this is prompted by the teacher's desire for a later repetition of such activities. And, although both EG and PAT are meant to be used in self-analysis by the teacher, he may not have projected "today" a future return to certain activities, so he can't rationalize the escalation of self-esteem "today" on the basis of not-yet-planned future repetition. So I treat P149 as non-translatable, especially since providing positive reinforcement is already dealt with in P145-148.

So is P149 a viable principle, NS?

Yes, it is, ZA. It covers situations where the teacher will want students to repeat activities, and tells him what conditions to create and control. One could, of course, translate this to say: Teacher who wants students to repeat given activities provides highly positive reinforcement at prior interaction between students and these activities.—This gets us to what is probably a most basic issue about the PAT, which will make more sense after you've had a chance to examine it.

The point I'm trying to illustrate is this: if you work your way through all 222 principles you'll find that not all are immediately translatable into teacher or student behavior. In order to create an assessment tool for looking at classroom instruction, a tool with a practicality the EG certainly lacks, one must translate the principles and the unit questions into observable teacher and student behavior.

I assume you aren't suggesting that I go through all 222 principles and translate them, NS.

I don't know how to answer you, ZA. The reason I chose the F-R unit is that I intend to go through it with you, so you can see how I arrive at that section of the PAT. Having done that, I'll "hand" you the complete PAT, just as I "handed" you the EG. But keep this in mind: I said you could probably ask unit questions other than those I ask; you may want to challenge the selection of principles and their paraphrasing by a non-psychologist; you may want to differ about what I regard as translatable principles; and you may even want to offer different translations. I suggest you follow me through the Feedback-Reinforcement unit. Then you can decide what to do. (See Table 1.)

Table 1 illustrates the transition from EG to PAT. The first of the seven columns is a numerical sequence for the Translations; this simplifies reference to any entry. The statements in the second column are in the order of the principles, essentially. What I did was to study a principle, make the Translation, enter it in the second column, and list the principle in the third column. Some statements, such as 1 and 2, have two principles each, though only one translation. That's because I see the one translation as pointing simultaneously at both principles.

The fourth column contains principles I consider not translatable, though generally related to the statements to which they are attached. The next two columns deal with translatable and non-translatable unit questions. The last column contains the numbers of the PAT questions which are derived from the Translations. Here you'll notice that Translations 6 and 8 are expanded into two questions, in each case derived from just one principle. Any questions, ZA?

Yes, I have three questions. Since you may want to establish a relationship among them, I'll state all three at once: (1) If one PAT question can point simultaneously (as you put it) at two principles, shouldn't you eliminate one principle or add one question? (2) If the apex of your effort to lay the foundation for and develop the EG is what you finally include in a tool based on observable behavior, why do you bother to include one "N-T" unit question and seven "N-T" principles, six of them associated with Translation 5? And (3) the basic question, as I now see it, is: Why did

Table 1

Feedback-Reinforcement Unit (EG): Translations

TRANSLATIONS	PRIN.		EG QUES.		PAT QUES.
	T	N-T	T	N-T	
1. T provides K with knowledge of results	145 148		a		127
2. F-R is individualized	164 165				129
3. F-R varied as to form	146 156 157				134
4. Individuals esteemed by Ks provide F-R	147				128
5. F-R is positive	150 152 175	149 154 155 163 170 171		c	130
6. F-R is specific and detailed	151		b		131 133
7. F-R is immediate/not long delayed	153				132
8. Ks learning to monitor/reward selves	158	159	d		135 136
9. F-R proportional to quality	160				137
10. Criteria of quality gradually increased	161 162				138
11. F-R given for Rs that approximate desired Rs	166				139
12. Partial F-R given to make Rs resistant to extinction	167				140
13. Continuous F-R provided in early stages	168				141
14. Consistency between K behavior and F-R	169				142
15. Guidance given in small amounts	172				143
16. Guidance given early	173				141
17. Guidance in symbolic form	174				144

you load us up with an impractical EG instead of going directly to your PAT?

Very good, ZA, very very good! Before I address myself to your questions, it makes more sense to "hand" you the PAT now, rather than later. So here it is.

PAT: Primitive Assessment Tool

A. Stimuli and Responses

	Tchr.	Obs.
a. *Stimuli* (Ss): Did the teacher		
1. create a definitive S situation?		
2. eliminate potentially competing Ss?		
3. relate present Ss to past learning?		
4. have S materials ready for use?		
5. anticipate the impact of Ss?		
6. individualize the Ss?		
b. *Responses* (Rs): Did the teacher		
7. translate goals into terminal K behavior?		
8. lead Ks to relate present Rs to past learning?		
9. anticipate the consequences of the Rs?		
10. elicit and parade erroneous Rs?		
11. extinguish erroneous Rs?		
12. individualize the Rs?		
c. *Communication*: Did the teacher		
13. communicate the S situation clearly?		
14. clarify the Rs at the outset?		
15. ascertain that the Ks knew what Rs to make?		
16. present the new learning in a familiar context?		
B. Readiness		
a. *Potential*: Did the teacher		
17. determine K potential for dealing with the Ss and Rs?		
18. provide for Ks who lacked this potential?		
19. provide for Ks who didn't need this experience?		
20. refine his perception of each K's self-image?		
b. *Achievement*: Did the teacher		
21. determine K mastery of prior concepts?		
22. determine K mastery of prior skills?		

C. Motivation

	Tchr.	Obs.
a. *General*: Did the teacher		
23. increase K need to reach some goal?		
24. create a need where there was none?		
25. develop an active K attitude?		
26. discern why some Ks were not motivated?		
b. *Physical Plant*: Did the teacher		
27. make proper adjustments in temperature and ventilation?		
28. decorate the instructional area tastefully?		
29. arrange bulletin boards to reflect current activities?		
30. arrange for optimum audibility and visibility?		
31. arrange seating to suit the needs of the learning situation?		
c. *Focus*: Did the teacher		
32. employ a motivation specific to the Ss and Rs?		
33. avoid directing K attention only at the teacher?		
34. direct K attention at the Ss and Rs?		
d. *Form*: Did the teacher		
35. arrange a situation in which the Ks could succeed or experience the normal consequences of failure?		
e. *Origin*: Did the teacher		
36. awaken or reawaken K interest in the new learning?		
37. optimize the use of intrinsic motivation?		
38. relate the Ss and Rs to what is real to the Ks?		
f. *Proximity*: Did the teacher		
39. exploit prior K interest in the content?		

	Tchr.	Obs.
40. arrange for a quick, light, vivid, active exposure to the new area?		
41. provide opportunities for overt bodily activity?		
42. provide opportunities for investigation?		
43. provide opportunities for adventure?		
44. provide opportunities for use in real life?		
45. stress improvement relative to one's past performance?		
g. *Polarity*: Did the teacher		
46. employ positive motivation?		
47. emphasize praise and minimize reprimand?		
48. vary polarity in keeping with K characteristics?		
h. *Strength*: Did the teacher		
49. employ a moderate degree of motivation?		
50. avoid excessive personal ego involvement?		
51. avoid excessive K ego involvement?		
i. *Variety*: Did the teacher		
52. vary motivation for individual Ks?		
j. *Timing*: Did the teacher		
53. re-motivate Ks when efforts seemed to diminish?		
D. Materials and Activities		
a. *Scholarship*: Did the teacher		
54. make no errors in facts?		
55. make no errors in concepts?		
56. demonstrate a clear grasp of the steps involved in the skills the Ks were to master?		
57. demonstrate a clear grasp of the modes of inquiry peculiar to the subject matter?		

b. *Materials*: Did the teacher

	Tchr.	Obs.
58. provide materials appropriate to the Ss and Rs?		
59. distribute materials at the optimal moment?		
60. arrange for effective sharing of materials?		
61. clarify the use and care of materials?		
62. arrange that K manipulation of materials facilitated learning?		
c. *Meaningfulness*: Did the teacher		
63. make the material meaningful to the Ks?		
64. elicit K feedback to determine meaningfulness?		
d. *Structure*: Did the teacher		
65. organize the material in a discernible structure?		
66. elicit K feedback re their grasp of this structure?		
67. encourage Ks to select their own structure?		
68. relate structure to K capabilities?		
69. present a general schema before dealing with specifics?		
70. isolate parts for attention?		
71. relate the parts to the schema?		
72. isolate specialized vocabulary?		
73. teach unrelated learnings separately?		
e. *Summaries*: Did the teacher		
74. provide for summaries of the learning?		
75. elicit summary statements from the Ks?		
E. Process		
a. *Attention-Distraction*: Did the teacher		
76. handle recurring or repetitious activities via well-rehearsed techniques?		
77. control controllable distractions?		
78. minimize the influence of non-controllable distractions?		

	Tchr.	Obs.
b. *Discipline*: Did the teacher		
79. organize Ks, spaces, materials, and equipment so that activities moved smoothly?		
80. provide for standards of behavior?		
81. use praise and reprimand within the time-space of the learning experience?		
82. delay responding to highly charged K behavior?		
83. use negative reinforcement to extinguish undesirable behavior?		
84. ignore Rs Ks are to forget?		
85. reprimand in private?		
c. *Media*: Did the teacher		
86. employ his own voice, gestures, and movements in ways that facilitated learning?		
87. serve as model of mature behavior?		
88. use materials and equipment which appealed to a number of senses?		
89. use materials and equipment skillfully?		
90. use the most concrete media of instruction?		
d. *Interaction Pattern*: Did the teacher		
91. listen and observe more than speak and act?		
92. arrange for maximum "doing" by the Ks?		
93. spread K participation?		
94. arrange for K contributions to have an impact on the substance and direction of the learning?		
95. elicit K involvement in relation to individual attitudes towards performing before others?		
96. arrange for private interaction with individual Ks?		
e. *Questioning*: Did the teacher		
97. phrase questions which were clear on first communication?		
98. wait for Ks to consider their responses?		

	Tchr.	Obs.
99. avoid filling in blank time with rephrased questions and/or comments?		
100. phrase questions which called for different kinds of comprehension and/or retention?		
101. phrase questions which stimulated Ks to critical thinking?		
102. encourage Ks to initiate questions?		
103. feel responsible for being able to provide answers to all K questions?		
104. deal effectively with questions which did not merit immediate consideration?		
f. *Competition-Cooperation*: Did the teacher		
105. stress competition with oneself?		
106. use competition only with older, average, or slow learners?		
107. foster cooperation?		
108. handle grouping patterns in ways that facilitated learning?		
109. guard the privacy of the individual where it does not interfere with the group?		
g. *Practice*: Did the teacher		
110. individualize practice in relation to need?		
111. arrange for practice to be done accurately and under full attention?		
112. have Ks practice Rs already learned?		
113. arrange for practice to be done in terms of the objectives to be met?		
114. provide for spaced practice?		
115. provide for practice periods of decreasing length and rest periods of equal or increasing length?		
116. use negative practice to extinguish habitual wrong responses?		
h. *Pacing*: Did the teacher		
117. adjust the learning process to a pace suited to the participating Ks?		

	Tchr.	Obs.
118. set time or work limits for tasks?		
119. make only moderate changes in timing?		
120. vary the context in which elements in a series are learned, if their recall would be elicited apart from the series?		
121. emphasize initial and terminal positions in a series?		
122. group and pattern material in a long and complex series?		
123. relate the amount to be learned to each K's memory span?		
124. interrupt learners near the completion of a task and without loss of self-esteem?		
i. *Accuracy-Speed*: Did the teacher		
125. stress accuracy on the initial R?		
126. stress accuracy before speed?		
F. Evaluation		
a. *Feedback-Reinforcement*: Did the teacher		
127. provide Ks with knowledge of results?		
128. arrange for persons esteemed by Ks to provide F-R?		
129. provide individualized F-R?		
130. provide positive F-R?		
131. provide specific and detailed F-R?		
132. provide immediate/not-long-delayed F-R?		
133. attach negative F-R to specific wrong Rs?		
134. vary the form of F-R?		
135. lead Ks to monitor their own Rs?		
136. arrange for material mastery to be its own reward?		
137. provide F-R proportional to quality of Rs?		
138. raise, gradually, the criteria for quality?		
139. reward Rs that are partially correct?		
140. provide partial, rather than 100% reinforcement?		

	Tchr.	Obs.
141. provide continuous reinforcement in early stages of learning?		
142. respond to given Rs consistently?		
143. arrange for Ks to discover things for themselves?		
144. provide guidance which permitted Ks to retain the initiative to act?		
b. *Success-Failure*: Did the teacher		
145. find that the Ks had learned to make the new Rs or improve existing Rs?		
146. involve the Ks in self-evaluation?		
147. provide each K with some degree of success?		
148. follow negative criticism with compensatory outlets for success?		
149. try to counter the negative impact of failure?		
c. *Retention-Forgetting*: Did the teacher		
150. relate new material to material already mastered?		
151. direct attention to material to be recalled?		
152. provide for over-learning?		
153. check on schemata Ks use to organize retention?		
154. tell Ks how and when retention would be checked?		
155. use recall, recognition, and relearning to test for different degrees of retention?		
156. arrange for relearning when recall and retention failed?		
d. *Transfer*: Did the teacher		
157. aim at the transfer of concepts and skills?		
158. guide the Ks to see how transfer occurs?		

Let's now go back to your first question. And since I've already indicated the overlap between P145 and P148 towards which Translation 1 points, we'll go to the next statement.

2. *F-R is individualized.*

P164. Any given reinforcement may have a different impact on different learners because their needs vary.

P165. Knowledge of results of their efforts has the greatest impact on better students, a greater impact on younger than on older students, and the least impact on poor students.

PAT 129. Did the teacher provide individualized F-R?

With the three sources thus juxtaposed, I think you can see why one Translation and one PAT question can point simultaneously to two principles. But can I then eliminate one principle? Obviously no, or else we'd have no issue to discuss. P164 suggests that F-R must be relevant to needs, whereas P165 deals with maturity and potential. They don't overlap; but they do imply that F-R be individualized.

Your second question asks about the need for "N-T" principles and unit questions, especially in relation to Translation 5 in Table 1. Let's juxtapose all these items for a clear view of the issue.

5. *F-R is positive.*

P150. Positive reinforcement for a response increases the probability of its occurrence.

P152. Informing the learner that a given response is correct results in greater progress than telling him that that response is wrong.

P175. Guidance should stress correct rather than incorrect responses.

(N-T)P149. Students are likely to repeat activities which originally raised their self-esteem.

(N-T)P154. Positive reinforcement reduces the learner's anxiety and facilitates his learning.

(N-T)P155. As the frequency of positive reinforcement for a given response is increased, so the probability of its recurrence is increased.

(N-T)P163. The frequency of a given response diminishes when positive reinforcement is withdrawn.

(N-T)P170. The absence of expected positive reinforcement is seen by the learner as at least a sign of disapproval or possibly a form of punishment.

(N-T)P171. Punishments do not necessarily weaken response patterns in the same way that rewards strengthen them.

(N-T) Qc. Does teacher treat incorrect responses as evidence of a need for re-teaching?

The three translatable principles all say that we should be observing the teacher providing positive F-R, as indicated by PAT 130: Did the teacher provide positive F-R? P150 is a general statement. P152 is more specific, and I debated a long time before deciding not to frame a separate, but corollary, question to PAT 130. P175 is a somewhat general form of P152; the difference I see is in the word "guidance."

Seagoe, the source of P175, uses "guidance" to represent the amount of stimulation and/or assistance offered by the teacher versus the amount of initiative the learner retains. (S-175) His description of "guidance" suggests that we are dealing with a process, used over a time-span, whereas P150 can be interpreted to be a one-shot feedback re a given student response. Therefore, I decided to retain both principles.

As to the N-T principles: We've already discussed P149, the fifth of the first five F-R principles. P154 tells us about some impacts of positive reinforcement; P155 relates frequency of reinforcement to probable recurrence of a response; P163 relates frequency of response to withdrawal of reinforcement; P170 describes what happens in the absence of expected positive reinforcement; and P171 is a statement about punishments. Whereas the information is valuable to the teacher, it does not suggest observable behavior.

"What valuable information?," you might ask. Well, take P154. In obedience to earlier translatable principles the teacher provides individualized positive F-R. But since "Any given reinforcement may have a different impact on different learners because their needs vary," (P164) he's now asked (by P154) to see whether the reinforcement he gave *this* particular student did reduce *his* anxiety and facilitate *his* learning. If teacher does not read the situation this way, then he has to vary the reinforcement. We could make a long-winded PAT question out of this, but I decided not to. Again, let's postpone the reason.

P155, P163, and P170 also offer valuable information: if you want a response to recur, increase the frequency of positive F-R relative to the number of times the learner makes that reponse; because the learner will make that response less often if you diminish F-R; and will be disturbed if he expects positive F-R and it's not forthcoming. Again there could have been some long-winded PAT questions, and again let's postpone my reasons.

P171 is a most general statement, is not immediately translatable, but says to the teacher: accentuate the positive, which we already know from other principles, but do so with a certain perspective in mind.

The non-translatable unit question is the shorthand for a somewhat longer issue. I included it in the EG because I believe that the first place to look for causes of ineffective learning is in the effectiveness of the teaching. Too often the blame is put on the learner. My unit question is meant to stress a teacher attitude, a readiness to examine one's own possible shortcomings, a willingness to engage in reteaching, before assuming that it's the learner's fault. And even then it may be a problem of Ss and Rs for which the K isn't ready, which are not meaningful to him, etc. Since I don't know how to phrase attitudes in terms of observable behavior, I put this unit question in the N-T column.

Now let's get to your third question. My response includes all the postponements above.—Yes, I could have gone right to a PAT, but one that would fall rather short of being a practical supervisory device. In addition to the 158 PAT questions, it would have had to include the 222 principles, plus such EG questions as the N-T one we just discussed. I was, and still am, and will be trying to aim for something analogous to what is called in baseball a "box score." The analogy isn't the best, but it may help clarify the relationship between EG and PAT.

Professional baseball has a full book of rules. To me the EG serves that purpose, not in its present form, but as a theoretical ideal. The better and more inclusive the units and questions, the truer and more complete the principles, the more the real approaches the ideal.

The box score is a non-judgmental, paper-and-pencil record of a game, from which a knowledgeable practitioner or fan can reconstruct what happened in every inning. I suppose that someone who is not perfect on the rule book can nonetheless read or write a box score, but a novice at the game can surely do neither. The PAT is not a record of an instructional session; it is full of judgments; and it can't be filled out or interpreted by a novice. But, if combined with a succinct chronological record of an instructional session, it can be most meaningful to both teacher and supervisor.

Furthermore, though I decided a long time back to focus only on the interaction in the classroom, I can no more omit questions and principles which best apply to pre-planning and post-analysis than I can omit the viewpoint embodied in that N-T question we've already discussed. So I see the EG as a kind of rule book and the PAT as a score sheet to be used only by those who know the EG.

> OK, NS, I understand your logic and have "received" but not "accepted" the explanation. I have specific questions about the PAT which I'd like to preface with a general one.
>
> When we applied the EG to the science lesson, we *did* evaluate the teacher and his instruction, despite the intent to probe the nature of the EG. But the EG is too cumbersome for general use, so you refined it to a PAT. Yet if the EG could be used to evaluate, aren't you being a bit coy about calling the offspring primitive, assessment, and tool?

It's a matter of precision rather than coyness, ZA. To value is to "determine the worth of," while to assess is to "set an estimated value on" (from my dictionary again). I'm not ready to say that I can determine the worth of someone's teaching. In financial transactions we can equate material objects and services to money, though even here there's no absolute scale for determining what an object or service is worth. In teaching there's nothing even comparable to money, so we can't set a price on any given effort. Ergo, I assess rather than value.

As to the science lesson: we evaluated, if we evaluated, neither the teacher nor his instruction. We did a thorough analysis of one lesson, but arrived at no definitive statement of its worth.

As to "primitive," ZA, I'm using it in the sense of "characteristic or imitative of the earliest stages; crude; simple; rough; uncivilized," because that's where we are in this business. Years ago, Biddle and Ellena said: ". . . we do not know how to define, prepare for, or measure teacher competence."* Whereas I don't see that developments in recent years now deny the accuracy of this statement, I do believe that I'm offering a definition of teacher competence plus a means for assessing that competence. That is, for me the competent teacher is the one whose "creation and control of conditions under which learners take on new patterns of responses to either old or new stimuli" are consonant with principles of learning. Presumably, the greater that consonance (as seen via the PAT), the greater the competence.

Then isn't the PAT at least an instrument?

No, ZA, because I'm quite certain that my 158 PAT questions are neither as equi-distant nor as equi-valent as the points on a ruler. I don't know that a score of 120 is better than a score of 119 or that being "right" on items 3, 5, 7, 9 is as significant as being "right" on items 2, 4, 6, 8. The PAT is not a research tool nor have I field-tested it to obtain a set of norms. The PAT is what I say it is: primitive, crude, simple, rough, in the earliest stages. And it's a tool, because an instrument is "a tool or implement, especially one used for delicate work or for scientific or artistic purposes." At this stage in the history of teacher competence we're not up to an instrument "used for delicate work." Ergo, a tool.

That seems reasonable enough, NS. May we now move to my specific question?

Before we do that, ZA, permit me another general prelude, with a musical analogy, for a change!

The supervisor is somewhat analogous to the music critic from some newspaper or musical journal. The critic at a violin recital, listening to an opus with which he's familiar, already knows what he will hear. He can even use a musical score to follow the performance. For him the hard facts are that the composer set

*Biddle, Bruce J. and Ellena, William J. *Contemporary Research on Teacher Effectiveness*. New York: Holt, Rinehart, and Winston, 1964 (p. 3).

down such and such notes, in unique phrases, with a variety of instructions regarding tempo, dynamics, etc. At the level of hard facts, two different critics at the same recital can probably agree on whether the violinist played the notes in tune and according to the other markings on the score. They will begin to disagree on the violinist's performance of ritards, accelerandos, etc., because either the composer did not provide (as composers generally do not) precise metronomic markings for ritards, accelerandos, etc., or because the critics differ about their own internalizations of such markings since (obviously) neither one sits with a metronome on his lap.

The point I'm trying to make, ZA, is that there are some hard facts (some "science") to music. Nonetheless, especially at the level of concert performance, the critics' final comments hinge much less on the "science" and far, far more on the "art." Did the violinist communicate the composer's intentions, at least as the critic interprets them?

The supervisor is in an even more tenuous position: there is no composer; there is no score; the teacher is more like a conductor than a single performer; yet the class is not at all an orchestra. Therefore, the supervisor's analysis is even more subjective and judgmental than that of the music critic. What's worse, the critic is independent of the performer, whereas the supervisor's role is to improve the teacher's effectiveness, with that very improvement being a reflection on the supervisor's abilities and talents.

The coda to this prelude is that many critics, both amateur and professional, can hear any given recital, permitting third parties to compare all published criticism. The supervisor rarely has any such company. The analysis depends on what he and the teacher can reconstruct of an instructional situation which takes place in real time and is never totally capturable even with hi-fi video equipment. So, teaching (as so many have said, so many times) is still largely an "art" and likely to remain so for the foreseeable future.

Therefore, the PAT is very much judgmental and subjective. Despite that, it does confine those subjective judgments to only 158 questions, organized into 33 units and six major sub-heads. The most salient point about the PAT is that I mean it to be used by teacher and supervisor as a kind of grid through which they filter the events in the classroom in order to come up with those nuggets which are golden enough to be retained in the teacher's repertoire of "creation and control," and in order to reveal those factors which are not consonant with learning principles.

My reasoning goes like this, ZA. Probably an ideal base for evaluating competency would be to decide on some new response pattern for a given group of learners, to pre-measure their ability to make such responses, to have the teacher try to teach them to make those responses, and to use a post-measure. The correlation between the pre-post differential and the teacher's teaching would then be significant. Comparing such correlations among many teachers would begin to tell us which constellations of teaching techniques are more effective than others.

As a supervisor, however, you cannot use such a research procedure in day-to-day supervision. Therefore, I reason, that if there *are* principles of learning that *do* tell us under what conditions learning *is* likely to be effective, then, if we see teachers creating and controlling such conditions, we should logically be able to gamble that the learning is more effective than it would be in the absence of such conditions. The PAT is directed at determining the existence of these very conditions. I've already agreed, ZA, that we don't know all of the principles of learning that research will eventually reveal, and that I'm not at all certain that the 222 statements I've collected will stand the test of time and further research. Both the EG and the PAT are tentative attempts at organizing what, in my judgment, we do seem to know into schemata for practical use by you and your colleagues.

> That's a rather long statement, NS, but it does answer my general question. Now the specific ones. First, I see that the PAT contains columns for teacher and observer. How are they to be used?

Since I've tried to phrase the question so as to elicit a yes or no response, I expect that teacher and observer can so respond. However, I recognize, as I'm sure you do, that both professionals might rather give a "gray" answer. It's also possible for them to agree on some scale, say with five representing total consonance and zero representing total dissonance. The symbols are of no consequence. I'm just providing space for notations, so that teacher and observer can compare notes.

You've used the work "agenda" for the points that teacher and supervisor decided to discuss at post-observation conferences. Are you saying that these two columns become the sources for an agenda?

Yes, ZA, that's exactly it.

You said a little while back that you've not field-tested the PAT nor developed norms for it. Does that mean that you've never used this PAT as a supervisor and/or that no one else has?

I've personally supervised a substantial number of student teachers in recent years. As a ZA, you should remember that I observed some number of ZA's each term and analyzed their teaching; and you participated with me in the analysis of recorded lessons. Unless you were in one of my most recent classes, you won't recall seeing a PAT. I made my analyses on the basis of current versions, without ever distributing a form. In fact, the very name PAT belongs only to the form in this discourse.

I suppose you can accuse me of promulgating a theoretical device as though it were already demonstrably practical. An invention ought to work for others besides the inventor, you might say. Well, ZA, I believe—no, I *know*—that it does. But that's not the crux of the matter. Let's review a bit.

A long time back, I said that I was proposing a framework for looking at teaching. All I hoped for (and still do) is that the concept of an EG with supporting principles would stand the test of time. I would be satisfied, I said, if only some of the 222 principles remained as truth. But the units and questions could change.

We both saw, after that long analysis of the science lesson, that the EG was not a practical device. So I've derived the PAT. To use it in a professional manner, however, will require not merely that teachers and observers understand the EG, but that they go back to the sources I've consulted, at the very least. The PAT, I said, is a kind of rule book. But I would no more hand a baseball rule book to a greenhorn in the sport and appoint him umpire, than I would hand the PAT to teachers and supervisors who lack a firm foundation in the field of learning. Merely understanding the EG is hardly the equivalent of studying the sources of the principles. So you have a homework assignment, ZA.

> You made me study one of your sources when I was a ZA, NS, but I will read the others. Now, another question. I can see some merit for retaining the identify of your six sub-heads, but is there really that much value in the 33 units?

There is, ZA. If either teacher or observer enters tallies against most of the questions in a given unit, that leads to a clear item on the agenda. In the absence of separate units, such constellations of tallies would be less meaningful. The best way to demonstrate this is to apply the PAT to a new lesson. So let's move on to that.

IX.

Junior High School Math Lesson

This one, ZA, took place in a conventional classroom, with movable furniture, but arranged in a traditional manner with all pupils facing the blackboard at the front of the room. Again, I didn't make a head count, but there were about 30 students, of both sexes. This was a ninth-grade urban class of brighter-than-average students, facing the prospect of a state examination some three months after the date of this lesson.

Boardwork was a central element. In order to clarify what you might have seen on a tape playback, I've labelled each use of the board with a letter symbol preceded by X (e.g., XA) and inserted that symbol in the text of the transcript at the point where each exhibit (ergo, X) was put on the board. The combination of exhibits and transcript will give you a quite clear picture of what appeared on the board.

TRANSCRIPT

Junior High School Math Lesson

0000	T	Question: What are we going to do today?
	K	(Answers, but many other voices are heard.)
	T	I seem to find a great deal of difficulty hearing her.
0011	T	(P–long pause) Go ahead.
	K	To learn how the Greeks multiplied.
	T	OK, why?
	K	Because they didn't use the same type of number system. They had, like, symbols for it.

0022 T Alice, how is that relevant? (P) Then repeat what she said. (P) It figures. What did she say? (P)

K I didn't hear her cause I was . . .

0037 T OK, repeat it (to the K who made the original reply).

K To learn how the Greeks multiplied because they used a different type of number system, they used symbols.

0046 T Why does it matter?

K Well, because in the Greek times they really, they really couldn't multiply as we do today. They didn't have decimals and their number system was very different from ours as we know it today, so they had a lot of trouble multiplying.

K Well, it's the basis for ours . . .

0112 T It's hardly an immediate basis. What period of time are we talking about?

K Hundreds of years before Christ.

0122 T Alright, say, safely, 2,000 years ago. Or maybe 4,000 years ago. Has a lot happened since then that would make this less meaningful? What has happened since then, mathematically? What are the developments?

K The Roman system, the Greek-Arabic system . . .

0149 T The Roman, the Hindu-Arabic. Alright. The operations performed by the Greeks are purely geometric. Before you can handle them you have to be able to construct perpendiculars, and that's where we're going to start today. All multiplication, the Greek way, is done by forming rectangles. Pretty obviously, you can't form rectangles without being able to form right angles. So we're going to start with the most simple construction. This is traditional; you can expect a question similar to it on the ninth year [state examination]. That's why it makes a more worthwhile topic. OK. What if we wanted to construct a 2-inch by 3-inch rectangle? How would you go about it? What would you start out doing? Someone gives you a nice handy little job to do: construct a 2 by 3 rectangle. You've got a piece of paper and all the tools that you have. What would you do? (p—short pause) Remember, it has to be precise, because the whole multiplication system will be based on how precise the rectangle is.

0258 K Well, I take a protractor and measure out the right angle first.

0302 T You don't have a protractor.

K I don't?

T What do you have? Look at what you have.

K Got a compass. (T—OK.) And I've paper, pen, pencil.

T OK. What else should you have?

K A ruler or a straight-edge.

0315 T (Giving K a ruler) OK, now you have a ruler. Go ahead.

K Well, ugh, I think you first construct your lines, 2 by 3, and . . . (T—You construct lines 2 by 3.) Yeah.

0330 T OK. We're going to have some weird inches. (Draws on board.) *XA.*

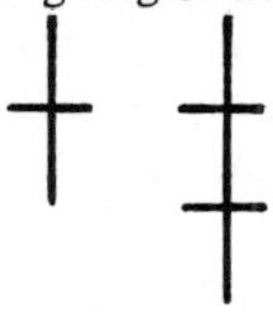

There's a 2-inch line; there's a 3-inch line. You just constructed 2 by 3.

K No, it doesn't go that way. (Class laughs) The 2-inch line should be the width and the 3-inch line the length. (T–Length and width.) Yeah.

0345 T Well, why don't you show me what you're talking about. (Laughter) Go ahead, construct. Remember: accuracy. (p) I'll allow your inches to be what you like, but it's more accuracy than . . .

K (interrupting) This'll be 2 inches (draws freehand). Here's the other two. *XB.*

T How do you know where to draw those other two inches?

K You have to measure first.

0410 T Alright. Take a ruler. Just for kicks, let's say that one blackboard inch is 4 inches long, so 2 will be 8 and 3 will be 12. Right? (K-Yeah.) OK, go erase. (K erases XB.) OK, we'll raid the drawer (for an eraser).

K (Begins to draw on board) (Street noises) First, there's the first line (uses the ruler this time) and the second line. *XC.*

0448 T Alright. Are there any comments at this juncture? Yes?

K The ruler's not straight.

T OK, that's true. What else can you say before he makes his mark, which he was about to do? Yes.

0503 K It's not like he could go to a different length, he could go to a different side; the bottom line wouldn't be the same as the top.

T What does he need before he can make his 3? (K-A right angle.) He needs a right angle; he needs a very accurate right angle. Where's he going to get a right angle from? With only the tools you are provided with. These are traditional, this is all you're allowed, and as a matter of fact, as I tried to point out yesterday, the compass I'm dealing with isn't even valid, because the Greek compass, when removed from the paper, collapsed, so that you couldn't use a compass to measure with. If you wanted an inch, another inch, another inch, you couldn't pick the compass off the paper. That makes life more difficult. OK. How's he going to get a right angle, with these tools? Aha! Yes.

0559 K He could use the edge of the ruler.

T The edge of the ruler. Well, they didn't even have rulers, they had straight-edges. But, uh, that would make for a very wobbly right angle. The edge of that thing isn't very wide.

0612 K Well, I think what you could do, you take the compass, put the point of the compass into the point on the end of the line and move it straight out using the ruler.

T Yes (to another K).

K You know, at this point you put the compass at the end of the line and turn it, so you would have a right angle.

T Do it. Have a compass (handing her the blackboard compass).

K (Goes to board and does what she said, but halts as she realizes she doesn't know where to end the arc. She laughs.)

XD.

T I hope you're getting the point of what the Greeks had to go through to do ordinary multiplication. (K–Yes.)

0707 T How do you know that's 90° and not 89.5°? But you don't. You're supposed to tell me how to do it.

K Well, I don't know. (Laughter)

0715 T Anybody?! (P) Nobody. Alright. This is the procedure. You begin with a line of two. How do you know it's two? We'll get to that shortly. Begin with a line of designated length, whatever that designated length is, and you extend the line. (Draws)

XE.

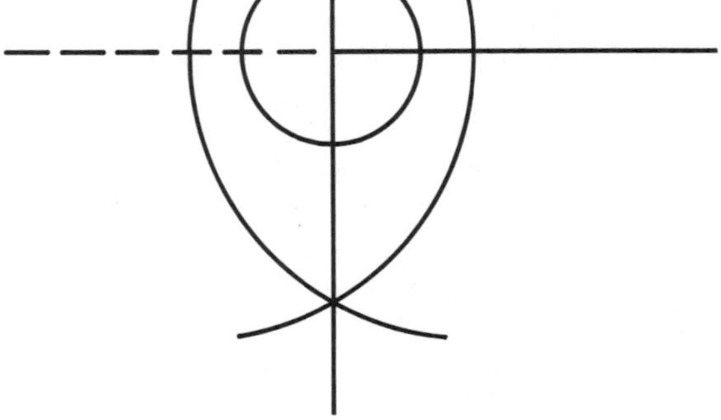

We have a straight-edge, so we can extend it as long as we like. Now that dotted or dashed line is necessary. But remember, it's not part of our two. Our rectangle is not going to start all the way over on the left end, past the dots; it's going to start right where it belongs. (0752) OK. At this point you can follow along on paper. Next step, placing the point of the compass at the end, just like June wanted to do, a circle is drawn around that point. (P–Ks working) (0822) The general name of this on the [state examination] is constructing a perpendicular to a line through a specific point on that line. What we're going to create is a perpendicular, right through that end point. That's what we're going to do. Now, one necessary factor is that the distance from this point, where the circle strikes our base line, is the same in both directions. How do I know it's the same?

0857 K Because the amount, the number of inches in the compass doesn't change. (T–Alright, and?)

K Doesn't it matter how far you go out?

T By the way, what is this little length called? (K–Radius.) (Pointing to a radius) (K–Radius.) Radius. And this one? (Pointing to another radius) This nice short little line?

K Oh, that one. A radius.

0926 T A radius. And what's true about the radii of a circle?

K They're all the same length.

0932 T They're all the same length. And, therefore, these two distances are identical. Next step: Opening the compass to a distance greater than the original radius. Now, how much greater than the original radius? Any amount greater than the original radius. Let's say, just for the heck of it, twice the size roughly, two or three times the size of the original radius. The point of the compass is placed at each of the intersection points separately. I'm going to start with this one. It doesn't matter which. And an arc is drawn. (Draws) Now I think Raul (tentatively raising his hand) already can see where the perpendicular is coming from. (p) Not yet though. Yes.

1026 K You put the other, you put the compass at the other point and start at the other point. (T–The other crossing point.) And then you just draw another arc. (T–Another arc.) (P) (T draws)

1041 T Now do you see the perpendicular we want? (p) Yes sir.

K They come to a point at the top and bottom. You just draw a line through them. (T does so)

1055 T Perpendicular. (P) At the end, just before June, we're going to do all the other constructions. This one we needed now. (P) Now there's another goodie we need. Yes?

K How did you know how much to open it the second time?

1115 T The same amount. (P) I've already violated one of the first precepts that I've started with; surprised nobody said anything. (p) Yes.

1126 K I thought the compass closes every time you pick it up.

T Yah, the compass closes every time you pick it up. I have goofed perhaps, have I? (p) How do I get around that? Remember, the compass can't be picked up and then moved to the other side and still have that dimension retained.

1152 K You just move it back and open it up again to where it was because . . .

T (interrupts) How do I know where it was?

K Because you can see where the other point was.

1158 T Alright. The nice part about the Greek compass is that it has two pencils, not one, and either pencil can serve as the center of the arc. So, I could start at one point, open the compass to the exact diameter of the circle, make my arc, and without ever leaving the paper switch to this pencil as the pivoting point (T is demonstrating all this as he talks) and make the other arc.

1235 T You see, having two pencils would be very useful. Their compass did. I'm going to repeat it. I said that the compass had to be opened to a greater distance than the radius, and I suggested twice the radius. If the point of the compass, which is one of the pencils, is put at the striking point, and the compass is opened to exactly twice the radius, an arc is made; then, without leaving the paper, the other pencil becomes the pivoting point, and another arc is made, the compass never has to leave the paper. (1313) OK. That's how you get around that little unpleasantness. You see, the Greeks had problems. (p) OK, so now we have our perpendicular. We have now a problem of how do you measure things. How do you know how long things are? What's 2? What's 3? We don't have rulers, we have straight-edges. We don't have inches, no such animal.

1340 K Make a little mark on a stick or something . . .

T Make a little mark on a stick. Well, they got around that, with their two pencil compass, by starting out with a base line. (Draws)

XF.

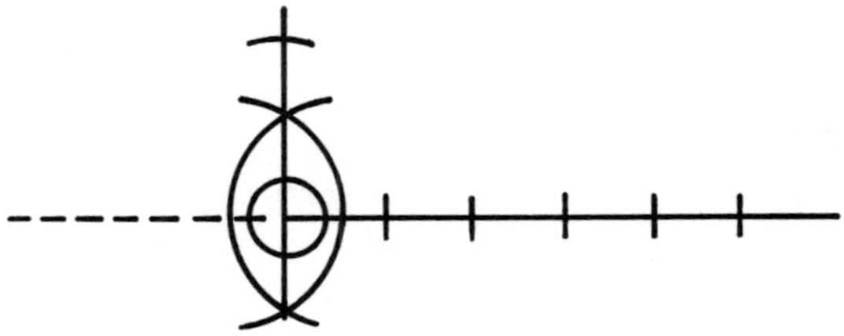

This base line was to be the place where the rectangle was constructed, right from the base line. (p)

1402 T With the compass open to any arbitrary length, with some mark set off as a starting point. If they wanted a 2 by 3 rectangle, they would take their compass and open it to any amount, mark one off, then use that as a pivoting point, mark off another, etc., and then do it right across the page. They could have three lengths, five lengths, 83 lengths, 900 lengths, immaterial. (1431) Then, they could draw their circle, strike it off and make a perpendicular; and finally, on that perpendicular, without ever leaving the page, mark off their single unit this way, again, again. That's how the Greeks did it. (1455) Now, for our purposes today, we're not going to get tangled up in what happens when the compass collapses. You're going to construct, traditionally, but with the tools you're used to, a compass with a point and a pencil, a ruler instead of a straight-edge. (1514) OK. Everyone, now to construct on their pages a line of length 2, let's say inches. Be careful, don't put it too low on the paper. You're going to need a lot of room below where you're constructing. There must be room left below it and a little room left to the right of it, as you'll see. So you're all to construct a 2-inch line, a perpendicular, and a 3-inch line. (1547) (Ks working; T circulates.)

1617 T I'm going to move quickly. If you feel unable to go through all the procedures of making a perpendicular, for the purposes of the rest of the period just draw a 3-inch line (p) and measure it, to be more accurate. (P, as T circulates.)

1645 T Finish off the rectangle, a perpendicular with the length 2. And finally, you don't have to worry about the last perpendicular; just connect the two end-points. (Draws)
XG.

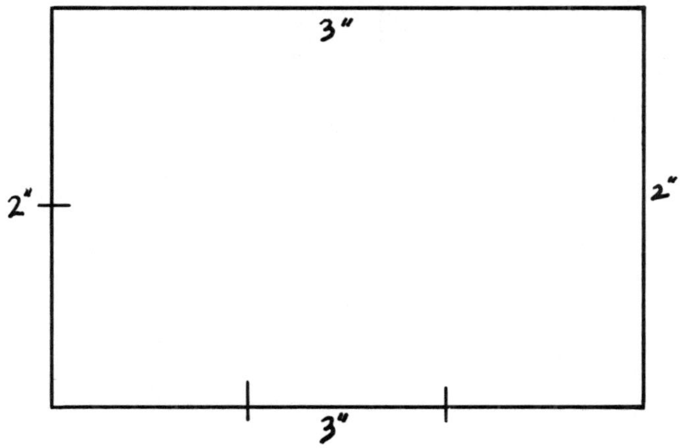

1658 T Alright. Now what in heaven's name does that have to do with multiplying? Is there anything on this board anywhere which is 2 times 3? (p) What is 2 times 3 on that board? Yes. (K–The area.)

1724 T The area of that rectangle is 2 times 3, and all multiplication, Greek multiplication, ancient, was done in terms of areas. If you could construct another rectangle, next to this one, with the same area that this one has, but with a side of one, what would that do for me? I'm going to repeat the question because half of you didn't listen. If I could construct another rectangle, next to this one, whose area was the same as this one, but one of whose sides is one inch long, what would the other side be, for me?

K Six.

1815 T It'll be six, which is the answer to the multiplication problem, isn't it? (p) That was how they got answers to multiplication problems.

1827 K The way he figured it out was by multiplying, by multiplying in his head.

T No, I'm not going to multiply anything. I'm going to draw another rectangle, without knowing that the answer is six, and when you go to the board and measure the length of the rectangle, what do you suppose it's going to be? (K–Six.)

1845 T OK. The procedure calls for–and I'm stuck because I've already messed up the board, so I'm going to try again, producing a 1-inch line. Produce. (Ks draw. T draws *XH*.)

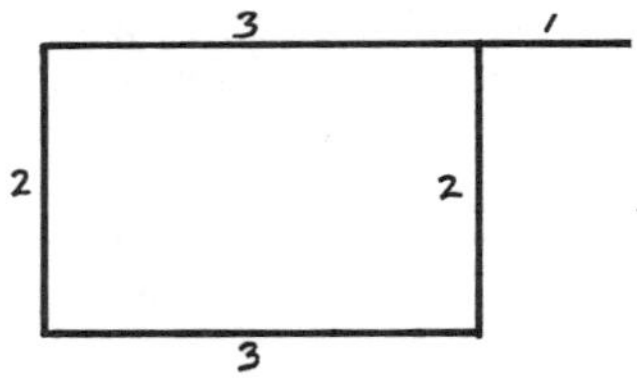

Drawn freehand by T.

You all have a 2 by 3 rectangle. You should all be producing a 1-inch line. (P) (Ks draw.) While you're doing that I'm going to make mine to scale, because the answer is meaningless unless it's to some sort of scale. (T draws.)

XI.

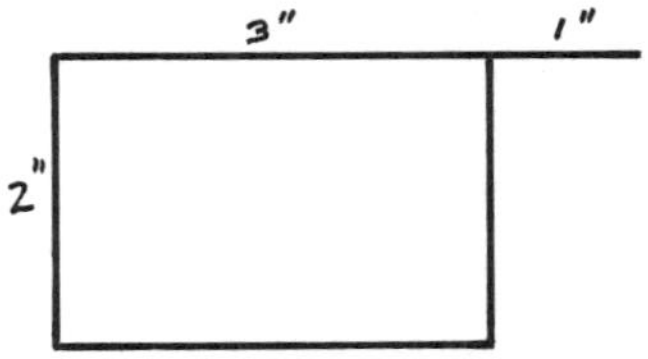

2006 T Can anyone see how I could finish this off? Be inventive, be creative. See what you can see.

K I don't think it's right. I thought you'd take however many inches was left on the top and put it by each point . . .

2032 T However many inches was left on the top . . . (K–No, ugh . . .) This is three (pointing to figure on board), and another one is four; this is two. Remember, you don't know the answer. Yes, it's six is what we're trying to find out.

K Just add them up. (T–Oh, that's pure luck.) Oh. (p)

2056 T No one can see where I'm going to get a nice long 6-inch line from, huh? (p) Remember, you know the answer ahead of time. You're not going to use it, except to help you think out. Yes?

2110 K The answer is 3 and 1 and a 2 . . .

T She said it. It's luck. It just worked out that way because the numbers are 2 and 3. What would this get you?

XJ. (*N.B.* Once the teacher has drawn figure *XI*, he continues with that figure. In order to make clear what the students are seeing at each step, this transcript reproduces each new configuration, as the teacher keeps adding to *XI*.)

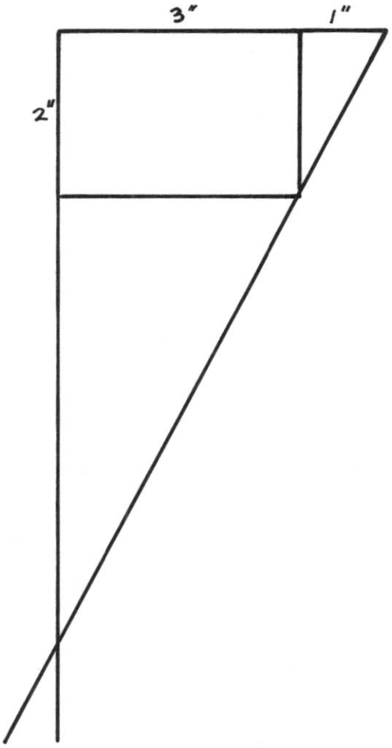

2136 K The line going down there is 6 inches.

K (inaudible) (T–It doesn't.)

2201 T Some of you ran out of paper. (P) But you did. (p) That makes 2, 3, 4. (T makes complimentary comment on their drawing.) You make good ancient Greeks.

2223 K Mr. ..... (T's name), it could be that (inaudible), where it meets the . . .

T (interrupts) Let's label it. (Labels drawing.) *XK.*

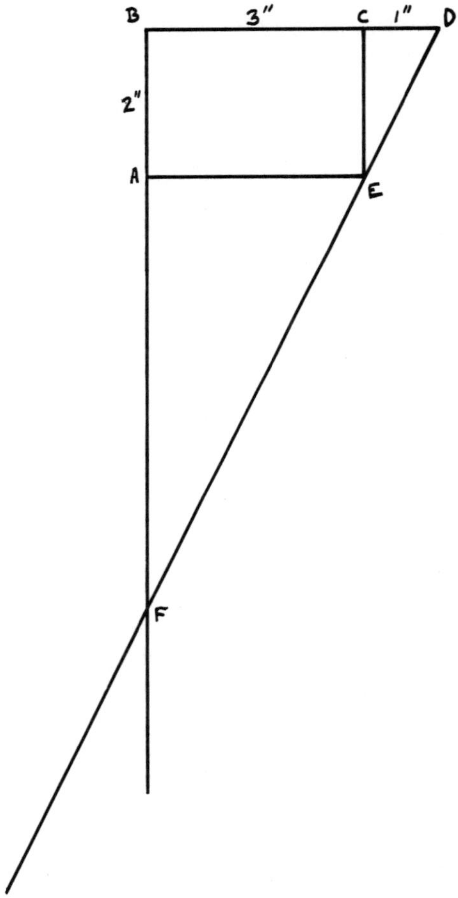

T Now what are you talking about?

K I think between B and F is 6 inches.

T You think BF is 6 inches. Well, measure it. What is it? You've got a good one (T to another K). What's BF? What's AF? What's BF?

K 8.

2258 T OK. Now what the Greeks actually did at this point. They didn't need to do it. They did it anyway. They finished this construction off, by actually creating, here; don't mark your papers, I'm doing this to show you; in here a rectangle.

XL.

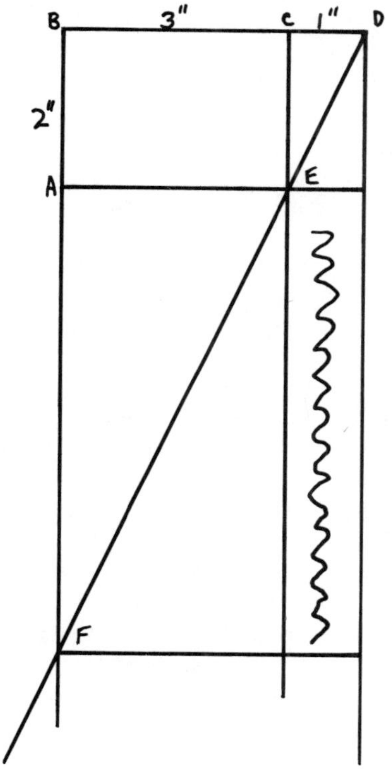

We're going to prove, tomorrow or the next day, why this created rectangle . . . which I'm going to create. The way you create it, another perpendicular, extend the line, another perpendicular, extend the line, you create a rectangle. We're going to prove that that rectangle has the same area as the original rectangle. It has a width of one and, therefore, its length would have to be the answer to the problem. We didn't need to go through all that, because our answer appears already: AF.

2358 T We don't need to finish off the construction of this rectangle. The Greeks did. They extended AE, they created a perpendicular at the bottom, another perpendicular; they extended CE; they built this rectangle by just drawing lines and perpendiculars. They actually created a 1 by 6 rectangle. They didn't know it was 6. The measurement came after this diagonal was drawn. The answer is there. (p)

2437 T Tomorrow we're going to take square roots, the way the Greeks took square roots; and then, possibly, $a^2+b^2=c^2$ will be a much more meaningful thing. When you think about how they had to multiply, and find out how they then went to take square roots, that makes the Pythagorean Theorem quite a development.

2505 T Alright. I want everybody to try a multiplication. But before, are there any questions? Yes?

K I don't understand the whole process.

T OK. Watch me. (T reproduces figure *XK* in freehand form as he talks.) First, construct a rectangle whose sides are the numbers you want to multiply. We wanted to multiply 2 times

3, so we created a 2 by 3 rectangle. We produced it. We proved it. We developed it. OK? (K–OK.)

2537 T How we produced it I demonstrated. Next, a 1-inch line was drawn, as an additive to either of the lengths. I did it across the top, but it doesn't matter. Finally, these two end-points are connected to the one, and the other base line is drawn. Your answer is that line. That's how it was done. The reasoning why it works is more complicated. A great deal more construction is required until a rectangle is produced here, and that's what we're going to talk about next time. OK? I'm leaving you sort of two-thirds of the way through. It's impossible to finish it in one day. OK, anything else? Yes?

2636 K How come the Greeks figured out something like that if they didn't even know how to multiply?

2641 T I have a better question. But how could they have figured out something like that (pointing to $a^2+b^2=c^2$)? Well, how do people figure? They had leisure. We talked about that; they had nothing better to do than to sit and figure. They had the people they conquered running around cleaning their dishes, sweeping up their floors. That's the way.

2709 T Alright. I want everyone now to multiply 2 times 4. I don't expect you to create perpendiculars properly today, with just about 2 minutes left, not even. Now, your homework will be on the board. Let's keep it small. Three multiplication problems, but you are required to create a rectangle in the specific, exact, ancient way. (P) (Ks work.)

2800 T I'm going to ask you to stop. Because we are so close to the bell. How would you handle a problem like 10 times 15 on your little pieces of paper?

K You could make it in proportion.

2815 T Yah. Instead of making it 10 inches, you could make it 10 anythings: 10 quarters of an inch, 10 half-inches, 10 eighths of an inch, 10 anything. But of course, the smaller the unit, the less accurate the final answer would be.

2833 K You could reduce it though.

T You could. OK. Two times 4 is now, and the homework is on the board. (P) (T circulates as Ks work. There is some general talking, with the T responding to individuals, but the words are inaudible on the tape.)

3035 Bell rings.

(N.B. The actual class period is longer than the transcript indicates. Some time was lost in setting up the TV equipment.)

Let me see whether I can apply the PAT to this lesson.

Go ahead, ZA.

I'll follow the pattern you used in the other lesson, focusing on each unit separately.

A. **Stimuli and Responses**

a. *Stimuli*

1. He had apparently laid the bases for the S situation the previous day, because the Ks knew what "we're going to do today" and why.
2. Although he was concerned about the noise level in the first minute, I wouldn't say he attempted to eliminate competing Ss of a context nature.
3. The context developed about Greek mathematics, the ability of the Ks to deal with the Ss and manipulate tools, plus the knowledge of what would be focused on in this lesson, all indicated a degree of continuity in instruction.
4. The materials were ready for use. (Except for a missing board eraser, ZA.)
5. Yes, and . . . and I'm not really clear, NS, on the question of anticipating the impacts of Ss. The science teacher didn't pass the fossil around for fear of it being dropped, and he avoided lecturing (we agreed), but just what are you looking for?

I'm looking for that use of stimuli which would alter, even temporarily, the focus of the interaction. A minor example would be the fossil: had the teacher arranged for it to be passed around from student to student and had it been dropped and broken before the fish fossil on it was so identified, then that would have had an impact on the lesson.

Our math teacher might have made a different impact had he said that multiplication, the Greek way, was difficult, that every state exam to date had included a significant number of questions on this topic, and that those who didn't pay absolutely strict attention today would fare as badly as their predecessors. Such statements would have created a tense context and made students anxious about an important future confrontation with an exam.

Early in my teaching career, in that school where I taught that music lesson, in the days before Gay Liberation, with an all-boys class, I used the word "fairy" in dealing with something. I forget what. I meant the word in its traditional meaning, but my boys reacted as though I had uttered one of the famous "dirty" words. The class broke up and the point I was making was totally lost—all because I hadn't anticipated "the impacts of the Ss."

Then would it be fair to say that our teacher threw in the bit about the state exam as added incentive to paying attention? After all, if he could fascinate the Ks with the sheer wonder of Greek multiplication, wouldn't that have been stimulus enough?

I agree with you. Whether he did so with malice aforethought, his statement about the impending exam would surely add some zest to the mere procedure of doing "what we're going to do today" anyway.

So let's say he didn't anticipate wild enthusiasm for Greek multiplication and threw in the state exam as an added stimulus.

6. There was no attempt to individualize the Ss. This was a whole-class lesson.

b. *Responses*

7. He did translate the goals into terminal K behavior. They were all to end up doing multiplication, the Greek way, using the tools permitted them on the state exam.
8. I have a question here, NS. PAT question 3, under the preceding unit, asks about relating present Ss to past learning. The question I'm now dealing with asks about relating present Rs to past learning. Could you expand on the difference between the two questions?

Stimuli are the entities to which Ks react, to which they make their Rs. Had our math teacher dealt only with constructing a perpendicular to a line in one lesson and then related this construction to Greek multiplication the next day, that would exemplify relating present Rs to past learning, Greek multiplication being based on having mastered the construction of a perpendicular.

For an example of relating present Ss to past learning we must go back to that sequence of music lessons which focused on form. When I brought in my classical records, they, as stimuli, bore no relationship to past learning. However, after the students had learned to hear form in their popular records, I could then expose them to form in marches, the latter now being stimuli related to past learning.

I think I see the point, NS, so I'll go on.

9. At a little past 1514 he tells them where to leave room on their papers (for the construction); at 2201 he comments that "Some of you ran out of paper"; and a little before 2636 he tells them that "I'm leaving you sort of two-thirds of the way through." More importantly, at 1617 he says what they can do today "if you feel unable to go through all the procedures of making a perpendicular." So he was anticipating the impacts of the Rs.

10. 11. I see these two questions as part of one large issue which also encompasses questions 50 and 51. May I postpone this discussion until then, NS?

Of course, ZA.

12. The Rs were individualized only in the sense that some students may not have been able to duplicate his procedures on their papers. At 1617 he says, "If you feel unable to go through all the procedures of making a perpendicular, for the purposes of the rest of the period, just draw a 3-inch line and measure it, to be more accurate." I interpret this to mean, since the work was to be continued the next day, he would then review the problem and give students time for construction. They would also be getting some practice via the homework assignment.

c. *Communication*

13. 14. 15. 16. I'd like to say that he did present the new learning in a familiar context (16) and that he clarified the Rs at the outset (14), but I also want to treat the unit as one large issue. A transcript doesn't yield conclusive data on clear communication. Does the tape help?

We could not have recorded each K's reaction to the situation. The tape shows that the students do attempt to use their tools to create both the perpendicular and the rest of the construction. The teacher comments that they would make good ancient Greeks and that at least one of them had "a good one," so I'm tempted to credit him with clear communication and with student understanding of what they had to do. As a supervisor, ZA, you would have been able to walk around the room and judge this for yourself.

Having completed the first sub-head, have you found anything you'd particularly want to discuss with the teacher?

There are two issues worthy of future exploration. (a) Since he individualized neither Ss nor Rs, is it likely that all Ks were equally ready for them, though I can accept that all Ks needed this instruction in view of the upcoming state exam? (b) Was he communicating effectively with his least able Ks?

Your first question anticipates the next sub-head, yet makes sense at this juncture. Both are interesting issues, ZA. Go ahead, you're doing fine.

Thank you.

B. **Readiness**

a. *Potential*

17-20. Except that he pretty obviously did not make any determination of individual K potential for dealing with Ss and Rs (which he might well know from each K's past achievements), I don't see how the reader of a transcript can score this unit. Unless you've omitted significant non-verbal teacher behavior, there's nothing in the verbal interaction to indicate that he made adjustments for those who lacked potential or for those who might not have needed this experience. Yet I would feel safer about my analysis if I had been in the room.

b. *Achievement*

21. 22. He made no determination of mastery of prior concepts and skills, but he may not have needed to. Again, had I been in the room I could probably have seen how many students were able to follow his constructions and replicate them on their papers. Is the tape revealing, NS? I ask for this reason: if even a tape misses certain essential features (essential to analysis, that is) then do tapes have any real value?

Without going into a long digression about videotapes, ZA, I'll just say this. The single-camera package generally available for on-site recording has limited capability, even in the hands of a skilled camera operator. It cannot encompass the entire class at once, nor can one position it so as to be able to capture each student's responses, unless one drastically reorganizes the normal seating pattern or one moves around the room with the camera.

I have recorded classes in our TV studio, using as many as five remotely-controlled cameras simultaneously. Even so, one can only record all that each camera sees by having a separate VTR (videotape recorder) for each camera. With only one VTR, one must select what gets recorded on the basis of a prior decision on the point of view for a particular recording. You do the same, under greater restrictions, using only one camera. But if you choose that focus in advance, you can then view the playback in the light of that focus.

I consider videotape facilities a marvelous aide for both teachers and supervisors and strongly advocate their acquisition by all schools.

You havent't asked me about agenda items from this area, NS, but I think the entire sub-head is not very open to observation, so I want to put it on the agenda.

C. **Motivation**

a. *General*

23-26. In your analysis of the science lesson, when you reached this issue, you cited P13, that an individual can be said to be motivated when he evidences some desire to attain some specified goal, and when the teacher recognizes and increases/intensifies such a desire, etc.

Your conclusion there was that if this is what motivation is, then the science teacher did not motivate the students. I could have commented at that juncture that the science teacher *had* motivated the students: to learn some things about fossil formation in order to pass the course. In the same way, the math students probably also felt a need to pass the course. They may even have felt a need to pass the state exam, a need he increased, *vis-a-vis* constructing a perpendicular, by his state exam comments.

But I must say that the transcript is again limiting as a vehicle for your PAT. In direct observation I could probably tell from nonverbal behavior whether the Ks were motivated to perceive the Ss and make the Rs, though such behavior probably wouldn't tell me "why some Ks were not motivated." Which makes me wonder: If your PAT is supposed to include observable behavior, are you saying that an observer can see whether the teacher discerned why some Ks were not motivated?

I do expect the teacher to be quick to discern *that* certain students were not motivated and to make an effort to engage their involvement. When and if I see the teacher altering the motivational situation for these students and being successful about involving them, I can guess that the teacher had put his finger on the difficulty, that he *did* discern why some Ks were not motivated. I can't be certain that he spotted the real cause, though the symptom seemed to have been cancelled out. If I do *not* see the teacher attempting to alter the motivational situation for non-involved Ks, then I must conclude either that the teacher is insensitive to this development (which is hardly likely) or that the teacher has been unable to discern why these Ks are not motivated (which is what I usually find to be the case). So I'm dealing with observable behavior.

Then I presume you will include the last possibility on your agenda, NS?

You presume correctly, ZA.

b. *Physical Plant*

27-31. I repeat here what you said re the science lesson: this unit has to be scored in person.

Let me add a few words, ZA. The focus of teacher and students was on the board and on students' worksheets. Temperature, ventilation, lighting, decoration, and bulletin boards were outside the frame of reference, were neutral in their impact. But everyone seemed to have a clear view of the blackboard.

c. *Focus*

32. I can't deal with this question, NS. We haven't agreed there was a motivation. I've always thought I knew what a motivation was, but now I'm not sure.

It is a bit of a problem, ZA. The R is the new response pattern the K is to take on, to which end he engages in activity, even if his body is at rest and he's only listening or observing. The S is the phenomenon in response to which he engages in the activity. He may be attending to a visual of some kind, such as a demonstration or an experiment; he may be speaking to a point, reading a passage, writing a reply to a question; drawing a figure; etc. The *reason* why he *does* anything is the *motivation*; which may be intrinsic because of its relevance to real life or its origin within the learner; and which may be extrinsic because of its irrelevance to real life or its origin with someone other than the learner. As some ZA's who've seen this tape have said: the motivation here may have been extrinsic, because the material was not particularly relevant to real life and because it did not arise from the students' need or desire to know how to multiply in Greek fashion; yet, students might well have had an intrinsic motivation to do well on the state exam (where high standing can lead to college scholarships), and the way the whole lesson was set into the context of Greek life could impel one to regard this as a real-life issue.

> That's a clear enough explanation, NS, but it doesn't answer question 32. In fact, it tells me how to address myself to numbers 36-38. I'll rephrase 32: was the reason-why-the-Ks-made-the-Rs specific to the Ss and Rs? Aside from his desire and success in obtaining silence and attention to what was being said, and aside from the remark about the state exam, what reasons did the Ks have to be attentive and to make the construction? In response to 23-26 I said that maybe they were looking to pass the course and to do well on the exam.
>
> Even though you've made "motivation" clear, NS, you haven't helped me with 32. How does an observer know, how would even the teacher know why the Ks were doing whatever they did do?

Maybe an example will clarify the point. I just finished reading an assignment turned in by a current ZA. It describes an elementary school reading lesson in which the teacher used an attractive toy to focus student attention on syllabication. The toy was an animal and the syllables were referred to as rocks. The kids were to have the toy skip from rock to rock as a way of counting syllables in particular words. Now, why a toy? Apart from whether syllabication is a useful tool in decoding, must one use an attractive object (an object unrelated inherently to the situation) to stimulate children to identify syllables?

Or take the case of games which are used as a format for dealing with specific subject matter objectives. All too often the object (for the kids) becomes one of winning the game rather than mastering material.

In our math lesson there was nothing extraneous to the issue at hand. So my answer to 32 is "yes." One can be tempted to fault him for throwing in the state exam, but he stated it as a simple fact, nothing more. What he seemed to be trying to entice them with is the idea that the Greeks managed to handle what was for them a complex operation because they were over 2,000 years behind us in mathematical history. He could have been most traditional by saying: The next topic in the text is making a perpendicular to a straight line . . . etc., so let's go ahead and see how that's done. Instead, he had involved them in an historic process, one culmination of which would be: (2437) "Tomorrow we're going to take square roots, the way the Greeks took square roots; and then, possibly, $a^2 + b^2 = c^2$ will be a much more meaningful thing."

Though I've given you some arguments to support my "yes" response to question 32, and though they may be convincing in this particular instance, I've not given you guidance transferable to other situations. In general, how does one know why students are or aren't motivated to attend to Ss and to make Rs? What answers there may be to this question are, for me, embedded in the principles under *Origin* and *Proximity* in the *Motivation* sub-head. These principles suggest the following:

- that intrinsic is probably superior to extrinsic;
- that relevance to the learner is a positive factor;
- that curiosity ought to be aroused;
- that opportunity to operate on the environment helps;
- that success in new experiences leads to the development of new interests; and
- that improving on one's past performance is motivating.

Therefore, in the "creation and control of conditions . . . , etc." teachers must so organize the learning situation that the above elements are working for you, not against you. And again I gamble: if a teacher functions in consonance with principles of learning, then I project that learning is more effective than if there is dissonance.

I can't read anyone's mind or heart and aver, without fear of contradiction, that students are or are not motivated by such and such elements. But if I see consonance with principles, then I gamble that learning will occur.

Again I plead for patience, NS. You seem to have committed all 222 principles to memory and are able to cite them whenever I need clarification. I'm beginning to see a little more clearly the real dimensions of the EG and the perspective it gives you on the instructional process. I'm also becoming aware of the implications of your definition of teaching. Once I truly make it mine, then all the rest seems to follow. But you're asking me to make a most substantial commitment, a commitment that moves me away from that familiar ambience I once referred to. Whereas I can still fall back on that ambience, just by putting this book down, I want to see where it will all lead. You *have* aroused my curiosity; this *is* relevant and intrinsic to me; I *am* operating on the environment and I seem to be improving on my past performance. So let's go on.

33. 34. Again I must go back to the science lesson, NS. You said of that teacher that the students were attending to *him*; they had no need or desire to know about fossil formation. Would you say that the math teacher was *not* directing attention at himself, but rather at the Ss and Rs? You said that what the science teacher did was a performance. Aside from the state exam, the math students had no more need for Greek multiplication than the other class had for fossil formation. In fact, that exam was apparently only going to test the construction of a perpendicular. Finally, going back to questions 10 and 11, didn't he really use approximately the first 7 minutes to set the stage for *his* explication? And if so, wasn't he therefore focusing attention on himself and his knowledge rather than on a guided development of a solution to the problem?

There is a delicate but significant differentiation to be made here, ZA. We've devoted a lot of words to the issue of what students do when the objective is to have them understand something. In the math lesson they had to attend to what the teacher did at the board and to his explanation of what he was doing, all in preparation for duplicating his constructions on their own worksheets. The material on the board and the teacher's words were stimuli. Without them they might not have been able to construct. And he stuck to the material at hand; no plays on words, no anecdotes, etc.

> Two things, NS. Are you now criticizing the science teacher for using humor, etc.? Do you want humorless instruction? And why the word "might" in your next-to-the-last sentence? You've so sensitized me to language that I can't let that word go by without comment.

Though humor isn't exactly my forte, ZA, don't conclude that I want purely intellectual instruction in dry, pedantic style. I'm not a member of the "learning-should-be-fun" school, because a great deal of learning, of taking on new responses to either old or new stimuli, requires application, perseverance, self-examination, re-orientation, giving up habitual patterns of thought and action, none of which is a particularly "fun" activity. So the more the process is leavened with humor, wit, vitality, enthusiasm, warmth, humaneness, and other such positive qualities, the more the learner is moved to be part of the process. But the first test is whether there is such a learning process, which is directed at learners doing things in order to be learning. That students are doing "fun things" is not a necessary indication that learning is going on.

There is no question in my mind that our science teacher is a very engaging man, a man of intelligence and intellect, flair and wit, vitality and warmth, a humane man whose lesson is, for me, a classic example of developmental instruction. I have no doubt that he has the ability to move towards the kind of teaching implied by the EG and the PAT. But his lesson doesn't tell us whether and what the students were learning.

Our math teacher is a different human being. His interaction with the students lacks the humor, wit, etc., etc., of our first teacher. Once he gets beyond the ego-flavored segment on parading erroneous responses, the interaction is largely impersonal. The focus is on the mathematics. The students are doing things, which can be looked at.

So, whereas the engaging qualities of the first teacher are missing in the second, the latter's required Rs are clearly observable, because the Ks have something to do.

As to the issue of "Without them they *might* not have been able to construct," I'm glad you picked it up, ZA, because mine was a deliberate choice of words. We cannot posit that this teacher's way of having students learn to construct the perpendicular and to complete the rectangle is the only way in which such an objective can be pursued. If we can assume that his students already know how to manipulate compasses, pencils, and rulers (a safe assumption, I think), then he could have proceeded as follows (at about 0300 into the lesson):

- Three students are sent to the board, each armed with compass, ruler and chalk. The rest work at their desks.
- "About one quarter of the way down on your papers, and similarly on the blackboard panels, rule out a horizontal line at least 2" long, using 4" = 1 blackboard inch at the board."
- "Make a dot on the left end of this line. Now extend this line to the left using dashes."
- "Open your compass to about 1" (or 4" at the board), set the point of the compass in the dot, and scribe a complete circle around this dot. Can anyone see how this might lead to a perpendicular?"
- "No? Then let's proceed. Open your compass to about 2" (8" at the board) and set the point where the circle intersects the extension in dashes on the left. Now make an arc from about 12 o'clock to 5 o'clock, like this." (Teacher draws clock face on board to explain his instructions.)
- "Now, without changing the opening in the compass, move the point to where the original circle intersects the solid line, and draw a complimentary arc from 12 to 7, but passing through 1, 2, 3, 4, 5, 6 o'clock. Can anyone see where the perpendicular is coming from?"
- K: "You connect the points at which the arcs intersect above and below the horizontal line."
- "Everybody see that? Any questions?
- K: "How do you know that you have a 90 degree angle"
- "Those of you that have protractors measure the angle. What is it? Oh, it is 90 degrees. Very good.
- K: "But how did it come out that way? Why does what we did produce a right angle?"
- "That's a good question, John, and we'll go into that tomorrow. Right now let's proceed to see how the Greeks used geometric construction in order to multiply." Etc.

What I'm illustrating here, ZA, is an approach not far removed from our teacher's manner and less-than-warm style. But, except for illustrating the clock-face instructions about the two arcs, which his pupils might have understood without the illustration, he would not be at the board, so only his words would be stimuli. The students at the board would give him a magnified sample of student seat work, which he could also be observing as he circulated. Wouldn't you agree that if he had proceeded in this manner you would not hesitate to answer "yes" to both questions 33 and 34, ZA?

> I wouldn't hesitate, but he didn't proceed as you suggest, NS, so what do I do now?

Another brief prelude, ZA, please. I think of you in the plural, though I address you in the singular: I see you as a former student (a real ZA) who may or may not have been exposed to some particular experience with me because I have altered my views over time; and I see you as a reader who never was a ZA. So I vary what I say depending on who's "talking" to me.

Real ZA's, especially recent ones, already know what a POC agenda is; they even know what the RAD cycle is. For the rest of you, please treat my references to agenda, POC, and cycle as the front ends of ligaments whose back ends will be anchored in the section of the discourse which will deal with the fifth and last of the questions I derived from defining supervision as the improvement of instruction: "By means of what techniques does one oversee, direct, guide, etc., the teachers? Who uses these techniques? Why?" End of prelude.

The answer to your question, ZA, is that questions 33 and 34 can go on the agenda for the POC, during which you might work your way around to some suggestion like mine. Although we're on the *Focus* unit of *Motivation*, just take a look at the last four principles in the *Feedback-Reinforcement* unit of the last EG sub-head. Can you see how my suggestion would earn the teacher some brownie points under *Evaluation*?

> I've looked and I see your point. Your suggestion does earn him positive responses on 33 and 34 but will also probably do the same on questions 141, 143, and 144. OK. Now to
>
> d. *Form*
>
> 35. I think that doing the constructions individually would be arranging for students to experience the consequences of failure. Whether they could succeed, I can't tell from the transcript. Only direct observation could tell me that.

e. *Origin*

36. The class knew what they would be doing this day, so I can't say whether they had an original interest in the subject matter.
37. But we've already agreed that one can go either way on the extrinsic-intrinsic continuum. So let's say that he aroused the curiosity of students about how the Greeks solved such problems. At least one K asked how the Greeks figured it out; and the teacher is aiming at their deeper appreciation of the Pythagorean Theorem.
38. Therefore, one might say that the Ss and Rs were related to a real-life situation the students could grasp.

f. *Proximity*

39. I guess I could have said, in response to question 36, that there was no evidence of prior student interest in this day's content. Nothing in the transcript indicates to me that he exploited or even referred to such an interest.
40. Nor did he arrange for a quick, light, vivid exposure to a new area, though both he and the students were active.

41-44. There was overt bodily activity, but hardly anything in the way of investigation, adventure, and use in real life. The two Ks at the board and the class at that point almost began to probe for a way of making that perpendicular, but he shut the process off.

45. There's nothing in the transcript on the question of improvement relative to one's past performance.

g. *Polarity*

46-48. Something just hit home, NS: in dealing with question 32, you, in effect, admitted that there was motivation; otherwise, how could you have answered "yes" to that

> question? Also I never really answered 23 and 24 (which ask whether the Ks *were* motivated) because I became so wrapped up in 26 and the Ks who *were not* motivated. So did he or didn't he motivate the students? Only a "yes" response will allow us to deal with the *Polarity* unit.

I answered "yes" because the Ks did listen to him and did do the constructions. Aside from the opening interaction with Alice, attention was not an issue. There were no discipline problems. So there must have been some influence at work to focus student efforts on the subject matter.

> Then I *have* caught you in a paradox! The science teacher had no discipline problems either! His students paid attention! With no instructions at all, they participated in the interaction, took notes, etc. Yet you say that his was a performance! But you don't level this accusation at the math teacher, though I think you're ready to agree that his parading of erroneous responses was really just a way of setting the stage for his explication.

Whenever students do what's expected of them, there must be some reason(s) why they do it. (Likewise, when they don't, there also are reasons.) But if teachers are to aim at intrinsic motivation, then the concepts and skills at issue must either be inherently interesting to students or must be related to real-life applications. Motivation based on pleasing teachers and parents and/or on passing the course are extrinsic, as well as being permanent elements in instruction, as contrasted with the transitory nature of any particular concept or skill.

Look, ZA, you've really warmed up to the process and are beginning to see how difficult it is to make a judgment that sticks. But let's see whether I'm contradicting myself.

In the science lesson the Ks did little more than listen, take notes, and talk (and only a minority spoke). They did not do the "doing" which would have led them to develop an understanding of fossil formation. (And there's no point repeating our long discourse on the whole issue of "understanding" something.)

In the math lesson the teacher could also have done all the

doing and had the students take whatever notes they could. Instead, he had them, at the very least, attempt to replicate the constructions he put on the board. I've already shown you how he could have had them do even more. He could also have pursued the process by cueing one or the other of the Ks at the board into a discovery of the proper procedure for constructing the perpendicular.

"But he didn't do either," are the words on your tongue. No, he didn't, and to that extent his was more a performance than it needed to be.

Let's face it, ZA. This matter of it being a performance is not a "To be or not to be" question; one is not *a-performer* or *not-a-performer.* There's a continuum here. The nearer an instructional situation is to maximum student "doing," the more consonance we have with principles of learning. But, keep this in mind, my very definition of teaching requires the teacher "to create and control conditions . . . ." One can't do this and yet be totally inactive. So it's a matter of degree. By that yardstick the math lesson was nearer to the student-doing end of the continuum than the science lesson was.

But, you will say, "You're comparing apples and pears, NS. They're both fruit, but they're not the same fruit. The science teacher's aim was conceptual understanding, whereas the math teacher's aim had an observable-behavior component."

True, ZA, no doubt about it. But I've already talked loud and long about how one might translate the aim of concept mastery into observable behavior.

I've been saying to many students in many education courses for many years that you have to ask yourself one special set of questions before you inaugurate an instructional situation:

> If, as a result of living through that situation, one can posit a student whose Rs can be rated 100% and one who can be rated 0%, how will they differ? How can I detect that difference? Can I also locate such gradations as 60%, 70%, etc.?

My thesis is that if you can't detect the impact of the teaching situation on the students, then you don't know what's been accomplished and where to go next. So, the more you aim at "doing" by students (and for me the so-called "aim" of every lesson *must* be a statement of what students will be able to do after instruction that they couldn't do before it), the better you will be able to create and control the next learning situation so students can progress towards mastery.

In that sense, the science teacher was much more a performer than the math teacher.

I hear you loud and clear, NS, at your vociferous best! Your words almost shout at me off the page. Discounting the vehemence, I appreciate the logic. And I must say it's persuasive. If I may use a drama analogy, you want the teacher to be the director, but you insist that the students perform the roles in the drama.

That's very good, ZA. It's an apt analogy because a sequence in learning is a kind of script.—Would you now go back to the *Polarity* unit please?

The polarity was probably mildly positive. Aside from calling Alice to account just as class began, there was no reprimanding; but beyond the "You make good ancient Greeks" (2201) and "You've got a good one" (2238), there was also no praise. Nor did he vary polarity in keeping with K characteristics.

h. *Strength*

49. You answered this one for me, NS, when you said that his manner was less-than-warm. Certainly there were no highs and lows.

50. 51. If you don't mind, NS, I'd like to finish off units *Variety* and *Timing*, because I want to engage you in that large issue which began with questions 10 and 11. OK?

OK, ZA, again I accept the postponement.

i. *Variety* and j. *Timing*

52. 53. There was no individualization of instruction and except for the compliments I just quoted he seemed not to have had to re-motivate his students. Now let's go back to ego-involvement.

The issue really begins with question 10: Did the teacher elicit and parade erroneous responses? First, what did he actually elicit? Well, one or more students tell him that the Greeks had a different number system and that they didn't multiply as we do today. Then he tells them that all Greek multiplication was done by forming rectangles, which you can't do unless you can construct accurate right angles. He poses the problem of forming a 2" by 3" rectangle and begins to parade what turn out to be erroneous responses. Two Ks offer solutions at the board, but neither one is correct.

What bothers me, NS, is the notation of laughter at points 0330, 0345, 0625, and 0707. Each time the laughter seems to be directed at a student's inability to meet the challenge of providing the right answer. Am I reading this into the transcript?

I don't think you are. The transcript doesn't record tone of voice, certain emphases in articulation, meaningful pauses, etc. But the entry at 0707 supports my non-verbal memories:

T How do you know that's 90 degrees and not 89.5 degrees? But you don't. You're supposed to tell me how to do it.
K Well, I don't know. (Laughter)
T Anybody? (P)

The impact on me is of a teacher-class relationship where teacher poses questions for students, permits them to attempt solutions, but without helpful cues; where students feel free enough to try, but where they fail; where failure may be laughed at, because it's permitted by teacher and tolerated by the individuals who fail; and where such failure sets the stage for teacher to show how it should be done. I'm not suggesting, ZA, that this is characteristic of all instruction by this teacher. Apart from recording this one lesson, I never saw him teach, either before or after. I'm simply generalizing on this lesson.

Well, then, so he elicited and extinguished at least two erroneous responses at the outset. And later on he twice responds to two different students who suggest adding dimensions 2, 3, and 1 to get 6, the answer to the problem. Altogether it seems to me that student attempts at creating that perpendicular are somewhat less an effort to parade erroneous responses than an effort to set the stage for the teacher's presentation of the proper solution.

But your last comment raises a side-issue, NS. I'm sure you will want to go back to see whether your generalization about this lesson is confirmed in others before focusing on such an issue in a POC. But what if I had been this man's real supervisor, his department chairman perhaps, and what if I knew for certain that he doesn't generally parade erroneous responses as a setting for his explication? Yet here you came in with the VTR and he seemingly did do so. What's my role, NS?

Since you claim to know his general practice, ZA, I can assume that you've observed him with some frequency, and that you've seen either the lesson or the tape, or else you wouldn't be in a dilemma.

Without launching us prematurely into the process I use in a POC, I'll just say this. At the next opportunity for a professional discussion of his instructional program you would get him to elaborate on why he chose to exhibit an interaction pattern which is at variance with his usual wont. There's no point in my writing a fantasy on how that discussion would proceed. But there is an issue here, an issue worth examining.

Collegiate colleagues have suggested to me that studio recordings, of the kind I mentioned earlier, are very artificial and hardly representative of day-to-day practice. They, and my teacher-students, also make the point that a supervisor rarely if ever sees instructional behavior which is truly representative of what goes on when only teacher and students are alone in the classroom. Therefore, recorded material, even when created on site and not in a studio (to which we used to bring teacher and class in the days before portable VTR's), has limited value in the training of teachers and supervisors.

To which I can make two responses: (a) In my studio-recording years I rarely recorded a teacher unless I had first observed that teacher teaching a very similar lesson (similar to the one we would record in the studio) taught to a class comparable to the one which would be brought to the studio. (I did this so I would know where to position cameras and mikes and how to record the lesson.) My experience was always the same: the teacher's methodology and interaction remained stable from the sample done back at the home school to the one we recorded in the studio. But the tension of being in the studio did exhibit itself in some exaggeration of a teacher's tempo of speech, pitch and timbre of voice, his pattern of movement around the room, the underuse or overuse of gesticulation, etc. Nonetheless, the essential professional content was unaltered and could therefore be used in teacher education courses. (b) But suppose I grant that no teacher creates and controls the classroom situation when there's a supervisor or college person in the room in exactly the same manner as he does when alone. If the observed lesson goes badly, then we attribute it to tension and work with the teacher to feel more comfortable under observation.

But if the lesson goes as smoothly as our match lesson does, yet is different from the teacher's normal practice, the question is: why the change? If that change is a conscious choice, which we would have to establish in a POC, then I must assume that it was made to match the presumed preferences of the observer. So, to get to your question, ZA, you and our math teacher would discuss whether he teaches this way when you don't see him, or whether he was nervous in front of the camera, or whether he presumed that I (the college person at the camera) had a preference for such an interaction pattern. If he sometimes teaches this way, when you haven't seen him, why? If, under tension, he falls back on such a pattern, why? If he made a conscious choice, why? No matter which question turns out to be appropriate, we have the basis for a professional discussion.

> You're saying, NS, that there's a stability in a teacher's practice; perhaps what some people call "style." That if the stability falters under tension, we work to reduce tension to re-establish the style before dealing with it professionally. But what if that style seems to be consciously altered only under observation, then I ask: why? But how would I know that, if the teacher always teaches the same way whenever I observe him?

You wouldn't know. You must deal with what you observe. My assumption is that you are either being shown the teacher's Sunday suit whenever you come, or the image he would like to leave with you. Either way there's a professional issue. However, I sincerely believe that this whole digression will cease to be an issue when you learn to supervise in the manner I will explain later on.

Again, I reserve judgment, NS, though I'm not sorry we digressed. Back to the analysis:

D. Materials and Activities

a. *Scholarship*

54-57. (It would be rather foolhardy for me to construct your response here, ZA. I claim no expertness in mathematics and can't say how well the teacher knows his material, etc. So I leave the judgment to those of you in the field of mathematics education.)

b. *Materials*

58-62. It's fairly clear that they had compasses, rulers, pencils, and paper, plus their counterparts at the board. There's nothing in the transcript about distribution and sharing, nor about use and care, so I gather that these are not relevant here. But I can't answer whether the manipulation facilitated learning. Can you, NS?

During the recording I was at the camera. I've already said that we couldn't record each Ks Rs. I did get onto the tape the efforts of some of the students at construction. Again, direct observation is superior to both transcripts and tapes.

c. *Meaningfulness*

63. When you dealt with this unit in the science lesson we went into a rather long philosophic digression whose major outcome, for me, at any rate, was your insistence on a social context for each segment of instruction. You said (on p. 102) that the science teacher was irrelevant in that lesson because "He didn't relate it to what they knew, not about the earlier material to which he had exposed them, but about the social and personal usefulness of such knowledge to the world at large and to these students in particular." In

> fact you began your discussion of the unit by saying that "*Meaningfulness* and *Structure*, which are really extensions of *Scholarship*, are probably the most crucial units in the entire grid."
>
> You also made a very emphatic claim (on p. 98): ". . . if I had to name one factor as being most responsible for lack of success in teaching I would not hesitate before saying: ignorance of subject matter."
>
> When I pressed you to exemplify a meaningful kind of instruction, you first described your music lessons, and finally indicated how you might have provided a social context for the study of fossil formation. I didn't argue the ignorance-of-subject-matter issue, because you're entitled to your opinion, and I don't regard opinions as rationally arguable. We don't have the same data base.
>
> What I got out of all that was that you have a powerful faith in the knowledge man has codified into the various disciplines and that you want your kind of "teachers" to be able to relate content to the social beings all students are. The science teacher, you said, didn't do that. Since I'm still struggling to put all this into a frame of reference I can grasp in fine detail, since I want you to respond on the assumption that I'm not a math expert either, and since you said somewhere that the supervisors using your methodology could help teachers even when they weren't fully knowledgeable in the teacher's field of instruction, how do *you* respond to the math lesson?

Actually, ZA, I think your grasp is already sufficient for dealing with the *Meaningfulness* in the math lesson, but I accept your conditions.

The math teacher had already provided the beginning of a social context. The Greeks, he said, had no ruler, no standard unit of length, nor did they have protractors. Furthermore, they lacked our much more sophisticated decimal system. Yet they not only managed to multiply, they even produced the Pythagorean Theorem. But, as I see it, he missed a golden opportunity when a student asked him how the Greeks figured out all that he demonstrated to them. Yes, he said the Greeks had leisure, so they used it to figure things out. But he closed that potential discussion instead of opening it.

I don't know what he could have said, ZA. I'm not a student of mathematical history, nor do I know what the Greek contribution was. But the teacher could already have been master of that material, and taken some time then (or postponed it to the next day because the bell was almost upon him) to sketch in what is known about the antecedents to Greek multiplication. Or he could have admitted to limited knowledge, but with a projection to filling in the gap for himself and for them. Or he could have dealt with the more general topic he counterposed to the student's question: "How do people figure?"

After all, apart from the requirements of the course and of the state exam, who needs to retain how to construct a perpendicular to a line and to create geometric forms in order to do multiplication? The social issue is, as the K put it: "How come the Greeks figured out something like that . . . ?" Dealing with this question leads to intellectual and aesthetic development. Following a set of rote procedures for constructing perpendiculars and rectangles doesn't.

64. Then you're saying, NS, that the Ss/Rs could have been more meaningful (as you define the term) to the students, and that he missed a golden opportunity to determine meaningfulness when he shut off that K feedback you just cited.

That's it, ZA.

d. *Structure*

65. There was a structure to the material. A math teacher or supervisor will know whether he chose the most appropriate structure. But I saw him go from the perpendicular to the rectangle to the steps in the Greek construction.

66. I don't know that he elicited feedback on student grasp of structure, but student involvement at certain points (plus your assurance, NS, that the tape shows the Ks constructing) can be viewed as important evidence. At 1041 one K knows where the perpendicular came from. At 1110 K asks how much to open the compass. At 1126 K remembers that the Greek compass collapses when removed from the paper. And so on.
67. But this was not a situation where students could have been encouraged to select their own structure. He wasn't dealing with an array of data to be organized for later recall; he was dealing with a geometric construction which required the completion of certain operations in a given order.
68. This was a whole-class lesson, as I've said earlier, with some limited adjustments to individual capabilities.

69-72. I find no indication of a general schema, parts of which were isolated for attention before being reincorporated into the whole, though there was some pointing to specialized vocabulary.

73. The issue of teaching unrelated learnings separately did not arise.—All of which is a rather inadequate response to a unit you hold in such high regard, NS.

Keep in mind what I said some time back, ZA: that both the Empirical Grid (EG) and the Primitive Assessment Tool (PAT) may need two observers, one specially skilled in content, the other on the rest of both assessment devices; or that one person would have to be skilled in both areas, with the latter being the more likely possibility. I would expect you, as the math chairman, to be able to apply the *Scholarship, Meaningfulness,* and *Structure* units expertly. I would also educate you, as a supervisor, to apply the rest of the PAT.

e. *Summaries*

74. 75. There were no summaries. If each K did

each construction, and did so accurately, then their replication of the teacher's constructions could be a kind of elicitation of summary statements by Ks. Only direct observation could have told me this.

E. Process

a. *Attention-Distraction*

76-78. Your transcript seems not to mention any "recurring or repetitive activities" nor any "controllable distractions." There is one indication of street noises, but I gather that the Ks were not distracted. Perhaps, had I been there in person, I might have noticed that some Ks were distracted, so let's chalk up another plus for direct observation.

b. *Discipline*

79-85. I find no way of using the transcript to determine my responses. The tape may provide some data on organization of Ks, spaces, etc.; the transcript does not. There seem to have been no problems.

c. *Media*

86. Once again the transcript offers no guidance, NS. Also, it seems to me I would need more than one observation to get some ideas about the issues this question raises.

87. But I do feel safe in saying that the segment we discussed on "parading erroneous responses" is an indication that, at least in this segment, he did not model very "mature behavior." Since it *is* a small segment, in just *one* lesson, I would have to reserve judgment until more data are available.

88. He and the students used the materials they had to use: rulers, compasses, etc. This use involved touching, seeing, and hearing (instructions). Smell and taste could hardly have been involved. But I do see now, NS, that if the students had only taken notes, they

would not have been touching the materials. So I give him a "yes" here.

89. Given the exhibits you duplicated from his board work, I project that he used the materials and equipment effectively. However, a math supervisor present in the room would have a more solid basis for a response.
90. Here, too, a math supervisor might have more to say, but teacher and students used implements and worked on writing surfaces. I don't see how they could have been more concrete.

d. *Interaction Pattern*

91. I've just leafed through the transcript, NS. The lines of type for the teacher's speech far outnumber those for the whole class. So he didn't listen as much as he spoke. Your p and P for lengths of pauses are better than nothing, but they're a far cry from what I would have seen in direct observation. So I must give him a "no" on this question.
92. We've already talked about Ks "doing" the constructions at their desks. Had he conducted the lesson as you suggested earlier, there would have been considerably more "doing" by the students. Which raises a question, NS: how much "doing" by Ks meets your requirements?

In preparation for becoming a music teacher, ZA, I took courses in brass and percussion, having already studied strings and woodwinds privately. I had the same excellent teacher for both courses. He never blew through a single horn or beat on any percussion instruments. He showed us how to put lips to a mouthpiece and how to hold drumsticks, then gave us verbal instructions, describing how our lips or hands had to feel and what the results ought to be. He also singled out those who were closest to his instructions to serve as models for the rest of us. In fact, I don't know to this day whether he could have gotten the results many of us achieved by the end of each course, which is, of course, totally irrelevant. *We* explored, *we* experimented, *we* acted on the environment, *we* discovered. *We* did the "doing" under his guidance. Which is partly why I described that alternative option for the math lesson. So I'm suggesting, ZA, that teachers need to limit their "doing" to those elements which provide a proper starting point for students. We could eventually have figured out how to set a mouthpiece on the lips or how to hold drumsticks, but it would have been pointless and a waste of time. Both tools are designed to be used in particular ways, just as string instruments are designed for "righties." So he had to demonstrate the design requirements. From there on we learned by doing.

That's an interesting point, NS. I hadn't thought of it that way before.

93. Then it seems obvious that he could have followed your earlier suggestion and had Ks at the board doing all the constructions. But what about time? Wouldn't your procedure, especially if he gave them time to "be inventive, be creative" (2006), have made it impossible for him to complete the Greek-multiplication-construction before the bell rang?

Especially since you're really not here to defend yourself, ZA, it seems quite unfair to infer that you have a commitment to "covering the material." But I have no choice. Let's look back at P124 and P125 under *Pacing* in the EG. P124 says: To learn to make the new responses required in a given learning situation takes time, the length varying with the learner's past experience and abilities and with the difficulty of the task. P125 says: Learning will not occur if the learner is asked to acquire more responses in a given period of time than he has the capacity to acquire. If you combine these two with the first sentence of P82 (The more time the learner spends in making responses, the more he learns.) you can see that time is something to be used in the learning process. It's not a measure of learning effectiveness.

Yes, I'm aware that P126 speaks of the value of setting time or work limits, but Seagoe (the source of that statement) suggests using time as a means of increasing intensity and rate. She's not saying that getting on with the content is more important than the learning process.

Since I've already raised a straw man, we may as well demolish him completely. No one can really say how much math a group of students ought to master in one semester. Seagoe (S-38) puts it this way: The interaction between the complexity of a learning problem, the learners' abilities in that area of learning, the degree of concentration of the motivation, and the extent to which the participating learners are affected by that specific motivation—that interaction determines maximal gains in learning by these participating learners. Therefore, the amount such learners *might* learn *may* be projected in advance; no one can *legislate* that the teacher and the learners have a joint obligation to convert that projection into 100% realization.—End of straw man.

This is another of those moments, ZA, when I don't know what words to put in your mouth. Oh, I hear you alright. You're saying that if an instructional program has a content (something I've already agreed to), then that content needs to be dealt with in some organized way. If teachers govern their pace by the speed at which the slowest students can move, the rest will be bored to tears. But if they give each student his/her unique time-span, then we must practically rule out any kind of group instruction. Etc., etc., etc.

We've already talked about open education and individually programed instruction. If we were now to go into how much subject matter content belongs in a Kg-12 curriculum, given the need for individual pacing, we would be going far afield. *If* one can use principles of learning as the basis for teaching and supervision, and *if* those principles withstand the test of further research, and *if* those principles then imply that certain ways of organizing schools, classes, curricula, materials, etc., are more effective than other ways, *then* we will have to make changes. But any such discussions are beyond the basic scope of this discourse, ZA.

I'd rather speak for myself, NS, and say that you lost me this time. I began answering question 93 by agreeing with your earlier suggestion about how the math teacher could have had Ks at the board to increase the amount of "doing" by students. Then I said, in effect, that the Ks couldn't construct as rapidly as the teacher, so the whole matter of perpendiculars and Greek-multiplication-construction would take much more time. So now

> you reply that there is no absolute amount of subject matter to be covered in any given semester, which is rather hard for me to deny, but that it's also a closed issue as far as this discourse is concerned. Why? If I'm chairman of a math department and have to lay out departmentalized programs for teachers and students, I have to have some basis for grouping students according to how much math they've "taken" and how well they've done in it.

Let me interrupt you here, ZA, though you obviously have more to say. This is, after all, a fantasy discourse. The words I generally assign to your part of the dialogue are words I've heard students say in my classes. And were we now in a class, I would also stop you.

The principles I have included in the EG are vouched for by the authors from whom I've derived them. Though each author may well have helped to establish one or more principles, none has done all the research necessary to establish all the principles in the EG. Therefore, at best they are secondary sources and my paraphrasings are thus tertiary. Whereas I'm willing to accept all the principles, until more research points to other choices, I can't trap anyone else into acceptance. And I would be, if I permitted our current discussion to continue.

Yes, the principles do suggest individualization and pacing, just as the principles on immediate-positive-specific feedback have implications for homework assignments. For me to engage you in a fantasy discourse on "So what shall we do about homework?" or "How much math is enough for a given period of instruction?" would assume that you have already accepted the principles and are ready to implement their implications. If, as a reader of this discourse, you become convinced of my major theses and wish to put the EG and PAT to work in your classroom or school, fine. But for me to assume that as ZA, my co-discourser, you have already done so would be to make this a work of fiction.

> I see the point, NS. So let me go on with the analysis.
>
> 94. He *could* have arranged for K contributions to have an impact on the substance and direction of the learning, but he didn't. He began the lesson as though he had this in mind, when he

sought K ideas on how to make the perpendicular, but as we both now agree, that effort was more of a stage-setting for his explication than an attempt to guide students towards a solution.

95. Even as a direct observer I would have to know each student before being able to answer this question. I could see how different Ks reacted to being involved, like the K in the science lesson who wouldn't make a second try at a response, but I couldn't tell whether the teacher was calling on those with least reticence about being active contributors to the group.

96. There was no need for him to talk privately with any student, except that Alice might have resented being called for lack of attention. I assume this question means that Ks who get out of line should be spoken to privately rather than embarrassed in front of a whole class. Yes, NS?

Yes, ZA.

e. *Questioning*

97-104. I followed your example, NS, and counted all questions, as you did in the science lesson. I count 36 original questions, five of which he restates once each without apparent intention, one he restates twice, and a seventh that he says he's deliberately repeating. I count just four K questions, the first (at 0302) hardly meriting inclusion, two others (0857 and 1110) being good substantive questions, and that very important one (at 2636) about how the Greeks managed to figure all this out.

Since the rate of repetition is low and since his rephrasings are not caused by lack of K clarity on what is being asked, then I give him a "yes" on 97. If your pause marks accurately reflect the flow of interaction, NS, then K answers follow quickly on T questions (98), so there's little or no time to fill (99). But the questions are not particularly challenging (100, 101). None arouses any K-K discussion. And with only three student questions, I can hardly credit him with (102) encouraging students to initiate questions. Therefore, 103 and 104 are not relevant.

f. *Competition-Cooperation*

105-109. This entire unit seems irrelevant as well. Nothing was said about competition or cooperation, and there was no individual privacy to guard (109) except Alice's. And I can't tell from a transcript whether he had appropriate grouping patterns (108).

g. *Practice*

110-116. Since practice is something one does in order to retain what one has already learned, there could not have been any practice here. I doubt whether even the Ks who replicated both constructions had thus learned them well enough to engage in practice. This, of course, omits those who didn't do full replications. But the homework assignment was for all to do, so at least some Ks were going to practice what they had yet to learn. So he did very badly on this unit, NS.

h. *Pacing*

117-124. I can't say anything positive on this unit. The transcript makes it clear that he moved at *his* pace, with only three K questions. I can't tell how many Ks had produced, successfully, his perpendicular construction, thus giving him a basis for going on to Greek multiplication. Yet he went on. Then he moved through that construction, though with some realization that not all students were keeping pace with him.

> Actually, NS, we ought to go back to the *Structure* unit at this point. If the "whole" consists of the complete Greek multiplication-construction, with proofs for the right angle at the perpendicular and for the equality in areas between rectangles ABCE and that 1X6 figure he constructed, then I find the *Pacing* and *Structure* both out of synchronization.
>
> If the state exam required student mastery of the perpendicular and the right-angle proof, then that could have been a "whole" all by itself, to be traced through, replicated, and practiced. In fact, they could have gone so far as to construct a 2X3 rectangle, with only a ruler and compass, building a new perpendicular at each corner of the rectangle. But that's not what happened. So the "whole" must have been the Greek construction, minus the proof of the areas. Then why have Ks replicate the perpendicular construction, which took time away from doing it all, including the proofs?
>
> I answer my own questions, NS, by saying that he never really defined the precise Rs he wanted the Ks to make in the time available, or else both *Structure* and *Pacing* would have been to his credit. Perhaps I'm doing him an injustice. Your tape is less than 31 minutes long. Surely the actual class time was closer to 40 or more minutes.

You've made a number of very incisive observations, ZA, the best one being the interdependent nature of at least some units of the EG. You're also beginning to grab off whole units rather than addressing yourself to single questions. That's progress.

You've hit on a key element in the lesson, the lack of a clear decision on the Rs. Being on camera didn't help, and we may even have delayed him by not being ready to record when he was ready to begin. I don't remember. This one decision affected the units you mention, plus *Practice, Questioning, Interaction Pattern,* and others.

i. *Accuracy-Speed*

125-126. So we can round the sub-head off, NS, by noting that he probably deserves "no" to both unit questions. Which leaves us with many items for that agenda.

It does, ZA, it does.

F. Evaluation

a. *Feedback-Reinforcement*

127-144. Aside from the likely irrelevance of questions 128, 133, 138, and 142, and his two comments on being good ancient Greeks and having a good one, I see no signs of F-R in this lesson. Do you, NS?

In answer to question 7 (*Responses* unit) we agreed that he translated his goals into terminal behavior. The Ks would end up doing multiplication the Greek way, with only the tools allowed on the state exam. You now seem to be saying that either we must draw back on that assessment or not credit him with consonant F-R behavior. Surely there's an unresolved issue here, an agenda issue.

b. *Success-Failure*

145-149. I agree, and also see why he must get a "no" on 145, leaving the remaining unit questions up in the air. If the Rs are not precise, then how can one respond to questions 146-149?

c. *Retention-Forgetting*

150-156. The last three questions are not relevant: they were going to continue with the material next time. Since I'm now sure that he didn't define precisely what the Rs would be for this lesson, there was no provision for overlearning (152) and no check on K schemata for retention (153). He focused on the material to be recalled (151) by that remark re the state exam, which in retrospect is not clear. Are the students responsible only for the construction of the perpendicular? For its proof? Possibly for something about Greek multiplication? And what would he expect in the next quiz or test?—Finally, as to number 150, I've already said there was continuity in the content, but he didn't specifically tie the new response pattern to material already mastered.

d. *Transfer*

157-158. There was some transfer between the perpendicular construction and Greek multiplication, but I'm not enthusiastic about what he did with it. The last question doesn't apply.

So let's see where we are now, ZA. Applying the PAT to a lesson led, as did the application of the EG, to the exploration of some new issues. Taking them in the order in which they occurred, we discussed:

- what anticipating the impacts of Ss means;
- how one relates present Rs to past learning;
- how TV equipment can be used in the classroom;
- how and whether teachers can determine the degree of K motivation;
- the distinction between S, R, and motivation;
- extrinsic vs. intrinsic motivation;
- the place of such teacher qualities as wit, vitality, humaneness, etc., in the instructional process;
- "doing" by teacher vs. "doing" by students;
- a teacher's instructional "style";
- what being meaningful-to-students really implies;
- time as a factor in the learning process;
- the interdependence of units in the PAT; and, generally,
- the relative merits of direct observation, recorded material, and verbatim transcripts.

I've abstracted these items from our discourse, ZA, to indicate that a professional interaction based on the PAT can lead to a professional discussion of truly professional issues. I'm being deliberately redundant in the use of one word to emphasize how the PAT gets us away from the too-typical POC in which the supervisor uses the time to list his commendations and to offer his recommendations, his suggestions for improvement. This idea will take on new meaning for you when we get to the supervisory cycle.

At this point, ZA, I'm caught in a dilemma. We've analyzed one high school science lesson using the EG and one junior high school math lesson using the PAT. Logic dictates that the next lesson should be in language arts or social studies, but at the elementary level. I hope you will go along with me in following only half of that dictum. As you can see from the Table of Contents, I'm going to build most of the exposition of the supervisory cycle around a series of POC's with just one elementary teacher. This will take care of examples in elementary education, as well as demonstrate what happens in successive applications of the supervisory cycle with the same teacher. So I'd like to apply the PAT to a language arts lesson, but I will be using a high school teacher again because his lesson will lead us to some issues we have yet to face.

X.

High School Language Arts Lesson

This lesson again comes from an urban high school class, an elective course in the Bible as literature.

There were some 22 students in the class, of whom 13 are identified by name in the interaction, with Douglas and Frances as the most frequent contributors, but with Douglas as the most significant speaker, especially in the latter portion of the lesson. The students who did not speak were attentive listeners. A number of those who spoke were not native speakers of English. The grammatical errors in a number of K contributions were recorded exactly as they were said.

The class sat in conventional rows, though the furniture was movable. The teacher was on his feet throughout the entire lesson, nearly always up front with the blackboard at his back. All students remained seated once they entered the room. The physical conditions seemed to have no visible impact on the discussion, but the teacher was clearly apprehensive (at the beginning) about being recorded and may well have continued to be so for the whole time.

As you will gather from the transcript, ZA, there was no board word. The entire interaction is in the verbal transcript; no written work, no fossils, no constructions, nothing but talk. So you shouldn't feel that direct observation would have been more advantageous. All that's really missing is how many hands went up each time he sought K contributions; no more than two or three, ZA, as I recall. With 13 students making contributions, he had substantial vocal participation.

The teacher saw the tape replay immediately after the lesson was over and said something to the effect that he was not pleased with the lesson. Since I was then making recordings for reasons other than their analysis in this discourse, I did not ask him for any elaboration.

Now you know almost as much as I know, except that I saw the lesson in person and have seen a number of replays of the tape, in addition to making the verbatim transcript. So here's that transcript. Please read it carefully, maybe even more than once, to get the full flavor of what happened.

Transcript

High School Language Arts Lesson

0000 T Pass in your homework.
K What homework? (Laughter; three or four Ks echo the question.)
T When you have passed in your homework, close your books and have only your Bible on the desks. (Still some laughter and general noise. Some Ks josh T for seeming to be apprehensive about being recorded.)
0057 T Alright, let me have your homework quickly, clear your desks, have only your Bible on the desk. (General noise.)
0115 T Now, the other day we were talking about faith. We were saying that I think one had the impression that many of you don't have faith in many things which people do have faith in. You gave me the impression, many of you, that you don't have faith in your parents, you don't have faith in the schools, you don't have faith in your teachers or our institutions, and when I ask some of you what you do have faith in—who can remember some of the answers that we received for that question: what do you have faith in? Laura.
0203 K A lot of people said they had faith in themselves.
T Alright, faith in themselves. What was another thing that you had faith in? Harry.
K I have faith in the youth of our day; youth.
T Alright, faith in yourself as a young person and faith in youth in general. Good. Mariano.
K (He seems to have said:) Faith in religion.
0237 T Good, that was another one. Some people. Felipe, can you tell us what you have faith in? You answered that question with a very good answer.
K Oh. I have faith in my mother; just a little bit, not too much. I have faith mostly in everything, but not too much.

T Alright. I think the other day you said you have a little faith in a number of things including your mother, yourself, perhaps God, perhaps religion, but perhaps you are holding back on your judgment for a while until you find out some more things.

0323 T Well, I want to go on with this matter and I remembered an expression from the Bible: Man cannot live by bread alone. (Pause.) Who can tell us what that expression might mean? Douglas?

K I think it means that (T: Take your hand away from your face.) I think it means that people need something to see them through because man himself is not strong enough and doesn't have the will to do things and to work, and he can't withstand, he can't survive without something to lean on, some religion or something.

0408 T Alright, good. What does bread mean in that expression: Man cannot live by bread alone? What does the word bread mean in that expression? Harry.

K By his own working, his own ways.

T Possibly. What else? Laura.

0425 K Just by having his physical needs taken care of. I think it represents his physical needs.

T Well, what might those physical needs be? Specifically?

K (Laura) Food and air and shelter and clothing and protection from nature.

T Good. Donald.

K The rest of the line says: For what proceedeth out of the mouth of God. Which means that, uh, which means that you need a guiding, that things around us, we need that, but we also need a guiding; and what proceedeth out of the mouth of God sort of is leading us to a better life.

0500 T Donald, you're so far ahead of us all. I was going to hold back on the last part and you went and ruined it. (Donald laughs with some embarrassment.) (p) Alright, I would like us for a moment to turn to page 427 in your Bible, to the Book of Ecclesiastes, and we're going to read a short passage here, page 427. The title is: Better To Eat and To Drink and To Be Merry. Assuming that bread means food, clothing, shelter, and all the physical needs that Laura says that you need, let us read this short passage and then ask ourselves what this writer would think of the expression, Man can not live by bread alone. Now, I'd like someone to volunteer to read the first two paragraphs. Alright, Harold.

K (Harold) From the top?

K (Not Harold) Right here.

T Better To Eat, Drink and Be Merry.

0600 K Then I recommended mirth, because a man hath no better thing under the sun than to eat, and to drink, and to be merry: for that shall abide with him of his labor the days of his life, which God giveth him under the sun. All things come alike to all: there is one event to the righteous, and to the wicked; to the good and to the clean, and to the unclean; to him that sacrificeth, and to him that sacrificeth not: as is the good, so is the sinner; and he that sweareth, as he that feareth an oath. This is an evil among all things that are done under the sun, that there is one event unto all: yea, also the heart of the sons of men is full of evil, and madness is in their heart while they live, and after that they go to the dead.

0656 T Alright, next, the next passage, I'd like a girl to read. Laura.

K For to him that is joined to all the living there is hope: for a living dog is better than a dead lion. For the living know that they shall die: but the dead know not anything, neither have they any more a reward; for the memory of them is forgotten. Go thy way, eat thy bread with joy, and drink thy wine with a merry heart; for God now accepteth thy works. Let thy garments be always white; and let thy head lack no ointment. Live joyfully with the wife whom thou lovest all the days of the life of thy vanity, which He hath given thee under the sun, all the days of thy vanity: for that is thy portion in this life, and in thy labor which thou takest under the sun. Whatsoever thy hand findeth to do, do it with thy might; for there is no work, nor device, nor knowledge, nor wisdom, in the grave, whither thou goest.

0803 T Frances, please read the last paragraph.

K I returned, and saw under the sun, that the race is not to the swift, nor the battle to the strong, neither yet bread to the wise, nor yet riches to men of understanding, nor yet favor to men of skill; but time and chance happeneth to them all. For a man also knoweth not his time: as the fishes that are taken in an evil net, and as the birds that are caught in the snare; so are the sons of men snared in an evil time, when it falleth suddenly upon them.

0837 T Now what do you think this writer would say about the expression: Man cannot live by bread alone? (p) When he says, A man hath no better thing under the sun than to eat and to drink and to be merry, what does he think of that expression, Frances?

K I don't think he thinks it's true. He doesn't believe in that. He believes that there's all that a man can do is eat and take care of hisself and be happy. I guess, he doesn't believe in it.

0914 T Alright. I would think so. He also says that the race is not to the swift and the battle is not to the strong. What does that tell us about his philosophy with regard to having faith and to not having faith? Frances.

K Maybe the weak shall inherit the earth.

T Possibly. But I don't think he says that either. In fact, I think he says sometime that the strong might inherit the earth.

0941 K It says not to the swift, not to the strong.

T Well, ordinarily we think that the fastest runner wins the race (K: Yeah.) and the strongest person wins the battle. Now what does this man say? (p) Where do you know of a case where the fastest runner did not win the battle, the fastest racer did not win the race, and the strongest person did not win the battle? Frances.

K The turtle and the hare in the fables.

T Alright, animals in a fable. Yes? Paul.

1019 K David and Goliath.

T Good. Another example? And don't we do, here in our times, don't we do bad things to some racers to see that they can't run as fast as they thought they could run? We do terrible things to horses in horse races. But this man would agree that all of life is not honest, all of life is not sincere, that the best is to eat, drink, and have a good time. Then we're safe.

1053 T Notice, too, that he speaks of . . . how does he compare men to fish and to birds? Look in the last paragraph, in the last few lines. (p) What kind of fish does he compare men to? And what kind of birds does he compare men to? Donald.

K Fish and birds that are trapped, that are caught.

1123 T And presumably that's his comment upon you and me and man. We are trapped animals. Our fastest runners don't always win the races. Our strongest don't always win the battles. Better to eat, drink, and to be merry. OK, and I would think there's a lot of evidence around for that kind of philosophy. And from some of the things I've been hearing in this room since the 2nd of February, I tend to think that some of you would agree with that philosophy. The fastest racer doesn't always win, the strongest doesn't always win.

1206 T Now I think it would be appropriate for us to read a selection by an American in which some of this we've been talking about is considered. (p) Please take this selection; read it through silently and then we'll talk about it. (Distributes sheets.)

1240 T Can someone tell us what a moor is? The title mentions I never saw a moor. (His voice is masked by Ks rustling the sheets. He seems to be saying that they might have read about a moor elsewhere.) Douglas?

K A moor is a people that live in North Africa.

T That is one meaning for the word moor. I think if you read this first stanza you will decide that that is not the meaning for the word moor. Frances.

1314 K I'm not exactly sure, but it's on the water, I think, not a docking, maybe, or a . . .

T Mooring is something you do to a boat. Yes. You tie it up. But I think this is a different meaning. By the way, quickly read this silently, then I'll ask someone to read it aloud. (P)

1342 T Alright, I would like someone to read. Donald, will you read this?

K I never saw a moor
I never saw the sea
Yet know I how the heather looks
And what a wave must be.
I never spoke with God
Nor visited in heaven
Yet certain am I of the spot
As if the charts were given.

1415 T Alright, now who can tell us what a moor is? (p) No one? Yes, Frances?

K A place.

T Yes, it's a place. What kind of place?

K It's on the water, usually, I think; I'm not exactly sure.

T Well, it's wet. It's not necessarily on the water, but it's wet.

K It's like mossy and grassy and I don't know.

T Swampy. Someone else? A moor? Harold.

K (Inaudible)

1447 T This moor is an almost uninhabitable place in England, where there are no trees, the land is very swampy and soupy, and most people don't live there. It's also unpleasant. It's too cold, it's too damp; they are lonely, foresaken places. The Bronte stories, some of them, take place out on the moors. Now, if this person, this individual, this writer, Emily Dickinson, if she never saw a moor, how does she know what heather is? And I'll just tell you that heather is a flower that grows on the moor. It has a purplish white blossom. If she never saw a moor, how does she know what heather looks like? If she never saw the sea, how does she know what waves must be; Paul.

1546 K By reading.

T One way. Good, yes. How else? Frances.

K She may have listened to stories that someone has told her and she believes in what the person has told her about them.

T Good, good. OK. She has read about them; she has been told about them. How else might she know about them? Mariano?

K She might feel, sort of?

T Might. But even without that, there is another simple way. She read; she was told. Harold?

K Dreaming of them; dreams.

1625 T She might've. Another more specific way, a purer way? Peter.

K She had faith.

T Well, we're getting to that. See you're way ahead of me here. Well, someone could have shown her a picture. She could have seen a picture and under the picture it said: this is a moor and this is heather on the moor. So, she never saw a real one and yet she knows. The same would be true for the sea. She may never have seen the sea, yet she knows what a wave must be. Alright, now look at the second stanza, and Harold, read the second stanza.

1711 K I never spoke with God
Nor visited in heaven
Yet certain am I of the spot
As if the charts were given.

T Alright, now, how does she feel that she knows about these other things if she did not see these either? She never spoke with God, she never visited in heaven, how does she know that there is such a place? Felipe.

K She have faith.

T Well, what do you mean by faith?

K She believe that is a heaven there.

T Believes. Harold.

K Well, maybe in her times of troubles she has a sense of security when she prays to God, when she feels that she's safe, like with praying Psalm 23.

1803 T Well, is this in the words here? Can you see that? Douglas.

K She's comparing it. She said first she never saw a moor, she never saw the sea, and then she says she never saw God either and never visited in heaven either, but she believes just like believes there was a moor and there's a sea.

T Well, what do you do when you have faith? What is it that you do when you have faith and perhaps what is it that you don't do when you don't have faith? I know that's a two-headed question. Harry's had his hand up. Let's see what . . .

K When you have faith you believe in what you don't see.

T Ah.

K So she has faith. She believes in it, but she hasn't seen it. She have heard of it. In the writings of the Bible, some of those people have spoke of seeing Jesus and seen heaven and going to heaven and having returned.

T Do you believe in things that you don't see?

K I believe, I believe in Christ. I go to church. (Class laughs.)

1903 T I mean, in terms of more everyday things. What, what are some things you might believe in although you did not see them? Because apparently that's one of the requirements of having a faith in something so that you believe where you don't see.

K Right.

T Now in the room the other day you all said: Well, I believe in myself. I believe in myself. So presumably you look at yourself in the mirror in the morning, getting ready for school in your slip, and you see something and you believe in it. And that's, well of course, that's the opposite, because that's believing when you're seeing. I'm trying to get at the other one. Now this Harold first, then the other Harold.

K I'd like to say, like last year the World Series, the New York Mets. Now people said the Mets were out, you know, were outstanding, that the Orioles was out over the Mets in pitching, hitting, and everything. So people have faith, they have faith in the Mets, that the Mets would come through. That's the way the guys in baseball see it in the statistics.

2008 T Good. Did that faith have anything to do with the Mets winning?

K I guess so. People came out to see 'em, so I guess that brought 'em all . . .

T What did that do?

K . . . that gave 'em faith, right?

T Gave, gave them what?

K Strength.

T OK, alright, good. Douglas.

K It gave them confidence, like because, you know, if you have people supporting you. That's what makes a team, what makes people go . . .

T Good.

K . . . like, like somebody is pushing you.

2032 T Good. Then there's a perfect example of where certainly nobody saw the Mets with the pennant or with the World Series. It just did that. Some of us hardly believe it now. But no one saw it. In fact, no one saw the future of the Mets, yet they believed even though they didn't see it. Harry, you had a point to make there, too. That sort of Mets example overwhelmed all of us. Alright, let's go on. Paul.

K When the men went to the moon, when they were coming back, they had faith.

T OK, and how did that . . . well, what faith did they have?

K Uh, God.

T Think so? K: I guess. T: Yes, Frances?

K They had faith in the men that sent them up, that, you know, that since they had sent them up, they ought to be able to bring them back.

2125 T Alright, but to be fickle, let's say, perhaps, perhaps they had a little faith all around, like Felipe here . . .

K Well, like, you know, they . . .

T A little bit.

K . . . like with their families, with the people that sent them up, a little bit with God; they just combined everything together to get 'em home.

T Would you think faith is kind of important to human beings, that got the Mets the World Series perhaps, that got the men back from the moon? When you speak of God and the matter of faith here, I am reminded that the minute those astronauts stepped on the deck of the carrier, someone said a prayer, and they, and they bowed their heads. That's quite unusual. I don't recall that happening in one of the other landings. (K says something.) That's right. They would salute the flag and sing the National Anthem. But this time they said a prayer. So, someone had some strong feelings about this matter. So here we are, good, with the matter of faith. Harry.

2226 K Well, when they said that prayer, they must of thought of something that was gonna happen if they didn't say a prayer before in the other ones.

T I don't understand.

K They didn't say a prayer when . . .

T When the other astronauts landed?

K Well, they said a prayer now because they thought something might happen.

2245 T Ah, very good, that's my question: Why did they say a prayer this time when the astronauts landed and not the last time? And not all the other times that the astronauts came back they didn't say one. Paul.

K Because, OK, because they were in trouble, and these two man, they weren't different man from the other two man. (T: Ah.) Maybe the other two man didn't believe in God, maybe these two man did.

2310 T Well, somebody else? Douglas.

K Well, I feel that, well, before they were depending on themselves. People have thing as when they believe in God, like, subconsciously, but when trouble comes, you know, but then this time they had some troubles, so they had to depend on God and themselves also.

T You ever had any trouble? Serious trouble, Douglas?

K No.

T But the other day you told us the only faith you had was in yourself.

K Yeah, but that's the way people are, you know.

2345 T Then I take it you haven't had enough trouble to get some faith in something other than just yourself. I'm very interested in hearing that comment from you because of what you said the other day. Frances.

K Just like you gave us that example of the lady in the elevator. Uh, when she was in trouble she started praying, you know, using a psalm. It's probably the same thing with them. As long as things go well, they don't need to pray. (T: Well . . .) Since there was also that superstition about the number 13 voyage, people are kind of leery about that, and . . .

2417 T OK, that's interesting. There was superstition there, there was fear. Paul landed on that very hard. There was fear on earth that all was over. Now, I would like everyone to turn to page 474 where we find the 23rd Psalm. Now, we want to read it and see what this class, (Ks begin to turn pages), see what this writing says to us about the matter of faith. Now I think you will probably find it says other things. But the part that interests me, when I think about you and reading this piece of writing is that if you don't believe certain things, then how is this psalm to have an effect upon you, and I am convinced that it does have an effect upon you. I am convinced that it had an effect upon the lady in the elevator, this lady in the stranded and stalled elevator between floors for two days. Well anyway, let's read it first to refresh our memory and then we'll talk about it. Now, I'd like to read this one.

2528 T The Lord is my shepherd; I shall not want. He maketh me to lie down in green pastures: He leadeth me beside the still waters. He restoreth my soul; He leadeth me in the paths of righteousness for His name's sake. Yea, though I walk through the valley of the shadow of death, I will fear no evil: for Thou art with me; Thy rod and Thy staff they comfort me. Thou preparest a table before me in the presence of mine enemies: Thou annointest my head with oil; my cup runneth over. Surely goodness and mercy shall follow me all the days of my life; and I will dwell in the house of the Lord forever. (p)

2638 T Now, we all know this selection and I have the impression that a lot of people respond very well to this selection, and sometimes they believe some of the things that are in here and sometimes they go along with this psalm whether they believe everything in it or not. First of all, I would like to know what a shepherd is. Douglas?

K That's the guy that in the Bible times used to take care of the sheep. He used to oversee the sheep.

T Yes. What kind of people are shepherds, usually? How are they pictured as a group of people?

K Well, say like poor people, maybe.

2726 T Poor, good, yes. Donald?

K They ranged all ages and they were very old and very young. They were strong; they were very strong. They had very little clothes. Well, you know, very ragged clothes. Impoverished.

2740 T Good. What else do you know about them? Frances.

K They were probably very, you know, a group of very responsible people or else they probably couldn't take care of the sheep very well.

T Good. What else, Paul?

K They carried long canes.

T Good. Why did they carry those?

K To keep the sheep, to keep the sheep, to herd them.

T With sticks, long canes, with a bend at the top, yes? Harry.

K They were the few that, they were always bothered by the marshalls, the pharoahs, the kings, they were always being taxed, you know.

2814 T OK. What kind of temperaments do they have? Now that's a hard word perhaps, but what temperament do you find generally in shepherds, Alfred?

K They were kind and patient.

T Good, why would they be that way?

K Well, sometimes the sheeps would get lost and they have to search for them.

T Why would that make them kind and patient? Why not unkind because of the bother of hunting for a lost sheep?

K They were very religious and everybody should . . .

T How do you know they were very religious?

K They were very forgiving, they forgave a lot of faults.

2855 T Wait a minute. We're talking about a man who works out in the country looking after the animals, and Alfred said they are kind and patient. How do you know?

K They really cared for the sheep they were taking care of.

T Well, what were they herding sheep for anyway? I don't want to get off on the matter of sheepherding, but I think there is something we must talk about. Douglas.

K That was their survival, their income.

T It's a business, and there is meat, there is wool. And what kind of an animal is a sheep? Is he a ferocious, charging-around, eating-up people? Paul, what kind of a person, what kind of an animal is a sheep?

K It's a real kind animal, you know, unhostile, you know. Can't do nothing. Have no way of protecting himself.

2950 T Very calm animal, at the mercy of just about every other animal, and that's one reason you need this shepherd is to protect them from bad, terrible things. Now, who are the sheep in this psalm?

K (softly) We are. (T seems not to hear.)

T Someone who hasn't answered. Now I have a few hands. Lavinia, I see a smile on your face. Who are the sheep in this psalm?

K Uh, I think the one who take care of the sheep . . . (rest inaudible)

T No, who are the sheep?

K The hungry?

K Man himself.

3027 T Right. You and me. Now, why is it good if you are going to talk about people, why is it a good idea to have a shepherd? Why is it a good idea to talk about a shepherd and sheep when you're talking about people and their troubles? (p) Alfred.

K A shepherd is always taking care of the sheep. (T: Right.) So, in this case, God is going to have the people.

T Alright, good. Yes, Douglas?

K A shepherd is this man, provides and take care and oversees the sheep, and so they use it, they say that, like, God takes care of man, and man depend, 'cause the sheep depend on the shepherd, so like in the same way, man depends on God.

3122 T OK, that's what this writer says. Whoever wrote this psalm, that is what he says. Is it an accurate comparison to compare you and me with sheep? (K: Yeah.) Harold.

K God has power over man. So there are good sheep and there are bad sheep. Some sheep'll run away, so God will have to come over and . . .

T I don't think you are answering my question. Is it good, is it a true comparison, a good comparison, an accurate one, to compare you and me and all people to sheep? Frances.

K No, I don't think so. (T: Why not?) Because sheep are docile and quiet, you know; they don't go around killing. Humans, you know, they have wars all the time, they're constantly killing men, women and babies, you know. Sheep aren't like that, you know. It really doesn't seem fair to them.

3219 T Well, is there any aspect of being human which is like being a defenseless sheep who needs someone to help you look after yourself? To help us all look after each other? Is there any aspect of being human which makes us like sheep? Yes?

K Our helplessness.

T Good. How are we helpless?

K Because, like, man is helpless, like sheep. He depends, he must depend on some other form, or higher, something higher than himself, whether it would be God or something else. Money or anything.

3303 T Alright. I'm glad to hear you say this (K, Douglas, laughs) because you keep saying things which are quite different from what you said the other day. Alright. I think the writer here assumes that mankind is defenseless in ways. And he needs help. And he needs some kind of help that you can understand. When you tell the story in terms of His help being like a shepherd and men being sheep helps. Now, what, what does this shepherd do for the sheep, keeping in mind what you need done for you? Look at some of the things at the beginning of the psalm. Donald, will you read the first two sentences for us, and I want you to watch for the things which man, which you need and I need, that apparently was provided in the psalm. Donald.

K (Donald) reads from "The lord is . . . to . . . his name's sake."

3418 T Alright, that's fine, thank you. That makes two sentences. Now, "I shall not want." What do you think that means? (p) Fred?

K This case is like wanting food, really.

3437 T Does it say food? (K: No.) It says, "I shall not want." Paul?

K He means that you don't have to ax for nothing because the Lord know what you need and He supplies every need.

T You will have no want because you've got everything you need. Alright, good. "He maketh me to lie down in green pastures." Now, what is there, that is, what do you need there, or what does that have to do with you or your life, even to this day? Harry.

K I guess that's because food is like farms and things.

T What in there would have to do with farms?

K Well, green pastures.

T Alright, green pastures, yes. Laura.

K Sleep and rest.

3530 T Good. Isn't that an important thing? Insomnia is a terrible thing. And to be able to lie down (p), what does it say? "He maketh me to lie down." OK, rest, very important. Douglas, what else?

K I think it means to have peace of mind and tranquility, because, like, you know, when you think of green pastures, you think of peace and tranquility.

T Why do you think of that when you think of green pastures? Good. Why do you think of the things you just mentioned, peace and tranquility?

3604 K Because that's what you have when you're lying down in green pastures, you know. (Laughter) Your mind is at ease; you're not worrying; you think of peace because, like, you have your own peace of mind and you don't think of, you don't think of harsh things when you imagine green pastures, like wars and things.

T Good. Why green? What does that signify?

K Because it's life.

T Ah, why life? Why is green, life?

K Because plants and people depend on plants.

3636 T Alright, very nice. Now, "He leadeth me beside the still waters." (p) Now, aren't all of these good things which people need? They need rest, they need relaxation, they need food, they need the hope that green gives. "He leadeth me beside the still waters." What does that give *you*? (P) Well, we read Noah and his ark the other day, read about Noah and his ark. What did we say about water there? Laura.

K It cleanses you.

3725 T Alright. What about still waters? How do still waters affect you, Douglas?

K Still waters might have the same effect as green pastures. Like it, you know, it soothes you and it, you don't think of harsh things. You walk by the water and it's still and your mind is at ease.

3745 T Alright, now. (p) I wanted to get farther through this psalm than we had gotten before the end of the period. I don't know; I never met anyone who didn't like the 23rd Psalm. I suppose there are people around who don't like it, because somehow or other, if anything has come through, if any piece of writing has come through to human beings to give them some satisfaction, to the man on the way to the electric chair, and to the lady in the elevator, and all of these things, somehow or other it feels, you feel better having read this, having memorized it, having recited it; but what do you do if you are an anti-religious person, if you feel as you have told me in this class numerous times, that you don't know about God and how God could stand by and allow the Vietnam War to go on and all those injustices, and how could He stand by and let slavery go on, and all the injustices to minority groups and all these things, how can you have faith in the elements of this writing, this short selection here, if you cannot go along with the first line, perhaps? Is it possible that you can have faith? (p) Well, what else do you have here in this selection which helps you respond to this writing? (p) Frances.

3934 K That even walking, you know, in the shadow of death, he's not going to be afraid, even though he knows that he might die, he wouldn't be afraid.

T What good do those words do to a person who doesn't believe he's that much of a sheep and he doesn't believe there is a Lord, or that there is a shepherd or anything else? Does that help him at a moment of death, the line that you just read about you walk (bell rings) through the valley of death? Alright, I want to continue with this tomorrow and I wish we had come a little closer to finishing it than we did. (4012)

Now, instead of analyzing the lesson unit by unit, let's take a step in the direction of the supervisory cycle.

When I observe an instructional session I use the Primitive Assessment Tool (PAT) to identify what I regard as the single or the two weightiest obstacles to greater success than I deem the teacher to have had. How I communicate this to the teacher I'm leaving to my later exposition of the supervisory cycle. So what I'd like you to do is to identify the obstacle or obstacles you see. I'm not going to ask you to state it or them, because I have not used this tape often enough to have accumulated a stock of student reactions. Instead I'd like you to compare your views with mine.

This was obviously one of a number of lessons in a continuum. The teacher refers to prior K statements on the matter of faith and ends by saying that he hoped to finish the discussion in the next lesson.

It was also a whole-class lesson, with no attempt at individualization or at determining individual readiness for the issue under consideration. (He might well have determined this prior learning.) I can't tell what the motivation was; it was also very likely set up in the preceding lesson or lessons. But the substantial vocal participation by more than half the class is some indication of student motivation. That that motivation is very likely intrinsic is indicated by the teacher's reference to a number of views expressed by students on where their faith is grounded.

Though the teacher talks more than the students, the focus is on an issue, faith, not on the teacher nor even on *his* views.

The materials are there and available as needed. You may wish to take exception to all the oral reading. You might even want to question his own reading of the psalm, had you heard him, because it was not a particularly effective rendition. You may also wonder why he let so many grammatical errors go by without a single attempt at correction, especially in an English class.

> Since you have yet to identify your obstacles, NS, I gather that neither the oral reading nor the grammar concerns you. Shouldn't an observer pick up at least on the grammar, let alone the oral reading of selections of which each K, presumably, had a copy?

In any given instructional session, ZA, a teacher should have defined, in advance, the new responses the students are to take on as a result of reacting to the stimuli embedded in the stimulus situation. Responses tangential to those sought are to be observed and noted by the teacher, but need not be dealt with immediately.

Let's go back to my earlier analogy to a football game. The object in the game is to score points and to win. But if your team's defense or offense is malfunctioning, you can't stop the game and run a practice session. You note what's not working as you hoped it would and focus on it in practice sessions between games.

I apply the same principle in the classroom. Had the teacher stopped to correct grammatical errors, he would have disturbed the momentum of the discussion as well as created an inhibitory stress for students who might then be reticent about speaking for fear of making more errors. In other words, only those Rs are given attention which directly impinge on the terminal behavior sought by the teacher. In this lesson, a digression of the kind you suggest, ZA, would not have moved the discussion along. In fact, he makes only one non-substantive digression (at a little past 0323) when he tells Douglas to take his hand away from his face. The words Douglas says just prior to the teacher's exhortation are somewhat muffled on the tape.

But how do you know that the teacher *perceived* the grammatical errors and stored them for later retrieval, NS?

I don't know, ZA. If I want to know, I'll have to ask him.

Your "if" suggests that you aren't especially concerned. Am I reading you correctly, NS?

You are, ZA, you are. If I were teaching a class to deal with the Bible as literature, I would be concerned with the idea-content of student contributions. If student vocabulary and usage stood in the way of their effective conceptualization and expression of the idea-content, I would clarify either one or both in order to promote conceptualization and expression. The teacher did that when it came to moor, shepherd, and sheep, but he let the grammatical errors go by because they did not handicap student contributions.

OK, I see your position. But how about the oral reading, especially the teacher's rendition of the psalm?

I can see a justification for oral reading in the principles dealing with the use of more than one sensory modality. Seeing *and* hearing the selections is especially beneficial for students who are not native speakers of English or whose abilities as careful readers are not quite up to snuff. And he obviously had both kinds in his class (by my observation, not by the verbal transcript). But I do think that teachers who mean to read aloud to their students should serve as exemplary models. This particular rendition was not such a model and is, therefore, an item for our agenda.

> Then I want to guess the obstacle you've identified. PAT question 7 asks: Did the teacher translate goals into terminal behavior? You're going to say that he did *not.*

That's very close to the mark, ZA. But let's develop a full context before dealing with your guess.

After the homework is passed in (and I don't know what the assignment was, nor what bearing it had on our lesson), the teacher (at 0115) recalls that they had been talking about faith and that the students reported having no faith in parents, schools, teachers, and "our institutions," but some faith in themselves individually and in youth generally. Mariano seems to have faith in religion; Felipe has a bit of faith in a number of things, but no great faith in any one thing. The teacher sums up their prior statements by saying (at about 0300) that "perhaps you are holding back on your judgment for a while until you find out some more things."

At 0323 he introduces "Man cannot live by bread alone" and begins to elicit student interpretation. The interchange with Donald (at about 0500) is most fascinating. Donald seems to have made a quantum leap to the teacher's unstated objective, earning the remark: "Donald, you're so far ahead of us all. I was going to hold back on the last part and you went and ruined it." Now what was the last part and what had Donald ruined?

Donald said (in part): ". . . we also need a guiding, and what proceedeth out of the mouth of God sort of is leading us to a better life." This is the tail end of his statement. If I interpret the teacher's rejoinder accurately, he implies, as an objective, that the result of their subsequent analysis of the Ecclesiastes passage, the Dickinson poem, and Psalm 23 will be just what Donald says, that man needs to be guided by God, man can't go through life alone, without Donald's "guiding" from God.

Another clue to the teacher's objective comes at just past

1625. This time Peter says, of Emily Dickinson, "She had faith." The teacher says: "Well, we're getting to that. See, you're way ahead of me here." And, as he did after Donald's comment, he goes back to his conception of a line of progress, as though he had not been interrupted. However, when the whole Dickinson poem has been read aloud and when he gets a carbon copy of Peter's remark (at about 1740: Felipe says, "She have faith."), he says, "Well, what do you mean by faith?" And just a bit later, at about 1820, he says: "Well, what do you do when you have faith? What is it that you do when you have faith and perhaps what is it that you don't do when you don't have faith?" Then, realizing that, in his desire to emphasize a central thesis, he has put the issue awkwardly, he adds, "I know that's a two-headed question."

The double question elicits the notion that faith is believing in what one can't see. In attempting to elaborate on this (at about 1930) he gets tangled up in believeing in what one can see, so he says: "And that's, well, of course, that's the opposite, because that's believing when you're seeing. I'm trying to get at the other one." At this point one of the Harolds provides a perfect example: the Mets (the N.Y. baseball team) who most unexpectedly won the World Series some time before this lesson.

Paul next (at about 2100) comes up with another example: "When the men went to the moon, when they were coming back, they had faith." Which hits a peak (at about 2150) with teacher saying: "Would you think faith is kind of important to human beings . . . ?" And comes full circle (at just before 2345):

T   You ever had any trouble? Serious trouble, Douglas?
K   No.
T   But the other day you told us the only faith you had was in yourself.
K   But that's the way people are, you know.
2345 T   Then I take it you haven't had enough trouble to get some faith in something other than just yourself. I'm very interested in hearing that comment from you because of what you said the other day.

This gets him to the 23rd Psalm, to the lady in the elevator, and ultimately back to Douglas again (at about 3230):

T   Good. How are we helpless?
K   (Douglas) Because, like, man is helpless, like sheep. He depends, he must depend on some other form, or higher, something higher than himself, whether it would be God or something else. Money or anything.

3303 T Alright. I'm glad to hear you say this (K, Douglas, laughs) because you keep saying things which are different from what you said the other day.

The final clue, and I think the only personal one, comes at 3745. "I don't know; I never met anyone who didn't like the 23rd Psalm. . . you feel better having read this, having memorized it, having recited it;. . ." He then summarizes the students' reasons for not believing in God: God allows slavery, the Vietnam War, and other injustices to happen. Wistfully he asks: "Is it possible that you can have faith? (p)" He ends the session with a question: "Does that help him at the moment of death, the line that you just read about you walk (bell rings) through the valley of death?"

My interpretation goes like this: The teacher, who probably believes in the concept of faith and has religious faith of his own, was concerned by what he had elicited from students in the earlier lesson(s). He projected that he could lead them to see what faith is and to demonstrate that their present views are open to reconsideration, if not to alteration. The Ecclesiastes passage was apparently meant to show students that there was some Biblical support for the views they had been expressing in class: (at about 1200) "OK, and I would think there's a lot of evidence around for that kind of philosophy. And from some of the things I've been hearing in this room since the 2nd of February, I tend to think that some of you would agree with that philosophy." However, what little discussion of it there is, is largely just between Frances and the teacher, and not firmly focused on what seems to be the teacher's notion: the author of Ecclesiastes believes that man *can* "live by bread alone," that he has no more need of faith than the students had been indicating about their own beliefs. The above-quoted statement is the teacher's summary of the purpose of using the Ecclesiastes passage. I infer, from the limited K involvement in the brief discussion of it, that they have only a hazy idea of the purpose of using the passage.

The teacher makes a quick transition to the poem. Here he succeeds in eliciting a definition of faith, plus two striking examples and a bit of marvelous insight from Douglas to the effect that people "get religion" when their own resources aren't enough to get them through their troubles. The elaboration of the psalm again leads Douglas to the admission that man needs to rely on some force outside himself: ". . . whether it be God or something. Money or anything." But of four alternatives offered by Douglas (God, something else, money, anything), the teacher selects only God. Then we get an elicited exposition of the promises inherent in Psalm 23, an expression of wonder by the teacher that people (students?) are not as affected by the psalm's message as he is, the summary of student views on their lack of faith in God, and an inconclusive terminus to a discussion cut short by the bell.

Now, did he translate goals into terminal behavior, ZA? If we project, as one goal, the definition of faith, then he elicited some definitions plus enough examples to make a case for the accomplishment of this goal. We can also project that he wanted students to understand (that word again!) the meanings in the poem and the psalm. If I had to rank his unstated objectives (which he might well have communicated to the class at the earlier lessons), the meanings would rank third, the definition of faith second, and something else first. The clues I listed some time back convince me that his first objective was to lead the students to a faith they denied, a faith not just in themselves individually, in youth generally, or in other institutions minimally, but a faith ultimately in God despite the injustices which so impinge on the sensitivities of the students in his class. The major obstacle to success lies in his not having projected that clearly as a goal, as his main goal, and to have defined, in advance, the responses the students were to take on.

That's a rather long and detailed statement, NS, which I'm glad I could read at my pace rather than hear at yours. The issue, as I see it, is not whether your analysis is absolutely accurate. Since even you never discussed the lesson with the teacher, we're both of us left without proof. It's a permanent riddle.

You have convinced me of at least this point, among some others: that you don't build a case to an empty conclusion. Had you conducted a Post-Observation Conference (POC) with this man, and could you now even just summarize it for us, and did that POC confirm your analysis, then all the foregoing would be meaningful. That's not the case, however. So what meaning are we to draw from all this?

That's an excellent point, ZA.

I have found that the crux of any instructional situation lies in the teacher's *perception* of what he's trying to do, not in the specific behaviors he actually exhibits in the classroom. No, I'm not, in one sentence, completely negating the PAT, which focuses on those specific behaviors. The PAT should make it possible to pinpoint the central issues in a lesson. I think that our analyses of the science and math lessons plus your guess about this one are significant pieces of evidence on this score.

The point I've been trying to make in this long and detailed statement is that the supervisor must learn to use the PAT to locate the central issue or issues. I was less than enthusiastic about pursuing grammatical errors, oral reading by students, and a less-than-effective oral rendition by the teacher. I just barely mentioned such positive features as pupil participation, intrinsic motivation, attention by the students, etc. Because with all the positive features, even the teacher was not satisfied. Neither was I.

Were I to focus on grammatical corrections, oral reading, or any other negative feature that a detailed application of the PAT would reveal, I would not be opening up a new path of growth for the teacher unless I centered our POC on the teacher's ability to define in advance the terminal behavior.

When you guessed that my obstacle(s) would center on PAT question 7, I said you were close to the mark. That question comes from the first sub-head, Stimuli and Responses, where the center of the mark is. As I run down the 16 questions in the sub-head, we'll see why you were close to, but not fully on target.

(1) He had created a definitive stimulus situation, carried over from prior learning. The focus was on faith, no distractions, no irrelevancies. (2) There were no competing Ss, and (3) present Ss were related to past learning. (4) the S materials were ready for use, but, (5) he did not anticipate that, in going from "Man cannot live by bread alone" to Dickinson's faith, Ecclesiastes would be a confusing and meaningless detour. (In not anticipating the impact of this stimulus, he also scored badly on the units Scholarship, Structure, and Meaningfulness.) (6) There was no individualization of the Ss, (7) only a partial translation of goals into K behavior, (8) though the lesson was part of a continuum of learning. (9) Because he hadn't resolved the issue of what responses the Ks were

to make, he obviously could not have anticipated their consequences. (10) There was eliciting and parading and (11) extinguishing of erroneous Rs, and the teacher was aware (12) that different Ks had different views on faith.

But (13) though the S situation clearly centered on faith, (14) he didn't clarify what the Rs must be, (15) nor ascertain K knowledge of what Rs to make. (16) Nonetheless, the context was familiar.

I've spelled out this sub-head, to convince you that I don't by-pass the PAT and make intuitive leaps to definitive judgments. A complete spelling-out would have to include the three units I mentioned above, but I'm assuming you see the point by now. That point is: using mastery of the PAT, the supervisor aims to identify the major obstacle(s) to greater progress by the teacher. At the Post-Observation Conference (POC), teacher and supervisor can determine how effective a judgment the supervisor made.

I included this lesson for two reasons. One I've already stated: the interaction is entirely verbal. The second is this: I wanted to convince you that the application of the PAT is not a long-drawn-out process, once one has mastered its contents. Our elaboration of this lesson-analysis is a good deal shorter than that of the other two, and would occur much more quickly in real time were I making the analysis in my head instead of discoursing it with you on paper.

As a reader of the book, ZA, rather than as my partner in a discussion, I urge you to study and master the PAT. If you can manage to record some instructional sessions on tape, then practice on its application would be possible.

If you are a teacher, applying the PAT to tapes of your own work would be most beneficial. You could "buddy up" with another teacher for mutual analyses of each others' tapes.

If you are a supervisor and mean to use the PAT with your staff, then each member should have a copy for study and mastery. Initial application could be on tapes of effective teachers or of teachers who have had experience in live demonstrations for other professionals. Teachers who volunteer for such tapes should have full knowledge of the PAT. It would be unfair to analyze their work with a tool on which they have not based their teaching.

Needless to say, full application of my analysis strand should begin with the Empirical Grid (EG) and with the sources for principles of learning.

XI.

The RAD (Retelling-Agenda-Discussion) Supervisory Cycle: Junior High School Music Lesson

We have now reached the second strand in our discourse, ZA, where we'll be devoting ourselves to the last question I derived so long ago from the definition of supervision as the improvement of instruction: By means of what techniques does one oversee, direct, guide, etc., the teachers? Who uses these techniques? Why?

Having demonstrated, explained, and discussed the RAD (*Retelling-Agenda-Discussion*) supervisory cycle to and with a large number of students over a span of many semesters, I learned one thing in particular: the whole process gets across to students much more effectively when I demonstrate first and explain second. Maybe it's another example of the old saw: one picture is worth a thousand words. So here's the picture.

I'm going to show you one last videotape, ZA, but this one will contain both a lesson and a verbatim transcript of the POC. Then we can discuss what you saw. But first, another prelude, an especially appropriate one, because you're going to see a music lesson.

Back in 1959 a two-phase project was begun at Hunter College (of the City University of New York). Its purposes and outcomes are not germane to our discourse. What is relevant is that I was a member of the project team in the first phase, and that we were contrasting supervision of student teachers via three techniques:

1. Supervisors sat in the classrooms, observed, took notes, and conducted POC's on the basis of these data.
2. Supervisors sat in a TV control room, observed via the three monitors available, while the three remotely-controlled, movable (pan, tilt, zoom) cameras recorded the lesson on videotape. The POC's involved viewing the tapes with the

student teachers. There was *no* direct, on site observation by supervisors.

3. Supervisors sat in the classrooms, observed, took notes. BUT, the TV equipment was *also* on and a tape was made simultaneously. The POC had as data both the tape *and* the supervisor's notes.

I served as one of three student-teaching supervisors in this first phase, with an assignment of 24 ST's over a period of one dry-run and three experimental semesters. To each of the six elementary classrooms in the project we assigned three ST's supervised by one supervisor, but each ST was in a different one of the three experimental treatments. Thus all three supervisors had the experience of all three treatment forms: direct observation, TV observation, and the combination of both.

The first tape playback always had a sharp impact on each ST: That's really not me! My voice doesn't sound like that. It's artificial. The cameras have a skewing effect. Etc., etc. One or two ST's even had to be coaxed into being recorded again. Since five observations were required for each treatment form, the two forms involving TV gave each ST time to adjust to the process. And they did.

A minority went even further: by about the third tape, some of my ST's said to me something like, "Let me analyze it before you do." And though their efforts were not totally successful, they did well enough to set me thinking.

I went from this first phase into the second phase of the project, which called for us to produce 12 recordings, each of which was to exemplify some aspect of the teaching of language arts and reading. For reasons irrelevant to this digressive bit of history, it fell to my lot to make these recordings. To get a final 12, I made about 30. And here's the reason for all this history.

In making this latter set of recordings, we agreed that no tape would be considered for use before being seen and approved by the teacher in the lesson. This gave me a new experience, that of an informal POC with each of a large number of courageous, experimentally-minded, experienced teachers. The sum total of all these discussions also set me thinking.

When I went back thereafter to the usual direct supervision, it was like watching a TV program with no picture; just audio. To remedy that, I began to develop what I now call the RAD cycle. The teacher had to be able to retell the lesson in order to personally experience something akin to a TV playback. My doing the retelling for the teacher wouldn't press him into the recall of visual and auditory images of what had taken place. And I had to give the teacher a first crack at analysis, just as some of my ST's had taught me to do.

For this first sample of the RAD cycle, ZA, you'll see a tape play-back. Thereafter you'll experience how Retelling works. Please read both transcripts, with special attention to the POC. I'm going to ask you to state what process I followed in doing it.

This is a seventh grade "required music" lesson in an urban junior high school. The teacher begins by putting on the board a few measures of musical notes, each measure representing a different meter. Her opening references are to these measures.

TRANSCRIPT

Junior High School Music Lesson

0000	T	(writing on blackboard)
	T	What am I drawing, three what-do-we-call-them?
	K	Umm, staffs. (T-No.)
	K	Measures.
	T	Three measures. OK. In each measure I have a different number of beats. (p) OK. If each one of these measures represented an entire song, we would say that this song moved in what? (T points to the board.) Or moved how?
	K	Moved in measures.
0027	T	Well, they all move in measures. We would say that this song, if this represented a complete song, this right here? What would we say about that song? It moved in four (K - Four.), in four-time. Alright, OK? What would we say about this measure, um? (T points to another measure. There is a long pause during which there is some indistinct K talk.) Oh, you know what I mean. Ah, Connie.
	K	In three-time.
0057	T	In three-time. OK. (p) And this song? (K - In two.) In two. OK. I meant you to tell me in what time you think is the song that I'm going to clap. OK? Here we go.
0120	T	Listen. (Claps one stanza of "America.")

0149	K	Four-time. (T - Four-time? What do you think?) (Another student) Four and two. (T - Four and two?) Yes. (K demonstrates by clapping.)
	T	OK, just let me say that all the songs that I clap will have one time, one time.
	K	Three. (T - Three.) (Another K - Four.) (T - Four.)
0210	T	Class, would you count for me? 1-2-3-4, 1-2-3-4, (class begins counting) and keep doing it. Now I'm going to clap what I clapped before. See if it fits. Or see if it feels awkward. (Class counts in four while T claps "America.")
0235	T	Dan, how did they feel?
	K	Wrong.
	K	Not very good.
	K	Yes, wrong.
	T	Did if feel correct? No. Let's try 1-2-3, 1-2-go. (Class counts in three.) (T claps "America.")
0257	T	Does it fit? Does it fit? (Class - Yes.) (Some few voices seem to disagree.) It doesn't fit? OK, well let's try this. Count again and I'll play it. I'll add which element of music? (K - Which should we clap? Three?) Which element of music will I add? By playing. (K - Piano.) (K - Piano.)
0316	T	Well, the piano isn't an element of music. It's not an ingredient of music. (K - Melody.) Melody, is an ingredient of music. OK? 1-2-3, ready-and-and count. (Class counts in three while T plays the first phrase of "America.")
0340	T	Does it fit? (Some Ks - No.) No? (Some Ks - Yes.) Really? What do you think would fit? (Ks offer a number of simultaneous and conflicting suggestions.)
	T	OK, to the ear it's very hard to distinguish . . . No, I'm sorry; I thought you meant the difference between four and two.
	K	(*inaudible*)
0403	T	Well, I'm accenting. (Plays a few measures, accenting the first beat of each, as she had done when she last played it.) We don't sing it like that. OK. Here's one more. What? Yeh.
	K	Are we (*inaudible*) some place?
	T	Possibly. OK. Listen! Tell me how this song is moving. (Claps) C'mon. My hands are getting tired. (T had clapped a long passage without K response.) (Ks laughs.) Yeh.
	K	Four. (T - Four? What do you think, Matt?)
	K	Two. (T - I have two.)
	K	Three. (T - Three.)
	K	Five. (T - Five. Well, it has to be one of those.)
	K	Two. (T - Two.)
	K	Three.
	T	Three. How many think two? (Some Ks raise their hands.) How many three? (Some Ks raise their hands.) (NB: The

camera could not be swung around fast enough to tell how many Ks raised their hands each time.)

0512 T Let's try three. 1-2-3, 1-2-3. (Class counts. T plays "Jingle Bells.") Does it fit? (Class - No.)

0539 T Let's try, let's try five. 1-2-3-4-5. (Class counts and T plays.) Does it fit? (Class - No.) No. That's how you tell how the song is moving. Let's try two. 1-2. (Class counts and T plays.) OK? (K - Four.)

0616 T Four? Well, what's four, basically? Two groups of (Class-Two.) two. To the ear it's hard to tell, very difficult to tell, if you're listening. Usually, when you're taking a song at a fast tempo, you would use... or if you want the song to be fast, you would use two instead of four beats in every measure. OK? Because four moves a little bit slower than two.

0649 T Now, I would like you to repeat after me. Let me see how alert you are. I clap first, then the class repeats. Ready? Listen, then clap. And-(Claps a pattern.) (Class repeats, with one "clinker.") Not bad. OOPS!

0716 T Ready, and, listen, again. (Claps another pattern.) (Class repeats, but with one extra clap. Class laughs.) OK, not bad. Listen to this one. I'll have to get you once. Listen. (Claps.) (Class claps. Again a few clinkers. Class laughs.) Alright. OK.

0755 T How about this one? (Claps.) (Class claps. Again, one extra clap in the last measure. A few Ks say "Oh" in disappointment.) It's alright. OK. One more. That was very good, very good. How about? Oh, this will get you. (Claps.) (Class does it sloppily, then laughs uproariously.)

0855 T Is there any person (Late K comes in), is there any person . . . Take it easy, don't be overcome (Said to late K's reaction to TV cameras) . . . who can do it perfectly? (Calls on one K. There is some random clapping in the room.) We're not ready yet. (K's name). (Some Ks comment.) Go. (He claps.) Good! Good! (Some laughter.)

0935 T And one more. (Still some laughter.) That was perfect. OK? Listen: (Claps.) Go. (Class claps.) (Class is not clapping together now, though the pattern alone seems not to be the problem.) Ah, what's different about that last section? (An announcement comes in over the school's public address system and all stop to listen.)

1007 T What was different in it? Yes.

K The beat changed.

T The beat changed. (K - Or the rhythm.) The beat changed? The beat was 1-2-3-4, 1-2-3-4. That was the beat. The rhythm is what I was clapping. Remember? Yes!

K The beat as (*inaudible*) changed.

T How did change? Connie.

K The number of beats.

1030 T The number of beats. Can you tell me specifically how it changed?

K The first time was . . . Can I clap it? (T - Yes.) (K claps a bit.) I'm not sure. The first one the last notes were four and the second one were three.

K The first one was four and the second one was two.

K You did one clap at the last beat.

1055 T OK. That's basically what they're saying also. I thought I clapped three and then two, but I don't even remember. OK? Ah (p). OK, what song am I clapping? Listen to the rhythm of the song that I am clapping and tell me if you can guess the name. (P) Ah (p) (Claps.) Don't call out. (K - Oh!) Just let me clap a little more so the others can hear. (Claps more.) Match the rhythm to the words. (Speaks as she claps.) (Some Ks guess aloud or try to volunteer.) Charles. (He says the name of the song.)

1158 T Right. Good. (Repeats the name.) OK, and how about this one? (Claps.) (K - OOH!—as if to say, that's a hard one to guess.)

1233 T Got any ideas? Tom? (K - Too long.) Too long. Lloyd.

K I don't know, 'cause I don't think it's one of the songs we learned.

T I think it is. (Another K says a name.) No. (2nd K guess.) No. (3rd) No. You're beginning to convince me that you're right. (4th) No. (5th) No. (6th) No. (7th) No. Now you're guessing. Did we not sing a song about chain gang in this class? (Class - No.) (K - I told you!) (K - *inaudible*)

1321 T You're right. OK. Here's another one. Here's another one. This one is popular. (Claps.) Try to put the rhythm to the melody, and you'll get the bridge, the middle part. (Still clapping.) And you'll see why I'm looking at you (Meaning a particular K, who says a name.) No. (K - Oh!)

1415 T I want you to hear it. That's not . . . (K - "I Am Woman.") I want you to hear it. You mean "I Am Woman." No. (K - I know what it is.) I'm going to call on you, because you did it the other way. Listen. Listen to the middle part of the song. You listening? OK. (Claps the middle part.) And so on. No idea? (Two Ks guess simultaneously.)

T "Touch Me In The Morning." (Claps and sings a few bars of the middle section.) (K - We didn't learn it.) No, we didn't, but you all know it. (K - Not me.)

1518 T OK, open . . . (speaking to one K) I'll have the words for you. I'll see you at the end of the period. Oh, open your books to page 122 and let's warm up our voices. (Ks open books and talk a bit.) (K - 123?) 122. Oh well, you see we need something to warm up on and we all know this. Now I want you to beat with your fingers. (T snaps her fingers.) Ready? (T snaps her fingers to the beat.)

1550 T (There is a brief interruption to adjust the teacher's lavolier microphone. Then she calls the class back to order.)

1645 T Now. Let me hear the beat. (Ks snap fingers.) 1-2-3 . . . C'mon Chris, I don't feel it. Don't you have any soul? C'mon. Ready. (T plays introduction.) Ready. (Ks make sloppy start on "The Erie Canal.") Ooh. Stop. Wait for me. (T plays introduction again.) (*1715*) Ready. C'mon. Ready and sing. (This time she leads them in with her voice as well. Song is sung through one stanza and the refrain.)

1818 T Ummm. Let's take it from "Low bridge . . ." Slower. 1-2-3-and (Class sings.) (*1844*) (T leads them into the second stanza with her voice. She is using her voice more, in addition to the piano, singing louder, to support the somewhat weaker performance, by the Ks, of the second stanza.)

1938 T OK. Now, on the board is written a song that happens to be very beautiful. Some of you may remember this, but it was popular.–Ladies in the front. If you have something to say to us, raise your hand. That goes for Harriet as well, and Lydia. (p)–It was written by a man named Don McLean. (T writes his name on board, over a panel containing the words of the first stanza of the song.) I think that's the way his name is spelled. And it's about a very famous person. Does anyone know who that person is? (K–Vincent Price.) (The song is actually "Starry, Starry Night.") Vincent Price. (Class laughs.) (K - It says Vincent on the board.) No. (Ks still laughing.) Well, at least he offered an answer. Well, Kevin, do you have any idea? Well, why is he poor? (She had apparently heard Kevin make such a remark.) Ah (p). Does anyone know? No idea. OK. He was a painter and his name is Vincent Van Gogh. (Writes it on board and some Ks read it as she writes it.) How many people have heard of Vincent Van Gogh? (Ks raise hands.) OK. What do you know about him? Know anything about him, Fred? Hm? (K - He had his ear chopped off.)

2108 T OK, he had his ear chopped off. Did he have his ear chopped off? (K - No, *inaudible.*) That's probably the story that most people know about Van Gogh. He was a painter. (K - Did he chop off his ear?) His hair? His ear. He mutilated himself. (K - He killed himself.)

2125 T Yes, yes. He, he, let me just tell you. He was a painter who was called an expressionist. He lived in the nineteenth century. And he was a very, like a lot of artists, how can I say it? He was temperamental. Do you know what I mean by temperamental? What do I mean? (K - He was like picky and very, he was upset and very high-strung.)

2158 T He was high-strung, that's for sure. And he was, he was a very creative person, naturally. And there were lots of emotions that he had inside that were conflicting and that bothered him, that he did not have a way to express. Huh. Van Gogh had a history of mental illness and he was in and out of hospitals a good portion of his life. His painting, his painting reflects some of the darkness and trouble, troubled conditions that he experienced. I have here some sketches, some drawings rather, and some paintings by him. It was said that he, he identified with peasants, he identified with those people who would not be in the mainstream, you know, of society, would not be the jet set. He identified with those who were poor; he did not have a lot. Simple people. Peasants. And he captured them beautifully. OK? Peasants. And you notice a lot of the works here are in what kind of colors? (K - Black and white.) Right, and they are what? (K - *inaudible.*) They're what? (K - *inaudible.*) Well, are they bright? (Ks - No.) How would you describe them? (K - *inaudible.*) (K - Can you tell us why he cut off his ear?)

2350 T Ah, I think there was . . . From what I read there's no specific . . . there are lots of stories that go around . . . like his girl friend was, she was upset. I don't hold to that. I don't know that that was exactly true. I don't think there was one specific incident that caused him to do that. I know that he had an argument with a friend of his, a painter friend, Gauguin, and uh, he did it. OK? (K - Did he die then?) Not as a result of that. No. Later on he committed suicide. (K - Like he cut off, because like . . .) (T interrupts.)

2430 T He was troubled. He was tormented. He was driven by something that could not be resolved. (K - He cut off his whole ear?) He just cut off his ear. I don't know if it was the entire one. (K - *inaudible.*) I don't want to go into how you do it. I'm not planning on doing it myself. So, yah. Excuse me. Fred, I'll wait a second. (Some Ks are talking.) (K - When he cut off his ear, could he hear and everything?) Yeah, I'm sure he could hear. This part is essential, it's necessary, but I'm sure he could, uh . . . (K - Why did he do it?)

2505 T He might not, I think he probably, I don't really know how much he cut off. (K - The devil could have made him do it.) The devil could have made him do it. (Class laughs.) Yes? (K begins to speak over other voices.) I'm sorry, Lloyd. (Ks talking.) (K - How did he commit suicide?) I really don't know, Lloyd. (K - How did he commit suicide?) (K - Was he a famous painter?)

2533 T Yes, yes. But I do want to go on. Could you hold on for a second? This song, "Starry, Starry Night," written by McLean, was inspired by one of Van Gogh's paintings, and here it is, a painting called "Starry, Starry Night." Now on the board, (pointing to it on the board) on the board is the first verse of the song that McLean wrote. (She reads it aloud.) (As she reaches the word "palette" in the second line she says:) Of course a palette is? (K - Where you have the paints and colors.)

2608 T Right. Where the artist mixes his colors. Agatha, where is it or what is it? What are we talking about then? (K - The painting and the colors.) Agatha, look at the blackboard. (Starts reading from the beginning. Completes the entire verse without interruption.)

2657 T What is Don McLean doing with words? Sara. (K - He putting, umm, he's like, (p), he's telling the man, (p), he's telling, he's describing a picture in words.) OK. He is doing . . . (K - He's expressing . . .what's the guy's name?) Van Gogh, Vincent. (K - . . . Van Gogh's feelings, he's telling Van Gogh *inaudible, 6-7 words* about how he paints his pictures.)

2736 T OK. Do you think that in that line, "Now I understand what you tried to say to me, how you suffered for your sanity," what do you think he's saying there? "How you suffered for your sanity." Charles. (K - Well, he cut off his ear because a guy who feels like that must be insane. So that's what he means.) OK, that's possible. Chris. Yes. (K - That he didn't have to commit suicide. He could have kept on going.)

2812 T Why do you think that? (K - Well, it's nice to live.) (Class laughs.) Based on that "Now I understand what you tried to say to me, how you suffered for your sanity"? (K - Well, he lived a miserable life sometimes.) OK, so you're saying basically the same thing Sara said. Yah?

K Well, because he was like a mental patient and everything. He was probably like very misunderstood, like you know he didn't want to live that much, you know, and so he was like, was like suffering . . .

T Right, right. (K adds three inaudible words.)

2845 K He didn't really want to live, so he probably didn't even want to live when he first started painting, he like found painting a way to forget about everything else, problems, and so he started painting. (T - OK, Phyllis.)

K Maybe he was saying, maybe he was saying . . . (T - Phyllis, would you speak louder?) Why should I go on after people do mean things and everything? And don't care what's happening. Maybe he felt like: why go on? (T - OK. Yes.) (Another K says something inaudible.)

2937 T OK. I must tell you that he had certain ideas about painting that he felt were correct and should be followed, and so forth and so on, and they were not necessarily taken immediately. Everyone did not immediately say: Oh yes, that's right. Let's go do what Van Gogh's doing. OK. I'll just take two more and let's go on.

K Well, I think he wanted to express all his feelings through his paintings, but sometimes he couldn't.

3000 T Right. So that he was left with no kind of outlet. (K begins to say something.) That's what you were going to say. I mean, imagine, if you have no way to express your hostility, your feelings, your happiness, love, whatever. What would happen? What would happen to you inside? How would you feel?

K Start burning up on the inside. You'd feel sad.

K Well, just think of how do you feel when a teacher says something mean to you and you can't say anything back? Well, you just want to hit, wouldn't you?

K Well, you give it back to her.

K Well, you take it out on someone else.

T He could not find an outlet for all of . . .

K So he took it out on himself.

3037 T Right. That's exactly what he did.

K Right. Like when a teacher yells at you and you can't say nothing to her, and someone comes and talks to you, you want to hit him.

T That must be why! OK, one more.

K (Begins, but T says: Excuse me, we'll wait. One second. Yah.) He probably had a lot of problems, maybe because he was like mentally upset. No one could really, like painting is really to be taken seriously, to pay attention to what he was saying. So he looked to painting as an escape and then putting all his feelings down.

3112 T I had to interrupt you, and can't stop. (Begins to play the piano.) The bell might interrupt me. I like you to sit until I finish singing the song, if the bell rings. (Plays the introduction.) If you know it, just listen. Not everyone knows it. Well, let me ask: how many people in the class do know it? (A number raise their hands.) Oh, that's enough to sing it with me. The rest of you just follow. And!

3138 (T and Ks sing the song. T stops them at one point.) OK, listen to that line. (Sings it and Ks join in. They complete the whole verse.)

3302 T Let's take it from "Catch the breeze . . ."

3306 Bell rings.

T OK, let's sing it. (They begin at "Catch the breeze . . ." and complete the verse again.) (*3358*)

3400 (Ks leave the room.)

Since we have three times now applied ourselves to an analysis as soon as a lesson was over, it may seem odd that I omit that step here. But I do so, ZA, in order to give you an uncluttered view of the RAD (Retelling-Agenda-Discussion) cycle. When that view is clear, we'll face up to the relationship between analysis (via EG and PAT) and supervision (via the RAD cycle). So please read the POC and prepare yourself to describe what I do in it.

Post Observation Conference:
Junior High School Music Lesson

NS Alright, Janet*, as I explained to you off camera, what I'm going to ask you to do is to make a critique of the lesson we've just both, you went, you went through and we looked at on video playback and to list for me what, in your estimation, you consider the strengths and weaknesses of this particular lesson, not of yourself as a teacher ('cause I don't know you as a teacher), just of what occurred here, without explanation or elaboration; and after you've listed them for me (I'm going to copy them down), then we'll talk about them. OK?

JG From the beginning of the lesson?

NS In any order you wish, whatever comes to mind.

JG The first thing that came to my mind is that the teacher spent too long on the clapping exercises.

NS Ummm. Go ahead.

JG Ah. In each category of clapping, the identification of songs, the identification of meter and, ah, repetition of phrases, possibly two examples would have been sufficient in each area. Ah. There might have been, uh, a little more solicitation from the children. They might have been, uh, it might have been more interesting had they been able to clap something for the class to repeat. Uh. (Clears throat.) The teacher, (p) the teacher's presence, I felt, was, was good, uh, uh, except that the teacher seemed a little bit formal to me. Uh. The (p), the transitions, the transitions between the singing and the Vincent part and the clapping could have come a little bit quicker, uh, and with less introduction: (p) Now we will do this. It could have been a little bit faster. I think that pace was the major criticism I have. Uh. (P) I liked, (p) I liked the class' rapport with the teacher. I thought they were very responsive. (p)

NS Umm, umm.

JG Uh. (p) Nothing else comes to my mind.

*The real names of all teachers and students in the entire book have been replaced by appropriate pseudonyms.

NS OK, there's no, there's no . . .

JG There wasn't enough of a variety in it.

NS Yes, but there's no limit on how little or how much. You could have made one statement or twenty statements. It doesn't make any difference; but if you think of something along the way as we talk, why please feel free to talk.

JG OK.

NS And since I took the notes, I know what you said. So let me say it back to you in the order in which you said it.

JG OK.

NS You said that the clapping exercises took too long, and you elaborated on it by saying that the examples of each of the various kinds of things could have been restructured to two each rather than as many as you had, and then it would have helped even more if you had solicited from the students the examples they wanted to clap for the class. (JG - Hmmm.) to guess, rather than your doing it all the time. Then you said that the teacher's presence was good, but you said that the teacher seemed a bit formal, that the transitions between the various kinds of things that were done in the lesson were long-drawn-out, should have been done more quickly, and you said pace was the thing that bothered you, without elaboration, and finally you said that you liked the rapport, the students were very responsive. Umm (p) well, let's, let's . . . You were more negative than positive. Of the eight statements you made, six were negative statements and only two were positive statements. Is that the way you perceive of yourself as a person? (JG laughs.) In the classroom, I mean?

JG In the classroom?

NS Are you always that critical of yourself?

JG Generally, yes. (NS - Umm.) Generally, yes. Uh. Of course, it comes over into the evaluation of myself as a teacher. (NS - Huh, hm.) I always think that I should be having the children moving and doing more creative things. Of course, that wasn't that type of lesson. I didn't intend it to be. But within that subject, there was lots of room for . . .

NS Now you refer to "that subject" and to "that type of lesson" in inverse order. What type of lesson and in what subject did you see this to be?

JG Uh, the subject was mainly ear-training, and that requires a certain amount of teacher-class response, uh, as opposed to a lesson where the children might be making or composing a song. Or playing instruments, creating rhythms on instruments, or learning to play the piano and moving around the room and having one class, one group, do a descant, where, you know, where the children are involved themselves, out of their seats, and so forth. Uh. That's the difference.

NS Now, it's interesting, that even though you had, as you might say, an aim or an objective or a kind of lesson or a subject area which dealt with ear-training, none of your comments dealt with whether you were, you worked successfully in that area.

JG OH! Ah. (p) I think that it was mainly reinforcement, uh, that I was aiming for. I had taught them previously what meter was. I didn't use the word today. I taught them the difference. I did give them what I considered to be the elements of music and I wanted them . . . that was quite a while ago, and I wanted to bring that back to their recollection and, uh, to see if they could do rhythms that were a little more complex than those that I did maybe six weeks ago (NS - Umm) uh, and they did. They did it successfully. And the review of an old song was, give or take a few measures, successful. (NS - Hmm, hm) I wasn't pleased with that song, you know. The moment we started to sing it I thought to myself: why did I choose this one? There were millions of others that were more interesting.

NS Let's hold off on the song for a moment, (JG - OK.) and let's see if we can fit into this projection you have, that is, the review of metrical material and their ability to do, to initiate, and to recognize different clappings for what they represented. Let's relate that to their being too long, too much time spent on the clapping, too many examples, not enough solicitation, and the issue of pace, which I presume is related to that. How do you see that assortment of things together?

JG You mean, how could I have gotten, how could I have accomplished my aim?

NS No, no. In view of what you said you wanted to accomplish, (JG - Right.) and in view of what you just said that your students were able to do, why are you being critical of yourself for taking too much time with the clapping, for solicitation from students when, as a matter of fact, they might not have offered a fine example? You know, of something? (JG - Um) And the issue of pace?

JG Um. Well, it seemed to me when I was watching it, that they were able to do a lot more than those rhythms that I gave them. When I was standing up there, I felt that the rhythms that I was clapping were appropriate and were on their level and so forth and so on. But looking at it and seeing how well they adapted to it, it seemed that I could have gone on to something . . . that I could have possibly gone on to notation of (on the board, not having them write it), but showing them how four-four looks and how it moves. I could have gone on to the next step, in other words.

NS Are you saying that while you were in the classroom, teaching, (JG - Right.) you weren't sufficiently sensitive to how well they were responding, and therefore you didn't proceed to do some of the things you are now saying you might have done had you had the sensitivity you have in looking at the tape?

JG Right. I think they're capable of doing more than I presented to them.

NS Now, you said that your objective had to do with ear-training. The song, "The Erie Canal," was merely something you did for diversion, I presume.

JG To get them warmed up.

NS Yeh. Ah, why then the movement to the song about Van Gogh?

JG I wanted to . . . well, that was the introduction of a new song.

NS Oh, I see. That was a separate entity.

JG Right. Right. I feel that, ah, sometimes I have one aim for the entire lesson. Other times I feel that, especially with seventh graders, they, you need more than one objective (NS - Ummm.) because the time spent is so long, and they need more to think about. (NS - Um, um.) So I . . . There are three verses to that song, and I thought I would introduce the first verse today.

NS I see. So that you were concerned with two different kinds of things: one was a review to see how well the students had retained over a period of six weeks of inactivity in this area the ability to recognize songs when clapped out (JG - Right.), uh, their ability to duplicate the clapping of different metrical patterns (JG - Right.) uh. Then there was a . . . It wasn't an application; it was simply a warm-up process of singing, preparatory to going to the song about Vincent Van Gogh. (JG - Right.) OK. I understand now. Then wherein is the . . . you said pace . . . it was a very pregnant statement you made, that pace was really the thing that got to you.

JG It seemed slow. Uh. I possibly could have spent less time on the rhythms, more time on, on pitch, pitches in the Erie Canal song, gotten into solo and chorus . . . class, uh, listening for: are we singing this flat or sharp, uh, and reinforce the . . . (inaudible word) that way rather than spending that much time on the first half, the first section.

NS Do you work with a watch?

JG Normally, normally, I don't. Normally, I think that because of the day and the cameras, and, huh, the fact that the class was switched around, I felt that they were my first class, and that class ends at 20 to (NS - I see.), and in my head I still had at least 10 or 12 minutes (NS - I see.) and when I finally realized it, this ends in 2 minutes, I said I have to interrupt you. (NS - Umm, mmm) So that's where the pace was off.

NS I see. So you were affected by the overall change in program.

JG Yes. Yeah. I didn't think I was nervous, but apparently I was.

NS Apparently you were. Since you normally don't have your lessons recorded (JG - Yes.), and therefore do not have the advantage of a Monday-morning-quarterback deal, where you can sit back and say: well, you should have done so and so; how do you decide within the framework of a lesson, while you're doing it, uh, that what you have planned to do has to be altered, either too much or too little is planned, uh. How do you decide whether to focus on . . . you know, as you suggested you could have focused on pitch, uh, whether they were singing the whole song properly. How do you make such decisions, mid-stream?

JG One way only and that's from the children. Their responses, if, if they are in a certain mood, I think I'm aware of that, and if I have planned a lesson and I think it's just the greatest song in the entire world and they're going to drop when they hear it, and they say: Ugh! (NS laughs) . . . (a few inaudible words) You have to. You can't say: you're gonna like this song or else you'll go the Dean. Uh. That's the only . . . that's why I'm there. To teach them. But not to . . . I'm not there to bore them and they're not going to learn if they're not listening. I don't mean just not talking.

NS OK. You're saying that . . . You're watching carefully to see what the student feedback is (JG - Right.), and the student feedback determines the pace *and/or* the content? Or the pace *and* the content?

JG If I've planned a lesson, if I've planned a theory lessson, and the class walks in and they are really up, and they've just come back from gym or they've just seen something in the auditorium or someone has just socked someone else down the hall by the water fountain and they're all over the place, they're not going to sit for a theory lesson, that says I hand out paper and we're going to notate, which can be interesting and can be fun, but they're not going to have the discipline to do that. So I'm going to have to sneak that . . .uh . . . concept in by some other means, such as singing a song that they know and saying: Well, listen to this chord, or listen to the melodic line; that's called a scale or whatever; or that's how that rhythm, when it's written down . . . (p) If you can't, if you really are . . . I don't teach by schedule. I am, as a person and as a teacher, uh, I don't adhere to schedules very, very well. Not at all. And very often I'll plan something and I can't be bothered with it. It bores me to think about it. So I'll scratch it and sing the entire period, and because I feel good about singing I can get them to feel enthusiastic about it, but, uh, I, I have to . . . gear . . . if I say, I have to teach this class quarter notes, eighth notes, and sixteenth notes by the end of the month because I have to keep them up with the class, and I want them to be able to do certain things by May, then I have to. So, if I'm going to teach it in a structured way, then I have to do it, quote, in a fun way; you know, games or songs. They love to sing.

NS OK. Now is it fair to conclude then from what you've been saying, that you have an overall commitment to have, to expose, I won't say to teach but to expose your students to certain technical elements, to certain performance elements, to certain listening techniques, etc.; ah, that you don't see yourself necessarily being bound to do any one of them even if you've planned it for a given day? Ah, but you do two things: you read the mood of the class as they come in, to see whether you can approach whatever you have in mind as you planned to approach it, but you might have to scrap it altogether, or whether you can get around it by beginning some other way. (JG - Right.) But that you feel sufficiently flexible so that you aren't tied down to these, to anything that's particular for that period. Umm. Then are you . . . You see, you're concerned with pace. You have said there was too much time on the clapping, there were too many examples, the children should have offered some, and pace; so that four of the eight statements you made, four of the five dealing with it that are negative, uh, all deal with the issue of pace in one way or another; well, not solicitation; so let's say that only three deal with pacing. Well, three out of six, three out of six is half your criticism that has to do with pacing. Ummm, and yet you adjust, you make the adjustment yourself in terms of the content. You can control that element. (JG - Content?) Yah. Where is the difficulty in controlling the pace?

JG The difficulty . . . when I am . . . (JG is hesitant.) . . . the difficulty in controlling the pace comes when I lapse in sensitivity to what my class is, to where my class is, in terms of attention and interest. Ah. If, if I, if I feel comfortable doing what I'm doing, it's very easy to continue. I feel very comfortable clapping, it's very easy to stand there and clap rhythms, and say, and make up songs. And I think that I got carried away in that area, and I think that that's how generally I would get carried away with pacing, by doing something that I feel comfortable doing. It's very easy to teach a lesson that you know (NS - Umm) and say I'm not going to scrap it, I don't care what happens. That's where it is, because the children will go where you take them. They will go willingly if it's good. And . . .

NS OK, then why are you critical of yourself for pacing? If you, if you say, that so long as you're doing what you are able to do well, and being able to do well means that your students are with you, what difference does it make how much time you spend on it? It's not as though . . . You haven't said you have a commitment in terms of a whole semester or a year program, that if there are 40 weeks of lessons, one a week, that you're gonna deal with, and that if you miss one week, heaven help you!!! If you're absent or they're not there, LOST!!! You haven't said that. Ah. Therefore, if the content is smaller than the volume of time, why worry about pacing? Why does it bother you?

JG It bothers me because when the pacing is wrong, it gets, it becomes tedious; it gets boring. Ah. And even if the children may not be disruptive, they still should not be subjected to my standing there and doing something that I feel comfortable doing for 20 minutes.

NS OK. Now let's bring this point to, you know, to a conclusion, if possible. Uh. What can you do, what perhaps should you do, to develop a kind of sensitivity to having done enough in an area and then quitting and going on to something else? That is, how, how can you be alert to your frame of mind vis-a-vis that of the students so that you know you've reached a point where you're now beginning to bore them? (p) In other words, if you had that kind of sensitivity, and it worked like a watch, a well-oiled machine, you would never be critical of yourself in pacing. You'd sense it and you'd move on. You'd be like a fine performer on the stage: when this isn't going, you do something else.

JG How . . . you're asking me, how can I tell you (NS - Yes.), within the class, now, not . . . (inaudible) (NS - No, no, within a particular class, obviously.) Well, of course, the children give you signals.

NS OK. Now what signal are you looking for that will give you the information you're interested in having?

JG Well, in a positive sense, when they are there, when they're with me, they're looking, it's in their eyes. They're not, uh, if you noticed in that, in the viedotaping, toward the middle and the end, there were children who were . . . (POC interrupted by an announcement on school's public address system.)

NS We were interrupted by a public address announcement from the principal. But let me see if I can recapture what we were talking about. Uh. I'm going to back up a little bit more because we haven't too much time for the rest of the conference. Ah. In looking back over the items that you gave me, actually, of the six negative items, umm, four dealt with the issue of pacing. Apparently it's a very important thing for you: the too long on the clapping, the examples, the quicker transitions (which is a pacing item), and the word pacing itself, or pace itself. So that, ah, that's half of all things you said. (JG - Yes.) Apparently this is a concern of yours. And again recapturing what you said: you feel very flexible in terms of content (JG - Right.) and in terms of methodology, which you can adjust to the mood of your students. You're critical of yourself because, either today because you were formal in terms of our presence, or maybe at other times, when you become involved in something which you enjoy doing and in which the kids move with you, you carry them along, you know, like a rapid stream; (JG - Right.) ah, you are saying that in looking back at this, especially in recorded form, you can see how you haven't been sensitive enough and the cut-off point should have been sooner. (JG - Right.) And I asked you how, from here on in, would you know where, what the cut-off point should be, and you said something about the student feedback or its equivalent would tell you. We were at that point.

JG Right. The student feedback is very essential. They become restless. Ahmm, they (p) will, ah, will . . . (p) That's basically it. (p) They, ah, they talk. (Bell rings.) They move around. Well, they will very often tell you. This class happened not to be very verbal, in terms of, you know, this is boring. Some classes will tell you. Ah. When I feel bored with something, I know it's time to move on. When I feel that . . . very often I'll be playing something and I'll say to myself: why is this important? It really isn't. Ahmm. And the quality of their answers, the quality of their responses I should say, dictates when it's time to move on, or what's not important to them. Some classes really only like to sing. Other classes really enjoy the theory, (NS - Ummm) the theoretical part of music. Umm . . .

NS Well, let me ask you, were you less sensitive today because of the TV cameras than you might normally be?

JG (P) I would like to say yes (said with a smile or a little laughter in her voice), but probably not.

NS Probably not. Well, then it seems to me, to round off . . . the bell rang and we can hear the kids in the hall . . . that if pacing is as important an issue for you and not as resolved an issue as content and approach, ah, then it seems to me that from here on in you might ask yourself two questions: You said you know when you become bored and you ought to ask yourself, as soon thereafter as you can, how did I know that I was bored? Because, you see, if your threshold for boredom is higher than theirs, they will become disruptive before you appreciate that they are bored. Your threshold should be lower than theirs, so that you can sense, in advance, that you're reaching their threshold, and if you cut at yours, which should be lower, then you will never bore them; you will change direction, content, substance, approach, and so on, (JG - Ummm) and you need to do some comparing, and the time will vary from class to class, (JG - Right.) the thresholds will vary. But if you can see the difference between theirs and yours, and try to keep yours on a tighter leash, so that it's lower and is reached sooner, then you make your changes (JG - Right.) and stop being critical of yourself in these areas. Yes?

JG That's a very good suggestion.
NS OK. Thank you very much.
JG Thank you.

Having read the POC, ZA, what process did I follow?

You began by asking her to give you, without elaboration, "The strengths and weaknesses of this particular lesson," which you said you would write down in the order in which she said them. Since you were able to read them back to her, I presume you did make such notations. I noticed that she referred to herself as the teacher, as though she had been an observer rather than the actual teacher.

You gave her complete freedom to make as many statements as she wished, in any order at all. Then you read the statements back to her and began by observing that she had made more negative than positive statements.

What stands out, as a clear omission, is that you did not say how you had evaluated her lesson, what was on your list of strengths and weaknesses, nor did you ever discuss any evaluative statements other than those she dictated to you. But you seemed to guide her in an analysis of her statements; you asked why this or that element was in the lesson; and you ended with the suggestion that her threshold for boredom should be lower than that of the students in any given class as a way of eliminating student boredom.

I also noticed that you never complimented her for anything in the lesson. Was that because you found nothing to compliment?

And one last observation: I saw no evidence that you had applied either the EG or the PAT to the lesson. Does that mean that this whole procedure is divorced from your "analysis strand," and that the only evaluation to be discussed is the one provided by the teacher? Didn't we agree, a goodly number of times, that we (not the teachers) could put items on the POC agenda as a result of applying either the PAT or the EG?

As I said, in the brief paragraph between lesson and POC, ZA, I want to give you an uncluttered view of the cycle. In due time I'll deal with where my analysis fits in, why I didn't compliment the teacher, and what happened to the supervisor's agenda.

Now that you've experienced the combination of lesson and POC, I can back up and tell you what I was trying to do and for what reasons.

Let's begin with an observation you can surely confirm or deny from your own experience, ZA, either as a teacher or as an administrator/supervisor. A school year is generally about 180 days long, each day consisting of some five hours of instructional time, making about 900 hours per school year. All the ZA's with whom I raise this issue say that no teacher is supervised 10 percent of that time. That is, the classroom instructional practices of teachers are not observed by supervisors at the rate of 90 hours per school year. In fact, ZA's report that few are observed even as often as once per month. They regard the 10 percent figure as fantasy, not reality.

Cogan makes a most useful distinction in this area. ". . . *general supervision*" (Italics his), he says, "subsumes supervisory operations that take place principally outside the classroom . . . *General supervision*, therefore, denotes activities like the writing and revision of curriculums, the preparation of units and materials of instruction, the development of processes and instruments for reporting to parents, and such broad concerns as the evaluation of the total educational program . . . *Clinical supervision* may therefore be defined as the rationale and practice designed to improve the teacher's classroom performance. It takes its principal data from the events of the classroom. The analysis of these data and the relationship between teacher and supervisor form the basis of the program, procedures and strategies designed to improve the students' learning by improving the teacher's classroom behavior."*

In discussing the supervisor-teacher ratio, Cogan says that ". . . the number of clinical supervisors in many schools . . . is inadequate for the responsibilities they hold." In addition to making available to teachers "the collateral services of other personnel" (such as subject matter specialists, psychologists, counselors, etc.) Cogan also says:

> As for inservice supervision, the estimate of the supervisor-teacher ratio required for clinical supervision will vary enormously, being related to the needs of teachers and the program of innovative and remedial instructional activities planned for a school, a department, or a school system. Nevertheless, one might venture to estimate the range as enough supervisors—resident and nonresident in a school—to provide an *average* (Italics his) of three or four hours a week for each teacher.

If we accept Cogan's higher figure, four hours per week, his explanations convince me that he means this time to include both actual classroom observation and out-of-classroom discussions and conferences. So let's say he's referring to two hours for observation and two hours for the rest. Therefore, even if a teacher teaches only 20 hours per week, then two hours of observation represent 10 percent of the time. So the teacher is still alone with the students 90 percent of the time.

My *major premise* is that clinical supervision (a term as applicable to what I'll be describing as it is to Cogan's material) should be directed mainly at guiding teachers to develop skills of *self*-supervision.

To achieve this objective, ZA, I have designed, demonstrated, and tested a three-part supervisory cycle, for each part of which there is a dual rationale.

*Cogan, Morris L. *Clinical Supervision.* Boston: Houghton Mifflin Company, 1973.

Step I. Retelling the Lesson

When I observe a lesson, ZA, I come equipped with a pad of paper and a pencil. The teacher whom I'm observing receives a full description of the cycle and its rationales and understands that I will be making notes of what I see.

I mark off a vertical column, about an inch in width on the left margin of the pad, in which I enter time. The larger remainder contains my notations.

	John Jones–4th gr.–Reading (date)
1000	
1002	
etc.	

I consider timing an important feature of my notes, because teachers are often unaware of how long they stay with an activity compared to the attention spans of their students.

I write my notes as rapidly as possible, in a kind of personal speedwriting, aiming to have enough data so I can later reconstruct all I've seen and heard. In parentheses I jot down those aspects of the interaction which strike me (at the moment) as worthy of consideration in the POC.

I leave room at the end of my notations for the Agenda.

I open the POC (Post-Observation Conference) by asking the teacher to *retell* the lesson, in chronological order, using the third person singular, referring to herself/himself as the teacher, Ms./Mr. Jones, she/he. This form of reference, I've found, tends to dilute the identification between the teacher doing the Retelling and that other self that did the teaching. There are two rationales for this activity:

a. *Training* In order for the teacher to learn to supervise himself, he must be able to recall what occurred accurately and honestly. Most of the teachers I have conferred with have no difficulty with recall, though a minority do lapse into the first person singular. I urge the teacher to put himself into the role of a TV camera and microphone and to retell what those machines might have recorded.

(This step can and should be shortened to a précis, once teacher and supervisor are convinced that the skill has been mastered.)

b. *Supervision* In order for teacher and supervisor to be able to analyze what occurred, they need to agree on the events. Ergo, the Retelling.

Step II. Agenda

I now ask the teacher to enumerate, to list without amplification or elaboration, how he would evaluate the lesson had he been sitting where I was and observing the events in the classroom. This is also to be done in the third person singular, for the same reasons as in Step I. The two rationales are:

a. *Training* If the teacher is to learn this procedure and to use it on himself in the absence of another professional, then he must be the source of his own critique.

b. *Supervision* I believe that one cannot begin to help another person to improve on his situation unless one begins with his perceptions of the meanings of what occurred. This is particularly true when the supervisor has more understanding of the instructional process than the teacher does.

As the teacher lists the Agenda items, I copy them down in the space I left at the end of my observation notes. Here I divide the page into two columns, thus:

+	–

I write each item down in the order given by the teacher, numbering the items consecutively from 1 onwards, but enter it in the column suggested or implied by the teacher. If the item seems to apply in both columns, or is neutral, then I still number it but write it across the middle.

Some teachers again succumb to a first person singular mode, but I help them to rephrase their statements. They're even more tempted to elaborate on each item. I ask them to hold back until all the items have been stated.

Step III. Discussion

I begin this last step by reading aloud the teacher's Agenda, in the order the teacher gave it, using his words (as nearly verbatim as I was able to note them). We then discuss the instruction he conducted, in first person singular. The key element in this discussion is that the supervisor is largely non-directive, perceiving himself as a well-polished mirror who reflects the teacher's contributions to the Discussion. The two rationales are:

a. *Training* If the teacher is to learn to apply the procedure to himself, there is only one Agenda he can use: the one he himself can supply. And if he is to conduct an internal Discussion with himself (during that 90 percent of the time), then he must ingest a supervisory role which is non-directive, which is a reflection of himself in a large mirror.

b. *Supervision* As I said in the parallel rationale for Step II, a supervisor has to begin with the teacher's perceptions.

Before you load us up with more material, NS, please let's pause for some comments and questions. Taking your ideas in the order given:

If you define Clinical Supervision as Cogan does, then, yes—no teacher that I ever knew received 10 percent supervision. There aren't that many supervisors on the staff. Using a combination of Cogan's figures and yours, 10 percent supervision would mean that a supervisor working 35 hours per week, seven each day, could devote four hours each to just eight teachers and have but three hours left for five lunch periods and other activities. I *understand* that Cogan meant the four hours to be a maximum allotment for clinical supervisors *and* for his "collateral services of other personnel." It makes little difference to me that the "other personnel" are not supervisors by title; they would be serving as supervisors by function. All of which leads me to see why your cycle is designed to teach teachers the skills of self-supervision. (Which reminds me that I haven't commented on where schools will get the funds to free each teacher from classroom responsibilities for two hours each week.)

Now I'd like to ask some questions about each step in the cycle, NS. Does Retelling in the third person come easily to teachers?

By and large yes, but some have more difficulty than others. Where such difficulties occur, the supervisor is advised to model the Retelling for the teacher. The teacher is encouraged to pick up the story whenever he's ready.

A more serious problem is the use of third-person form for first-person substance. For example, a teacher will say: "The teacher began the lesson by following up the work he and the class had begun yesterday." That is in third-person form, but not in content. Camera and microphone could not report that yesterday's work was being followed up. They could report that the teacher began by asking the class what had been accomplished yesterday and what had been projected for today. That event would have been observable by a third person.

Or a teacher might say: "The teacher led the class through a review of the various musical meters they had been studying, because she wanted to establish that as a base for today's learning." That, too, is *verboten.* Camera and microphone have no way of discerning what the teacher "wanted" to do. They can only report what she did.

But isn't a teacher's motivation germane to any analysis of what took place?

Of course it is, ZA. But as you said, it's germane to *analysis,* not to the Retelling. When, during Retelling, supervisors permit teachers to go into past or future events, into their reasons for what they did, or into their rationales for the activities, the objectivity and accuracy of recall break down and the POC gets sidetracked. Remember, I'm after accuracy in recall largely because I want the teacher to remember precisely what occurred. This is what the students experienced, and it's their experience which is central to the learning process.

But what if the teacher omits or distorts some of the events in the classroom while doing a third person Retelling?

When events are omitted, I have the choice of filling in the gap or not doing so. Omissions can be emotion-laden, like a confrontation with a student, a loss of control, a serious error in content or process. If this is our first POC, I would make a note of the omission. If the next lesson I see contains no such lapse, I can assume that the first one was not usual for this teacher and reserve judgment until other observations yield more data. However, if a similar lapse occurs at the second observation and is again omitted from the Retelling, then I see that something conscious is at work. Unless the lapse is potentially of lasting harm to teacher-pupil relationships, I'll wait for a third lapse. If the teacher still omits the matter from the Retelling, then I'll describe all three lapses in the third POC and note that they were each omitted in Step I. Do you have any comments? I would ask.

If the teacher omits some inconsequential item, I'll let it pass. However, if the teacher omits something which is not an emotion-laden lapse but may well be crucial to an effective analysis of the instruction, then I will fill in the gap during the Retelling or find an opening for it during the Discussion.

Beginners in the method are best advised to note omissions, except where a teacher has obvious difficulty in recalling the events in the classroom. My secondary students run across this difficulty more frequently than the elementary ones do; secondary teachers often teach the same lesson to two or more sections of the same course on the same day and have trouble sorting out the details of the one observed by my student/supervisors.

As to the matter of distortions—I've encountered none of any consequence. If I did, my strategy would be to find some appropriate point in the Discussion for suggesting a correction.

Though I grasp your response, NS, one statement in it seems to conflict with the supervisor's well-polished-mirror role. If the teacher omits from his Retelling some emotion-laden item from three consecutive POC's, you call his attention to them. Forgive the comparison, but your advice sounds too much like that "Mirror, mirror on the wall, who's the fairest one of all?" who gave that lady some feedback.

That's an amusing comparison, ZA, so there's nothing to forgive. One rationale for each step in the cycle is labelled "Training." If the Retelling is to be as brutally honest as the camera-microphone combination, and if the teacher is to learn to supervise himself, then absolute honesty is crucial. Therefore, I have to be able to lead the teacher along a path to mastery, but I do so with caution. I wait for "three strikes" before, in a sense, saying "You're out."

Then, as I understand your position, NS, you want a Retelling which is a verbal substitute for an audio-video tape, and you want it in third person to establish the kind of distance that exists between a teacher and an audio-video tape of the lesson being retold.

That's right, ZA.

Your implementation of the supervisor's role during the Retelling, NS, clear as it now is procedurally, nonetheless leaves me with some unresolved feelings. I don't see any problems in keeping to third person form and content, in noting omissions and distortions, or in modelling the Retelling, but how do you decide that a "lapse is potentially of lasting harm to teacher-pupil relationships," what makes a Retelling omission "inconsequential," what determines whether an omitted item "may well be crucial to an effective analysis of the instruction," and how do you find "an opening for it during the Discussion"?

Cogan gives a superb answer to your question,ZA:

> A *Caution.* This book is an attempt to set out in usable form the rationale and procedures for systematic supervision of teachers. The word *usable,* however, requires an explanation. The book is not usable in the sense that a person may study it and learn directly how to become a clinical supervisor. The compe-

> tences needed by the clinical supervisor are generally too complex and too difficult to master in this fashion. For the very large majority of people, the professional competences of the practicing clinical supervisor must be learned in an extended program of preparation that includes a carefully planned and supervised practicum, that is, in a systematic and critically examined induction into practice. During the induction process, which is individualized for every candidate, the future supervisor is helped to examine the rationale and practices of clinical supervision and to relate them to his own behavior in his own style.
>
> In sum, for most people, this book and a "textbook course" on clinical supervision are inadequate as preparation for practice. Supervisors must build their competences through supervised practice related to a carefully examined rationale. In the latter process this book may be useful.*

You, ZA, were a student in my class, coming one evening each week for 150 minutes for just one 15-week semester. Depending on my practice in any given term, you conducted two or three POC's, recorded them on audiotape, and submitted those tapes to me, along with your description of each lesson and your evaluation of it. I read your words, heard your tapes, and wrote you an individual response for each POC. Doing that for as many as 30 ZA's in a class took an enormous amount of time, and was still no more than one small step to mastery. By no stretch of the most egotistical imagination can that be equated with Cogan's "extended program of preparation that includes a carefully planned and supervised practicum." Only in such a practicum can I even hope to create and control conditions under which you may learn to make the judgments you enumerated.

> Then let's go on to the second step in your cycle, NS. Here you ask the teacher for a self-evaluation. What confuses me is that you call it an Agenda, a term we've been using to denote what a supervisor might want to discuss with a teacher *after* the supervisor's EG or PAT analysis of the lesson. So are there *two* agendas?

When you read both Goldhammer** and Cogan†, you'll find

*Cogan, *op. cit.*, pp. 9-10.

**Goldhammer, Robert. *Clinical Supervision: Special Methods for the Supervision of Teachers.* New York: Holt, Rinehart, and Winston, Inc., 1969, p. 57.

†Cogan, *op. cit.*, p. 10.

that their cycles have five "stages" and eight "phases," respectively. Goldhammer has a "Stage 3: Analysis and strategy" in between the observation and the POC; Cogan has "Phase 5: Analyzing the teaching-learning process" and a "Phase 6: Planning the strategy of the conference" in between observation and POC. It should be obvious from the long analyses we made of the three lessons that the RAD cycle can not exclude either Goldhammer's "analysis" or Cogan's "analyzing the teaching-learning process." And I will be discussing with you how I deal with "strategy" or with "planning the strategy of the conference." I excluded both analysis and strategy from the formal RAD cycle description because each of its three steps has a dual rationale, a point I for one can't make as a basis for the other two supervisory efforts.

So, yes, there are *two* agendas, the supervisor's and the teacher's. The latter is elicited after the Retelling. The former requires a longer statement.

The most significant item to keep in mind is the premise undergirding the RAD cycle: teachers are alone with students over 90 percent of the time, so that the cycle's *prime* objective is to help the teacher master a process or method of self-supervision. Therefore, although a supervisor should make a full-scale PAT analysis of an observed instructional situation, *his* agenda should be restricted to the identification of that single element (or, at most, two elements) which seem (to the supervisor) to stand in the way of professional growth by the teacher.

> Before you even explain *why* my agenda should contain only one or two elements and *how* I select them, I must register a complaint. Your analysis of the science lesson and mine of the math lesson sifted out a number of agenda items—though, come to think of it, you did emphasize relevance in the science lesson and you did ask me for a single major obstacle in that Bible lesson.—Alright, I withdraw my complaint, but I would like an explanation.

If you juggle science, math, English, and music lessons simultaneously, ZA, you'll see that I wasn't leading you astray. The science lesson was irrelevant because it lacked a social context; it was not meaningful to Ks, as I define the term. The math lesson didn't allow for enough "doing" by Ks and didn't pursue the social implications of the issue raised by one student. The English lesson missed because he had not decided in advance what the students' Rs should be. The music lesson's problem was a teacher threshold higher than that of the students. Yes, I know. Each lesson had other problems. But look now, ZA, at the characteristic common to each single failure above: each one is *not* a criticism of just the one lesson we observed; it's what I call an *overarching factor applicable in a great many future lessons.*

And that's the key element in my conception of the supervisor's "strategy" or "planning the strategy of the conference." Just *because* my aim is to teach (to take on a new response pattern), and just *because* the teacher is being guided into self-supervision during that 90 percent of the time, I choose to use the analysis of any single lesson as the basis for generalizations which apply to a great many lessons.

The music teacher did have other problems:

- The teacher improvised the clapping patterns she had the students duplicate, and there was no solid indication that they progressed in difficulty. She *could* have prepared patterns which went from simple to complex.
- The same thing is true of the songs she wanted students to identify merely from her clapping of their rhythmic patterns.
- There are other songs that might have served as a more effective introduction and warmup to the new one about Van Gogh. Again, she improvised instead of doing rigorous planning.
- She engaged in much too long a discussion of Van Gogh's history, for which she was prepared neither with the necessary data nor for those parameters of a discussion which could serve as meaningful context for learning the new song.
- And she was generally guilty of "doing what comes naturally" to her rather than following a carefully planned program of studies.

Yet I was sympathetic to her unique situation, having faced it myself. You can't really engage students, especially in musical activities, if they're "all over the place" because of some event that precedes their arrival in your room. So a certain degree of flexibility and improvisation is necessary, based on a clear conception of the "responses" you want students to "take on" over the semester they're with you. All the more reason why you must be specially attuned to the students' threshold. Which is why I pursued that as the chief item in our Discussion.

> You've now made a major statement about your conception of the supervisory process, so I need to pause to digest it, NS. You're saying that you write as detailed notes as you can manage to get down about events in the classroom, that you do make at least a full PAT analysis of those events, but that you somehow try to select one or no more than two major obstacles to greater success in the learning process. So I have two questions: (1) How do you decide what the major obstacle(s) is (are)? (2) Why do you seem to neglect the specific problems you've just now enumerated?

Your second question can be answered in fewer words than the first, ZA, so let me do that now.

The music teacher I observed was a person who volunteered to have me come in. I was not on the staff of her school. In addition, neither of us knew each other, nor were we going to have a continuing relationship. Therefore, I could not tell how typical of her general practice was the lesson I observed. So I could not assume that the apparent absence of simple-to-complex sequences in replicating clapping patterns and in recognizing songs from clapped-out rhythms was necessarily typical. She herself was critical about the clapping exercises and suggested that there "might have been, uh, a little more solicitation from the students." I made a "light touch" reference to student solicitation by saying that "they might not have offered a fine example . . . of something." To which she responded with: "Well, it seemed to me when I was watching it, that they were able to do a lot more than those rhythms that I gave them. When I was standing up there, I felt that the rhythms that I was clapping were appropriate and were on their level and so forth and so on. But looking at it and seeing how well they adapted to it, it seemed that I could have gone onto something . . ."

So here was a teacher who was not sufficiently sensitive to student responses to alter her stimuli mid-stream, though she had the sensitivity to see the issue in a TV playback. Her name for the problem was "pace." It was not the issue I would have selected.

The major obstacle I identified was the last one of the five items I listed for you just a while ago: that she didn't follow "a carefully prepared program of studies." In PAT terms, she hadn't clearly identified the Stimuli and Responses.

And here we come to a major element of the RAD cycle. As I clarify it, I will be answering both your questions, ZA.

As you've already noted, the PAT is so ingrained in my mind that I can apply it even as I observe. Thus, I make parenthetical notations, in my rapid note-taking, of items which become the source of my agenda. Before the POC I decide which of them (or the combination of some or all of them) will become my one or two major obstacles to teacher progress.

But as I hear the teacher's Agenda, I make rapid calculations. If her Agenda contains an item or items which overlap mine, then I'm in luck, because I have direct access to the introduction of my major obstacle into the Discussion. In this POC I had no such direct access, so I worked entirely with her perceptions. Yet note carefully, ZA, how much she revealed about herself in just one POC. In the order in which the revelations came, this is what I heard:

1. She is self-critical (six negative, two positive items).
2. She wasn't pleased with her selection of "The Erie Canal."
3. The students should have done more.
4. She was not sufficiently sensitive while facing the class.
5. She sets up more than one objective per lesson.
6. She was affected by the change in program. (In order to accommodate me and my schedule, and because she wanted to be recorded with a particular class, her schedule of classes had to be altered.)
7. The cameras made her nervous.
8. She goes by the moods of her students.
9. She doesn't teach by schedule.
10. Her own lesson plans sometimes bore her and she scraps them.
11. She can lapse in her sensitivity to K feedback.
12. She feels free to do what's comfortable for her.
13. Yet says that her students should not be subjected to her exercise of such freedom.

14. She can tell that Ks are with her when "they're looking, it's in their eyes."
15. She questions her choice of songs even as she's playing them.
16. She goes by the quality of K responses,
17. But admits that she was no less sensitive under recording conditions than she normally is.

The nearest she came to my major obstacle is in #9, that she does not teach according to a schedule; or, as I put it, she didn't follow a carefully prepared program of studies. But she also had reasons for the two clapping exercises and the two songs. Had I even hinted at my major obstacle, I would have been challenging her head on, which is hardly non-directive.

Such a challenge would have required her admission that the clapping exercises were improvised, that they had no simple-to-complex hierarchy, that "The Erie Canal" bore no relationship to Vincent Van Gogh (she questioned its selection, but not as a bridge to Van Gogh), and that she was ill-prepared for the pre-singing discussion of the Van Gogh song.

In place of a challenge, I reflected back to her the major concern she had about pacing. It seemed to me (right in the POC itself) and seems to me even now, that pacing was an oblique admission that the flow of activities in the lesson was somehow awry. So I worked with her perceptions, as the rationale of the RAD cycle requires, but I also led her to a perception she might not have reached on her own.

(Pause) I've just now done what you did a number of times in our discourse, ZA. I've backed up to read your last statement, your two questions, and my attempts to answer them. And I haven't quite done so.

Then why didn't I erase my efforts and start again? Well, because what I've said is part of the answer.

I seemed to have neglected "the specific problems you've just now enumerated," yet I didn't, as my list of her revelations indicates. When we were discussing the lack of attention to grammatical errors in the English lesson, I said that "only those Rs are given attention which directly impinge on the terminal behavior sought by the teacher." The same dictum applies when the supervisor is "teacher" and the teacher is "learner." As supervisor/teacher I set up only one or two objectives (major obstacles) for the POC.

The teacher's many revelations indicated how stimulated she was by our Discussion, but she would leave with a diffuse focus unless I zeroed in on one or two major issues. I settled on one: hers, only partially mine—pacing, which I converted to "threshold."

Why threshold? Because if I can get her to maintain an attitude of awareness to the contrast between where she is and where the students are, then that could serve as a brake on her doing what's comfortable for her (#12), so that students won't be subjected to her exercise of such freedom (#13). If she feels less free "to do her own thing," and becomes more aware of K responses, then maybe we'll get a positive impact on my major obstacle, a planned program of studies, a proper specification of Ss and Rs.

This is hardly your most direct response to a question of mine, NS, but I think I now see that you didn't fully neglect all of the specific problems I mentioned in my second question. Your eye is on your major obstacle, which peripherally includes attention to what the teacher also happens to reveal. And in keeping with your well-polished-mirror role, you try to reflect to the teacher the meanings you see in her Agenda, especially her emphasis on pacing.

One POC is really only an introduction to your conduct of it, especially the Discussion segment, so I'll see what your series of POC's with one teacher will reveal. But you really haven't answered my second question in so many words: how *do* you decide what the major obstacle(s) is (are)?

Essentially I've answered that question, ZA: by applying the EG or the PAT. In each of the four lessons we've now discussed we applied one or the other and came up with dissonances between events in the classroom and the conditions which would have been consonant with principles of learning.

Obviously, NS, but you came up with more than one dissonance per lesson. By what criteria did a single one become the major obstacle?

You have every right to be a little sharp and impatient with me,

ZA, yet my response won't reduce either reaction. I can't give you a formula, except for either the EG or the PAT. Apply them and you'll come up with some number of dissonances. I choose that one or those two that, in my idiosyncratic view, are most likely to lead to greater success if converted into consonances. The final test of my choice is in the real classroom situation, in Cogan's advice for "an extended program of preparation that includes a carefully planned and supervised practicum."

I believe that my "teacher" should be concerned with the intellectual and aesthetic development of learners. This requires strict initial consonance with the units on Scholarship, Structure, and Meaningfulness. You can't create and control conditions for learning unless you know your material, unless you have a structured grasp of its concepts and modes of inquiry, and unless you can make it meaningful to learners. When you're master of the first two, there's a chance you can do the third one, not a guarantee. Then you can probably move to clear definition and communication of Ss and Rs, determine readiness, etc., etc.

I've already taken two strong positions, ZA: on the role of "teacher" and on ignorance of subject matter as the single most pervasive reason for teacher failure. We haven't argued either premise, because all one can do *is* to argue about them. One is a philosophical position, and the other is a conclusion based on experience as seen through the lens of my philosophical position. In Cogan's practicum I stand a chance of convincing you by direct demonstration. On paper we reach an impasse.

However, I can give you a better answer to a question you haven't asked: Once you elicit an Agenda from the teacher, how do you decide where to begin your non-directive role as a well-polished mirror? Well, here are some guidelines:

1. You must *listen* to what the teacher is saying. As a well-polished mirror you must be able to take in the teacher's image completely and accurately, or else your reflection will be only partial.
   a. You do this by freeing your mind: you have your notes of the observation; you've made at least a PAT (Primitive Assessment Tool) analysis; you have your agenda; and you've selected your major obstacle(s).

   Now you listen to and observe the teacher.

2. The *order* of her Agenda is meaningful.
   a. It may begin with negatives, perhaps because it's-better-if-I-admit-to-it than if-you-point-it-out-to-me.
   b. It may begin with positives to indicate some self-assurance about what she has accomplished.
   c. The first or the last item may be the most significant.
   d. Or, the really significant item may be inserted rapidly and casually, so as to give it as little weight as possible.

   But the order *is* meaningful. One of the reasons for reading the Agenda back to the reader first is that it gives *you* a chance to think about that order as you read.
3. *Repetitions* are important.
   a. A teacher may be listing the same Agenda item in a number of ways, as the music teacher did re the factor of pacing.
   b. A teacher may literally restate the same item.
4. *Most important* is what the teacher singles out as her *big concern.* The music teacher focused on pacing.
5. The *best guide* is the sum total of the Agenda. Its length and content are a total communication pattern. After all, you've asked her to analyze her own classroom situation. The Agenda is her way of telling you not only what her strengths and weaknesses are, but how much she's really willing to tell you.

Always keep in mind, ZA, that my major premise is ultimate self-supervision. In addition to mastering the Retelling step, the teacher needs to learn the process of honest self analysis. Therefore, your role is to listen, to reflect, to clarify, to support, because these are acts one can perform on oneself. You don't attack, because you don't want to teach her to attack herself.—My experience with all the recorded POC's I've heard is that the kind of listening I'm discussing is a most difficult response to elicit from trainees.

So my first answer to my own question about where to begin the Discussion is to listen and observe.

My second answer is that you "read" what the teacher is saying and doing.

When I transcribed the music lesson POC, I had the choice of cleaning up her conversation and mine by omitting the hesitations (hm, uh, ah, etc.), the repetitions, the unfinished sentences. You wouldn't have known that I had done so. I didn't do it–in fact, I wish I could have inserted the whole audiotape into the text–I didn't do any of that just so you would get as as much of the flavor of the POC as cold print permits. So, if you listen to every utterance, if you observe bodily movements and facial expressions, they too will tell you what the Agenda and the Discussion mean to the teacher.

A third answer is to try to determine what the teacher needs. The music teacher needed support. She *has* good rapport with students. She *does* know her musical material (despite the pre-discussion of the Van Gogh song, which both of us studiously avoided). She plays the piano and sings beautifully. I project that she would have scored well on Scholarship and Meaningfulness, but not very well on Structure, if I could have seen a larger segment of her instructional program. She's conflicted: "I always think that I should be having the children moving and doing more creative things," which she later elaborated into ". . . making or composing a song. Or playing instruments, creating rhythms on instruments, or learning to play the piano . . ." etc.

But if that's what she "always" thinks, why a review of ear-training, a warmup song whose very selection she questions, and why such a poor lead-in to the song about Van Gogh? Well, the cameras and the change in schedule upset her, but she was honest about all but the prelude to Van Gogh in her Agenda.

Therefore, she needed some support from me, and I tried to do that at the start by reassuring her that she needn't be self-critical. She could convert her sensitivity, to herself and to her students, by putting her threshold for boredom on a tighter leash.

> You're saying, NS, that you did all this consciously during the POC, that it's not a Monday-morning-quarterback rationalization of what you did do? And if the answer to my double question is yes and then no, how could you have exercised that much control, and can you teach it to me?

I say, for the third time, that Cogan is so right. You can't learn clinical supervision (or being a doctor, lawyer, Indian chief . . . and teacher) from a book. The last question I put into your mouth, ZA, is one of the final questions ZA's ask me, after my demonstrations and their POC's. The answer is: yes, it's a conscious act and you can learn it. Even in just three practice POC's I have found two or three ZA's in each class who've made a remarkable adjustment to the RAD cycle. I attach no scholarly or legal evidence; you'll have to take my word for it.

> OK, I reserve judgment. But let's go back to two earlier issues. In my initial reaction to the POC I noted that you ended with the suggestion about her threshold. How can a well-polished-mirror-supervisor make any suggestions at all?

My major objective for Step III (Discussion) is to model a supervisory role which the teacher can ingest. Therefore, I try to show her how one can combine her own insights (her Agenda) into a deeper level of insight. And please note this, ZA: I didn't suggest any very specific actions, such as how to bring students into a song (after playing the introduction) without using her own voice; how to introduce the Van Gogh song; how to set up a simple-to-complex clapping progression; etc. These are relatively minor alterations in instructional practice; they're not major perceptual changes. Altering them would not have any significant impact on my major obstacle. If she *had* defined Ss and Rs properly, then one R would be an effective "entrance" by Ks after an introduction without her vocal intercession; and two proper Ss would be the introduction to the Van Gogh song and the clapping progression. Therefore, if I can permanently alter her perceptions to include the effective identification of Ss and Rs, then I would be able to note her progress through her own (independent) arrival at the very suggestions I didn't make.

> OK, then the last question (for now) has to do with compliments. Since you now admit that she did some things quite well and that you wanted to provide her with support, why no compliments, no statements of approval?

Most of the students in my supervision classes accept my premises, rationales, and techniques, much as their experiences in their schools provide no exposure to these ideas. They have great difficulty accepting the absence of compliments. My rationale goes like this:

The POC pattern we're discussing is a professional communication between two professionals. Its major objective is the application of the whole process by the teacher to himself during that over 90 percent of the time when the supervisor isn't there. When the teacher applies the RAD cycle to himself, he must be the source of his own bouquets. Ergo, I would be defeating that very purpose by establishing a dependency relationship between teacher and supervisor.

However, I have not been able to convince ZA's of this position. So I do provide support, as in the music POC and in the others you are yet to read. But I also respond to teacher needs. And where I see a need for direct approval, I do provide it. Were I functioning in a school as an administrator/supervisor, I would gradually wean the teacher away from this need. I am thus applying two EG principles:

P157. The learner can become overly dependent on a particular reinforcement or on a singular form of reinforcement.

P158. Learning to monitor his own responses and to reward himself are important steps forward for the student.

My supervision-classroom RAD demonstrations have not been done with one single teacher over a long enough period to either clarify or prove my point.

XII.

Elementary Social Studies — Post-Observation Conference #1

The three POC's in the Elementary Social Studies series were all made with a single teacher (AC), in an elementary school located in a "disadvantaged" area; but the POC's are reflective neither of this fact, nor of the pupils in AC's class, nor of the fact that it is a combination fifth-sixth grade class. Both AC and I knew we were attempting to fulfill my need for material for this discourse. At the same time, I was carrying an unstated obligation to render AC some professional return for her efforts. I think, ZA, that although you will "hear" only three of the five POC's AC and I held, you will see that I made a professional return.

AC had been a student of mine in a masters-level course, but had not been exposed to either the Empirical Grid (EG) or the Primitive Assessment Tool (PAT) prior to the POC's. I had tried to use ZA's (students in supervision courses) as "subjects," but I decided that their interactions with me would not be parallel to those you, ZA, would encounter, should you be convinced enough to try using the RAD (Retelling-Agenda-Discussion) cycle with teachers unfamiliar with my whole approach. So AC, in that sense, is a "fresh subject." But she did have over four years of teaching experience when our POC's began.

I deliberately avoided learning anything about AC's class, school, administration, instructional program, etc., because the RAD cycle can function effectively without such knowledge. When you apply RAD in your school, ZA, you will have the added advantage of full briefings in all relevant areas, so your application should be even more effective.

Finally, I must confess in advance that I made some tactical errors at various points in my conferences with AC. Since I'm going to let you read the transcripts and react to them before I make any comments, you will have first crack at spotting my transgressions.

But why didn't you use un-flawed POC's, NS?

For a number of reasons, ZA:

a. To demonstrate some of the errors one can make.
b. To show that the procedures have sufficient leeway, so that making such errors does not vitiate the whole effort.
c. To demonstrate how tempting it is to be the usual supervisor, who feels a need both to sit in judgment as well as to be the source of valuable suggestions to the teacher.
d. To prove that a supervisor (NS) brought up under what I now think of as the "old way" of conferring with teachers, has yet to rid himself of the urge to talk more than the teacher.

The major positive reason is in the outcomes of these particular POC's, whose results speak for themselves.—So here's POC #1. It begins with a full transcription of the notes I took as I observed.

	Audrey C . . . . . . 26 Ks P.S. . . . . Rm. . . . . Class 5/6 Combination 2/--/7-
1030	(When I came in I was not recognized nor greeted—as per my request of AC. AC was just switching Ks from one pattern to another. Ks sat quietly, reading or working from reading materials. AC had an individual K at her desk and was giving him reading instruction. Ks not only quiet, but actually at work.) (Room well decorated with pictures of well-known paintings, each labeled. Over front blackboard is a full-length display of "Famous American Authors" in the form AUTHOR Famous Works Clothing closet bulletin board covered with charts on musical instruments, math, spelling, language arts. Rear wall has very large chart with material showing baboons, at different ages, in different sizes, apparently to scale, with each size titled.

Display table at rear has a K-constructed model of a tropical area, with flora and fauna in paper and clay. Mobiles are suspended from overhead light fixtures.)
(On front blackboard, in extreme right panel, is:)

Schedule
1- Science - Mr. . . . .
2- Math
3- Reading
Group 1-, 2-, 4-] BL
Group 3-, 5-, 6-] Library Books
4- Social Studies
Lunch
5- Music
6- Research

1053 First K back to seat. AC calls another K for individual work.
1104 Instructs all Ks to cease current work and put books away. Ks do so. (*Some socializing now.*) Four Ks come to AC with some issue which is quickly disposed of. (*No sense of tension in the Ks or in AC.*)
07 AC comes to front and center. Now goes back to her desk. Back to front and center. 'Everything back and away.' (*NB-Single quotation marks denote that the quotations are approximate, not precise.*) Ks have nothing on their desks.
08 'OK, we've been studying baboons for a while.' AC reviews roles of troop members by elicitation from Ks. Many volunteers. AC repeats K contributions.
10 Gets the full list of troop members. K asks question re infant classification. AC refers class to chart on rear wall and adds data, orally. 'Now that you know the names of the troop members, you will write clues. Each group will get 20 cards to write.' Reads aloud a sample clue card and a K guesses the troop member to whom the clues refer. AC gets Ks to volunteer an elaboration of why the K was correct.
13 Same procedure with the second clue card.
15 Ks are to write clues. AC specifies such items as age, color, etc. Ks are to do this in groups of 4 or 5, but no more than 5. AC asks them to choose their own groups and Ks begin to move to different locations. AC says that groups may be 3, 4, or 5 in size, but still no more than 5.
1117 Ks now set up in 7 groups.(*Did they group selves by grade?*)

AC explains: Ks will write clues, but the cards will cover a whole baboon troop, with each type of group member represented and in the proper number of each type in the group. K asks re the number of cards. 'Each group gets 20 cards, with clues to be written on the front, and the back left blank. Tomorrow groups will identify from other groups' clue cards, which member is meant.'

20 K asks re each group's functioning. AC lets each group do the task in its own way.

21 Public address announcement. AC and Ks listen.

22 'Any more questions?' Ks ask some questions and AC answers. (*Some restlessness.*)

23 'William has a question. Martin, do you want to listen?' AC gets attention and answers questions. Says she will come around to answer other questions.

24 AC distributes envelopes of cards to each group. Ks begin to talk in their groups, primarily discussing the assignment. AC circulates. Talks to a group; to two Ks; to another group.

27 Volume level of talk subsides considerably as Ks begin to write as well as to talk. AC still circulating. Back to the group she began with. Now to another group. A different group, at which I can hear her. AC asks this group whether they've decided how many cards to write for each troop member before allocating cards to each K. AC moves to another group and seems to ask the same question.

1131 AC now at the 6th of the 7 groups. Cautions some Ks to keep the noise down.

35 Returns to the first group she was with, then to the second group she visited. Back to the first, which has 5 boys. (*Are they 5th graders or poor students?*) (All Ks are obviously motivated to do the task. Why?) (*All doing it without exception. Why?*)

38 AC goes to another group. Reads completed cards.

39 Same with another group; and another.

41 Now goes to the one group she has not visited. Reads their cards. (*Why so late to this group?*)

43 Responds to an individual K. 'When your groups are finished, put the cards into the envelopes. Be sure each group member is represented.' Goes to another group.

44 AC looks at her wristwatch. Goes back to the first group. (*Some Ks have finished; seem to be at loose ends; walk quietly around the room.*) AC goes to another group; another group.

47 Two Ks return from outside the room. AC goes back to first group. To another group. More Ks have finished.

48 'Alright, will everyone sit down, if not already seated.' Ks do so and become quiet. Calls on each group and asks for the status of their work. Most have finished. 'People who have

	finished, choose one K to bring up the envelopes.' The groups who had not finished had one or two cards each left to do.
50	AC signals class by putting lights off and then on. Collects the envelopes. 'I think you found something out by doing this. Some of you found it easier. When you exchange cards tomorrow you will be able to identify clues that other people found. You will see the hierarchy more clearly. Those who haven't finished can complete it in the research period after lunch.'
1152	One girl leaves the room with her coat. AC collects one more envelope. One group still working. The rest come quietly to attention, hands folded.
53	AC sends Ks to clothing closet and then to the line-up for lunch. Class lines up in very good order, with a minimum of talking.
56	AC and class leave the room.

As you can see from my notes, ZA, I was very much impressed with the rapport between teacher and students, especially since AC is a gentle person and seemingly not the usual disciplinarian. The Ks seemed to be ready for the task, and motivated to do so (for reasons not immediately obvious to me). The purpose wasn't clear to me nor did it seem to be clear to a number of the Ks, though they all applied themselves unreservedly. Because I chose not to move around the room, I could not tell how effectively each group functioned, but AC's movements provided some rather clear clues. There would be no feedback until the next day, so the Evaluation subhead was not relevant. But because AC's instructions about the clue cards were not clear to me and because some of the groups seemed to require additional elucidation, I made my major obstacle the Communication unit under the S & R subhead. There are four questions in this unit:

"c. *Communication:* Did the teacher

13. communicate the S situation clearly?
14. clarify the Rs at the outset?
15. ascertain that the Ks knew what Rs to make?
16. present the new learning in a familiar context?"

All four of them were part of my major obstacle.–Now for the text of the POC.

Grade 5-6 Social Studies: POC #1

NS 0000 The procedure that I follow is directed at helping teachers to learn to supervise themselves. The chances are that if you are seen by anybody at all, by a supervisor, it's probably with great infrequency, maybe once a month, maybe twice a year, or some (you know) rather minimal figure. (AC - Umm.) So I've developed this scheme by means of which I hope to teach teachers to supervise themselves; and I use this material in a course that I teach in Supervision. And it's a cycle, because there are other people with cycles; so this is a cycle too, aah, but this cycle contains only three steps. I'm going to ask you, uh, to try to recall . . .

AC Three steps?

NS 0045 Three steps . . . I'm going to ask you to try to recall for me what happened during the Social Studies lesson. But, of course, I have the notes here so that, if I need to, I can refresh your memory. Aah. You're welcome to see what I have at any time . . .

AC It's a lot.

NS 0100 Well, this is description material; you know, what your room looked like (I have a drawing of the room), and so on. [NS leafs through his notes.] You're welcome, you know, to see what's there at any time.–And after you've described it . . . And I'd like you to try to describe it as a third person, in the third person singular. You can talk of yourself as the teacher, Ms. C . . . . ., Audrey, she. Try not to say I. This creates a perspective, a distance, you know, between you and the person who did the instruction. (AC - Umm.) And then I'm going to ask you to list, enumerate without elaboration, what you would say in self-evaluation (what you did well; what worked well; what didn't work well) in any order that it comes to you; but just to list the items, not to elaborate on them; and then I'm going to write them down in these two columns: one is plus, the other is minus. I'm going to decide whether you're making a positive or negative statement; and I'm going to write them down. And then after we're through, after you've given me as many as one item, ten items, as many as you wish, I will read them back to you. That'll end the second part of the cycle. I also want you to do that in the third person singular: you know, the materials were good, the teacher had rapport, whatever–again in the third person singular, not referring to yourself in the first person. After we're through with those two steps, and I've read you the list (which I will call the Agenda), then we'll talk, directly, person to person.

AC OK. (NS - OK?) AC - OK.

NS 0230 So, why don't you go ahead and tell it to me, aah, in enough detail so that if I hadn't seen it I could get an idea as to what I would have seen. Then I'll munch, and you'll get a chance to do it afterwards. OK? (AC - OK.)

AC The teacher told the children to put their various reading materials
0245 away at the end of the reading period, and waited until everyone was
quiet, and then began talking about what they were going to do in
Social Studies today. She elicited from the children the various
members of the baboon troop, which is the topic that they have
been covering in Social Studies; and after she had gotten this list (to
recall in everybody's mind all the members), she told them what
they were going to be doing during this lesson, which was (p) (short
pause) writing clue cards for the various troop members, in a group,
which they would exchange with another group the next day, during
Social Studies. And the purpose was to see if they could (p) really
identify the various troop members by their different roles, or ages,
or whatever, so that the meaning of the troop would be clear to
them. (p) She then told them to choose their own groups (p)
anywhere from three to five members, no more than five members.
The children did so, in a not too orderly fashion. Umm. She then
handed out the envelopes with the cards, (p) gave them some ideas
that they can keep in mind as they were writing the clues, directed
them to write only on the front part of the card, told them that they
could organize the groups in whichever fashion they found success-
ful. (p) Asked if there were any questions. There were quite a few
questions before people actually got started; and then I told them
0505 that I . . . and then the teacher told them [slight laughter in her
voice as evidence of failure to stay with the third person format]
that she would come around and help them if they had problems
while they were working. The activity lasted . . . The teacher's
directions lasted about ten or fifteen minutes and the activity itself
lasted the remaining half hour. Teacher summed up, very briefly, at
the end, and then the lesson was over.

NS OK. AC - OK?

NS Ah, yeah. You, you attempted once to say "I" which is very good
0537 for a first effort, and there was one point where you came close to
the line when you talked about, ah, what the purpose was. Umm. It
0557 was only partially clear to me as an observer what the purpose was,
ahm, and it was only partially clear that you gave them instructions
on the purpose, and what you were saying mostly was what was the
purpose in your mind, on the teacher's mind during this. It's very
difficult to maintain that kind of separation. (But, for a first effort,
it was very, very good.) The whole point of this is, Audrey, that if
you and I do this more than, you know, this once, as soon as I see
that you can recall a lesson in great detail, you'll just quickly
summarize it, in two or three sentences, and that'll be the end of it;
because the idea is not to do it over and over again, but to see
whether a teacher can accurately recall. Once a supervisor is clear
that a teacher can accurately recall, there's no point in rehearsing it
over and over again. OK? (AC - OK.) As you munch (and don't

worry about it because it will give you time to think between bites), umm, try to tell me, in any order that comes to mind (p) (and remember: no elaborations) the points (AC - Umm.) you want to make about the lesson.

AC In first or third person? NS - In third person, yes.

AC The teacher was prepared and had materials ready. (p) (NS - Yes.)
0714 Umm. The lesson (p) . . . The teacher thought it was a good idea to work in groups in this particular lesson because it lends itself to group work rather than individual work.

NS Well, I don't know that . . . That's what you think was on the
0746 teacher's mind. What you're saying is that doing this kind of thing in groups was, was effective. (AC - H'm.) Alright. (P) (long pause) OK? Take your time. (p)

AC It is very difficult to put it in the third person at this time, at this
0813 point.

NS Alright, if you can't, you can't.

AC Ah. Looking back, I'm not sure if too much time was wasted in the
0821 way they got into groups. (P) The method of, of choosing their own groups was purposely done that way, but . . . and I don't know if that can be done in a more efficient manner (if they're choosing their own groups) or not, but a little bit too much time was wasted, I thought, at that point. (NS - Uh-hm.) From what you said before, I don't know if the purpose of the activity was clear to them. It was clear in my mind. I'm not sure if I expressed it either well, well enough, or perhaps even at all, in so many words, to them. I thought I [p—as she realizes that she's using first person] (NS - Go ahead.) I thought I gave enough directions before we started, but considering the amount of questions that there were, umm, it seemed that something wasn't clear enough at the beginning. You know, perhaps I could have, could have said more.

NS You're elaborating now, Audrey, on the main issue.

AC Once they got into the groups, some of the groups, uh, really needed
0938 more help than others, but that's as far as I know to be a fact. I think the groups worked well. I was glad I did it that way. Umm. I wish I had left a little bit more time at the end to tie it together and tell them what was going to happen tomorrow. (P) (P) I felt, I felt comfortable walking around (NS - Uh-huh.) answering their questions and helping them where necessary, but that's about all I can contribute right now.

NS (P) Did you find this a rather difficult thing to go through the first
1036 time?

AC Yeh, I did.

NS Alright. I meant to ask you earlier: were you comfortable with my presence?

AC I'm glad you came in earlier and were sitting there, rather than just walking in for the Social Studies, 'cause I almost forgot you were there (NS - Yah.), after a while.

NS It also gives me time, 'cause after all I'm not your regular supervisor.
1058 I don't know what you do. I don't even know why this is a 5-6 class, and I'm not going to ask this. It's not germane. I like to come in earlier because it gives me a chance to put a teacher at ease, to look around for myself to get a feel for what's going on. You haven't travelled around to as many classrooms as I have, so you aren't aware of what one can see by seeing, you know. (AC - H'm.) So, while you eat, let me read back to you the Agenda you gave me. Ah.
1141 You said that the, that you had prepared–I'm going to talk to you directly–that you had prepared, you were prepared, and that you had the materials ready. I consider that a positive statement. You thought that the working in groups was effective, ah, but you also thought that maybe, that the kids took too much time to get into the groups, that the method you chose for having them group themselves might not have been as effective, at least in terms of time, if that's a measure. You weren't certain that the purpose was clear in the students' minds and you said that was sort of triggered by a comment I had made before. Then you went back to saying that the groups worked well, ah, but that some needed more help than others; that you should have left more time at the end for a summary of what was accomplished and projected into tomorrow; ah, but that you felt comfortable circulating from group to group and answering questions. (p) You look quizzical.

AC Hearing them in that order just sounds (p) . . .

NS That's the order in which you said them.

AC I know. I know. Hearing it read back, it . . . I jumped around a lot. I can't . . . (p) In other words, what I said about the lesson (p) jumped from my feelings, to the work, to the method. I don't know. It probably doesn't make any difference.

NS (overlapping the last sentence) It doesn't make any difference
1322 whatsoever, and it's not a problem. (AC - OK.) Alright. (P) You made a couple of statements about which you had reservations. Umm. Of the seven statements you made, three of them deal with
1415 groups. First you said you thought working in groups was effective. Then you said maybe they took too much time to get into them. Then you said that the groups worked well. Some needed more help. And even your last statement is basically associated with the grouping idea: that you felt comfortable going around and working with groups. (AC-Right.) Oh, I think it's fair to say that of the seven statements you made, uh, four, more than half, are concerned with the whole grouping idea. Ah. Is this the first time your kids have gone into groups this way. Audrey?

AC The first time they've gone into groups this way. Usually . . .

NS Let me ask the question in two parts: Is this the first time they've gone into groups? Or the first time they've gone into groups this way?

AC It's the first time they've gone into groups this way.

NS Can you tell me about the first time they've gone into groups? That is, I shouldn't say that. They've apparently experienced grouping before. (AC - Yah.) How did the way of going into them today differ from the way they went into them in the past? Because that's what you were unhappy with.

AC They were allowed to choose . . .

NS This is in the past or in the present?

AC In the present. Today they were allowed to choose any group
1527 member they wanted and there was no directive where to sit or anything of the like. Other group work that they had done has either been fifth graders separated from sixth graders or just by tables, and being told, you know, you sit at Table 1, you sit at Table 2. In other words, I've always chosen the groups that they worked with. Today was the first time they worked completely on their own. I mean, they worked out the groups completely on their own.

NS Ahm. This is the first time you've granted them this much leeway, is
1604 what you're saying? (AC - Yah.) Ahm. Why today? Why not yesterday? Why not tomorrow? I mean, you know, why not two weeks ago or three weeks from now? What led you to decide that at this point they were ready to make this choice?

AC Because one of the negative points on that past grouping, other
1625 than . . . Separating fifth and sixth graders is totally different, because that has to do with, you know, the grade level of work. But, in the past, one of the negative points has been that group members have friction with each other. And why today? I don't know. Because it was just a group situation that I knew was going to happen and I figured: why not today, you know. Seeing what would happen when they worked with people they wanted to work with. (NS - Uh-huh.) I think today's grouping was really . . . It couldn't have succeeded if they didn't interact completely, that I felt that this would be a good time to see.

NS Perfectly logical. So why are you unhappy with it as a first effort? It
1715 didn't take very long. (AC - Umm.) Seeing that they were choosing, they chose rather rapidly.

AC Did they?

NS H'm? Yes. I can, I kept time, uh. I kept time. Part of my system is
1729 that I record time, (AC - OH!) so I know when each thing happened. Now, you began with the groups . . . umm . . . You said to them, ahm . . . [NS is searching through his notes.] You came to the front of the room at seven minutes after 11 by my watch, and you waited a little bit, went back to your desk, came back to the front. You said: Everybody, put your things away. At 11:08 you said: OK, we've been studying baboons. You went into the story. Then you elicited the list of the troop members; ah, you read them the two clues; and at, at, in nine minutes, in nine minutes time from the time

you began your explanation, not from the time you told them to get into the groups . . . In fact, you said . . . at 11:15 you were still explaining and in about (AC - Two minutes?) less than two minutes time they were in their groups. This is the value of keeping this kind of a record, you see; so that your conception of how much time it took them is skewed. (AC - Umm.) By being an active participant in the situation, you couldn't tell. You didn't stand there and say: two minutes. So, it took them very little time, actually. For a first effort I thought it was quite good. (p)

AC I thought it took them longer than that.

NS Well now, you have a wrist watch, so you can keep time. You might,
1906 as a matter of curiosity, knowing what I observed today, if you do this again, see how much time it does take, and you'll get a feeling for how much time it takes, since you now have a standard against which to work. (AC - OK.) So that takes care of how much time it took. Ahm. You said: the method. What was the, your criticism of the method? (p)

AC Umm. Just in the group that sat over here. There seemed to be a
1940 little arguing about who was going to be allowed in the group. But that was, that was . . .

NS This group? (AC - Yah.) I made a number of notes. I find it
1952 interesting. You went to that group first. I called it Group #1 in my records, not knowing what their numbers were, because you later . . . because apparently they had numbers. (AC - Right.) But I noticed that you gave this group more attention than any other, in terms of the number of times as you circulated you came back to them. I also found it interesting that after you'd been to all of the groups, all but one of the groups at least once (AC - Umm.) and this one two or three times, you finally came to (AC - To that group.) to this group, which seemed to need no help whatever anyway, but you came to them last. Uh. Had you, was that a conscious choice?

AC Yes. Well, (p) I really intended to go around to each group once. I
2035 skipped over that group because that group needed help when I was ready for this group, and then I completely forgot about them, (NS - Umm.) probably because they were working so well (NS - Uh-huh.). But it, it wound up to be a group of girls who I know are conscientious . . .

NS That's exactly what I figured. They looked like they were conscientious workers, so there was no need to pay attention to any of them.

AC The two groups that I found that needed the least help were this
2104 group and that group over there. This group was finished very quickly. (NS - Umm.) One of the things that I'm not going to know until tomorrow is how . . . You know, I read a few of the cards (NS - I noticed that.) and this group had excellent clues, but I'm not going to know what all the clues were until we do it tomorrow, and how

well . . . It's going to be difficult in judging work: are the clues written well and can the other groups just not identify, or is it a question that they weren't good clues to begin with. So that's going to be . . .

NS So *that* you'll find out tomorrow. Umm. But just to give me a little
2147 background: these, this class has been pursuing the study of baboons as a social unit (AC - Right.) and (AC - From the *"Man, A Course of Study."*) . . . Oh, you're using *"Man, A Course of Study,"* with all the films and everything? Very good. It's an interesting course of study; I'm familiar with it. Uh. And you've been using it for some time? (AC - Yes.) Umm. Now you also said you felt comfortable about going around and answering questions. Why did you feel you had to comment? I was curious as to why you made a comment on it, since you had had groups before. Haven't you done this in the past?

AC (p) Yes, well, you just said to mention anything . . . I don't know
2229 why it came into mind.

NS Well, that's why I'm curious.

AC I don't know. Probably because at the beginning you said about . . . if I want to mention rapport or anything. So I just felt that I had. It's not a question of not having it in the past. That's one of the things I also had today.

NS Is it that you're unclear about your role at that particular point? In
2257 the instructional process?

AC On how much, you know . . . if they're really having difficulties, how much should I feed them. Umm. But it worked out well. Some, like I said, some people, really, I wound up saying to them: well, whom are you trying to write about? And then, if I mentioned one or two things, they said, oh yeah, alright, now I'll be able to write a clue, when I mentioned a few points about that particular troop member. But, umm, it worked out well, that I didn't have to say much before they knew what to write.

NS Do you follow any particular train of thought when you go around
2331 to groups? By that I mean: there are a number of possibilities. One can sit down with a group and mainly listen to the interaction process and see how effectively it is functioning, and then just leave them there and going on to another group and waiting to be invited into the interaction, or projecting yourself into the interaction process. In other words, in this particular case you could have gone around to the groupings and checked to see how well they were doing. I don't mean "checked" by asking. By simply listening to see how the interaction process was functioning, and then deciding that it was OK. It wasn't the greatest or the worst, but it was alright, they were making progress and there was no need . . . You were letting them work out their own problem. Ah. Or you could go to a group and find that the interaction process was functioning rather

inadequately and then trying to provide direction. Have you, have you thought that process through?

AC
2435 I really didn't, until I wound up going around, and that's what I ultimately wound up doing with this group, with that group, with the group in the back. Uh. They didn't need any particular help in getting started. This group did. This group gave out cards and were starting to write clues but had never said, you know, how many of each member are we going to write about, who's going to write what. So I found that I really had to sit with them and tell them: make a list of the troop members and decide how many of each member you were going to write, and then . . . you know, so I really directed that group.

NS
2518 I see. Now your explanation originally didn't contain the full explanation that you apparently must have had to give to some of the groups. Some of them were able to work with the instructions you originally gave. You told them that they were to . . . ahm. You first elicited from them, uh, the various troop roles. And once you got them all, you repeated a complete list. And then you asked, some child asked, about infant classifications, and you responded to that. (AC - Right.) Ah. You referred to the chart on the wall back here (NS points to rear wall.), so they could get further clarification. And then you told them they would write clues and you described the cards they would get, ahm, and . . . but it seemed to me at the time, in listening, that considering what they ended up doing, what I was able to hear you say to a group that was sitting near me, it became a little clearer to me what the assignment was, that apparently you entertained them with questions and at some point you cut if off and let them go on and then decided to answer the questions; you said you answered the questions as you went around.
2639 What I'm trying to say is that, ah, there wasn't a full explanation (AC - At the beginning.) at the beginning, see, and that some students, therefore, needed further assistance, while others understood the shorthand and grasped the idea quickly (you read a couple of cards and, you know, explained them), whereas others needed more assistance. (AC - Umm.) Again, the question is: how far had you projected all of this? Had you decided for yourself in advance what instructions you were going to give, before the students went into the groups?

AC
2723 Yes, I, I, and I thought that I had decided enough, you know, that what I wound up saying was going to be enough, but I found . . . that's what I said before . . . I found that there were so many questions once they started the actual grouping, that my preliminary explanations could have been clearer, or might have been clearer, not necessarily longer, but clearer.

NS But clearer. What does that suggest for the future? (p) If anything?

AC That I should put more time into it and time not in a way that . . . I

2800 should put myself in their shoes, perhaps, and think of the questions that they'll come up with, relating them to my explanation at the beginning, you know. Alright, here's my explanation. Once I say it, what kind of questions might they have? And then try to rethink what I'm going to start out saying.

NS Alright. That's one possibility. Are there any other possibilities? (P)
2830 (P)

AC I don't know.

NS Well, you used the second possibility today. What did you do?

AC Give an explanation and then say: if there are any more questions, I'll answer them as I'm walking around.

NS And so, when you found that the initial instructions weren't fully
2856 adequate for every group, you answered each group's questions individually, which is what you did today. A third possibility would be, ah, that you could go around quickly and scan each group to see what problems arise, ask the class to cease activities for a bit, and say: The following questions have arisen in a number of groups (AC - Umm, umm.) and, ah, here they are. Let's address ourselves to them, you know . . . So that if you didn't have, if your explanations weren't totally clear at the beginning, you could either come by a clearer understanding for each group by addressing each group or you could save time, for every group, by trying to see what problems they were encountering on a quick survey, stopping class, answering the questions, and then having the groups go back again. That would save individual explanations in each of the groups. (AC - Umm.) I'm
2957 not saying that one method is superior to another. I'm simply saying these are strategies of various kinds (AC - Right.) and there is, there is no necessarily greater merit to an initial crystal clear explanation, (AC - Umm.) and then letting them work. Ah. They're getting a task, ah, and they try to work around it. Then as their questions, as questions come up, they either try to resolve them or you answer them and it gives them another opportunity to resolve their own procedure, which in itself is a learning process. (AC - Umm.) Do you
3032 follow what I'm saying? (AC - Uh-huh.) So, depending on what your objectives are in group work, apart from the actual product, there's a process involved here (AC - Umm.), and if you're concerned as much with the process as the product (AC - Uh-huh.), then it is possible to play around with the process: a brief explanation; see who gets it, so they can work on their own without listening to a long explanation, an explanation that's too long for them; and giving attention to individual members.

AC So that's why I cut off those initial questions. They were getting
3057 jumpy and they weren't listening to each other anyway.

NS OK, so you can, you can play with this, if you continue using this group arrangement, to see what is the optimal distribution of time between initial questions . . . answering questions for each group

individually, or again answering questions for the whole group after
the initial explanation, and that will begin to tell you how much
explaining you must do so that most of them can get started (AC -
Uh-huh.), so you can minimize, you know, so you can keep that to
an optimum minimum; and then those who need special attention
can get the special attention while the others are already to work, at
3147 which time you can discover what the best pattern is. (AC - Umm.)
Now, ahm, let's talk about this issue. You said that it was triggered
in your mind by what, by the comment I made earlier, ahm, that it
might not have been clear in the students' minds what the whole
thing was about (AC - Umm.). (P) I have never seen you teach
before, so I don't know how you function. How do you decide in
what terms to project the purpose or the objectives for an activity to
a class?

AC (P) I don't know if I understand what you mean.

NS Well, when you give students their assignment, whether it's in
3236 reading or math or social studies or whatever, some certain amount
of time has to be devoted to projecting instructions as to how to
perceive and then finally to attack the tasks. [Bell rings.] (AC - Five
more minutes.) (p) How do you decide how much instruction to
give?

AC (P) I don't know how to answer. It really depends on what they're
3313 going to do, or on how complicated what they're going to do is, I
mean. Hopefully, my purpose of doing it is what I want them to
finally learn through the whole thing. But, umm, direct it just as
much as I think they'll be able to do in order to do the individual
work or the group work.

NS I'm not asking the question very well, though you've answered it as
3341 best as you can given the way I've asked the question. Let's take
today as a case in point. What they are finally to do . . . the ultimate
objective was for each of them to produce twenty cards. (AC -
Right.) Each card was to contain a clue that would identify a group
member by role, by age, by sex. (AC - Right.) Ah. And that the sum
total of twenty cards produced was to make certain, was to include a
reference, a clue, at least one clue for each troop (AC - Troop
member.), troop member, ah, so that the major, the major task was
to produce twenty cards, but the cards were to include clues for
each role of troop membership; (AC - Yes.) and since there were
fewer troop members than twenty, therefore there could be more
cards per troop member . . .

AC Well that, yeah. Right.

NS And the more complex the role of the member, the more clue cards
3447 there might be for that particular one. (AC - Right.) So that, ahm,
this kind of a breakdown of the task (AC - Umm.) should have been
a key to the projection of the instructions: A. How many troop
members, how many troop roles are there? Seven, eight, whatever

the number is; but there were twenty cards. So if there were ten troop roles, then there could be an average of two cards per troop member.

AC Oh, no. That wasn't even clear to you. One of the things that they
3523 learned was, umm, that even though the central male . . . I don't know if I'm being too specific right now . . . even though the central male plays the most important part in the troop, there aren't more central males in the troop. They were supposed to come up with a ratio of troop . . . in other words, each baboon troop that we studied has a certain proportion of troop members, um, not necessarily the most dominant troop member has, has . . . there aren't more central males in the troop than there are infants, even though they're the most important. They were supposed to remember, or figure out as they were going along, the ratio; and that's how they were supposed to divide the twenty cards.

NS They already know that from the past study, ah, the hierarchy
3617 within the troop? (AC - Right.) Then what you are saying . . .

AC And this was supposed to make it a little clearer.

NS . . . that the higher a troop member is on the hierarchy, the more
3627 likely it would be to have more clue cards for that member. (AC - Right.) And they were to have understood this. (AC - Right.) OK. What I'm trying to say is that in projecting the objective for a group's assignment, it seems to me that these various ingredients (AC - Umm.) need to be clarified. You identified all the roles. If you had also identified the hierarchy, it might have been clearer to the weaker group or groups what the assignment was. (AC - Umm.) Do
3705 you follow what I'm saying? (AC - Yes.) So that if you are clear in your mind about these various criteria by means of which you will judge the twenty cards, then these criteria are projected in advance or even put on the board (AC - Uh-hm.) so they can judge whether their division of the cards or their allotment of cards to each troop role or member would come close to the hierarchical pattern.

AC In other words, when the groups get the cards, when the other
3730 groups get somebody's cards tomorrow that's going to be one of the things we're going to look at. In this particular troop that another group made up, are all the troop members not only represented, but represented in the right proportion? (NS - Alright, but you see . . .) Will the troop be able to survive, let's say, in the savanna?

NS . . . what I'm saying is this: if that's a criterion to be used tomorrow
3754 for the group's work today, then that criterion should have been projected initially. (p) That would be part of your objective. So there are two criteria so far. One, that every troop member is to have at least one clue card, and two, that the number of cards per troop member should bear some relationship to his hierarchical status within the group, because those are the criteria you're going to apply (AC - Tomorrow.) tomorrow, and that wasn't clear as far as I could

3830 see. (AC - Ummm.) See what I'm getting at? (AC - Yah.) Alright. Since the time is close to being up, ahm, let me see if I can summarize what I was trying to do. One of my objectives in conferences of this kind is related to the fact that even if I teach people to supervise in this fashion, they still can't come with much greater frequency than they come now; though obviously they should come with greater frequency than they do now. But since there's a lot of time between observations (AC - Umm.), that if the teacher is going to self-supervise, that the analysis of any one lesson is so generalized that the outcomes can project to a number of lessons. Follow? (AC - H'm.) So, I was trying to get you to discuss grouping in general terms, so that it would have some bearing for grouping in the future, the time element, for example (how long it takes to get into groups), your role vis-a-vis each group, the projection of instructions (which applies to group work or to any other kind of work), ahm, and the topic we didn't get a chance to discuss: whether there was enough time at the end, (AC - Umm.) how one times, how one spreads the time out in a given instructional session. So that we can come up with statements which themselves project over a longer range of time. Do you follow?

AC I follow.

NS Now, as to the matter of having enough time left at the end: had you decided in advance what you would have wanted to summarize?

AC I wanted to . . . Well actually, one of the things I wanted to say at
4013 the end probably could have been said at the beginning, in that tomorrow, you know, we will see not only can you identify from these clues, but see if the troop will be able to, like I said, survive in a savanna. Are the troop members represented enough? (NS - Uh-huh.) Too much? You know, are there too many infants or whatever? That was something that I never said at the beginning. So that's going to be difficult to do then, tomorrow. But that's what I intended to come up with, you know, why they wrote these cards and what we were going to do with them tomorrow . . . I had intended to stop the whole thing at 10 to 12, and if all the groups were like that group or this group, we could have done that. But I saw that so many . . . two or three groups still had so many cards to do that I just kept them writing. I don't know that that's ever really, um, able to be resolved; there are always slower ones than . . . you know, some people are always done quicker than others.

NS Well, this is a general problem that all teachers have. When you
4123 assign a number of students a given task, some will complete it sooner than others, and part of the general planning in any instructional session is to allow for the pace at which different groups or different individuals work, (AC - Uh-hm) and deciding at what point, what's the optimal point, at which to stop for a summary, knowing that some had finished and been finished for

> some time and some would still be working, and thats a difficult decision to make. (AC - Umm.) But one has to experiment with it to see. Another possibility, of course, is to have a clock in the room, which unfortunately you don't have, and to say: Look, you're going to work in groups until X time and whatever you finish you finish. But that's the target time; and then we will summarize; and whatever you haven't finished you will finish at this and this time. You told them later that they could do it this afternoon before the research period, but that again was something that could have been in the initial instructions. (AC - Yah.) But it's a general problem. It's not just specific to this particular lesson. (AC - No.) Alright. Let's just take the minute that we have (4235) . . . (I asked for her reaction to the supervisory method, not realizing that the tape had run out.)

I'd like to begin with your notes, if I may.

By all means, ZA.

You came in at 1030, but began your "observation" at 1053. Why?

Teacher AC was not a volunteer. I was impressed with her involvement in the course in which she was my student and asked her whether she would want to be a "subject." She hesitated for a number of days. She admitted to being rather uneasy about adult visitors and yet sensed that our interaction could benefit her as much as me. So she finally agreed to serve. We also agreed that I would appear in her room prior to the start of the SS lesson, particularly at my first observation, so she would have time to forget I was there. We discussed this matter briefly between 1036 and 1141. Please note that I took on some of the onus for appearing early, saying that it served me as well as it had served her.

OK. Do I recall accurately: what you put in parentheses and underline in your notes [*italics in this book*] are those items which might be some bases for your Agenda?

That's right, ZA. But since I write them down as they occur to me, as I am then (at that moment) reacting to the situation, their meanings and values are relative, not absolute. As I apply the PAT to the entire lesson these notations take on their appropriate meanings and values. You know by now, having read the POC text, that only some of those notations surfaced in the interaction.

That's true.—You provide a very sketchy application of the PAT as a kind of coda to your notes, NS. Is that a model for us?

No, ZA, not at all. You can't tell from the time markers on the POC, but there were no more than about 10 minutes of elapsed time between the dismissal at 1156 and the start of the POC. For reasons of mutual accommodation and because I could not be as accessible to AC as a real supervisor on the staff, we agreed to an arrangement for all my visits: Social Studies would be taught the last period before lunch and the POC would be done during lunch. The real supervisor should arrange for a sufficient hiatus to allow him to make a careful application of the PAT and to make a decision on major obstacles.

Alright. Since I've already had one practice session with the PAT on the math lesson, I can see that I'll need more than 10 minutes. Now I have some questions and comments about the POC itself.

May we regard your allotment of time to the various parts of the POC as a model of some significance?

No, not in any specific sense. Here's a breakdown of the POC:

Instructions to AC	4:22
AC does R	2:52
AC does A	3:22
Digression re NS presence	1:05
AC and NS do D	30:54
	42:35

There are only two conclusions I'd like you to draw, ZA: that step D should take up the largest segment of time; and that even in a first POC, with a teacher totally unfamiliar with RAD, one can give D this largest segment. I make no recommendations on specific allotments for each of the three steps.

If you make no specific allotments and if (as I assume) you don't sit there watching the clock, NS, how do you avoid long segments for R and A?

Largely by seeing to it that there are no judgmental statements and digressions during R and no elaborations of Agenda items when I elicit A. That automatically leaves most of the time for D.

> I see. Going back now to the beginning of the POC, I have two procedural questions: do you regularly make drawings of the rooms you visit? and Would you really show your handwritten notes to the teachers you observe?

Keep in mind, ZA, that I'm not a "real" supervisor, that I observe in a number of schools and classrooms each year, and that I would lose track of some of the data if I didn't make sketches of the seating arrangements and the availability of boards, displays, centers, etc. A "real" supervisor in a single school is on the scene and needs no such reminders.

Showing my notes is a different matter, one about which I've changed my mind. Most teachers whom I meet in POC's don't ask to see my notes. The few that have made remarks about them generally have gotten the same offer I made AC just before 0100 ("You're welcome to see what I have at any time."), but neither she nor any of the others have ever taken me up on my offer. I have now ceased making the offer. The descriptive material is neutral, of course, and would create no problems, except for deciphering my hieroglyphics. But the parenthetical notations, if seen by the teacher prior to that particular POC, would upset the very concept of the RAD cycle, since the teacher would get a glimpse at my agenda. It's not that my agenda is top secret, which it is in a way, representing as it does my perceptions of the instructional process; it is that the teacher has to learn to be the source of his own Agenda during that over 90 percent of the time when I can't be there to observe. So I think I'm being more honest now by not making any offers.

> Seems logical enough, but I'll have to see how it works for me, NS. Another procedural question is this: I think I recall you saying some time ago that your rereading of the teacher's Agenda begins step D. Yet in your statement which ends before 0230 you say, ". . . I will read them back to you. That'll end the second part of the cycle." It's probably a rather minor issue, NS, but it needs clarification.

It is a minor issue. At the time I did these POC's, that's how my thinking went. I have since changed my mind. The Discussion begins when the teacher ceases to be a 3PS, a "third person singular," which is when she hears what her Agenda sounded like. In fact, AC's reaction (at 1248) to my rereading was instrumental in my change of mind. I now regard the rereading of A as the opening move in D.

> OK. Now, just after the statement I cited above you say: "... you know, the materials were good, the teacher had rapport, whatever ..." You are suggesting two possible Agenda items, both of which she later *does* make part of her Agenda. Again, is this a model for us to follow?

No, ZA, it's the first of my self-confessed transgressions. The immediate stimuli for some of my longer statements in these POC's are AC's non-verbal reactions: the look on her face, her periods of silence, her gestures, etc. I sensed that she didn't quite catch on to my request for an Agenda. So I selected two items that I (as the observer) could identify as positive features: she *did* have good materials, and her rapport with the Ks was most impressive. My *present* thinking is as follows: (1) The best ploy is to suggest nothing. If the teacher doesn't know where to begin, the supervisor can ask something like, "Have you ever seen someone else teach? What are some criteria you applied in deciding how effective that instruction was?" As soon as the teacher offers some, you can tell her to apply them to her situation. (2) A second tactic is to be ready with Agenda items that could apply to some other kind of instructional situation. For example, you might imagine having observed a gym class where it would be appropriate to comment that the procedures for putting on sneakers, gym suits, etc., were well-rehearsed and took a minimum of time; that the teacher had isolated a particular sub-skill for special attention before re-integration for use in some game like basketball; and so on. As you can well imagine, musical examples come easily to my mind.–Of course, once a teacher becomes even partially knowledgeable about the PAT, there is no longer any problem here.

> I'm still not totally clear on your role during each step of the POC. You made a deep impression on me with that reflective mirror metaphor, yet you seem quite active in both the Retelling and the Agenda steps. At 0537, for example, you tell her that she veered from

the 3PS format, and at 0557 you even make a judgment about what turns out to be your major obstacle. Would you resolve this seeming contradiction for us, please?

As I've said before, ZA, the teacher needs guidance, feedback, and reinforcement to achieve mastery of Retelling and of producing an Agenda consisting of short, unelaborated statements. Therefore, the supervisor is more of an activist in these two steps. Ergo my statement at 0537.

The one at 0557 is my second, and much more significant, transgression. I heard this tape within an hour after AC and I recorded it. I couldn't then nor can I now determine why I violated my own strictures. She needed correction on the issue of saying what was on her mind, which an observer could not know; but I had no right to make any judgments at that point. Overeagerness, maybe. I don't know. I do know that it's wrong.

Then your transgression lies in going beyond providing feedback on how well the teacher did a 3PS Retelling without her making statements which only she, as the activist rather than as the observer, would be able to make.

Yes, ZA, that's all I should have done, but didn't.

Then let's move on to the next point. At 0714 she begins her Agenda with the first of your suggested items, pauses, hesitates, then makes another activist, rather than observer, statement. At 0746 you transform it into an observer statement. At 0813 she finds it difficult to continue in 3PS. You forgive her. And at 0821 she resumes doing A, in a mixture of activist and observer formats, mostly activist. At just before 0938 you caution her not to elaborate, so she completes her Agenda entirely in first person. What do you make of all this, NS?

One of the reasons I chose to use AC's tapes is that some problems arose in them which I had not encountered, to the same degree, in other POC's. This makes the tapes atypical, but gives us an opportunity to clarify the usual by facing up to the unusual. It should be clear now why I transformed AC's first Agenda item: she needed instruction on how to speak as an observer. But she was unable to do so. Had I stopped to instruct her at greater length, we would likely have had a very poor Agenda. So I gave higher priority to her Agenda than to the 3PS format. Since I could not determine, on the spot, why she was having this difficulty, I tabled it for the moment. (The issue gets more extended treatment in another POC.) I cautioned her not to elaborate at 0938 for reasons we've already discussed, ZA.

> That's right. I remember now. You want an Agenda free of elaborations.—After you read the Agenda back to her, you note (at 1415) that four of her seven statements deal with grouping and both of you go into a long development of this issue. OK. I *also* can see that four items deal with grouping, but that raises a new problem. When we discussed the music lesson you said that when a teacher's Agenda overlaps your major obstacle(s) you're "in luck, because I have direct access to the introduction of my major obstacle into the Discussion." (p. 257) So here's AC playing right into your hands by taking up your transgressional hint and listing the communication of purpose as her item 4. So why didn't you begin with that?

Good question, ZA, good question. Before I answer, let's look at her Agenda in an exact transcription of my notes.

+	−
1-T was prepared and had materials ready.	3-Maybe Ks took too much time getting into groups.
2-Working in groups was effective.	4-Was the purpose clear in Ks' minds?
5-Groups worked well, but some needed some help.	6-T should have left more time at the end.
7-T felt comfortable circulating and answering questions.	

Her #1 was a direct reflection of my cue, so it was not worth any consideration. Although she could easily have followed that up with my second cue and made her fourth item #2, she didn't do so. Her real desire was to discuss grouping, so she commented on grouping in four items. I would have been utterly insensitive to her needs had I begun with my major obstacle. The teacher's explicit and implicit needs are the prime criteria for determining which Agenda items are chosen for discussion.

As it turned out, I had read AC accurately. What's more, she wanted feedback on what turned out to be an experiment, a new grouping arrangement in which she was relinquishing what was for her some substantial amount of control, and, most significantly, an experiment conducted during my first visit to a teacher who was very uneasy with other adults in her room. One of the indications of how unsure AC was about the experiment was that she made an unreal estimate of the time it took the Ks to choose new groups. As Seagoe says in P186 (p. 65), the learner who is succeeding underestimates the passage of real time: ". . . time seems short . . ." The one who is failing (or is as apprehensive as AC must have been) overestimates. For him ". . . time seems long . . ." Fortunately, my time notations made it possible for me to give her precise, objective reassurance. I could say more than, "Oh, it really didn't take very long." In fact, ZA, I even complimented her: (at about 1900) "So, it took very little time, actually. For a first effort I thought it was quite good." AC needed reassurance. I gave it.

> But weren't you rather abrupt (at 1906) about dropping time as as issue? ("So that takes care of how much time it took.") And where does "the method" issue come from? It's not on her Agenda.

I made a big to-do a long ways back in our discourse, ZA, about the relative weights I assign to form and substance. At 0821, when AC was giving me her Agenda item #3, she made two statements about "time was wasted." Sandwiched in between them was an incomplete judgment about the method of choosing groups. I could have made that a separate Agenda item. However, since she seemed to see time and method as a single entity, I kept to her perception. But once I could divorce time from method, I moved quickly to do so, because the experiment was not concerned with how long it took, but with the new method for choosing. For me, time was form; the rationalization of the method would be substance.

But (at 1940) she says two sentences about method and is into her third when you cut her off. Is this a third transgression?

Yes, though not as serious as the second. Again, I was over-eager. Her last Agenda item had puzzled me ever since she uttered it. The statement came after two long pauses, as a kind of after-thought (at about 1015). To say that AC "felt comfortable walking around answering questions and helping them where necessary" implied, to me at any rate, that she had felt either uneasy in the past or more at ease today than she had expected to feel. Either way, it raised an issue.

But I postponed facing it until we had dealt with Agenda items 2, 3, and 5: working in groups was effective; the Ks took too much time getting into groups; and the groups worked well, but some needed some help. AC told me she had used grouping assignments before today's experiment. Surely she must on those occasions have moved from group to group to answer questions and render assistance. So why item 7?

Although I made a specific inquiry into the item at just before 2229, we were actually discussing it from about 1930 to about 2110. The topic was her criticism of the method, which led to my description of how she had moved from group to group with what frequency, and her account of her interactions. AC said she had planned to visit each group once, but forgot about her plan as she responded to different needs in different groups. I wasn't aware of it during the POC, but as I now read the transcript, doesn't it strike you, ZA, that AC tries to close off further discussion of how she circulated and what happened?

Perhaps. At 2104 she uses two sentences to sum up which groups needed the least amount of attention. You say "Umm." Then she changes the topic. She won't know "until we do it tomorrow" how effectively the clues were written. "It's going to be difficult in judging the work," she says. "Are the clues written well and can the other groups just not identify, or is it a question that they weren't good clues to begin with." And here *again* you close off an avenue of discussion. For a non-directive-reflecting-mirror you seem to do a great deal of directing, NS. And what's wrong with discussing what she won't know until tomorrow? Wasn't the writing of good clues the very pattern of new responses the Ks were to take on?

That's two questions at a time, ZA, the second of which requires fewer words. On principle I will not discuss what I haven't observed. So yesterday and tomorrow are generally not germane, except as they become relevant to our exploration of teacher perceptions about what it means to teach. The greatest danger of launching into a discussion of either yesterday or tomorrow is that it permits us to escape facing up to today. Yes, I could have said: "You saw a number of the cards. Were the clues written well? If so, why are you concerned with what will happen tomorrow? If not, how will you face that problem?" Which would have violated my principle. We would be projecting to events that had yet to occur and which I would not observe.

I don't follow you, NS. Are you forbidding us to respond to teacher needs for guidance on planning for the future? If so, on what grounds?

No, ZA, I'm not doing that, nor have I any grounds on which to do so even if I wanted to. AC and I were nowhere near ready to face tomorrow. When a teacher and I have fully explored today, there's every reason to respond to a teacher's desire or need to project ahead. AC wasn't asking me to do that with her at this point.—That's the first half of your second question, ZA.

As to your statement that writing good clues was the new response pattern—you're right, it was. Had I considered AC's change of topic a desire for a discussion of the clue cards, we could have talked about it and maybe even worked our way around to how the writing was related to her manner of communicating instructions, which was my major obstacle. But we would then have skipped over my interpretation of the real meaning of her last Agenda item.

You made the comment any number of times, ZA: a transcript is no substitute for personal presence. I *heard* and *saw* AC pause after item 6 on her Agenda. She was hesitant about telling me something that truly concerned her. Then she said something, but what she said was only a reflection of her real concern, not a direct revelation of it. So it had to be exposed to full view.

Now, as to your very fundamental question: do my actions

belie my words? Am I really the non-directive-reflecting-mirror that I tell you to be?

Well, ZA, I may have made a tactical error by assigning a name to my actions. "Non-directive," "reflecting," and "mirror" are names for passive responses to someone else's behavior. And I do want you to adhere to that kind of role as much as possible. Ergo, my self-confessed transgressions. However, my basic aim in the whole cycle is to have teachers take on a new pattern of responses: to Retell honestly, chronologically, and in uncensored detail; to make terse, unelaborated, uncensored, un-withheld Agenda judgments; and to face up honestly to all the judgments via Discussion with a supervisor who is there (in part) to model a pattern for such Discussion. I'm trying to "teach" people something. So I must create and control conditions under which . . . etc. Therefore, when I sense that a teacher is veering from an open confrontation with some basic and/or maybe unpleasant issues, I cease to be non-directive.

> You may be right, NS, about the matter of assigning names to your actions. Non-directive-reflecting-mirror makes it sound as though you are more passive than active; yet you do have an objective which calls for more than passivity on the part of the supervisor.—So, I think I understand, better now than before, what your role is and why you moved AC back to the issue that bothered you: her last Agenda item. And I must say that it does lead to a very fruitful discussion. What I don't see, especially since you had only 10 minutes in which to prepare for the POC, is how you came to be so ready with the three alternatives for projecting instructions. Had you made, in advance, a decision to offer her and discuss such alternatives?

That, too, is a very basic question, ZA. The RAD cycle, when I arrived at it, was actually a rationalization for what I found myself doing (and having to do, in response to teacher input) as I conferred with teachers from that "Phase I" project and beyond. I've also said to you more than once that this is my current view of something or other. I keep observing and conferring with teachers. As I hear the tapes, as my ZA's hear them, I try to understand why I do what I do so as to explain it to myself and my students. I must confess that I can't rationalize every act of mine. I can't tell students why I do what I do every time I do it. To that extent I'm less than effective in arriving at useful guidelines for prospective supervisors.

So I don't know what prompted me to ask (at 2257): "Is it that you're unclear about your role at that particular point? In the instructional process?" The key word is "role," which was my unpremeditated translation of her last Agenda item and the aura surrounding her way of saying it: "(P) (P) I felt, I felt comfortable walking around (NS - Uh-huh.) answering their questions and helping them where necessary, but that's about all I can contribute now."

I'm going to make a point about punctuation here, ZA, a point crucial to further discourse. A recorded POC has no precise punctuation. *I* enter it into transcripts as *I* hear tapes. So maybe AC meant to put the period after ". . . where necessary," so that "but that's about all . . ." would be a complete sentence. *I* heard the whole statement as one long sentence, with a last clause beginning with "but." That implied to me, at the POC (and now), that the clause modified the sentence, not all seven items on the Agenda. Had the clause been meant to serve as a modifier of the whole Agenda, I would have heard: "I felt, I felt comfortable walking around answering their questions and helping them where necessary." Then perhaps a p or a P, plus something like "That's about all I can contribute now." As I heard it, the last clause modified item #7, as if to say: this is my assessment and ("but") I'd rather not go into an elaboration of why I felt that way. This is what I sensed, ZA; it puzzled me; and I assigned it a high valence as a communication from AC. She was conflicted on opening the issue up for further probing and yet, as her response to my "role" question reveals, she was unclear "On how much, you know . . . if they're really having difficulties, how much I should feed them." It was this particular question of mine which turned up a broad, overarching issue: how does one prepare oneself for communicating to students the Rs they're expected to make in such a way that the explanation, in length, detail, and complexity, is optimal for a whole-class lesson with a rather wide range of K aptitude?

What I gather from your long answer to my question, NS, is that you have no precise answer. You seem to shy away from the word, and yet what you do is intuitive. And if it is, then how do I come by it?

My dictionary defines intuition as "the ability to perceive or know things without conscious reasoning." In that sense I perceived, without stopping the POC to think the matter through, that "role" was the issue. I can't offer you a principle on the application of which you would arrive at the same point, ZA. Once again we need Cogan's practicum in which I could discuss your conduct as a supervisor. I've given you all the conscious reasoning that went through my head right at the POC.

Then there's no point in pursuing that matter any further, NS. But there are two final issues that interest me, procedurally. First, from 3627 to 3830 you give her some rather precise directions on how she might have identified the hierarchy within the baboon troop and even suggest having it put on the board, because the criteria she would be applying tomorrow (as the cards are read aloud) weren't clear to you today. So not only do you make a judgment, but you offer two specific suggestions. Why, NS?

When one is trying to sell a new product as a better substitute for an old one, the customer has to be specifically persuaded that the new is in precise ways as good as the old one and even better. So I tend, in initial POC's with teachers (to all of whom my way is absolutely new), to do a bit of what the old does, which is to offer specific suggestions. The thesis is that it takes a little time and experience with the RAD cycle to become satisfied with overarching outcomes which one must translate into specific acts on one's own.

I presume that the judgment you refer to comes at the middle of the 3627 statement, when I say ". . . in projecting the objective for a group's assignment, it seems to me that these various ingredients need to be clarified." And I admit that it is a judgment, but it is also a suggestion.

My intent in having no more than one or two major obstacles is to be able to arrive, in just one POC, at one or two overarching generalizations for the teacher to grasp, to accept, and to implement. Implementation, however, means going from the generalization to some specific application. If RAD is to work, then the teacher must take on the behavior pattern: "I can translate a generalization into specific applications." Where it seems appropriate, I model such a pattern of behavior to the teacher. This was one such model.

> You've not been that direct with me, NS. After persuading me to be a non-directive-reflecting-mirror, you've gradually chipped away at it until there's not much glass left. Why?

First of all, ZA, I hope your metaphor is hyperbole, and that what I've added is a rather carefully constructed frame around it. Whatever I want the teacher to learn, she has to learn by doing it. Ergo, the less I talk and the more I reflect back when I do talk, the more I facilitate the teacher's learning process.

But (in a new paragraph, with a strong accent on the first word), *but* I don't come to a POC empty-headed or empty-handed, ZA. Real ZA's know that I'm a very opinionated person. I've also made that very clear in this discourse, and have built judgments into the Primitive Assessment Tool (PAT) and the Empirical Grid (EG). Were I a real supervisor in a real school, I would have clear commitments to certain kinds of instructional programs, to teacher in-service growth, etc. The very fact that I derive my whole system of assessing teaching from a single definition indicates that I'm hardly likely to accept other definitions unless they can be rationalized as fully as I've rationalized mine. Et cetera, et cetera, et cetera. I come to the POC to teach a teacher, to create and control conditions under which the teacher will take on new patterns of behavior. The single largest process element is "non-directive-reflecting-mirror" because that's the pattern I want the teacher to follow in talking to herself when the supervisor isn't there, as he isn't for over 90 percent of the time. But I also want to achieve each of the goals for each of the three steps, goals that I summarize for you on page 291. To do that, I *control* conditions; I am directing; but only to reach that one or those two overarching generalizations which the teacher may be able to apply to much instruction that I will simply not have time to observe.

> I hear you loud and clear again, NS. But even that statement creates a new problem. You had *one* major obstacle. But when you summarize (at about 3900), it

becomes clear that you discussed items #2, 3, 4, 5, and 7 of her Agenda (having rather ignored #1), and that you will still take time to discuss #6, "T should have left more time at the end." Since you had already dealt with your major obstacle by the time you summarized, why a coda based on #6? And, are we supposed to deal with each and every item on the teacher's Agenda?

No, I don't mean to suggest that you deal with each item. No, the supervisor makes a selection, as I hope to demonstrate in subsequent POC's.

Actually, #6 isn't, strictly speaking, an Agenda item, any more than #7 was. No observer could say: "T should have left more time at the end." An observer might say, negatively: there was no time for a summary; or, the teacher did not elicit a summary. AC's #6 looks to be 3PS in form, but is actually first-person in content. So I asked her, why? and learned that she (not an observer) had projected using more time for a particular kind of summary. Which turned out to be related to our earlier discussion of my major obstacle, in addition to raising a brand new issue: pacing.

The answer, ZA, is to select from the teacher's Agenda. I've already set some criteria. They're in the discussion of the Music POC. But I do feel it important to respond to first-person-content utterances, because they help me build a portrait of the teacher's instructional perceptions.

One final word. On page 291 you asked me "how you came to be so ready with the three alternatives for projecting instructions" and I never answered you.

I've already explained why I came to define teaching in neutral terms (no matter who does it, with whom, under what circumstances, etc.). I see RAD as an equally neutral system. No educator (or educationist) expertise is required for guiding teachers to meet my criteria for effective performance of R and A by the teacher. Someone skilled in non-directive interviewing techniques could play the supervisor's role quite effectively during D. But it takes prior experience as a teacher, plus expertise in educational process and content, to be an effective supervisor of classroom teachers.

Having taught some length of time myself, ZA, I have accumulated a sizeable hoard of ideas, one of which surfaced when AC and I discussed the communication of purpose.

XIII.

Elementary Social Studies — Post-Observation Conference #2

Once again, ZA, here's a transcription of my notes:

Audrey C 27Ks
P.S. . . . . . . Rm. . . . . . .
Class 5/6 Combination 3/--/7-

1030	Room in darkness as I came in. Class had just begun to watch a film. (I could tell by looking at the film cassette, ZA.)
1100	Discussion of Netsilik Eskimos just seen on film. On blackboard were questions put on before film was shown, to which, presumably, the Ks were to pay attention in the film. Discussion consisted of responses to two questions, plus questions raised by Ks or contributions made by them, such as: 'Where did they go to the bathroom?' (*Ks were talkative at times and had to be called to order, but it was not a matter of discipline, merely enthusiasm for the topic.*)
10	Discussion still in progress.
12	'OK. We're going to be studying about three parts of Eskimo life: (*Ks restless.*) their technology; social organization, family life, extended and immediate; and their world view, the different kinds of myths and beliefs.' T elaborates on these items. 'The first part we'll do now is their myths and beliefs. We'll start with songs and stories.'
14	Asks Ks to pass out certain books. Says she'll play a story on a record. Ks begin leafing through the books.
1116	'You can read along if you turn to p. 11. You're going to have to listen to the record and read along.' 'Can we calm down a little bit?' Plays record: "Thunder and Lightning." While record plays, T writes on board: What do these stories tell us about the Netsilik inner world? Why would the Netsilik want to explain these things?

1120 'OK. This is one of the myths they really believe in.' Each group is to read a story to the class. They must decide how to do the reading-aloud, depending on the presence of quotations and how the paragraphs are organized. Each group will be responsible for a dramatic reading. 'As a group you'll decide what this tells us about the people.' T assigns different pages to different groups. (*Today's groups are simply the tables at which they sit.*)

23 Ks begin to read and discuss.

25 T turns lights on and off and cautions them about loud voices. T lists on board the stories and pages to be read. Begins to circulate. Has to shout to get attention. 'You can't begin to organize your thoughts this way.' T repeats the assignment. (*T herself speaks with more volume than the room requires even when the Ks are quiet. Why?*)

28 Continues circulating. Ks are discussing the dramatizations. T is at table #6.

33 (Responds to monitors who have come in, and makes a written entry as they wait.)

34 Goes to front and center. 'You have five more minutes to get ready to do the readings.' Is at #3.

37 At #5.

38 'Alright. Will everybody sit down and quiet down?' Ks do both. 'Which group would like to read first?' Group #2 volunteers and T calls on them. All attention is on group #2. They begin, with one K reading aloud, then a second, third, and fourth. The Ks read well. 'OK, that was very clearly done. Can you tell me, after that one reading, how day and night came to be?' K in another group responds. T accepts the answer and compliments the K.

41 Group #4 volunteers. T comments that it's 'not necessary for us to be reading along, since they've rehearsed.'

42 Group #4 reads. A girl is the narrator, two girls are sisters and two boys are brothers in the story.

44 'OK, what do you think of that?' Ks seem to be appreciative. T compliments the group. 'Who became the sun?' K: the sister. T asks similar factual questions about the selection and calls on individual Ks to respond. They do so.

45 Group #1 performs, with two Ks reading aloud individually and a third responding to one of the questions on the board. T compliments them, and comments on a K in #2 who simulated a tree growing out from the ground up.

48 Group #5 performs, each K reading a stanza dealing with a different animal.

50 One K reads too much and T comments on that. She wants the books closed, so the performing group can have the class's full attention.

1152	Group #3 volunteers. Then a K in #2 asks, 'Can we do this again?' T: 'Do you enjoy it?' Class responds affirmatively. Now #3 performs. (*What is the value of this reading aloud?*)
54	'OK. That was a little bit hard to hear.' T elicits meaning of poem.
55	'This is one of the most important spirits, the one group #6 will read about.' Group #6 performs. One "audience" K wants to follow along in the book. T says they'll be able to read the books since they may take them home. Group #6 continues performing, K by K.
58	'OK. What did you think of that story?' Ks groan. 'Those are myths, in which we may not believe. Is the spirit friendly?' Ks: No. 'What if a spirit is powerful but not friendly?' This elicits the response that they would respect such a spirit. 'Respect in what way?' K: Through being afraid. T elaborates on this.
59	T turns to the board. 'I think the first question has been answered.' T explains her opinion. 'Why is it good that we have a chance to study about their culture?' K: We can study the feelings of other people. 'We're going to read more.' K: Not in the same groups! T: 'OK. We can worry about that another time.' Has Ks put books in their desks.
1201	K asks a question. T has him repeat it. The question is about being an orphan. T elicits responses and singles out the main point. Another K responds.
03	T begins lining them up for lunch dismissal. (*Why so long on one topic, with Ks in their seats all that time?*)

The parenthetical items in my notes, ZA, don't serve as a direct indication of what I identified as the major obstacle. The five items note a talkative enthusiasm on the part of the Ks, a grouping by tables, a desire on my part to find meaning in the teacher's volume of voice, a question about the value of reading aloud, and another question about an activity which kept the Ks in their seats for so long. But my major obstacle is Scholarship, with special attention to PAT question 57: Did the teacher demonstrate a clear grasp of the modes of inquiry peculiar to the subject matter?

In order for me to rationalize my choice I need to make references to the POC, which you have yet to read. As you do, please keep the following points in mind:

a. The lesson must have begun at about 1015-1020, because the teacher needed time to direct their attention to the five items on the board, items she mentions in the Retelling.

b. Though I began taking notes at 1030, I judged that the film showing began at about 1025.

c. The film ended at about 1055 and was followed by some 17 minutes of discussion of its contents.

d. The teacher began on a new tack at 1112, an effort which was finally terminated at about 1200.

e. I saw this new tack ('We're going to be studying about three parts of Eskimo life: their technology; social organization, family life, extended and immediate; and their world view, the different kinds of myths and beliefs.') as the more inclusive statement, as the statement under which one could subsume both the film and what the Ks were to get from it. Yet the teacher made no effort to relate the film's content to the 'three parts of Eskimo life,' going instead to a more active K activity involving the dramatization of the poems and stories. And note, ZA, that the Ks were restless at 1112, when she announced the new task.

Please read the transcript, so we can discuss it.

Grade 5-6 Social Studies: POC #2

NS I don't know if you remember from last time, so I'll remind you
0000 once again. I'm going to ask you to retell what took place. Uh. I came in at the time you were showing the film; so you can begin with what happens after you show the film; and, um, since the purpose of that part of, of this . . .

AC Oh, you started from then?

NS I started from about eleven. You were . . . I didn't . . .

AC You started from the discussion or you started from . . .

NS From the discussion.

AC Oh! I didn't know that! OK. Huh.

NS Um. Since last time, when I heard your tape–I've heard it a few
0034 times now at home–I, um, you obviously knew how to retell, so it doesn't have to be very detailed, but the highlights of what took place today, (AC - Uh-huh.) if you can remember.

AC OK. (p) Before the film I had directed them to be as aware as they
0054 could of the five specific things: what the man, woman, child do in

the film; how they care for their young; and how they caught their food. And that was the way that I tried to direct the discussion afterwards.

NS Try to remember: I want it done in the third person.

AC Right. (NS - You forgot.) (p) Um. So the teacher started the
0124 discussion by asking one of the specific questions: what the men in the film were doing. And the discussion (p) kept going in that direction. The children answered. (p) It wasn't just a question-answer. Some of their answers produced other questions by the children, and (AC sighs deeply.) some of the questions led to a "why," (p) that I thought could be answered by the children reading some of the stories and legends that the Eskimos believe in. So after the discussion on the film, which I think lasted about 20 minutes, the children were told that they were going to read these specific myths in groups and there was a sort of dramatic presentation to the class about what they . . . no . . . a dramatic presentation of the story to the class, with the idea that this would hopefully get them to learn a little bit more about what makes the Eskimo culture what it is.

NS Let me say a word about this third person retelling because I don't
0307 think I quite got the idea across to you. The purpose of a Retelling, as far as I'm concerned, is that (p) this method is designed so that if a supervisor were to come, let's say, once a month as I'm doing, (AC - Um.) huh, is that the teacher would acquire the technique of being able to select a segment of a day, some portion of a day, (subject area, if that's the way you function) and to be able to sit down after class and, as thoughts go very rapidly through your mind, say what happened. This happened, that happened, yes, yes, I remember. Remember it accurately and thoroughly, (AC - Uh-huh.) and to try to think of it as though someone else had done it, as though you had sat and observed instead of being the teacher. So that when you do this to yourself alone, because the whole purpose of this is to teach people to self-supervise, you'd be in a position to recall accurately what took place, or any teacher would, who would be subjected to the technique, and then, in the second part, would be able to evaluate this as though the teacher had been observing herself or himself teach.

AC I guess the only area that I'm confused about is why it can't be (NS -
0427 In the first person?) retold and still evaluated if I'm saying it . . .

NS Well, because I think it's important . . . I think? I *know* from the
0440 many many years that I've done this with lots and lots of people that it puts a certain distance between the teacher and the lesson. The technique arose out of TV work I had done many years ago in a project where students saw themselves on videotape (AC - Uh-huh.), and because they saw themselves on videotape they had the objective Retelling. See what I mean? They were separated from the

film. In fact, they said: That's not me. (AC laughs.) I don't look like that. I don't talk like that. Well, that's how the idea came to me, that since tape is generally still not available to everybody; certainly it's not going to be available to every supervisor to come walking in with a machine (AC - Hm.), big nuisance. So I had to find a substitute for that and the substitute turned out to be having the teacher retell. I also found that when teachers retold it by saying: the teacher did so and so; he or she; Miss Jones, Miss Smith, whatever it was—that it put a distance, a social distance, between the teacher who did the lesson and the teacher who retold the lesson. (AC - Hm.) So that the Retelling and the third-person-singular in both the Retelling and, um, what I call the Agenda, the self-criticism (AC - Hm.) puts a certain distance between the person who is the activist and the person who becomes the self-observer, so to speak.

AC So that the ego isn't involved. (0608)

NS That's right. That's exactly the point; so the ego isn't involved. (AC - Right.) And when you once get the drift of it, you'll see that it does do that for you. (AC - OK.) So let's assume that the lesson—since I know what it was and you obviously remember what it was, try now, if you can, to give me a list of how you would evaluate it. And, again, I'm going to write it down. Try to do this for me in just single statements, that is, with no elaboration. Something like: (uh) the materials were there, you know; whatever you want to say. And then we'll go into the elaborations of them. OK?

AC The materials (NS - Well, . . .) (AC laughs.), the materials were there.
0650 This was—I don't know if it's necessary—but this was the second time they saw the film.

NS I wouldn't, an observer wouldn't know that.

AC Oh, alright. I thought (slight hesitation at the realization that she
0705 said "I") the discussion went really well. They were all anxious, most of the time, to respond and answer. They seemed to have been really paying attention to what went on in the film. (p) (NS - Huh-hm.) There were some questions or some statements that I felt got off the track but obviously were something that they wanted an answer to, and wanted to, wanted to deal with. I didn't really want to prolong the bathroom discussion, but it was something that they were curious about, so, and I could understand that. I get thrown off, though, when I don't expect (Laughter in her voice.) these kinds of questions.

NS Again, let me interrupt you. Umm. If I were, uh, doing this as a third
0801 person, I could say that the materials were there; I could say that the students seemed to be anxious (eager, I would have said) to respond. (AC - You wouldn't know . . .) The students . . . That's right. The students seemed to have paid attention. I could tell that sometimes they got off the track when they asked about the bathroom, because that was not in the film. But I wouldn't know that you were

bothered by it. (AC - OK.) So try to do this as though you were me and I wouldn't know what's on your mind.

AC OK. Ahm. When it came to the question of why certain things
0837 happened, which was (p), ahm, a question about two specific things that had to be with the ashes and why he moved away, I, the teacher then went on to explain that we would be dealing with their world view of things by reading these booklets; and (p) ahm, I don't think (p) I'm really, I'm really projecting too much (NS - Alright.) into this. Huh. When they got into the groups, there was (p) active participation. They really, they really got into what they were doing. Some of the children wound up not participating in the presentation of it, in two groups, but in general I thought that they organized quite well. I did very little directing as to how they were going to present it, you know. Uh. They did this amongst themselves. And I thought that one group in particular did a really good job as far as the presentation, when they decided, when they broke it into
1025 narrator and actual speaker. (p) For the first three presentations the children were into listening. I don't know if they were, if they really wanted to read it themselves or if they weren't following as well and that's why they wanted to do the reading. But I redirected them back to listening when I thought that the (p) object of it, which was listening to another group do it, was lost. So I told them that they had to close their books and get back to actual listening of it. But when I asked questions about what was read, they were able to answer. The lesson itself went longer than I though it would go. Huh. I was planning to be done by about five to 12, and, as it was, I think it was 12 or a few minutes after 12 by the time we got finished. But they really enjoyed doing it, which came out when one boy asked if we could always do it this way, and most of them seemed to also say that they enjoyed it. Um. The only objection was that they wanted the groups to be different the next time. (p) I think that learning did, did take place, (P) in an enjoyable fashion. (1207) (P, P)

NS OK. There doesn't have to be more and you can always add
1218 whenever you want to. (AC - OK.) You still have difficulty separating yourself from yourself, (AC - Yes.) which you didn't have the last time, strangely enough. For some reason or other, today's lesson, ah, sort of pulled you into the operation of things. You can't separate yourself from what you did. (AC - Right.) But I'm going to re-read this to you as though you had made the separation, just so you'll hear what it would have sounded like had you separated yourself from the circumstance.

AC I–can I just say . . .? I think one of the reasons is that I had a lot
1247 more to do this time. I mean, I was–during the discussion I took part, I directed the questions. Last time was strictly group work and I really didn't have as much participation in what was going on,

which might have a relationship to why I can't separate myself now. (NS - Yah.) But (p) I don't know.

NS Well, well, let's see what the possibilities are, because, after all, uh, I,
1312 as the observer, could make an Agenda, and not having been involved, I could make the statements that I would have wanted you to make. Now, except for one point that you made that I'll have to catch off the tape, because I'm not quite certain what you said. I'll tell you where it is, but you may be able to recall. The first thing that you said—and I'm going to try to say this as a third person—the first thing that the teacher said was that the materials were there. The students seemed to be eager to answer and, um, seemed to be paying, seemed to have paid attention, I presume, to the film. Aah. In the discussion, ah, the students sometimes got off the track, um, um; that is, they got off from what the film dealt with. The film didn't deal with what happens when you go to the bathroom, and the students asked a question or two of that nature, which was apart
1413 from what the film dealt with. Then there was a point that I didn't catch. Then, after that, the teacher said there was active participation in the groups, ah, but in some of the groups, um, some children didn't take a role in the presentation. Ah. One group, um, did a really good job. Ahm. The children listened without reading along with the presentors during the first three presentations, but thereafter seemed to be inclined to want to read silently along with the class and the teacher had to stop and redirect and tell them that the groups had prepared the presentations, so it was only fair that the class listen to them. Ahm. (P) But when the teacher asked some questions, it was obvious that the students, though their minds seemed to be divided between listening and paying attention and
1509 reading (AC - And reading.), they were able to respond. However, the lesson was longer than the teacher—ah—well, that would be hard for a third person to say, that the lesson was longer. That's something you felt. (AC - Uh-hm.) Ah. A third person wouldn't know that. Ahm. The teacher, the students seemed to be enjoying it, as evidenced by the fact that one boy asked if they could continue doing it this way, ah, and suggested that a different grouping arrangement might be desirable. Ahm. And, um, as an observer, one could say that learning did seem to take place because the children seemed to know what went on in the film, and so on. Ah. (1553) It seems a little clumsy, in my retelling, you know, in my restating this, ah, because so much of you, as the teacher, is involved in the statement. Ah. I think it's a matter of practice, of learning to think of yourself as someone else (AC - Um.), and that's the real technique behind, the real rationale behind this, to create the separation between yourself and the individual . . . What I found, Audrey, is that, for example, if you let a person retell and at the same time begin to criticize, they get hung up on points and never produce a

long Agenda, and therefore the full scope of what they might want to say about a lesson doesn't get said. So I, I don't permit a mixture of evaluation and retelling. Also, when you, when, if you permit elaboration of a point when it's made, again there's a chance of getting off on it without producing the Agenda, the full scope of it. So that the idea of the technique is to, is to remember: This is what happened. Now, if I were a third person looking at it, without knowing what I had done yesterday, what I planned to do tomorrow, or why I did what I did today, what would that person have seen and said about it.

AC 1713 So when you're retelling it, what happened, you're retelling it in third person. When you're doing the Agenda, you're evaluating it, also doing it in the third person.

NS 1722 (overlapping) also in the third person. And after that we talk here. The idea is that if the supervisor knows what to do in this third step as I call it, the Retelling being the first and the Agenda being the second, in this third step–the idea then becomes that the teacher ingests the role of the other discussant and can sit down and say: So, OK, so the materials were there; and so on–so? (AC - Um) (p) And if there's been a successful set of experiences in this third step of the cycle, then a teacher can come away from the self-analysis with something in the way of thought for the future. We'll come back to it after we've talked a while about this. OK? (AC - OK.) (1812) (p) The last time I was here you also had a grouping arrangement. (AC - Right.) Ahm, and we talked for some time about how quickly the kids went into the groups. The last time wasn't just as it was today. Today it was: whatever table they sat at was the group they were in. Whereas last time was the first time that you let them choose their own groups, which is what one of them said they'd like to do again. Ahm. But here again you were, you were concerned with groups. I would say, let's see, the, the, the materials . . . was not one of them. Ahm. You said there was active participation; one group did a really good job. Ahm. You had to redirect their attention to listen to the groups. Ah. They did listen to the presentations, because they could answer questions. They enjoyed doing the thing in groups. Ahm. So that a lot of this again is a concern with the way the grouping arrangement works. (1916) (AC - Um) The one, the two statements you made that deal with the substance of what was learned is that they were able to answer the questions and at the end you said that learning took place. Ahm. The only other things that were neither group nor learning is that the materials were present and the lesson was longer, which I said was a statement you made on your own, in a sense, rather than as the third person. Ah. But looking at this, ah, of the eleven items you listed, one of which I didn't record properly, ah, you're again concerned with the way the group functions vis-a-vis what you want them to get out of this. Ah. And that the other is what they got out of it, the learning of it. (AC - Um.) (2008) So, let's talk a little again about groups, because apparently (p) the way you group the kids and what you get out of the grouping arrangement, ah, is of some concern to you. For example, (p) another person might have commented on, ahm, how well they recalled each of the items in the film. Another observer might have said: the teacher had five questions on the board and they seemed to, they responded very well to the first; on the second one they were able to get, (p) get fewer inferences. See what I mean? (AC - Hm) In other words, someone else might have made a different kind of analysis, based on the five questions. (AC - Right.) (2058) Ah. Someone else might have been concerned, therefore, more with what the content outcomes were. But you weren't saying that. I'm not saying . . . I'm not suggesting that you ought to have. (AC - Uh-hm.) I'm simply pointing out why (AC - What could have been said.) what could have been said, and yet you didn't; so that obviously, that you didn't say it, means either that your mind doesn't give that a high priority or you make assumptions about it, (AC - Um.) because when one looks at the Agenda, the grouping feature is again very important to you. Why?

AC I think that in the past my teaching has basically been I-talk–you-
2138 listen. Uh. You know, I could picture today's thing going on a lot differently. Ah. Either as a whole class or, or really with me dominating the scene, and I'm really trying to get away from that.

NS That's an interesting statement. Ahm. (a) Why are you trying to get away from it? and (b) Where are you going that's better than where you've been?

AC (Laughs.) I don't, I don't know for sure if where I'm going is better
2214 than where I've been. I think that a lot of what I've read and a lot of what I've heard and a lot of what I am, perhaps, trying to believe in (and I'm not so sure that I believe in it yet), is that, you know, learning can really take place even if all the wisdom doesn't come from my head. (NS laughs.) And I am really–I took a survey of their opinions of the first half of *Man, A Course of Study,* when they were just dealing with the animal section, and some of the answers were very interesting. But, I do think they learned a lot from that section. And a lot of it was the group work type of thing; but I'm still not totally convinced by the whole thing and I'm kind of convincing myself as I do it.

NS You're wrestling with what is essentially your role in the classroom,
2314 aren't you? (AC - Right.) And you seem to be saying that you are still basically emotionally married to a certain role, (AC - Hm.) but intellectually you've been subjected to a certain amount of input from readings and other sources which seem to suggest an alternative, (AC - Right.) and intellectually you're examining the alternative, intellectually you're testing the alternative in some ways

through various grouping patterns, ah, but subjectively you aren't convinced yet. (AC - Right.) Ah, let's talk about it because it's a very, it's a very important, very important issue. Umm. What is your emotional commitment, the one you're wedded to, about the role of the teacher? (P)

AC
2408 Probably a lot of it is based on, on when I went to school, and you know, what I know as school being: the teacher is up there, this is the lesson today, and you do it; and then, like I said, you listen and you get some more facts and everything has to be, um, judged by and approved of by the teacher. Ah. I went to Catholic school, and this is the whole, you know, pattern. But I am taking a course now in the theory of Open Education and I've done, you know, various readings down at Hunter. And whereas I'm, I'm definitely not ready to do completely individualized opening, um, like I said, I'm just trying to (p) get myself to, to step back and guide where they're going, without, um, I don't know, pushing it into their heads, kind of, you know, making them understand that they can learn by helping themselves and discussing with their classmates. One of the things they came up with on the survey, that they found the hardest to do, was express themselves, which had a lot to do with their age and their shyness, too. But I think it also has to do with . . . that they're asked to do that very little, um, in general, not just here, but, you know, in their years before. They don't hold very high regard for the opinions of their classmates; and I imagine that has a lot to do with both the way I carry on and what they're used to before. You know, if the teacher says "That's right," then it's right; but if another student says "Yes, that's right," they look to me and want to know: Is that right? And it's that . . . this course of study has really pointed that out to me. I'm learning it, they're learning it, I mean, just about. I didn't know anything about baboons or chimpanzees or salmon or herring gulls before I started this year, and, ahm, I think that, that was one of the things that helped me see that, that I'm not just the source of wisdom. That there are other sources, and, and I've been enjoying it. (Laughter in her voice.)

NS
2642 (P) OK. You're not the only one who faced this–who has faced, and is facing and will face the problem. What do you think you're moving to? Have you gotten any kind of a hold on the direction?

AC
2703 (p) Ahm. Hopefully where they'll be a little bit surer of themselves, in what they do, and know how to attack things, how to find out certain things, other than thinking of just one source for an answer. I don't really know if that, you know, if there's more, at this point, in my mind than that, that's clear, anyway, you know, that I can express. Ahm. You know. I still basically feel that I'm responsible for them, for a year, in what they pick up, and, and what they leave at the end of June having accomplished. Ahm. I'm not convinced, and I don't know if I should be convinced, that this could be done if

I took even less of a role than I'm trying to take now, you know. We visited a mini-school last week as part of this course (p), where the class in itself was just so different. We didn't see it functioning; we went at three o'clock. But just the way it's set up. And we saw the agenda for the day. At the beginning they get together. Then, after that, for an hour, they're allowed independent choices, doing whatever they want, with absolutely no directions at all. Then, supposedly, they're semi-directed to work in a particular area. I, I can't, I can't see myself at that point yet at all and I don't think I would ever really be, um . . . I just feel that a certain amount of stuff has to be covered and I'm not convinced that the children would do it if at some point they weren't directed to it.

NS Alright, you haven't been eating, so why don't you go ahead. Ahm.
2915 (p) Let me put it in another context, Audrey. (P) When kids come to school, (p) regardless of the mode of instruction, highly directed or at the other extreme, seemingly non-directed, (p) would you agree that initially somebody, somewhere, has to make a projection as to what these kids will leave with at the end of June, as you put it?

AC Do I think that's necessary? (NS - Yes.) Yes.

NS OK. Do you suppose that the people in Open Education don't have a
3003 set of objectives, something that the kids are going to leave with in June?

AC (p) I think that they have a general set of objectives. I don't, I don't
3014 see how it could be specific, because if a child is going to basically choose all the time what he's interested in, ahm, (p) then . . . and I know that children learn better if they're interested in what they're learning than if they're forced to learn something that they think they have no use for. I think a basic framework is needed and I don't see how you can relate the two.

NS Alright, let's make it very specific. Today's lesson. Uh. The children
3058 saw a film on the Netsilik Indians, Eskimos, in the *Man, A Course of Study* program. When I came in they were watching the film. It ran at least a half-hour, (AC - Right.) half-hour. Ahm, and, uh, thereafter you were concerned with whether they had gotten certain things out of the film. (AC - Uh-hm.) (P) Ah. What did you want them to get out of the film? (p) You don't have to list them all. Just list a few.

AC That different members of the family definitely have different
3141 functions. That their way of life is different than what we know, or at least that one segment of the way they were living is different. (p) That there are certain rituals and taboos that were shown in the film that they didn't know at that point were rituals or taboos, but which I wanted them to get out later. Um. And where these things came from. Basically, from the myths and the . . .

NS Alright, let's ask a more basic and general question: why should they know all this?

AC (p) Well, dealing with the course of study that we're doing, they're

3233 basically in June going to hopefully get an awareness of what really makes humans human. Um. They've studied the animals, they've studied the lower forms, rising all the way to the baboons, and now they're dealing with a more primitive human society, umm, hopefully with the awareness that, you know, it's evolved to a more advanced, progressive way of living; but they still should know the things that came before it so that they can understand where they've gotten to now. In other words, the Eskimo culture, from what I understand, from what I've read, is far less sophisticated than where we are now, but could be understood so that they see that we weren't all, um, put on the Earth to do the same thing, that people have progressively gotten to where they've gotten because of the culture that they live in.

NS At some point this year, will you tie down the, the myths the kids
3351 read today, (AC - Huh-hm.), some of the myths (where we came from and so on)? Will that be related to our myths?

AC Yes, they're supposed to branch out now into several types, you know, the Greeks, you know, and what different cultures have derived that . . .

NS So that they've studied organizational patterns in animal groupings
3423 that function as groups and not as individuals. They're now into a less sophisticated culture and presumably they'll come into our more sophisticated culture at some later date, and presumably, that the mode used to study those cultures, whether animal or human, the modes of study would be applied to their own culture.

AC Right. You know, with the animals it's basically just observing.
3443 Ahm. What I'm going to try to deal with, with the Eskimos, is that when you're dealing with human beings, even if it's, if it's as, as primitive a society, perhaps, as the Eskimos, that more than observation is needed. They have to really understand what makes the culture, and what makes their world view what it is.

NS Well, our time is almost up and your kids are going to be
3524 coming . . . (AC - Oh, are they?) Let me leave you with something because we haven't really, we've only just brushed the surface of the whole issue. Between now and the time I come back again I'd like you to ask yourself a question and see what answers come to mind. Presumably you hope, as a matter of professional pride, that a result of associating with you for a year's time, a school year's time, your kids will in some measures be different than they would have been had they not associated with you. (AC - Huh-hm.) And there are many many differences, obviously, that you're going to be looking for. (3607) Let's fix on *Man, A Course of Study* as a, you know, as a thing to tie this whole issue to, because if, if we go through the whole curriculum it would take forever. See if you can spell out for yourself what it will be or ask yourself a simple question: Supposing you could postulate that in your class there's a student who will

learn 100% of what you want the individual to learn, and that some other one will learn almost zero or very very little compared to the other one. How, in looking at them in June, will you be able to tell the difference? What will the 100 percent learner be able to do that the one who's learned very little will not be able to do? (AC - Uh-hm.) And then, if you can begin to spell out the difference between the top learner and the bottom learner, how will you know, how will you be able to measure that difference, identify the difference? And then when you've identified the differences, we can then talk about whether the method—going back now to the role of the teacher—whether the method used, which involves of course what the teacher's role is and how the teacher functions, can be altered, given the outcomes. (3735) In other words, if the outcomes remain stable, if they're the non-varying elements, and you set them up, these are the things you want to achieve—can they be achieved only by your perception of yourself as a teacher? Can they be achieved in this other method, in this Open Education method? Somewhere in between along some continuum? Because, it seems to me that (p), you see, let's say, for example, you meet someone in the street and they say: how do you get to 42nd Street and Fifth Avenue? Well, they can use the self-discovery method. Obviously, they can go wandering forever and finally end up at 42nd Street and Fifth Avenue. But if they want to get there (NS snaps his fingers to indicate getting there quickly.) you say: Look, you make a right turn, go down that street to 42nd Street, make another right turn, in three blocks will be Fifth Avenue. That's the end of it. That's very directed, because that guy wants to get there as fast as he can and you want to help him get there as fast as he can. (AC - Hm.) (3829) On the other hand, if he mainly wanted to explore Manhattan, just wander around, and he had six months to do it, so he takes six months to do it. You know what I mean? (AC - Right.) So that the method is related to the objectives to be achieved. The two people both want to get to 42nd Street and Fifth Avenue, but one is in a great big hurry. That's part of his objective. The other wants to explore, see many things, and ultimately end up there, and doesn't care how much time he spends in between because he expects to see other things along the way. (AC - Huh-hm.) So that, depending on what the ultimate objective is, the directiveness, you see, of the person with the information, is related to where the individual wants to reach, where he wants to get to, and how soon he wants to get there. Do you follow?

AC I follow.

NS So that if you spell out the objectives, then we look at the role that
3916 the teacher needs to play in sometimes giving very precise directions and sometimes allowing time for exploration. Do you follow? (AC - Right.) And that the role of the teacher is not a role that's absolute,

regardless of the objectives, but is related to where the kids are to go. (p) Alright? (AC - Hum-hm.) OK. Let's stop here. (3944)

You've given us a great deal of material to digest at one swallow, so I'd like to go through everything in the order of your presentation, NS.

Once again you came in early, but apparently either too early or too late. Had you come in at 1015-1020, when you presume the film prologue began, and left at about 1110, you would have seen AC prepare the class for the film and discuss its contents with them afterwards. Or, had you come in at 1112, you would have seen a lesson which you describe in your notes, starting from 1112. Seeing either one alone would have given you an entirely different perspective. You could not then have seen "this new tack as the more inclusive statement . . . under which one could subsume both the film and what the Ks got from it."

I raise the issue for *you* only because you raise an issue for *me*: when do I arrive and when do I leave, when I come to observe?

If you can control your arrivals and departures with precision, which is not always possible for real supervisors, then your timing should be based on what you and the teacher have agreed is the entity to be observed. Structured instructional situations, with true beginnings and endings, should be seen in their entirety. Traditional teachers teach "lessons" as total entities. Open Education teachers do have planning sessions with their children, and these can be viewed as unique entities. Or, the periods of independent activities can be regarded as entities. The test is what the teacher defines as the beginning and conclusion of an instructional session.

On the other hand, even trains and planes don't run precisely on schedule; so teachers can't expect of themselves and their students that they will be ready for the to-be-observed instructional entity at precisely the promised time. Therefore, supervisors and teachers need to be flexible: supervisors need to feel free to arrive before the promised time to be sure to see the whole sequence; teachers need to feel free to begin a sequence at the promised time (or earlier) even if a supervisor has yet to arrive. Both will have to learn to rely on the teacher's Retelling to bridge gaps missed by the supervisor.

However, you do make a good point about AC's lesson: I could not have raised the particular issue about "this new tack" had I arrived at 1015 and left at 1110 or had I come in at 1112. Since I came in when I did and saw what I saw, and since AC aimed at a tie-in between the two segments (at about 0200: ". . . some of the questions led to a 'why,' that I thought could be answered by the children reading some of the stories and legends . . ."), there was good reason to deal with the whole of what I saw as one entity.

OK, NS, I see your point. Now, I'm curious about your parenthetical notes, since you claim to apply the PAT even as you observe. Your first comment is about Ks being talkative and having to be called to order. I presume that's your response to the *Interaction Pattern* unit in the *Process* sub-head. May I gather that your concern is not that the Ks are voluble, but that one cannot carry on a discussion with more than one person talking at a time? You're not suggesting, are you, that you like quiet classrooms, NS?

You may gather the first impression and take back your second, ZA. What Ks are "doing" should be related to the response pattern they are to be taking on. The discussion of the film was meant to serve as a vehicle for answering the five questions on the board.

Your next two comments (that the Ks were restless at 1112 and that the grouping was by tables) are clear enough, but why the notation about the teacher's volume of voice?

If you haven't already noticed the phenomenon, ZA, then you might experiment. My observations indicate that any central figure in a social situation can under- or over-stimulate the participants by effective control of volume, pitch, tempo, pauses, etc. It seemed to me that AC was at that moment unaware of the amount of sound she was producing. Since I never noted this again, there was no issue.

Now that you've explained, NS, I think I've also observed the phenomenon, but I will do some experimentation to confirm your comment.—What really puzzles me most of all is how you arrived at Scholarship as the major obstacle. A transcription can't tell me (except via parenthetical notations) that Ks and T are talking thus and so, or that Ks are grouped by tables. I'd have to hear and see those in person. But even from a transcription I can ask, as you did, what was the value of reading aloud and why AC kept them in their seats doing listening, observing, reading, and speaking for over 90 minutes. Both questions deal with what Ks are "doing," which should be related to the new response patterns. So if we both object to what Ks are doing, then aren't we contesting AC's ability to "translate goals into terminal K behavior?" (PAT #7) And, if so, how did you get to Scholarship, NS?

PAT #7 is the key issue, ZA: the translation of goals. And for a change we're back to "understanding" again. So let's listen to AC:

0054 . . . Before the film I had directed them to be as aware as they could of the five specific things: what the man, woman, child do in the film; how they care for their young; and how they caught their food. And that was the way I directed the discussion afterward.

0124 . . . Some of their answers produced other questions by the children, and some of the questions led to a "why," (p) that I thought could be answered by the children reading some of the stories and legends that the Eskimos believe in.

So the Ks were to understand what the roles were in daily activities, in child rearing, in food gathering, and to arrive at another level of insight via the stories and legends. The new response pattern was basically "to understand," though that word does not appear in the POC.

I concluded (and only a transcript of the lesson itself could provide clear evidence) that a teacher more fully prepared in the content could have led the Ks to a clearer perception of what roles are and to connections between roles and cultural beliefs. I wasn't saying that AC made no translation of goals into terminal behavior; she did do that to a degree. She would do better only when she herself had a deeper grasp of the material. My estimate of that grasp turned out to be accurate, ZA. She says (in the POC, just before 2642):

> I'm learning it, they're learning it, I mean just about. I didn't know anything about baboons or chimpanzees or salmon or herring gulls before I started this year . . .

Although I'm jumping ahead, ZA, it was this comment by AC that caused me to drop any effort to discuss my major obstacle.

I may want to discuss that item again, when we get to it, so I won't respond here. But let's go back to sequence. I have questions about the POC itself.

After you review the procedure briefly, AC raises the issue of "you started from then?" You tell her you began (taking notes, I presume) from the discussion, which seems to surprise her. Why didn't you pursue that, NS?

I didn't see that it was an issue. She wasn't keeping track of my arrivals, and I didn't want or ask her to do so. Therefore, I wasn't concerned by her lack of recall. And even if I had been, I'd still have gone directly to the Retelling and Agenda, holding my concern in suspense until the Discussion. My major purpose is always to model a total cycle. A teacher applying the cycle to herself would know which segment of instruction she was recalling for analysis.

Alright. The next point is that you had anticipated a smooth 3PS Retelling. Instead, AC had difficulty "separating yourself from yourself," as you put it. Since this was only your second POC, why did you assume that success at the first meant that the Retelling could be foreshortened?

Please believe me when I tell you that I was deliberately experimenting, hoping to prove that a supervisor should *not* make the very assumption you suggest I made. One effective Retelling indicates "mastery." What is needed is overlearning via practice in order to insure maximum accuracy in future responses. So I expected that AC would not be able to give me an accurate précis, which would then lead us to a more detailed Retelling. This is meant to demonstrate to both participants that it takes practice to move from full details to a brief summary. Unfortunately, I ran into a more serious problem: AC could not separate herself, neither in the Retelling nor in the Agenda.

Then why didn't you have her do the Retelling over

again by modeling part of it for her? Why did you launch into the history of the cycle?

For a very basic reason, ZA. I believe that I can modify behavior, large chunks of it, by altering perceptions rather than by working directly on the behavior itself. And again AC contributes some effective data:

0608 AC - So that the ego isn't involved.

I had a second reason, for which I must use a musical example, for a change. If you have ever sung in a chorus or even in a music class, you might have run into a conductor or teacher who said: "That's not good. That's not what I want. Let's do it again." Or: "I want a happy sound. That's not a happy sound. Make it sound happy." A chorus or a class determined to be and desirous of being cooperative, will "do it again" or try "to sound happy," but the results will be acceptable only by pure chance. If one rendition is unacceptable to the conductor, then somebody is out of tune, out of tempo, too loud, too soft, etc. Unless those performers who are responsible for a rendition being either "not good" or not "happy" are told, most specifically, what to do differently, then various self-selected performers will make their own alterations, which, except by chance, will cancel each other out, and result in further conductor dissatisfaction.–So there was no point in having AC do it again unless I could, on the spot, determine why she did it "wrong" in the first place. And I couldn't stop the POC to think about it. Ergo, I tried to work on her perceptions by having her relive my experiences with me. Her "ego" comment indicates to me that I made some headway here.

Then what are we to conclude from your experiment?

That no teacher is to be instructed to foreshorten the Retelling on the second effort. How many successful Retellings will prove that the teacher needs no more practice? Frankly, I can't give you an exact answer. How many times does a child have to spell a given word accurately before you cease checking him on it? You'll have to judge for yourself. When you think the teacher is ready to do summaries you can tell her, when you make a date for an observation, that you'll be asking for a summary. If she's not successful, you can go back to complete Retelling, or you can model a summary for the teacher. The problem may not be recall itself, but how one summarizes it.

I get it, NS, I get it. I notice you did model the Agenda for her, twice, in fact: once after she had made a few statements and a second time when you reread the Agenda. Why?

I was concerned, ZA. I had devoted a long time to the rationale between Retelling and Agenda. She seemed to understand the 3PS rationale, yet she reverted to first person in making the analysis. So I wanted her to hear how it might have sounded, in part and in whole, in 3PS. At 1247, before the total rereading, AC suggests the reason for her difficulty. And again, since I couldn't take time to make my own analysis, I accept, but don't discuss her idea.

Then we're supposed to conclude that you will not deviate from rather strict pursuit of RAD, unless you can identify the cause for particular teacher behavior.

True, ZA, true. When you read the POC #3 transcript, you'll see that I do return to the issue.

OK. Now once again you suggest "materials" as an Agenda item. Though I presume this is another of your "self-confessed errors," why do materials come to your mind first?

You're right about the error, ZA. And I guess I regard that as a rather non-controversial item. Very few teachers set out to teach without control over the availability of materials. Again, I should *not* have suggested anything at all.

OK. But we come now to a major question I've been saving up to ask, preceded by a rather small one: Why didn't you stop AC as she was giving you her Agenda, when you found you had missed a point? In fact, you missed a point which had a direct bearing on Scholarship, a major obstacle you had by then already identified and should have been alert for.

I have neither explanation nor alibi. I don't take notes that rapidly; I did miss just what you say I missed (0837: ". . . When it came to the question of why certain things happened, which was . . . a question about two specific things that had to be with the ashes. and why he moved away, I, the teacher then went on to explain that we would be dealing with their world view of things by reading those booklets; . . .") and should have asked AC to pause. I didn't. I made an error.

> Then my major question, NS: Had you perceived and recorded that statement, a statement which gives you direct access both to Scholarship and to a discussion of what turns out to be two parts of a single rather long lesson, would you still have chosen to discuss grouping? And yes, I do remember that the commandment is to discuss what's on the teacher's mind first.

Before I answer, let's examine a transcription of the Agenda as I wrote it down, with the missed item enclosed in parentheses:

+	–
1-The materials were there. 2-They were anxious to answer and seemed to have paid attention. (4-T said they would be dealing with their world view of things.) 5-Active participation in the groups; but some individuals did not take a role. 6-One group did a really good job. 7-Ks listened during first three presentations, but they wanted to read along, so she had to re-direct them.	3-Sometimes they got off the track: e.g., bathroom.
8-But when she asked questions, they were able to answer. 10-Ks enjoyed doing it. One boy asked about doing it this way again, but in different groupings. 11-Learning did take place in an enjoyable fashion.	9-Lesson went longer than she planned.

I began my categorization of her Agenda at 1812. I noted that today's grouping was by tables, not by free student choices, and that items 5, 6, 7, 8, and 10 deal with grouping. I regarded the latter half of 8 and all of 11 as matters of the substance of what was learned. You're welcome to look upon my categorization as stretching the point, just so I *could* discuss grouping. After all, you might say, items 1, 2, 3, 4, part of 8, and all of 9 and 11 did *not* deal with grouping. So a careful categorization would have shown that six-plus items out of eleven did *not* deal with grouping. Then why discuss grouping?

Because, ZA, I did not catch item 4, thus leaving five of the ten items on grouping, and because of a better because. AC had experimented with a new grouping arrangement on my first visit, an arrangement in which each group's task was rather more complicated than today's. Yet today, when she must surely have noticed the Ks' restlessness and might easily have made room to release some energies by student selection of groupings, she played it safe. So I sensed that the issue of teacher's role was still on the agenda, just as it had been at POC #1, and again I hit pay dirt!

That you did, NS; I must agree. Fascinated as I am by the substance of that discussion, I do remember that we're discussing the supervisor's role, the process of RAD, rather than the issues raised by how the teacher taught. So I have only three questions to ask: At about 3607 you tell AC to ask herself "a simple question" about all that a 100 percent student will have mastered in a school year. Do you really think that's a simple question?

No, ZA. It's an easily-phrased question with a rather detailed and complex answer. I didn't intend for AC to provide the answer. I wanted her to see that the teacher's role is not invariable, that it depends instead on the goals of instruction. I was implying (and could have made it explicit had AC been fully exposed to my definition of teaching and what that encompasses) that when one creates and controls conditions leading to the acquisition of new patterns of responses, then those responses condition the teacher's role.

Alright, that sounds reasonable. My second question is: what is the breakdown for each part of this POC? You supplied it for POC #1.

It goes like this, ZA:

Instructions to AC	00:54
AC does R	02:13
Instructions to AC	03:43
AC does A	05:28
Discussion of A	00:54
AC and NS do D	26:32
	39:44.

So, despite the problems with 3PS, we devoted about two-thirds of the POC to Discussion.

> Finally, then, NS: Since I'm not likely to be part of a Cogan-type practicum with you, and since I am now a practicing "real" supervisor, how do I make such productive choices as *the* items for Discussion?

The most effective method I know of is to record your POC's just as I did. Only you won't need to transcribe them. Listening to them alone or with a supervisor-colleague would be very useful. As a matter of courtesy, you might let teachers hear the tapes you made with them.

My most major piece of advice is to efface yourself during R and A. Guide the teacher into effective 3PS statements, then sit back and listen hard. If you listen most attentively, if you are *perceived of* as an attentive listener, and if you respond to what is *really* being communicated to you, then you will elicit ever more meaningful statements.

XIV.

Elementary Social Studies — Post-Observation Conference #3

Audrey C.	26 Ks
P.S. . . . . Rm.	(Seating unchanged)
Class V/VI Combination	4/--/7-

1038 As I came in, each K was in a seat. A distribution of "The Data Book," some sheets and cards was in progress. Ks were apparently to look up tools in "The Data Book" to see what they were made of. There was an issue as to whether Ks were to work alone or in pairs, but after explanation about each K doing his or her own work, the Ks got down to work quietly.

40 Ks working.

43 T, responding to one K's request, tells whole class what a word is on a particular page. Ks "buzzing" as they work. T circulates.

43 She asked one group how they worked downstairs (*but I don't understand the reference*). They respond. She looks at what individual Ks are doing.

48 T circulates, Ks work.

52 Two boys come to Social Studies display on rear wall to look at the material there, and discuss among themselves the content of the items on the bulletin board. T still circulating and assisting Ks.

54 T is checking the work of two boys who claim to have completed something. She discusses it with them. Rest of class is working, with a certain amount of content-related talk at an acceptable level of volume.

1056 T now talking to 2 other Ks.

58 T goes to rear closet and gets some paper. Calls to attention. T asks how many have finished and come up with answers. Some Ks raise hands. T says those who have finished will go to something else. T reviews with class: they had studied in the room, had gone downstairs, and had now studied tools. They

Board Work

Panel 1

Girls' Kickball 2:00 Teams 3 & 6

Panel 2

Tool—any object that performs

useful work for man by

modifying the physical → pollution

→ superhighway etc.

and/or social environment → easier to job

(ex) automobile

Panel 3

Tool	Useful Work Done to Modify Environment
	*Paper/Animal Skin String/Sinew Sticks/Bone *

Panel 4

(1) Make a container for a pack of loose Eskimo cards.
(2) Make a gift for a friend that will make him happy.
(3) Make something that will be fun to play with.
(4) Make something that has a pleasing sound.
(5) Make a model of a tool that the Eskimos use.

would now design their own tools using paper, string, and sticks in whatever quantity they needed. She explains that Eskimos made tools when they had a need. She will put problems on blackboard and Ks will choose to make a tool to solve a problem. Ks are free to make an effective tool, using the three materials in any way they wish.

1102 K: Can we use glue? T: No. Explains that Eskimos had none. They may make tools they saw downstairs. The tools may also resemble those on the cards distributed earlier.

04 T explains that she has sticks of plastic and wood, but Ks must use one or the other. Paper is "Eskimo skin;" strings represent tendons of animals; and sticks are animal bones. K: Are we allowed to use scissors? T: Yes, but no glue or tape. 'Any other questions?'

06 'If you are finished with your list, then put it and "The Data Book" in your desks and go get materials.' T now says they may work in teams (*seemingly a change of mind*). Ks go get materials. T writes on board, panel 3.

09 While she's doing Panel 4, someone comes to the door and tells her something. So she makes an entry on Panel 1.

10 T has now completed Panel 4 and reads it aloud to class. In response to a K, T says they may make a second tool if they have time. T distributes scissors to those who raise hands.

12 T circulates. Ks work.

13 T circulates. Some Ks say: "Look what I'm making!" T looks. (*I note: String is too thick for the thin paper being used and for the dimensions of the sticks. So how did she choose the materials? Did she herself make a tool in each category, using these materials?*)

18 Some male adult enters. He and T transact some business at her desk for about 30 seconds. He leaves. T circulates.

20 K brings her his creation and they discuss it. Another K calls her to attend to his creation. They discuss it. Ditto with another K.

22 T calls class to attention. Repeats what each item of material represents in Eskimo culture. K: But we have no nails. This remark not discussed. T redistributes some material from one K to another.

23 T adds to Panel 3. Continues circulating.

24 Explains task individually to one K. Another K brings her his creation. "Oh! That's great!"

26 'I think it's getting a little bit too noisy.' Allots 10 more minutes to finish tool. Then Ks will stand up and explain their tools. 'Think about what you will say when you stand up to explain it.'

27 Two boys begin to scuffle. T: 'Oh, not another one?!' Manages

	to soothe both quickly, yet with minimal interference. T: 'One a day is sufficient.' Goes back to circulating.
1129	(*Ks now at work since 1107.*)
31	T circulates. Ks work.
36	T: 'Will everyone please sit down!' Ks do so. 'If you're not finished, put the material down. You'll finish tomorrow. We will now look at those who have finished.' Ks are to explain the problem they selected. T calls on class by tables. At table 5 a K shows "harpoon." T asks him to discuss it in Eskimo terms. He does. T suggests to another K what would make his "boat" float as a kayak does. She looks it up in "The Data Book." (*Why didn't she have all material put away and completed products brought up front, so all Ks would give their full attention?*) One K has made four items, all of which he demonstrates. T discusses how Eskimos might have solved his problems.
42	'OK. You made a lot of things.' K describes the arrowhead he made.
43	T calls on another K. He describes his creation in Eskimo terms. T comments on it. K also made a "tent." T asks what else he needs. Another K mentions a tent pole. T elaborates on the idea.
45	'Who else is finished?' 'Let's take a look at Nancy's for a minute.' K guesses that it's a woman's knife. T has Ks criticize it. T: 'She is not finished.' Gets other Ks to suggest what Nancy might do.
47	Another demo by another K. Same procedure.
49	Another demo by another K. This involves a tool made by another K which T has been demonstrating.
51	'OK, we'll look at two more before lunch, the finished tools. (Bell rings.) We'll put them on the table in the rear.' Another K demonstrates.
52	'What were some of the problems in doing this?' Ks: We needed glue. It's hard to tie a knot. T comments on how to tie.
53	Another K demo. Ks and T comment on it. Another K offers his "tomahawk." T: 'We'll look at the rest tomorrow.' T issues instructions about putting finished tools on the rear table, etc. Assigns different Ks to collect the various unused materials.
56	Clean-up begins.
1202	Class goes to lunch.

I had *three* major obstacles in mind, ZA: AC's inability to do R and A in 3PS; the progress she was making on resolving her conflict about her role in the classroom; and the tension set up in whole-class instruction when two different tasks are assigned in the face of individual student pacing. Only the last, of course, arose from this particular lesson. I had also decided to find an opening to ask whether AC had pre-tested her material by making the kinds of tools her students were to make.

And, for the record, this is how the time went in the POC:

Recapitulation by NS	03:14
Instructions and R modeling	03:41
AC picks up on R	04:43
Instructions	01:02
AC does A	02:51
AC and NS do D	26:23
	41:54

Grade 5-6 Social Studies: POC #3

NS Umm. What I want to say first of all is that I always have the
0000 advantage over you, apart from the fact that I'm the observer here. I have the tape, and I can always listen to the tape; and I do. I listen to it once immediately after I record it, and then I listen to it again before coming. I heard it this morning. (AC - Oh!) So that, what is a memory to you, overlaid with many other things, is to me very fresh, 'cause I just heard our conversation this morning. And one of the things that happened last time, in contrast to our first time, was that you had difficulty on two counts: the first was that you couldn't really explain, really describe the lesson too adequately in the third person, the way I wanted you to; and also you couldn't give me what I call the Agenda in third person singular, because you
0058 couldn't divorce yourself. (AC - Huh-hm.) And when we talked about the latter, which is more important to me than the former in some ways, ahm, you, you thought that the reason that it happened was that in the first lesson that I observed you were, as you were today, walking around, not as involved, but in the second lesson you were more involved, and therefore it was harder to separate yourself from what went on; but I just thought I'd throw this in, not for discussion, but for you to think about. That in view of what we actually talked about, which is the um, you're going through a process or rethinking your whole approach to your role in the classroom, ah, that what you did last time, was so important, or in

some ways a very important test for you of which way you're going to go, that this whole matter we've been exploring, the role that you have in the classroom, has enough emotional overtones for you, so that the more deeply you're involved in a particular process, the harder it becomes for you to separate yourself. (0205) In other words, if I were seeing you teach in the way that you used to teach (AC - Huh-hm.) to which, on the tape, I said you were emotionally wedded, (AC - Huh-hm.) um, you would have no difficulty recalling, because it would be what you normally do. You wouldn't be in conflict. Whereas now, at least the last time, (p) you were so invested in the method you were using, which was a trial, you know, (you're still in trial and maybe going to another level of classroom organization) that I think the inability to describe was in some measure due to, especially to evaluate, was due to, uh, this emtional involvement. You might just think about it. I'm suggesting, um, that the more one is caught up in what one does, the more difficult obviously it is to separate oneself and be observer and activist at the same time. And that's probably what happened to you last time. (AC - Hm.)

0314 Now today, what I'd like to do is tell you where I came in, because it's always difficult to tell exactly what I was looking at when I came in, and then—that will give you a chance to munch a little more—and then I can describe what I saw, in part, to start the description off; and then you can complete the rest of it. It shouldn't take us too long, because a lot of it was the same activity over and over again.

0342 Anyway, as I came in, (I came in at 10:38 by my watch) the kids were in their seats, the teacher had apparently distributed the data book which comes from the *Man, A Course of Study* series, (AC - Hm.) and a sheet and some cards, and I gather at the time as an observer (both of us were observers at this point), as an observer I gathered that the students had apparently been asked to look at the tools in the data book to see what they were made of; and there was some discussion as to whether, ah, they were to work alone or in pairs. After a brief explanation by the teacher, the children got down to work and worked rather quietly for a couple of minutes. Then the teacher, responding to one student's request, told the whole class—she stopped them from what they were doing—what the word was on a certain page, and the kids went back to work. The teacher began to circulate, go around the room, you know, and stop to talk to each student. Ahm. She asked one group how they had worked downstairs, and again, to the observer, the reference was totally unclear. They responded. She looked at what individuals were doing. And the teacher continued circulating and the students continued working. (0501) Two boys came to her. No. I saw, the observer saw two boys going to the Social Studies display at the back of the room to look at it because it had—they discussed it because it had some relationship to what they were working on; they discussed the content and how it affected the job they were doing; and the teacher continued to check what individual students were doing and discussing with them what the work was.

0529 Then considerably later, 20 minutes later, ah, the teacher went to the rear closet, got out some papers and some other materials and another segment of the class began. And at that point I will let you (as the other observer, in a sense) continue the discussion. (0545) I just want to say that in the meantime, ah, the observer noted that there were some items on the board. One was a definition of a tool, and then, in another panel, there was a chart or the beginnings of a table of some kind, with a narrow column for the word "Tool" and a wide column which was headed "Useful work done to modify the environment," ah, which may have been related to something else. At any rate, when the teacher went back to the closet and got the materials, ah, she stopped the class from working and said: How many of you have finished and come up with answers to your problems? Some students raised their hands. And she said: Well, those of you who have finished will now go on to something else. And then she began to clarify for me, for this observer at any rate, what had happened. Apparently the students had studied, had begun on this work this morning in the room, had gone downstairs (wherever downstairs is), and apparently there was a place where they could look at tools, and they were now going to do something as a result of those two joint experiences. I'm going to ask you to continue this, again in the third person singular. OK? (P) Don't tell me what the students had done downstairs. As an observer neither of us would know. OK?

AC OK. The teacher wanted to (p) . . . the teacher wanted to begin
0655 explaining the purpose of the activity that they were doing with the data book (p) by explaining to them that the next assignment they were going to do was design their own tools. She told them that they would have only the choice of three materials: paper, sticks, string. And that there were going to be five problem choices on the board. They had to choose one of those choices, and after they had chosen one of those problems that they were going to apply themselves to, they were to pick as many materials as they needed to design a tool that they could use in that way. Those that were finished checking their list as to makeup and purpose of the Eskimo tools, were to begin designing their own tool. And if they weren't finished checking their list, they were supposed to continue checking their list. Um. At that point the excitement that was aroused at that point made many more people . . . it seemed to the observer that many more children were automatically finished checking their list than were really finished. (0845) (NS - Huh-hm.) But they chose their materials. They chose them before the list on the board was finished, which (as an, as an observer) they were just anxious to get their

hands on these things. They didn't look first what they might need, you know; they didn't think out first (from an observing standpoint) what they would need, what they were going to do, and what they would need to do it. They were just anxious to get started. There was a question if they could use anything else to put the things together and the teacher replied that glue was definitely out, but they could use scissors, since, uh, Eskimos probably would have use of cutting materials when they made their tools. That was supposed to be the purpose of them designing this tool. (0942) (p) I think the teacher this time made that clear to them, that the materials that they were using were representative of what the Eskimos would have and only what they would have; and that that's what they were supposed to keep in mind as they made their tools. They went about working. There was some question as to whether or not they could work individually or in pairs. At first the teacher said: no, individually. But she then changed her mind and said that no, if you want to work in pairs, you can. Umm. Everybody was involved right away. Like I said, the checking of the formal list was finished and (NS - Yes, in a big hurry.) (AC laughs.) and they really, um, and they really seemed to attack right away, you know. (1045) There was only one boy that the teacher saw that wasn't really getting at it. He was sticking with his list, probably be . . . well, you wouldn't know that; I would . . . probably because he didn't know what to do, so he would rather stick with something that was nice and concrete: checking a list. But—and—when the teacher thought the time was up for the work, at least for this session, she asked those that weren't finished to stop working on their tools, that they would have a chance to work on them tomorrow, and asked everybody to pay attention as those who were finished would say what it was and demonstrate the purpose of it, or explain the purpose of it.

NS Alright. You're getting better at it, at the third person singular
1138 approach. It's a little difficult for you still to separate yourself from what goes on. I think you've gotten the idea. It'll take a little more practice. (AC laughs.) But then you recall once again that the purpose is that you are to be able to separate yourself from the activity (AC - Right.) so you can really examine it outside yourself, and that's the discipline I'm trying to instill in you. Alright. Now last time also, when we were dealing with making up what I call the Agenda, that is, the self analysis, you also had difficulty separating yourself from the person who did the teaching. (AC - Right.) And you had difficulty stating in the third person, from an observer's point of view, how you would analyze the lesson. (AC - Right.) So try . . . I won't suggest this time what you might begin with; I did last time. I won't suggest anything this time. I'll give you absolutely free rein. So go ahead and make, without elaboration, whatever statements you want to make. I'll write them down and then we'll talk about them.

AC 1240 The teacher (p) was very clear as to what (AC is speaking hesitatingly.) they were going to be doing, the materials (p), the purpose for doing it. One thing, from an observing standpoint, was that the stimulus was so stimulating that it interfe . . . nobody wanted to finish what they were supposed to finish. They all wanted to get right to what they were doing. (NS - Hm.) (1321) Aanndd, that should have been considered: that if this was supposed to be stimulating enough to do, that the children should have been able to begin it when this was presented. (NS - Huh-hm, alright.) (P) It seemed that the children all understood, ahm, (p) but they had to make this connection between the fact that the materials they were using were representative of something else, and (p) they were really all putting a lot of effort into what they were doing. (P) (1427) At the end, the teacher raised the question as to whether or not anybody found (p) this difficult in any way and, um, by the two answers that were given by two different students, it seemed that this, there were problems that arose that many of the children had, and, um, I think I pointed out to them the fact that the Eskimos really had to be pretty ingenious to make the tools that were necessary for what they needed, and that this wasn't quite as easy as it might have looked beforehand. (1515) (P) (P) (P)

NS 1531 Alright. You only broke down once. You said at the end here, you went into "I" on this last statement. (AC - I did? I didn't know I did.) You were OK up to that point. Alright. Here's what the teacher said, you know, in self analysis. The teacher said: The teacher was clear as to what the students would do and what the purposes were of doing it. I assume that you meant that the teacher communicated (AC - Right.) this to the students effectively, which I put down as a positive statement. Negatively you said that the students wanted to get right to the new task, um, that the teacher ought to have considered this in, in the procedure, ahm, so that the students would have been able to get to the second task when it was presented without the second one interfering with the completion of the first task. Then positively you said that the students seemed to understand that the materials they were to use were representative of the materials that the Eskimos would have used in this effort. Ahm. Then you said that the students put a lot of effort into their work, which I considered a positive statement. Then the last thing you said was that the students–and this I write across the middle of my chart because I consider this a neutral statement–that at one point near the end the teacher asked whether the students had had problems in doing this second task, but the teacher pointed out to the students that the Eskimos would have to be very ingenious using the limited materials available to them, ah, to make up the things they had to make up, and that the task the teacher gave the students wasn't really as easy as it looked initially. Um. (1720) Now it's a very interesting Agenda you've created here. It's quite different from the others that we've dealt with in the past, because all of these are oriented now to, to the situation as in this lesson; that is, they're oriented to the content of what took place today. (AC - Umm.) You're not discussing grouping arrangements any longer. For the moment, at any rate, we're past that stage. Your concern was that the task was clear to the students, that they understood what was going on, that they put a lot of effort into it, that they appreciated how difficult it was for the Eskimos to do this, what they were trying to do; but the one hang-up was that the transition from task one, let's say, that list and the cards and so on, to task two, took place in an awkward way perhaps, an awkward time. (AC - Um.) You want to elaborate on that?

AC Just that transition? (NS - Yah.) I guess, from the standpoint of a
1818 stimulus-reponse type of thing (NS - Huh-hm.) I wanted them to really be excited about what they . . . should I say "I"? (NS - Yes.) . . . I wanted them to really be excited about what they were doing, ahm, and I'm glad they were, but I should have realized that if they were going to be so excited about it, they should have been able to get right into it and, um, the only other way that I . . . Everybody obviously was going to finish that checking of the list at different times, so that the only thing that I could have done to make it a smoother thing would have been at the beginning of the checking of the list, to say: this is what you're going to do first; this is what you're going to do second; and explain all of that before they started checking their lists, so that they would have to finish and maybe would have given them more of a stimulus to finish the checking of the list faster before they went on. But I know that there are about 10 of them that had really finished checking and I really wanted that list checked accurately and carefully before they went on. And I didn't allow for the excitement that took place.

NS This is a problem that teachers always face when they're work-
1943 ing . . . Let me stop in the middle of a sentence. This takes us back to our earlier discussion of the method you were accustomed to when you were a student. You had made reference last time that you had gone to Catholic schools (AC - Right.) and you were accustomed to a certain role for the teacher. You're still largely functioning in that role, in that you are working with your class as a whole on any given issue, although the work was individual in terms of the making up of those tools, the facsimile tools. (AC - Huh-hm.) (2018) You're working with the class as a whole and you always run into the problem, you always will run into the problem when you do that, that some will finish a given task sooner than others. The question is: what do you do with them? When do you make a transition to the next task in such a way that allows those who finished to go on to it and yet those who didn't finish can finish

what they're doing? And it's a very difficult problem to resolve when you have, as you had, 26 students in the class today for this to happen. As you said, 10 students were finished with the earlier task, and how do you maintain their pace of learning and so on? Ahm. (2058) I wish, I wish I knew an all-encompassing answer that I could give you that would once-and-for-all resolve the problem. I don't know of an answer (AC - Um.) and, um, I'm not certain that one has to expend a great deal of energy looking for an answer because, ah, as a matter of fact, most of the students really didn't finish the second task either. (AC - Right.) When you asked at the end how many had finished, a minority of the class had actually finished and they will still have to. Which means that at the time they, those that had not finished the second task, come back for a period of work in this area, they may be among the ones who didn't finish their first task; so that when you come back to this again there'll be two kinds of people: those who finished the second task and may not have finished the first, and so there'll be people (AC - Hm.) working on one task or the other simultaneously. (AC - Huh-hm.) So it's not too serious a problem, but there is a question of the competing stimuli, (AC - Huh-hm.) which is one of the things on the chart that I gave you and it is a difficult thing to resolve as to just when you bring in another task, when you're working with the class as a whole.

AC What do you think about what I said, you know? If I had presented
2212 it together at the beginning?

NS (p) Well, you said that if you had presented both tasks at the
2222 beginning, ah, the knowledge that the second task would come up and it might be a more interesting one, would speed up the work, or would increase the pace at which the students were doing the first task, (AC - Huh-hm.) in their eagerness to get to the second one, which, if you explained it in advance, would look very enticing. (AC - Right.) Well, obviously we can both anticipate what some of the things . . . What do you anticipate might have happened?

AC Some of them might have done it well and fast, and some of them
2249 might have done it (NS - Fast!) fast. (Both say the word simultaneously and laugh.)

NS So you see, each choice has its own consequences. (AC - I know.)
2258 That's why I say I don't know of a nice formula to give you which would solve the problem. (AC - Huh-hm.) If you continue to work with the class as a whole, you're always going to encounter this difficulty, no matter what the two tasks are. (AC - I know.) If the second task seems less enticing than the first, then nobody is going to be in any great big hurry to get to it. (AC - Right.) If the second task is more encompassing, more interesting than the first, they'll sort of skimp on the first one in order to get to the second one. Ahm. (p) (2335) I don't know off-hand of a nice smooth transition one can make. I think that this is something you'll have to

experiment with and see, ah, what balance you can strike between tasks. Ah. There's another consequence also and that is that the instructions for the second one are rather complicated.

AC They might be forgotten (NS - That's right.) and might have to be re-explained.

NS So each choice has pluses and minuses to it. You have to strike a
2358 balance somewhere. (p)

AC I think one of the reasons why my Agenda wound up the way it has
2407 is that you asked me to focus on one particular, I don't know, grouping (?) from your PAT. The one that I focused on, which is one of the areas that I was pretty poor on in the other two, was communication, (NS - Huh-hm.) and that's where I tried to be really accurate and clear.

NS Well, do you feel you were?

AC Yes. (NS - Huh-hm.) I don't think that . . . there were a few
2438 questions, but there weren't half as many as previous times. I mean, the children could really get right down to work and, ah, the three or four questions that I had, after I finished explaining, were easily answered, and thereafter there was really no problem.

NS And, therefore, you were able to say that you were clear on what
2502 you wanted the students to do, for what reason, and that you gave your instructions in clear terms; and I would say that the evidence is that they did understand and that they did go to work on it, (AC - Hm.) and what they produced at the end was indicative of, some value in isolating a portion of the PAT, ah, to see whether you can make it function as you like it to function. (2533) Ahm. (p) The, this idea of making tools, replica tools, fascimile tools, with, ah, materials which in their own way are even more limiting than the ones that the Eskimos had (AC - Right.) because they're not at all related to what the Eskimos had to do in real life, ahm . . . What did I start to say? (p) Ah, yah. The . . . You said the purpose was clear. What did you have in mind? Why were the kids making the facsimile tools?

AC So that they could realize that the Eskimos made the things that
2613 they made because they had a need for a harpoon or a leister or a tool bag, but they were very limited in the materials that they could make these things with, and they had to, without going to the store to buy it, they had to think of a way to get these materials together in such a way that they would really work. (NS - Hm.) Ahm. Now the tools that they made won't be able to be tested to see if they work, but they did have to keep in mind, like I pointed out with the knife, you know, it was very easy to do the paper on the bottom but then there were people that realized that you couldn't have the paper, which meant the skin, at the bottom, that you had to know what type of thing would work for you on it.

NS By the way, the word leister, I've heard it a number of times. How
2707 do you spell it?

AC Leister, l-e-i-s-t-e-r.

NS And what is that?

AC It's a, it's like a spear, but it has two prongs at the end . . .

NS Oh, is that the one that looks like a trident? (AC - Right, right.) The one they caught the fish with. It's that Y-shaped device (AC - Right.) with which they caught the (AC - The fish.) fish. Yah. I see. Ahm. (p) (2735) Let's, let's spend a little time on, on the larger role, you know, the larger issue that we were talking about at least in the other two sessions. Ah. Where are you up to now? Where do you stand on, on your role in the classroom? (p)

AC They've been doing a lot more . . . group work. These past two
2752 weeks have been crazy weeks, with all this testing business, you know. (NS - Oh, you had the city-wide tests.) Yeh. Math one day, reading another day. Ahm. My schedule has . . . I don't know why . . . there've been meetings every other day. My prep was changed, was changed to the second period, which is why they went downstairs today. It was supposed to be after lunch, but it was changed. So, they haven't really been normal weeks, but I have been doing more grouping and we have one hour of independent, quote, activities, which isn't really too independent, at this point. They're limited to the . . . like, if I give them seven choices, you know, they can pick one of them. I'm still telling them what they can choose from, but, ahm, I'm trying to make them at least do that much, (NS - Huh-hm.) you know, have the responsibility of choosing what they want to work on, knowing that what they choose, they have to finish; and, ahm, sticking with what they choose. (2920) It's interesting that some of them can really choose different areas every day. I don't know if it's because they want to vary what they're learning or if it's, if it's not quite as intellectual, I mean, if it's a bore doing what they did the day before and want to go on to something else. There are some children who pick the same type of activity every day, and then I kind of go up to them and suggest: well, maybe today you should pick something from a different area. But, ah, it's worked and it hasn't worked. It's worked in that I feel that they're (p), they might be learning more because they've chosen it, and because they want to do it for that time. (3015) I find it awfully difficult to get to any kind of correcting, you know. If it's the type of correcting they can't do themselves, and there are things that they can, you know. They can correct it and show me their corrected stuff. But if it's something that they can't do themselves, because I don't have answer keys prepared yet or whatever, then I find it awfully hard to really check all the work, and I'm certainly not at the stage where I can say that it's not necessary for me to check. (NS - Huh-hm.) So that part is hard. (3047) I'm talking a . . . it's not really a course. In District . . . [*I've omitted the number deliberately, ZA.*] they're opening up a new school next September, quote, in Open

Education. It's a new school being built and that's what they . . . they don't have classrooms; they have the whole corridor thing; and on Monday afternoons we go there. We heard Lillian Weber, etc., etc., and one of the things that we had to do for them was prepare a (p) . . . how we were, quote, opening up our classrooms somewhat. So that's my attempt to open my classroom. (Said with laughter in her voice.) (NS - Huh-hm.)

NS Are you conflicted in, in, on this issue? Does it bother you in any
3123 way that this, that moving in that direction will not permit you to cover, quote, unquote, all the material you'd like to cover?

AC Well, at this point I feel that if I'm still putting the choices up there,
3144 that I'm, I'm directing them basically where I want them to go, you know. It's just not: come in and do whatever you want. Reading comic books or whatever is still not one of the choices. So in a way I still feel that I'm "covering." Um. Of course, not everybody gets to everything; but if they're getting into something and they're getting something out of what they're doing, then I feel pretty happy with that. (NS - Huh-hm.)

NS One last question, because we have only another five minutes or so.
3224 (p) When I left you last time, I don't know if you recall, but as I say I heard the tape this morning, ahm, I left you with a question. I said that, that one of the ways to look at the problem of your role in the classroom, what methodology you adopt, will depend on where you want to end. (AC - Right.) If you could, if you could postulate that the outcomes would be in the form of two students, two exemplary students: one would exemplify 100 percent achievement; and the other one a good deal less, near zero, or considerably below; and that if you could measure both of their accomplishments in terms of the outcomes that you have, then the outcomes would dictate . . .
3335 [We were interrupted, briefly, by a colleague of AC.] I said that if you could postulate the existence of two such students in June, then we could examine, knowing what the outcomes are going to be, we could try to examine whether the methods you're using are methods that get you to the goals. Remember that I said to you that if someone wants to get to 42nd Street and Fifth Avenue, that depending on how quickly he wants to get there (AC - Right.) and what he wants to do along the way, it would determine which way he would go, the directions you might give such a person. In the same way, I said, we couldn't rationally evaluate the effectiveness of your methods until we could both decide on where you wanted to end up. And, I said, one way of deciding this is what would a 100 percent student end up with (AC - Right.) as compared to zero or close to zero percent students. Then, if we could measure the difference, (AC - Huh-hm.) then we could see whether the methods you have been using are efficient in that they help you get to those goals. (AC - Right.) Have you thought about that?

AC No. (Laughs.) Umm. Not, not to any . . . I don't know if it's to
3434 enough . . . but that I think that 100 percent students would just be so aware that there's so much to learn and that the teacher is not the end-all for the answers, and they would really think out and be aware of the different resources and sources that they can go to for their answers, the teacher perhaps being one of the sources, but not being totally dependent on that person, whoever she or he may be, you know, in whatever grade, you know, for all the answers.

NS (Huh-hm.) Did you ever hear the, the phrase "process education," (AC
3525 - No.) as opposed to "content education"? (AC - Oh!) Or when I say process-oriented as opposed to content-oriented? (AC - Yeh.) In what context did you hear it?

AC Well, I don't . . . I know what you mean though, (NS - Huh-hm.) that you're more (p) . . . You're dealing or you're focusing more on how you do than on what you do. (NS - Hm.) Right.

NS And what you were saying for this 100 percent student was a process
3600 outcome. You didn't say that he had to master all the math, for example, (AC - Right.) or all the social studies, amass X number of facts, master X number of concepts, (AC - Huh-hm.) but you put it in terms of, of his awareness of what a learning situation entails, (AC - Huh-hm.) what problems he had to solve. You didn't say those words, but that's what you were implying. And what resources he would go to, (AC - Hm.) and the teacher was only one of the resources. (AC - Huh-hm.) So you were stating what technically is called a process outcome, (AC - Hm.) rather than a content outcome. Because you obviously could have said that a student would have to learn 250 spelling words, you know, and would have mastered this much math, etc., etc. You didn't say that. (AC - Right.) So you were stating a process outcome. Well, you might try to think . . .

AC They have to be related though, don't they? (3656)

NS Well, let me suggest a frame of reference in which you might think about this, so that we could, in another discussion like this, ah, try to go beyond the specifics of a lesson like this (AC - Huh-hm.) to the more general form of the question. For example, you had a process outcome here. You were concerned not that they made the tools that they were; that they could function, because there was no way of testing the facsimiles; but you were concerned with having them appreciate the fact that the Eskimos were faced with some rather unique problems, with very limited materials available to them, no technology to speak of. And so, when they began to make the facsimile tools, given the limited materials they had, they were to appreciate how ingenious, you said, the Eskimos had to be to solve their problems and that, you see, is a process outcome. They didn't learn . . . A content outcome would have been to learn to make real good tools, you know, that could be tested functionally. That would be content. But you were concerned that they appreciated the difficulties that the Eskimos faced, and how ingenious they had to be to use the bone and sinew and so on in order to achieve the end result that they had to achieve just to survive. (AC - Right.) That's a process outcome, rather than a content outcome. (p) (3821) You see, one could turn this around and say: well, what I want the kids to learn is the 10 most important tools of the Eskimos, you know, their names, how to spell each word. That's content. Whereas process is the other side of the picture. (AC - Huh-hm.) So, at least for me, now, you're beginning to think, (maybe you've been doing it for some time, I've no evidence,) of the process outcomes for your students.

AC 3847 (Hm.) I think I do that in math too, quite often. Like, I'm not so much interested that, ahm, 2 plus 2 is 4, especially in word problems, you know, what is (bell rings) what is the method that you had to use to get the answer, you know. Like I find myself stressing that a lot. But I don't think I just do it in this. (NS - Huh-hm.) But I don't think that . . . I mean, I do want them to, to learn content too, like . . .

NS 3919 Alright, let me just make . . . let me finish this conceptual framework, then you'll go get your kids. If you think of content as something to chew on and as process as the perfection of the art of chewing (AC - Huh-hm.), then that's the essential difference. For example, if one outcome is to be able to state a problem, identify the relevant resources, come up with a solution, test that solution against the problem you began with to see how effective it is, then this problem, can be a mathematical one, (AC - Scientific.) a literary, it could be a scientific one, (AC - Hm.), but the essential ground rules would be the same: the problem, the relevant resources, the procedure used, the testing of the, of the solution, (AC - Hm.) but the area wouldn't matter. You see what I'm getting at? (AC - Right.) (4016) So that if you think of content as the thing you do in order to achieve a state of health or something (the state of health is the measure of the value of the exercise) (AC - Huh-hm.) and what the exercise is, is not . . . this choice is then measured by what it does for you to gain the state of health. In the same way, if the end result is to be the ability to define a problem, then a lot of things can be used in order to, to develop a skill in defining the problem; but the skill, you see, is a process. (4049) The skill is always a process, (AC - Right.) whereas the content is memorizing the facts, the names, the dates, the places, the events, and so on. (AC - Hm.) And one can use that content simply as something that you chew on, work with, but the end result is not the content, the end result is the process. Now, if you think of your work in those terms, you'll achieve somewhat more clarity as you pursue this, and what processes you want your children to be masters of at the end.

AC 4121 I find myself asking myself that question a lot more, you know, in preparation for this, ah, than I had weeks ago, saying to myself: what is it that I want them to learn at the end? What are they doing this for? You know, not just: oh, this is a good idea, so have them do it. (NS - Yah.) So I think I'm picking up.

NS Good. Well, if you feel progress is being made, it makes me happy that it's taking place.

AC A nice feeling.

NS OK. Thank you very much.

AC OK. (4154)

Once again, you came in early, NS, and saw a transition between two different tasks, and it was that transition which became your major obstacle. In POC #2 the fact that you arrived at a certain time made an important difference. Is that a coincidence?

I don't think so. Obviously, since there is more traditional instruction being done than any other kind, I've seen more of it than I have of Open Education, for example. My objective conclusion, based on that experience, is that, given a free choice, I'd like to come in near the end of one instructional session, see a a complete session, and a piece of the next one. This is clearly most possible in self-contained elementary classrooms. However, I get almost as much insight from observing departmentalized secondary school instruction, when I come to see lesson B but arrive 5-10 minutes before lesson A ends and stay over into the beginning of lesson C. The adjustments Ks and T have to make when moving from task to task, within one room or between two rooms, offer interesting data for analysis. You might try to follow that pattern to see what you get, ZA.

Sounds like something worth trying, NS. Having read your description, the POC, and the material in between them, I notice that you got around to discussing all three major obstacles, but not whether AC had tested out the materials in advance by making sample facsimile tools herself. Since your notes contain two parenthetical comments on this one issue, it must have been of some importance to you. So why didn't you deal with it? When you discussed with AC the making of the tools you could have brought the matter up.

Yes, I could have, ZA. At 2613, AC tells me why she had Ks make facsimile tools. Her perception of it was that the Ks were to use *that* one of those available materials (paper, sticks, string) which best represented what the Eskimos would have chosen from among skin, bones, and sinew. As she says, in making a facsimile knife it was easy to use "paper on the bottom but then there were those people that realized that you couldn't have paper, which meant skin, at the bottom, that you had to know what type of thing would work for you." The student had used paper (i.e., skin) as the knife's cutting edge, which is not functional in Eskimo terms, and both she and some of the Ks saw the problem.

The new response pattern was to create facsimile tools, which, if made of real Eskimo materials, would function. Therefore, the measure of success was not whether the facsimiles functioned, but whether the equivalent representational material was selected. And the Ks were to explain what they had made and why they had used which materials. Therefore, pretesting might have led AC to find thinner string and to offer better "problems" to choose from; that she did not do so seemed to have no significant impact on the learning process. So I didn't raise the issue.

Actually I was misreading AC's purpose when I made those notations. When she told me what her purpose was, it became clear that my questions were picky and basically irrelevant.

But shouldn't teachers pretest materials?

Oh yes, definitely! But if I'm to raise the issue with AC, I want to do so when the absence of pretesting turns out to be a major obstacle.

I see.—Let's turn now to the POC. You begin with your recapitulation of AC's problems with 3PS in doing R and A. At about 0058 you say that eliciting a 3PS Agenda is "in some ways" more important than a 3PS Retelling. That implies to me that because analysis is more difficult than description, you value one over the other.

That's it, ZA.

But I don't have a ready explanation for your decision not to discuss with AC your thesis about the reasons for her difficulties with the 3PS format.

Well, ZA, I had listened to her tape and taken time to think the matter through. I couldn't count on AC having thought about it, so we were unequally prepared for a rational discussion.

Fair enough. But this is our first encounter with an element outside the three steps of RAD. Are there other such elements?

Your question opens up a rather large issue, ZA. Were I a real supervisor/administrator bent on instituting RAD (Retelling-Agenda-Discussion) in clinical supervision of the faculty, I would begin with the EG (Empirical Grid), the PAT (Primitive Assessment Tool), and principles of learning. Using recorded and live material (demonstrations of teaching) I would devote some major segment of time to the mastery of 3PS (third person singular) description of what others have done. Then we would focus on 3PS Retelling of one's own efforts, followed by 3PS analysis of other teachers' efforts and by 3PS Agenda of one's own teaching. Only then would I demonstrate the whole cycle with a volunteer on the staff. By the time I reached the point of doing all supervision via RAD, the staff would have largely mastered the 3PS format. So there would be little or no need for the recapitulation in AC's POC #3. I had given AC no such instruction outside of our POC's; there was no time. Ergo, my conferences with her contain digressions made necessary by the absence of such instruction.

I see your point, NS. Now, at 0314 you begin modeling a Retelling for AC: AT 0342 you very precisely indicate when you came in and what you saw. I gather you did that in response to AC's reaction at this same procedural point in POC #2.

You gather very well, ZA.

Thank you. At 0501 you go into a rather detailed description of what *you* saw two boys do. I see a connection between that and what AC retells at 1045 about the one boy who continued checking that list. Would you care to comment, NS?

Yes, ZA. I made no errors in this POC of the gravity of those in the other conferences, but I did pull this faux pas here. Truthfully, I was impressed with the Social Studies chart on the rear wall and with the fact that the boys were seeing and using the connection between its contents and the task AC assigned them. I should have found room in the Discussion to give AC positive feedback on both items instead of implying it in the Retelling. AC missed the positive-feedback-meaning of my remarks. She saw me as including small details in the Retelling, so she added something I (as the other observer) could not have seen: the boy sat all the way up front; I sat all the way in the back.

That raises another question, one we talked about during the music lesson discussion: how detailed should the Retelling be?

My stock answer to that frequently-asked question is: in enough detail so I could visualize what took place if I hadn't been there to observe. The question arises for me very often because I do live and recorded POC's for ZA's and they do recorded POC's for me. In "real" supervision all *you* need, ZA, is enough detail to convince you that the teacher accurately Retells what you observed. With practice you'll arrive at what's comfortable for you.

OK. Then just two more comments on the Retelling. At about 0545 you say you will let AC pick up the Retelling, but then you talk until 0655. Why?

Frankly, I got a little wound up, ZA. I did want to include the material on the board, because it was related to the content of the lesson, but I should have quit right there. The last reason I gave you (p. 266) for using AC's conferences was to demonstrate that supervisors trained (if trained at all) in what I call "the old way" are prone to do most of the talking. I still have the habit, as I'm sure these POC's clearly prove, and am determined to break it.

What hope is there for me, NS, if you haven't reached an acceptable level of supervisory input?

You, ZA, can begin by recording your POC's, whether you're a real supervisor conferring with a teacher, or you're a teacher conferring with a colleague. And while you do so, you have the full array of procedures and rationales I've been elaborating on over so many pages. I had to invent the process for myself and have only recently begun to discipline myself to obey the proper half of the old maxim: Don't do as I do; do as I say. So you're ahead of me in some ways, ZA.

That's a comforting thought, except for those ZA's who've been using "the old way."—But to go on. My last comment on the Retelling is AC's rather pointed reference at 0942 that she clearly communicated the Ss and Rs to her Ks, a point you both elaborate on in the Discussion.

As to the Agenda. You also deliberately refrain from suggesting sample Agenda items (at a few sentences before 1240). At 1531, before re-reading the Agenda to her, AC indicates she was unaware of having slipped into first-person format in the last Agenda statement. Do you have a comment, NS?

First let me say that you're learning to read in between the lines very well, ZA. That's good. As to AC's departure from the format, it's par for the course. Holding one's own efforts at arm's length and doing a 3PS analysis takes more practice than AC had up to this point, especially considering her initial difficulties. She did even better in the remaining two POC's, (which are not included here only because they raised no new issues for you and me to discuss, ZA).

Thank you for the immediate, positive, and specific feedback, NS.—At 1720 you comment on AC's "interesting" and "quite different" Agenda. Am I right in seeing a connection with her revelation (at 2407) that you had asked her to focus on a given PAT unit and that she used the one on Communication in the first sub-head?

After the second POC, I gave AC the PAT for the first time, with only a brief account of what it was. I did ask her to select one unit, to see what would happen. The result was a new kind of Agenda and a modest demonstration of the value of singling out a unit for emphasis in self-analysis. I'd like to say parenthetically here, ZA, that I've deliberately stacked the cards against myself in this series of POC's. Had I used an enthusiastic ZA volunteer, fully briefed on EG, PAT, principles of learning, and with experience in doing my three required recorded POC's, any successes we achieved in demonstrating RAD for this discourse could easily have been attributed to what that ZA was bringing to the conferences. Therefore, the music teacher, AC, and the Open Education teacher whose POC appears next, were all "fresh subjects."

So, yes, the connection you see is really there. And at 1720, I acknowledged, I gave AC immediate, positive feedback; and at 2407 AC felt free enough to change topics and to go directly to this issue, at which point I let her be the source of her own feedback, which I then reinforced.

> And now my last two questions about this POC. At 2058 you say you don't have "an all-encompassing answer" to AC's problem of a smooth transition between two tasks. Apart from whether there is an answer or not, which would take us away from the process of RAD and into a content which you won't want to discuss anyway, what would you have done if you did have an answer?

I would have tried to lead AC to it. But that wasn't my concern. I was trying to show AC that traditional whole-class instruction has inherent limitations for which there are no real solutions. To me this was related to the conflict she was going through on her role in the classroom, the most overarching issue of issues in the entire series of POC's. Therefore, I led her back to this issue, asked her whether she had thought about the question I had left her with at POC #2, and ended up with process-vs.-content education.

> That was my last question. When you listed as one of the three major obstacles the issue of role, had you already determined where you were going to lead her?

No, ZA. I make no such specific commitments in advance. I am not purely a reflecting mirror in that I do have strong commitments to certain philosophic positions, of which I've already told you much more than you probably want to hear. But the specifics of what I do depend on what steps the teacher seems ready to take. AC isn't ready to give up on her responsibility "to cover" the subject matter content. But she is open enough to test a new approach intellectually while still married emotionally to another approach. So I offered her a way: what would two contrasting students be able to do after a year with AC? She offered a "process" outcome, which opened the door to "process education." And what I said to her was hardly an on-the-spot invention.

Way, way back, on page 20, I said to you: "*IF, and that's the single most significant IF in this business,* if schools and colleges *do have* goals for students—goals translated into curricula and courses-of-study —then teachers must have designs for teaching, or else anything goes." I see this as the absolutely central issue in all schooling. There's no rational way for opting between one methodology and another; there's no way teachers can be held accountable; and there's no way to implement the current hobby horse (competency-based teacher education, CBTE; or performance-based teacher education, PBTE) unless we agree on the goals of schooling. Yes, the principles of learning emphasize individualization of instruction over and over again. To me that carries as little weight as the observation that kids should begin learning a foreign language in elementary school, because the earlier you begin . . . etc., etc. What if a society is determined to suppress individuality? (I don't see that the do-your-own-thing philosophy has exactly led to social responsibility, justice, equity, and so on.)

Now don't misread me, ZA. I can't make the *teacher's* central goal intellectual-aesthetic development and simultaneously favor the suppression of individuality. That would be sheer madness! But that *I've* made up *my* mind on *my teacher's* central role is hardly of much consequence on even a local-district scene, let alone a national one.

So, I arrived at a neutral definition of teaching and simultaneously claim that principles of learning apply equally to every member of the homo sapiens family. There is encyclopedic knowledge in the world. What anyone suggests for emphasis is a suggestion, not a scientific commandment . . . etc., etc., etc. We went through all that for openers.

Therefore, a teacher's role depends on the goals set up for the students. I don't see school leaders doing such a bang-up job of defining the goals of instruction. Until, and if ever, they do, I'm for intellectual-aesthetic development, which is *process,* not content, education, and I will assess instruction both to see that it's consonant with principles of learning and that its efforts are rationally aimed and guided.

Finally, therefore, what I said to AC was not an on-the-spot invention. It came from the very core of my being as a teacher.

XV.

Open Education Post-Observation Conference

You'll need just a few words of explanation before reading my notes and the POC itself:

1. Dawn H. teaches in a school housed in what was originally a commercial building. One remnant of that era is a sealed freight elevator shaft. As I came in, two Ks were painting on the bolted doors to that shaft.

2. Dawn's classroom is located off a large area, used by a number of classes, an area she calls "outside" in the POC.

3. The school is fully air-conditioned. There is carpeting all over the building. But Dawn's room has no windows. Its setup differs from the traditional classroom, but she does have a desk, and there are two tables for small-group instruction, plus a corner with pillows, one wall of blackboard, and a number of bookshelves and storage cabinets.

4. I had visited Dawn once before this POC, to ascertain that she was in an OE program and that she would cooperate in doing the POC. At that time I did tell her, rather sketchily, what RAD was about, but I said nothing about EG, PAT, "strands," etc.

5. On the day of the POC I came at 0845, the arrival time for the Ks, and stayed until about 1110, when her student teacher took the Ks to the library. Then Dawn and I conferred.

6. It's purely coincidental that teacher AC had a combination 5-6 class, and that DH has a 2-3 class. I've already told you how I came to choose AC, the only one of all the teachers in our discourse that I actually selected. DH was made available, then made herself available to me. As you'll see, she was an excellent subject.

So here is the transcription of my notes, followed by the POC.

	Dawn H	25 Ks
	P.S. . . . . Rm.	
	Class 2-3 Combination	5/–/7-

0845 Some Ks have already arrived and are doing some socializing. Two are painting on an elevator door in a room adjacent to the classroom. (*Ks call her Dawn.*) As Ks arrive, I copy the blackboard material. (See the next page, ZA.)

55 More Ks have arrived. T is discussing things with individual Ks. Tells K his plan won't take two hours to complete. Two Ks are in pillow corner doing some writing. Now six Ks are seated in four different locations in the room doing some writing. T discusses work with one of them.

0904 Three Ks check their plans with the T. 'It's nine o'clock, so I want to meet,' T announces. She asks a K to ring the bell. K does so. Ks assemble on floor in center of the room facing T's desk. T asks Ks about some kind of notes and some paper, which sends a few Ks looking for the items. (*Is this their planning session?*)

07 T calls attention to the need to have spelling words in by the afternoon. Book orders are discussed.

09 T asks them for a place to keep certain papers. K suggests a spot, which T accepts. She reads Joe's topic to the class, after asking him for permission. There is some laughter during a discussion on the elimination of human wastes. T wants to go on, but Ks are still embarrassed and are in a laughing spree. T stops and they stop. T completes reading the plan.

12 Some Ks wanted to work on the telephone. T says the IPI's are ready to be worked on. She mentions the need to care for plants.

13 Last reminder about museum things needing illustration. The class will have two classes visit them on Friday to whom they will have to read something. T will bring a camera.–T changes the topic to homophones. She goes over board panel #1 with the whole group. (*She says that DO, DUE, DEW sound alike.*) K defines DEW. T enters definition on board. T now says that DEW is not a true homophone for the other two. Elicits definition of DUE, then DO.

20 Deals with BORED, BOARD in the same way. Ks suggest ideas on their meaning. (*T not ready herself with definitions, suggesting examples of usage instead.*)

23 Now deals with HORSE, HOARSE. (*Is there no dictionary available?*)

24 COARSE, COURSE.

27 Still discussing last two words. Some Ks suggest CLOTHES,

Board Work

(1)

due
dew
bored
board
horse
hoarse
coarse
course

(2)

Tuesday, May ___, 197___

Good morning,

Please put your homework in the top bin and give book orders and "picture money" if you have it for me.

Rose will be late this morning. She'll be in by 10:15.

Write your plans for the day immediately. Plan on two hours of work.

Have an industrious day.

Love, DAWN

Remember (3)

*Some museum reports need illustrations.
*Add new homophones to your workbooks.
*Have you worked in IPI, lately?
*Pet people–Sunshine cages need cleaning.
*How are your plants?

(4)

Skill Groups Today

M Dawn	R	Math	Rose	R
Paul	Lucy	Sam		Anita
Pat	Gene	Ralph		Sam
Louise	Paul	Anita		Louise
Lucy	Ralph	Leah		Karl
	Pat			Shari
	Louise			

IF there is time

Blanche
Sam
Emil

CLOSE as homophones. (*All these seem to be words Ks have trouble with in their writing.*) (*T does not deal with differences and variations in the pronunciation of these words.*)

0929 T now announces she wants to work with a math group. Calls for those whose plan books need approval. Other Ks go about their tasks.

32 T still approving a K's plan. (*How does she decide what belongs in each K's plan? How do Ks know what to include?*)

41 T finds notebook on floor. Shows something interesting in it to two Ks.

44 More checking of plans.

47 T and five Ks are now seated at the arc-shaped table doing math. Ks are decoding large numbers.

53 Student teacher arrives. T and Ks in the math group play a game involving the decoding of numbers and some computation.

1000 (I voluntarily involve myself with some Ks who are trying to drill holes in plastic bottles.) T instructs these Ks to get on with their overall job. The math group has now moved its game to the center of the room, on the floor, and more Ks have joined the game. The ST assembles a group. T assists the math group. Now moves the group and its game outside to the larger room so as not to disturb the ST and her group.

07 Two Ks return to the classroom. T tells them to move on to another task. T now assembles a group of just two Ks who are doing long division. They sit at the arc-shaped table.

14 Has Karl move from across the room to the table because he's wasting time where he is.

16 T moves over to help Karl. Tells him what to do. Goes to the large room to check on what the Ks there are doing. Returns. Checks the work of two Ks. Checks another K's work. Goes back to helping Karl. As she works with him, three other Ks are waiting to get her attention for their work.

22 T checks a K's work in math. Explains the task to him. Now there are more Ks waiting to be checked.

27 More checking. (*T shifts gears very often.*)

29 Ks in large outer area do some horsing around. T comes out to check.

32 (*How does T keep track?*)

35 Ks who have been playing the math game on and off, in the outer room, return to the classroom with the game. T has them put it away.

40 T is out in the large room checking on the work being done there.

45 In the outside room I observe two Ks playing. Three others

join them. T comes out to see. Ks stop playing. T checks on the progress of their work.

1048 I return to the classroom. T is sitting on the floor with five Ks, doing a section in "My Weekly Reader." She asks the Ks to read the front and back pages. Four other Ks come along and ask to be given copies. T does so.

55 Ks have read a selection silently. T and Ks discuss it.

1105 T breaks off from this group. Bell has rung so class can go to the library. T: 'OK. Start your comments, please.' Apparently the Ks have to evaluate how they carried out their plans, so T can check them. (*How are these data used?*) Ks are writing.

07 Ks whose comments are checked are to begin cleaning up. T collects the plan books. (*What criteria does she use in checking them?*) T has Ks clean up. Most do so. A few stand around talking. T: 'How many did not get to your wordbooks today?' Some Ks raise their hands. T says she'll give them time this afternoon.

10 T inspects the room. "Looks pretty good." ST takes over. T and I leave for the POC.

Grade 2-3 Open Education POC

NS 0000 What I'd like you to do is to recall this morning's events and to reconstruct them verbally, speaking as though you had been the observer, not the teacher. Try to imagine that you were me and to describe what happened from an observer's point of view.

DH You want me to describe what happened as though I were you, speaking as the observer.

NS Yeh, speaking of yourself in the third person, if possible, as DH, Ms H, or the teacher, she; and, you know, it's a long, long morning, so I don't expect you can recall intimate details, but the general outline of what took place.

DH 0037 OK. The kids came up in bits and drabs. Some of them started, ahm, working on a, on a mural basically on an elevator door. Ah. One of them started to work on his, his daily plan. The teacher told him to start early because he has a difficult time attending to it. Ahm. So Gene started that, pretty much as soon as he came in. Ahm. Then the bulk of the kids came up and (p) many of them read the board, which is what the teacher expects them . . . The teacher expects them all to do that. Those that read the board started, some of them started on their plan immediately and others had to be coaxed and reminded. (0135) Umm. Children put their things away, got their homework out, ah, and got themselves organized, till about nine o'clock, at which time the teacher had the bell rung, so that the kids would know to come and meet. Kids met at the center and sat down, (deep breath) and the teacher gave announcements about reminders of things, uh, shared a, a project proposal that the kids have started to work on, used it as an example to read to the other kids, uh, and then continued a, a unit on homophones, having the kids define them and having the kids discuss what the words mean, and asked that the kids write them in their wordbooks, ah, as reminders, some time during the morning. When the planning meeting broke up, let's see, the kids then were asked to write their plans for the day. They write individual plans, and after they're written they're brought to the teacher. They were brought to the teacher for approval and for discussion. Ahm. After the plan books were approved, most of the kids started their own work. (0203) Ah. The teacher worked with five students on, ah, reading numbers greater than a thousand, and taught them a game to reinforce that. (p) Ahm. The game, (p) the game was, got a little noisy, so she sent, the teacher sent the kids outside to finish the game. Ah. The student teacher had come in, around that time, (NS - Uh-hm.) yes, around that time, and she started working with her reading and math groups. Um. The teacher helped, basically helped kids who came up to her for help, in between working with the kids that were playing the game and helping kids get moving. There was a group of kids that were working on costumes and were having difficulty with it, and they were, they brought it into the room to work on it, but weren't making much progress, and, as it turned out, they had used up most of the time they had allotted for the costumes, working on a problem of getting a hole in plastic. (She laughs.) Um. (0424) (p) Let me recall. Math group. Ahm. (Deep breath.) Then the teacher worked with two kids on, on division, aaannnddd called over another kid who wasn't working well by himself to sit closer to her so that she could keep an eye on him and help him when he got stuck and, you know, help him get on with his work. Ahh. (0502) Also, one of the children came back from the game and wanted to continue his work for the day and the teacher helped him with his math book which he's having difficulty with. Ahm. After the, after . . . after the kids in the math group looked like they were OK for a while, the teacher went out . . . Well, the teacher was going outside periodically to check what was going on out there. Um. (I don't think there's anything special that went on out there.) But, toward the end of the morning she called a reading group, ahm, to meet and read from a news magazine, at which point (spoken with laughter in her voice) it was eleven o'clock and the day was over.

NS Uh-Huh. Alright. Considering that you were pulled in so many
0553 different directions, you recalled very well. Ahm. Is this (NS is hesitant.) a typical kind of morning? With the lesson plans and with the kids writing their comments on them? (DH - Yes, yah.) [A few words of NS are covered up, on the tape, by DH's response.]

DH Yah. The kind of thing that goes on is typical of what may happen
0608 on another day with the, ahm, the gym period interrupting, or, ah, a long term group being pulled out to work (NS - Uh-huh.) like on a play that's been brewing . . . (Teacher's voice fades away.) But the format's the same.

NS Format's the same. OK. We'll come back to that part of it. Now I'm
0632 going to ask you to do the harder thing, which is to still imagine, uh, that you were me and that you were watching and to imagine that you had to somehow arrive at an assessment of how effectively this was going on, and to make, at least initially before we discuss them, some terse, brief, unelaborated statements of how well or perhaps not well at times the whole process worked today. But say them from an outsider's point of view, uh. You see, you as Dawn, the teacher, knew always what happened yesterday. You know what you expect to happen tomorrow. You know what was on your mind, what was on the kids' minds perhaps. I wouldn't know any of that because I wasn't here yesterday. (DH - Yes.) and I won't be here tomorrow, and I'm not Dawn. So try to make these statements as though you were me, looking at them, at this scene, from an outsider's point of view . . .

DH . . . without knowing the progression.

NS . . . without knowing the progression, yes.

DH That's not easy. (Said with laughter in her voice.)

NS No. (DH - Ah.) (p) Well, if you had seen this as a supervisor, what might you feel you would like to comment on, that you would compliment the teacher for or might want to suggest that things be altered in some way? But only make it in brief statements, because we'll come back and take care of the elaborations afterwards.

DH Yah. (p) Um. I would have liked to see, to have seen more structure
0755 for some of the . . . two of the boys and one of the girls, that there were kids (p) who don't function well in this kind of environment and need to be given . . . specifically: do this, do this, and don't get up till you're done.

NS Uh-huh. You can see this as an observer? (DH - long pause) Well, yes, OK. I would agree with . . . (DH - Yes, I think I can.) . . . Karl . . . Go on.

DH Ahm, and Gene. (NS - Uh-huh.) Ah. (p) As a supervisor I would have wanted to see more . . . (P) I don't know. I was going to say, more interaction among the kids in terms of helping each other, (p) in working out problems together. (p)

NS Alright, we'll come back to it.

DH Ahm. (P) I think I . . . that the individualization of activities would
0927 be a strong point. (P) (NS - Uh-huh.) (P) (P) (P) It's hard. (p) It's much easier to be critical as the teacher. (Said with laughter.) 'Cause I am, but . . .

NS You'll get a chance to do that too.

DH OK. (P) (NS - Hm.) (P) (P)

NS Well, there's no set number that I require, Dawn. You can make one
1023 statement, you can make twenty, and I've had people do both. (DH - Yes.) Ah. You've made three, essentially. Uh. If you can't think of any right now, (DH - OK.) as you talk further on, if any others come to mind, we add them. OK. Now from here on in, even though I'll be allowing you to add poi . . ., you know, other items, to this list which I call the Agenda, there are three things you said. I'm going to read them back to you and from here on in we'll just talk directly, without, you know, you're Dawn again, you know, (DH - Uh-huh.) not somebody else (DH - OK.) watching yourself teach. (1058) Now what you said was that you would have preferred to see more structure for at least two of the kids you mentioned by name, perhaps others, and more interaction among the kids along the line of them helping each other and working together, (DH - Uh-huh.) on joint efforts, and, ah, and that individualization of activities, however, you regarded as a strong point in what went on. Umm. (p) (1123) Now, of course, the, the individualization was obviously tied into Gene and Karl's need for more structure. Uh. There's a kind of a, a balance between those two things. On the one hand, you're individualizing; on the other hand, you're saying that for some, that individualization has to have a stopping point in that they can't . . . or are you saying that? You know, what are you saying?

DH Yah. Well, I just feel that, that the work of all the children in the
1155 class has been individualized. (NS - Uh-huh.) A particular need of Gene's and Karl's is that, ah, whereas other children don't have a place to sit, Gene and Karl need their own space and they need, ah, more direction. That's their need; a personal need, as opposed to an academic need. (NS - Uh-huh.) It's a, it's a way that they work better. (NS - Uh-huh.) Their skills are . . . I meet their, their academic needs just as I would meet any other child's academic needs on an individual level, (NS - Uh-huh.) grouping when there's been other kids that need the same thing. And it isn't, it isn't so much academic; it's not that they're particularly behind (NS - Uh-huh.); it's more of a behavioral thing, that, ahm, Paul, Gene, and Karl need centering, need their own space, and they need, they get lost more easily. They need to be reminded by presence, by space, by things, you know, to attend, whereas other children can handle more noise and more freedom; (NS - Uh-huh.) and I've found it very difficult to provide as much structure as they need, their physical structure, the quietness of the room, of the group. (1327) Then again we've had a perfectly quiet room to the point where I was jumpy (Said with laughter.), that I couldn't handle it. Umm. It helped, but it's a strain on everyone, the kind of atmosphere we . . . hopefully kids working and helping each other and playing with each other. There's a certain amount of noise that goes on in the classroom. It's very difficult for

these kids to work with it, so we've compromised. They let us know when it gets out of hand and we, you know, play it by ear. Ah. They're the only children who have their own desks, their own place to sit, to help them with their organization, 'cause they're having trouble losing themselves and losing their books and losing everything. So I've done . . . as much . . . as I really can do, given the kind of teacher I am. My feeling is that they need a different kind of classroom, and that I, at this time, don't really know how to set up a second classroom, that there's just . . .

NS Well, there's just no space for all that, and you have the room you
1431 use and the outside area, (DH - Uh-huh.) which, of course, is a traffic area for other people, and, ah, your room isn't that large that you can give up a corner for just two out of twenty-some-odd kids that you have in your classroom. It's rather difficult.

DH It's a problem.

NS Are you suggesting here that, um, (p) that this, that the informal structure in which you function (although it's formal in many ways), ah, is not for everybody?

DH Oh absolutely! It's not for every teacher, it's not for every child. (NS
1508 - Umm.) Ideally, (DH accents the word and says it with laughter.) I feel a classroom teacher should be able to meet every kid's need, (NS - Umm.) but in reality (Again accented and accompanied with a laugh.) it just doesn't happen. (NS - Uh-huh.) Ah.

NS Why do you feel that "ideally"?

DH (p) Oh. (P) (p) It seems to me that it, uh, that a good teacher should
1532 be able to . . . I mean, if you have twenty-five individuals with twenty-five different needs, and to a large extent a teacher is required to meet these needs. See what I mean? I guess, it's just part of the feeling that a teacher (Said with a laugh.) should be able to do it and that it's my personal lack that I haven't figured out the way. But I know that there are successful open classroom teachers, you know, that are able to deal with, with diverse kinds of children and their needs. (1630) Umm. (NS - You seem to be suggesting that . . .) I just feel that I can't, (With a laugh.) that I'm not at the stage where I can, can cope with many, many different types of children; that this particular kind, the kind that needs superstructure and quiet and requires constant direction from me, ah, is very hard for me to deal with, you know, and . . .

NS And, and you see this as a lack within you?

DH (p) Yah, umm, (NS - How would you feel . . .) Because I've, because I've swallowed this, this idea of what an open classroom teacher is, I think, and I know that there are successful open classroom teachers.

NS What if I . . . You have a combined second and third grade. Your
1721 kids are around seve . . . (DH - Seven, eight, nine.) Uh. Supposing I threw a four-year-old at you? Would you feel obligated to meet the four-year-old's needs?

DH I was teaching first, second, and third grade . . .

NS No, no, no! With these same kids. No, no, no! If I threw a four-year-old in with these sevens, eights, and nines.

DH I don't think being . . . would . . .

NS So why can't you be willing to regard Gene and Karl as kids who
1752 aren't up to, as mature, the level of maturation of the others? In other words . . . (DH - No, no, I see . . .) why are you beating your breast rather than saying that there are limitations on, on the grouping arrangement, that the guilt isn't yours, but the guilt lies in the fact that there aren't enough sections, perhaps, in the school, you know, enough different classes, ah, to accommodate to such kids who are sufficiently different, as a four-year-old would be with your seven-eight-nine-year-olds, (DH - Yeh.) that the fault isn't in your lack of skill or professional competence, but rather in the fact that the grouping arrangement isn't adequate to the situation.

DH (p) Really, that (She laughs.) makes a lot of sense. (DH sounds
1838 relieved.) Yeh.

NS Ah, you know, you may be right. I don't know. I, I, I visited you once before and, and this is the first time I've spent actually watching you, ah. For you to take on a, a guilty conscience for something which may or may not be your fault, or for you to strive to meet an obligation which is not simply idealistic but may be actually unrealistic will always mean that you're going to prescribe failure for Dawn. (p)

DH That happens a lot. I think it happens a lot anyway . . . Teachers in
1907 general (NS - Uh-huh.) . . . I think we see ourselves and we allow parents to see us as being 100 percent responsible for what happens to the child, (NS - Um.) the growth and development, if the child isn't mature enough, it has to do with the fact that . . . or isn't functioning well . . . it has to do with the fact that the teacher is doing something wrong, as opposed to the child, (NS - OK.) something within the child, or some other event's going on. (NS - Uh-huh.) I think we allow that a lot.

NS Well, I'm, I'm suggesting to you that you give it some thought. That
1947 I think that where a teacher is, is at fault, where realistically the teacher has to face that responsibility. When a teacher is likely not to be at fault but takes on the guilt for it and the blame and is really not in a position to do anything about it, ah, then a teacher is always guilty of the fault, but thoroughly frustrated, with no outlet, you know: What should I do next? I don't know what to do. (DH laughs.) Well, the answer is: there's nothing you can do, so there's no reason to feel that way.

DH (p) Yes, but . . . as a mere teacher, you know . . . who am I to say: I
2020 have really explored all possibilities. I mean, I feel it's, it's too easy not to feel that way and say: It's my personal limitation, that there are lots of successful open classroom teachers in many other

situations than a school for our kind of children. Ah. It's very easy to.see it as a, as a personal lack than saying that no one else can do it. Must be possible (DH laughs.), you see.

NS
2101 Yah. It's a difficult line to draw. Of course, it's an easy cop-out to say: It's not my fault, you know. It's a harder thing to say: It's a child's fault. Because the child is so young and how can one escape one's adult responsibilities and say: It's the child . . . must be the child rather than me. So the tendency is to say: It's me. But I think one needs to learn to walk the line, a realistic line, and say: What am I trying to do? To what degree is the, is the difficulty inherent in the situation? Which, which includes the kinds of children that are there, the facilities that are available, the program, and so on. And what, what . . . Since every child brings himself to the situation, what does a different child, any particular child, bring, which may create problems for the rest of us because of the unique baggage that's brought in, that simply doesn't fit. It doesn't belong in any of the cubbyholes, you know; it doesn't sit on a chair properly; it won't fit under a table. You know what I mean? (2202) (DH - Yah.) And to make a realistic assessment of where the difficulty is. Because you see, for as long as you don't resolve the problem, then you're hung up on a, on an issue, and you waste psychic energy saying: Well, it's my fault; I'm not making it work; I can't be a very good teacher, or at least I'm not that good a teacher. Ahm. On the other hand, you may be able to do nothing about it and really have to learn to accept that be able to do nothing about it and really have to learn to accept that that's the situation, and that rather than tying yourself up in a knot and saying: (NS beats his breast as he speaks.) You know, I'm . . . my fault, you beat your breast, I'm doing something wrong. I'm not doing well enough. I'm not as good as some other open classroom teachers. (DH laughs.) You have to look realistically at what's possible and to accept that this is as far as you can go, given the circumstances. So that it really isn't a matter of your competence; it's a matter of the situation. (2257) So that if you have twenty-five (or whatever number of kids you have), you know, twenty-three of whom can, ah, do a great deal of, ah, on their own, through self-direction, and the only thing you said here is that you wish that they would, instead of just going off by themselves, they would assist each other more (and we'll come back to that), uh, there are these two kids who can't do this. Ah. And since you don't sit anchored in a chair, so that you, you know, you can't, can't put 'em on either side of your desk the way a structured classroom teacher can do, ah, then they don't belong or they will get less out of it right now and in time may get more without, you know, your concerning yourself about it.

NS
2354 Ahm. Let's move on to the other one because we'll be rehashing the same thing. You said that you wished that the kids would interact

more with each other, helping each other out in working together on joint efforts . . .

DH As opposed to coming directly to the teacher.

NS Oh, that's not what I . . . Oh, you mean . . .

DH That's the . . .

NS You mean, for them to resolve whether they've done something satisfactorily, whether it's right, or what?

DH Many of the things they go to the teacher, or (NS - To you. You can
2425 say: to you.) Yeh, to me for help, (NS - Uh-huh.) they can really get the same kind of help, the same pats on the back, the same kind of thing from another child, or this is what we would have done or tried to do.

NS Does it have the same meaning, though?

DH (p) Ahm. (P) Not in all cases, no. But in many . . . many areas, you know, that kids ask: How do you spell this? or: Will you check and see if this problem is correct? or: So-and-so is making noises. Ah. (p)

NS If you had to . . . If I knew your roster of students; not just by
2525 name, but really knew who they were, would you be in a position to make a list of all of your kids, ah, in the order, in the rank order of, ah, the most self-sufficient down to the least self-sufficient, so that the most self-sufficient would say: I did this right; I don't have to ask Dawn right now; I'm pretty sure it's right; if not I know whom to ask, ah, and when I get a chance, when I've done all of it, I'll take the whole thing over to her instead of running over for every little thing. Do you have any kids who think that way? (DH nods in assent.) Alright. Now then, could you, if you had to, make such a list? (DH - Yeh.) Have you ever tried making one? (2614) (DH - No.) Well, you see if (p), if you want someone to perform in a certain way, what, what do you do?

DH Make the ground rules very clear.

NS And then what?

DH And reinforce their doing it.

NS OK. You reinforce the behavior pattern you find acceptable. Here's
2633 a behavior pattern that you'd like some kids to engage in, more so than they have. You want those, for example, who are more self-sufficient to serve in the capacity of an alter-Dawn; and you want others, who are less self-sufficient, to accept them, under certain circumstances, in and within certain parameters, as substitutes till they can get your attention with regard to certain factual things: Is this spelled the right way? Did I do this correctly? My drawing . . . uh, whatever. Ah. So you have two problems: those that are on the low end of the scale need to be reinforced to accept the approval or at least the advice on correctness from others; *their* behavior has to be reinforced to serve that function without threat to themselves because they're displacing you (which can also be a threat to such young children). And it seems to me that what you . . .

DH We did the first one, but not the second. We made . . . At one of our
2738 class meetings there was a great deal of concern, upset, about the fact that I was . . . The kids felt that I was with Paul and Gene and a few of the other kids too much of the time, too much; there wasn't enough of me to spread around. And the kids said: Why don't we Xerox Dawn? That was their expression. And we did. We made a list of children who could help in the capacity of handwriting and math. These are the kids who really did well enough to help. We made this whole list of people to go to when in need, (NS - Uh-huh.) when I was busy. Ahm.

NS What happened to the list?

DH I don't know. Somehow it disappeared. I think it got covered up.
2819 Ahm . . . I . . .

NS Did you reinforce the list?

DH No, no. That's . . . When I think about it now, (p) I . . . it was . . . it
2825 was, it was a negative thing; that people go, I was irked, but the praise on the other hand for having done it and the positive reinforcement for doing it . . . Another thing was the insistence that I will not answer this kind of question. You really know who you can go to for help, you know. I feel that, that (p) I was working in two directions. I was saying on the one hand: Do it. On the other hand, I continued to answer the questions and be irked and think to myself: Why don't you? But rather than insisting on, you know, and saying: I won't answer this question. You can go to Corinne or Sue.

NS But you see, there are a number of problems involved here. First of
2913 all, I wonder, have you really accepted Xerox copies of you? Junior Xerox copies. That is: Does it really sit well with you, deep inside, that certain seven-eight-nine-year-olds can serve your kind of function on a very temporary basis? That's a question that only you can answer by internal examination. (DH - Yah.) The other point, and the other point is this: When you came in you didn't write a daily lesson plan today. What you wrote on the board is one thing. But you didn't submit a plan to someone else as to how you were going to spend your morning. Right? The kids submitted a plan to you. Each of them had to have your approval. OK, I'm Corinne. (Apparently Corinne is one of the kids who can do these things.) I'm Corinne. You've approved my plan. One of the things I'm going to do is homophones, or heavens knows what. Now here I am, busy doing my thing that I have to do to fulfill my plan, and suddenly up comes Joe Brown or somebody and says: How do you spell so-and-so? Well now, when they interrupt you, you're the teacher; but Corinne has a responsibility *not* to be the teacher, but to be the student who at the time is doing the fulfillment of a lesson plan that she made for Dawn. Now, does her lesson plan contain space for assistance to other students? Does it?

DH I see what you're saying. Yah.–No, it doesn't. It's . . .

NS OK.

DH It's very flexible and, in fact, when we sat down at the end of the
3047 day, I have them add to the lesson plans other things that happen, because we don't expect that the day is going to go as scheduled: I got hung up on this, or I helped so-and-so, to add the things and other ways the time was spent. So there's a sort of an assumption there that this kind of thing will go on. But, in truth, it isn't stated exactly.

NS OK. So if you want what you say you want, that is, if you want
3118 more interaction among the kids, that they're helping each other, working out problems together, you have to reinforce this behavior, ah, on two levels: for those who seek the assistance and those who can offer it; and maybe on a rotating basis. There may be some things that Corinne will need someone else's assistance on, so that you don't get a status, you know, situation going in your classroom. Ahm. You also need to internalize your . . . to look internally at your feelings to see whether you're willing for this to happen, to accept that if Corinne said it was spelled correctly, which is a problem. And the other is to build into the commitments, if everybody is going to write plans every day, to build into their commitments those who will be the Xerox, junior Xerox copies of Dawn, uh, something which indicates their availability, so that if, for example, if homophones were to be reviewed today and the expert on homophones is so-and-so and such-and-such, then that gets built into the lesson plan. If you're doing homophones and I'm busy, why don't you check with Geraldine or somebody. It gets built into Geraldine's plan. See what I mean? (DH - Yes.) But you haven't structured this into the situation so that it . . . and you haven't continually reinforced it, (DH - Right.) and therefore it's not going to happen until you do reinforce it. (DH - Uh-huh.) OK? (DH - Yes.) (3300)

My first question has to do with what your major obstacle was (or obstacles were). But, in imitation of you, NS, first a prelude.

You supply no details on DH's interaction with the two math groups and the one reading group, and with individual Ks. But the segment from about 0914 to 0929 in your notes, when the whole class is assembled, gets the most detailed treatment plus a total of five parenthetical comments. You seem rather deliberately to be suggesting that in 2 hours and 25 minutes of observation you focused most on whole-class instruction. Yet I'm sure there's a better explanation.

Yes, there is, ZA. Open Education is very oriented to small-group and individual instruction. There's also a tendency for any visitor to get pulled by the kids into what's going on, and I succumbed at one point because I'm somewhat handy with tools and the kids who were trying to make holes in plastic bottles were so obviously in need of help. But I had told Dawn that I wanted to stay aloof and she introduced me, when they assembled, in a manner to suggest that I not be involved, and I wasn't.

I also didn't want to have a distorting impact during a first (and only) observation. So I never sat close enough to small-group instruction to record details, nor (of course) did I dog DH's heels to listen in on her interactions with individual Ks.

But the 0914-0929 segment was conducted like a traditional whole-class lesson, so I could hear and see it in full. Ergo, the detailed notes.

Well, then, since you had the closest look at this time segment and made the largest number of parenthetical comments about it, was this your major obstacle?

No, ZA, and here's why. I made 13 parenthetical notations, which are regrouped here under headings I've just invented, to simplify reference to them.

1. *First Name Basis*
   a. "Ks call her Dawn."
2. *Class Assembly*
   a. "Is this their planning session?"
3. *Homophones*
   a. "She says that DO, DUE, DEW sound alike."
   b. "T not ready herself with definitions, suggesting examples of usage instead."
   c. "Is there no dictionary available?"
   d. "All these seem to be words Ks have trouble with in their writing."
   e. "T does not deal with differences and variations in the pronunciation of these words."
4. *Daily Plans*
   a. "How does she decide what belongs in each K's plan?"
   b. "How do Ks know what to include?"

c. "How are these data used?"
d. "What criteria does she use in checking them?"

5. *DH's Flexibility*
a. "T shifts gears very often."
b. "How does T keep track?"

That doesn't mean that I somehow managed to observe Dawn and her Ks, to make notes and parenthetical comments, apply the PAT, and go through an intense internal dialogue on what my major obstacles would be. No. That would have been impossible. What I did arrive at was an informal version of the "headings I just invented" and decided that my candidates for major obstacle, in that order, could be Daily Plans, DH's Flexibility, First Name Basis, Homophones, and Class Assembly.

That's a rather unexpected ranking, NS. But let's see if I can find my own road to the answer. When you first explained the RAD cycle and stressed the need to select one or no more than two major obstacles, you emphasized that the choice must fall on something you called an overarching factor which could apply to many lessons. If I apply that notion to your list of candidates, I should arrive at an answer.

Very good, ZA. Go ahead.

Then the answer is obvious, yet just a bit confusing. "3. Homophones" is the most specific candidate. If I understand the total import of your five comments, the obstacle here is Scholarship, though dealing with homophones as particularly as these comments suggest would not be so overarching a factor. But if so, why isn't it last among your candidates, or if the issue is Scholarship, your most important unit in the PAT, why isn't it first?

All five headings are candidates for major obstacle. But there's a logic to my rankings. In reverse order, *Class Assembly* is surely a routine, daily affair, as indicated by the instructions to have the bell rung. But I saw only one sample of this daily activity. In fact, I wasn't sure that she meant it to be a planning meeting until she so identified it, a few sentences after 0135 in the POC.

Let me interrupt you, please. Supposing Dawn had said, at 0904 of your notes: "It's nine o'clock, so let's have our planning meeting." (instead of '. . . so I want to meet.') Would that have changed anything, NS?

No, ZA. I assumed it *was* a planning meeting. What I said in my head was: Is *this* (?!) their *planning* (?!) session? In other words, I saw it as an *attempt* at such an event, but concluded that it didn't meet my criteria for such an appellation.

> If I ask you the obvious question (Why not?), I suspect you'll give me a brief lecture on planning, maybe with some dictionary references thrown in, but this time I boxed myself in. So: Why not, NS?

I will try to be brief, ZA, but I do need to refer to my dictionary again. "*Plan* refers to any detailed method, formulated beforehand, for doing or making something." Which tells us nothing at all about who the *planners* are, should be, or must be. However, my prejudice says that when a teacher assembles a whole class for a "planning meeting," especially with Ks who write individual daily plans, why then *both* teacher *and* Ks are the planners. Yet look at what happens during this event:

1. DH asks for some notes and some papers.
2. DH calls attention to the spelling words which must be submitted by that afternoon.
3. Book orders are *discussed.*
4. DH asks for a place for certain papers, and accepts one K's idea.
5. DH reads Joe's proposal to the class despite their embarrassment at part of its contents.
6. *Some* Ks say they want to work on the telephone.
7. DH says that the IPI's are ready to be worked on.
8. DH says that the plants need care.
9. DH announces a last reminder about illustrations.
10. DH announces a visit by two classes.

So, Dawn, in addition to her instructions in Panels 2, 3, and 4 on the board, initiates eight of the ten items in this "planning meeting." The Ks initiate just one, #6, and both teacher and Ks discuss book orders. And, oh yes, in #4 she accepts one K's idea about where to house certain papers.—Which hardly merits my calling it a "planning meeting."

What stirs up my prejudice, ZA, is that I've seen altogether too many traditional (mostly elementary school) teachers, who apparently recognize that pupil-teacher planning is a "good thing" to be doing, who put a list of the day's activities on the board, who read or have the list read aloud by a pupil, and who then seem to be satisfied that they've done their duty and earned some self-awarded brownie points for the effort.

You reminded me a long, long way back that I want pupils involved in decision-making in the classroom. And I certainly do. To me it's an essential element in intellectual development. But for me to label it "planning meeting" or "pupil-teacher planning," I must see and hear Ks making decisions, plans. Can I get you to agree that that's not what I saw and heard, ZA?

> OK, I concede the point. But since decision-making by students is so important to you, and since Dawn's planning meeting doesn't meet your criteria, why is it your last item on the list of candidates?

Let's review the circumstances under which I observed Dawn. This was going to be my one and only observation. (We had actually established contact months before I finally did come, but a series of events in both our personal and professional lives forced us into numerous postponements.)

When you said you would try to find your own road to an understanding of why the list of major obstacle candidates had the order I gave it, you remembered one of the criteria for the identification of a major obstacle. A second one is that it actually seems to be blocking the teacher's further development. And, thirdly, in a single and only POC the choice has to fall on an item that is not only overarching and a block, but also on one a supervisor can do something about in just one session.

So I had only one sample of planning meetings, much of it given over to whole-class instruction on homophones. And whereas Scholarship was the real issue in the homophones segment, I would be challenging Dawn's scholarship, again on the basis of very little evidence. However, on *Daily Plans, DH's Flexibility,* and *First Name Basis,* I had 2 hours and 15 minutes of evidence. Neither of the last two could qualify as a block. DH seemed to have no problems with being called Dawn by her Ks, and she shifted gears rapidly, apparently able to retain the data she acquired. Both items qualified as "overarching," but neither had the immediacy of being a block.

That leaves *Daily Plans* as the major obstacle. In a first POC, especially when I have no background on a teacher's ways of functioning, I generally choose the most pervasive issue I can find and attempt to have the teacher expand on it during the Discussion. Had Dawn not given me so marvelous and revealing an Agenda, I would have sought a bridge to *Daily Plans,* hoping that her elaboration of how this was done on other days would lead to as intense a Discussion as we actually did have on the two negatives in her own Agenda.

> You keep adding new bits of information on how you operate the RAD cycle, so that I can't be successful in applying what you said before you make your next new revelation.

I admit that I do make new revelations, but surely not in an attempt to keep you from succeeding. I don't have a whole set of do's and don't's about RAD to offer you, ZA, nor would I want to try to overformalize the process. I add new items as the occasion warrants, when the revelation is functional in the given circumstance. What all this confirms once again is the need for a practicum.

> I'm more than convinced about the need for a practicum, but I want this discourse to yield maximum returns. So before we analyze the POC, please explain your views on *First Name Basis* and *Homophones.* The other three I'm clear on.

OK. Here goes.

"1. First Name Basis." The use by Ks of a teacher's first name comes under the "Media" unit, question 87: Is the teacher serving "as a model of mature behavior?" Now, though there are some parents who permit and encourage the use of their first names by their own children, and though I have no Principles of Learning (PoL's) to support my obvious opposition to such behavior, I wonder what the instructional gains are. I also wonder what the rather young DH (a teacher with four years of experience) will do as the older teacher twenty years hence. Dawn is now not quite old enough to be classed as chronological peer to her pupils' parents. In twenty years, if she's still an OE teacher of seven-eight-nine-year-olds, she'll be somewhat older than the parents of those future students. Will she and those (younger) parents be as comfortable about her being "Dawn" then, as her current (and older-than-Dawn) parents may be now? In sum, if we

do something which cuts across the grain of a culture, there ought (at least) to be a gain for the break with that culture. What's that gain? I saw none.

> That's an interesting position you take, NS, though you open yourself up to the label "old fashioned." I don't know, and you seem not to have investigated: how are other teachers in DH's school addressed? And what if she and some younger teachers follow her practice while the older ones insist on the usual titles? I know we're digressing, but the issue piques my curiosity.

The absence of PoL's is some indication of the priority of the issue, though you're as familiar as I am with the practice: superordinates use subordinates' first names; but generally not vice versa. My guess is that even seven-eight-nine-year-olds are aware of this cultural phenomenon. So when a superordinate (a teacher) gives up her last name, she's in effect trying to diminish the social distance between herself and her subordinates (pupils). Before you extend this into a quarrel about their being her subordinates, just recall what I said in the POC: They wrote plans for *her* to check and for *her* to approve; she didn't write plans for *their* approval. She decided when to have the bell rung, when the three different groups would come to her; etc., etc., etc. So that functionally and in incontrovertible reality she was the adult and they were the children. Then why create a fiction by calling her Dawn?

As to *"3. Homophones,"* here's my view: Homophones are words that sound alike but are spelled differently. To declare that two words have such a relationship implies that both conditions are met. My dictionary says that DO rhymes with WHO, and that both DEW and DUE can rhyme with WHO and FEW, in that order. That makes the latter doubly-true homophones, but only for those spellers who consistently rhyme both words with WHO *or* FEW, or who are aware of and sensitive to *both* pronunciations for *both* words. But children who suggest CLOTHES and CLOSE for consideration as homophones, and children who are *not* asked to sound out *both* pronunciations to demonstrate their grasp of the oral criterion for homophones are *not,* in my book, candidates for a study of homophones. What they *do* need is to learn how to spell the words which they can accurately use in terms of what they mean.

> Now I see, even more clearly, why Scholarship is your top priority unit, NS, and that DH is also guilty of improper definition and communication of stimuli and responses. So let's begin with a seriatim discussion of events in the POC.
>
> Dawn responds very, very well to your request for a 3PS Retelling, but her remarks at 0927 puzzle me. She seems to be saying that viewing herself from a teacher's vantage point would have been easier for her than doing so from the supervisor's position, to which you respond with: "You'll get a chance to do that too." So: (1) Why did you instruct her "Well, if you had seen this as a supervisor . . .?" (2) What do you make of her distinction between teacher and supervisor viewpoints? And (3), why did you make a promise (and not keep it, so far as I can see) that "you'll get a chance to do that too"?

At 0740 Dawn responds to my long paragraph of explanation of a 3PS Agenda with "That's not easy," with an embarrassed and uncomfortable laugh, and with a quizzicality my notes don't reflect. So I offer her the alternative, seeing herself as a supervisor might, which leads to her making three Agenda statements.

Your second and third questions bring us back to the High School English lesson, with its grammatical errors. I hoped that she would clarify what sounded like a difference in vantage points (teacher, supervisor) as the POC proceeded. So I made a projection that we would. We didn't. Had we had a continuing relationship and more POC'S, I would have been prepared next time: "Dawn, you've now given me an Agenda. Last time you seemed to distinguish between supervisor and teacher perspectives. If I understood you correctly *then,* are some of *today's* items from one or the other perspective? Or did I misread you?"

I am saying, ZA, that at a single POC, especially the first, some things are as "off course" as the grammatical errors in the English lesson were. I took note of the issue, but it was not germane (at that point in the POC), nor, more importantly, would I have been prepared for dealing with it. So I projected that she would reveal the difference. She didn't. Nor did I finally see that I had missed a significant issue.

What strikes me with greatest impact, NS, is that you protect yourself here, just as you did once or twice with teacher AC: you don't go off in directions new to you (and, in one case, new to AC). The reason seems obvious, but is it?

It's not really a matter of protection, ZA. I'm not trying to shield myself from being drawn into a discussion I don't expect to occur. The whole discourse is surely an indication that I'm not at a loss for words, a fact to which real ZA's can readily attest. In addition, I can fall back rather well (if I say so myself) on the 100 percent reflecting mirror tactic. No. Nor am I protecting the teacher from unexplored possibly treacherous terrain. In parliamentary terms, we'd be "out of order"; there's "a motion on the floor" and those who get the floor must discuss the motion. I'm trying to teach teachers, and current and prospective supervisors an ordered arrangement of three events, each to be lived through according to its own rules. So we must do it uniformly and consistently. Since I can (as I demonstrated above) easily get at the new issue next time, in a controlled fashion (when the major obstacle may well turn out to be the teacher's perception of supervisor vs. teacher views, a perception antithetical to both EG and PAT), there's no point in an unplanned exploration "today."

You sound as though I touched a tender spot. But your response is most instructive. Thank you.

Back to the POC. I can see why (at about 0800) you hesitated about accepting her first Agenda item as one with 3PS content and why you changed your mind. Apparently you were aware of only one boy who needed this treatment, not "two of the boys and one of the girls." Which is probably why we get mention of Gene and Karl, but not of any girl. Yes?

You read it most accurately, ZA. But also note this: In the third, fourth, and fifth sentences of the very opening of her Retelling, she identified Gene as a child who needs to be told "to start early (on his daily plan) because he has a difficult time attending to it." Contrast this with the fact that I made an observation within a few weeks of the end of the school year, and keep this fact in mind when our "seriatim discussion of events in the POC" reaches the first item in her Agenda.

I see what you're leading up to, so we'll table the item until then. But there's a new procedural development here, NS. At about 1023 you seem to be saying that though the 3PS format ceases after you reread the Agenda, you will allow her to add more items. The point you hint at but don't clarify is this: if DH had wanted to add items to A during D, would you have insisted on both 3PS content *and* form?

I think you just want to hear me say it; you know the answer: Yes, in both content *and* form. Why? Because I'd really rather not have any items added during D. In a real "real" situation, where I'd be using RAD with teachers trained in PoL's, EG, and PAT, (about which Dawn heard nothing from me) I would expect the teacher to have come to the POC *after* having applied the PAT to herself, so her Agenda would not need to be carried over into D.

That's a new one, NS. You've never said that before.

Yes, it's a new one, ZA, but a totally predictable one. In a real "real" situation, where I'm truly training teachers in both of my strands, I would expect teachers more and more to do most, if not all, of RAD as a monologue. As I conduct RAD POC's, I'm as responsible for consonance with EG and PAT as any teacher with whom I confer. In order for me to live up to the demands of the Evaluation sub-head, I must ultimately do the equivalent of listening in on an attempt by the teacher to apply all of RAD to herself/himself. And to be a 100 percent student in my "school," you must end up applying RAD successfully to yourself. Ergo, training must be strict and disciplined. R, A, and D each serve different purposes and must be carried through according to their unique requirements.

Beginners (like Dawn, AC, and the music teacher) *may*, if they have to, put some of A into D, but only as beginners.

I did know the simple answer, "yes," but not the rest of it. Of course, it's in your usual logical style, but I probably couldn't have made the total projection myself. So let's move on.

At 1155 in the POC, Dawn launches into a long explanation of the unique needs of Gene and Karl, which leads to your suggestion (at 1752) that she not feel guilty about a situation which is not, or may not be of her own making. I don't see why you were so ready to absolve Dawn of guilt. I'm taking you at your word that your first visit to the school and to Dawn was purely procedural and that you did not then make any other judgment except that she was an OE teacher who was ready to do a POC with you. Weren't you going out on a very uncharted limb?

Not really, ZA. Just listen again to Dawn, as I paraphrase her statements. She took particular note of Gene at the very start of the Retelling. She didn't have to. She was responding to other Ks at that time and could as easily have made a more specific statement about the mural painters or other children and their individual activities. She didn't. She was alert to Gene's needs, and so late in the school year at that.

Then, as she explained the Gene-Karl difficulties, beginning at 1155, she was very perceptive. "They need to be reminded by presence, by space, by things . . .," and there had been much effort expended to meet the special requirements of this rather small fraction of the total class. The majority even agreed to curtail itself in different ways just to meet these few of their peers more than half way.

On top of all that there was Dawn's reaction to being pulled in so many different directions by different children. She was more than simply patient. The word "patient" has the "grin and bear it" feeling about it, for me. Dawn neither grinned nor bore it. She was vital at all times. How could I not grant her a kind of absolution?

When I did so, ZA, you might recognize an unvoiced, hidden agenda of mine, on which I've already expatiated in great detail: the "whole child" issue. When I got her to expand at (1532) on her "I feel a classroom teacher should be able to meet every kid's need, . . ." (at about 1510), I was really discussing that very issue. Which is why I asked her what she would do if "I threw a four-year-old at you?" Do you still see me climbing out on an uncharted limb, ZA?

I guess not. As you've said before, NS, you were responding to a teacher's need. But before we leave this segment of the POC, may we just back up to a little before 1508? !t seems to me you make a parenthetical judgment when you say: ". . . that the informal structure in which you function (although it's formal in many ways) . . ." I'm not questioning your conclusion. There are structured (ergo formal) elements in her classroom: the groups in Panel 4 on the board; the class meeting at nine o'clock; the whole business of writing, executing, and commenting upon the daily plans; etc. Were you trying to point out to Dawn that she was more structured than she seemed to suggest she was?

Exactly, ZA. It was my attempt at providing her with some feedback relative to the Gene-Karl issue. I didn't mean it as a judgment, though it can be read that way. I was implying that even for the majority of the class there was a certain amount of structure, so that the differences between the majority and the minority of the pupils was more quantitative than qualitative. But Dawn was listening to the main issue, my question at that point, and not to the words I've set into parentheses. Or else she agreed and saw no need for comments.

Just one last probe at this matter that you've now labeled "absolution." At 2101 you begin a rather long statement on the issue. You finish it at just before 2354. But you do so by closing the matter without giving Dawn any chance for a response. Why?

That's a good question, ZA. Having heard, transcribed, typed, read, and reread the POC more than once, I could see that my abrupt move to close off one Agenda item and move to another would be a point you might want to challenge.

Let's assume I'm Dawn, but a Dawn who's been through an in-service program with full training in PoL's, EG, PAT, and RAD, and I'm now doing a POC with myself, in my head. There's no one else talking to me, so I'm playing both roles: I did the teaching, but I'm now "supervising" myself. How do I discipline myself to stop rehashing an issue and move on to another one?

If I, NS, the supervisor, don't model for the teacher so important an element for application in that over 90 percent of the time that a Dawn will be alone, where will she learn it?

You've reopened an old kettle of worms again, NS. After persuading me that I must be a non-directive reflecting mirror, you began to chip away at the role.

> When I accused you of doing that, you chided me and said you were merely putting a frame around it. And just a few pages ago you spoke of uniformity and discipline in RAD, because each step has its own rules. Now, when I point to how controlling you were, at this juncture, with Dawn, you have a new rationalization. (I was going to say "alibi.") I must say: you've pretty much lost me, NS.

Let's back up, all the way to the beginning of this "supervisory strand." After I "showed" you the music lesson and the POC, and after you had described what the POC process looked like to you, I devoted some pages to ancient history and ended with a detailed statement about Retelling, Agenda, and Discussion. I provided you with a dual rationale for each step.

The "training" rationale for each step is that a teacher needs ultimately to master accurate, chronological 3PS Retelling; to state an Agenda in brief, unelaborated statements; and to conduct an internalized discussion with an absent supervisor. The "supervision" rationale begins with a Retelling which spells out an agreement between teacher and supervisor on what really did transpire during the observation; continues to a teacher's Agenda, in order to get her/his perceptions; and ends with a Discussion based largely on these perceptions. You're not having difficulty with R and A; only with D.

In order to master the skills involved in carrying on a Discussion with herself, the teacher needs a model of how a supervisor takes her Agenda and converts it into a new insight into her and her students' instructional behaviors. Part of that re-direction (which is an active, not a passive, function) must obviously include the discipline of ceasing to beat a dead horse and moving on to another part of the Agenda.

All this may well be a product of my own experiences, and those of many of my students, where "supervisors" (?) operated rather uniformly on the basis of "five goods and five bads." You had to receive *com*mendations for successful efforts and *recom*mendations (meaning suggestions) from the supervisor's presumably large repertory of ideas about "good things to do." That made the supervisor not only active, but gave him license to engage in monologues with an audience of one at each POC, if there was a

POC. All too often the aftermath of a so-called "formal observation" was a written report, in multiple copies, detailing the "goods" and the "bads."

I want to reverse roles: the teacher is licensed to do as much talking as possible, because he'll do all of it in that over 90 percent of the time. But, in order to do so, effectively, he needs a model. So it's not a question of "control," but a need to model the new response pattern the teacher is to take on. The longer you'll meet with a given teacher, overy many POC's, the less modeling you will do.–Have I found you again, ZA?

> I think so, NS, but whereas you have a compass in your head, I can still barely make out the dial and pointer on mine. But let's move on.
>
> At 2354 in the POC you pick up her second negative point and misunderstand it at first (which I found very reassuring). However, you regain your footing and presumably "model" for DH a long analysis of the issue she's raised, leading into a projection of what she might have done, half of which, it turns out, she actually did. And after she explains how the list got covered up, you begin a new analysis of "a number of problems involved here." You state the first problem as a question, and restate it, again as a question: "Does it really sit well with you, deep inside, that certain seven-eight-nine-year-olds can serve your kind of function on a very temporary basis?" Dawn's response is "Yah." Which at least shows that she was following you, but "yah" doesn't tell me what her detailed response might have been. I don't know whether she's answering your question in the affirmative or acknowledging the preceding sentence: "That's a question that only you can answer by internal examination." Couldn't you have stopped and said something like: "Dawn, to which of my sentences are you responding?" and given her a chance to see whether she even wanted to address herself to the issue?

Yes, I could have, ZA, but to what avail? Had it sat well with Dawn that some of her immature second-third-graders could be Junior Xerox copies of her, would she have struggled with herself about carrying out that policy?

DH 2825 No, no. That's . . . When I think about it now, (p) I . . . it was . . . it was, it was a negative thing; that people go, I was irked but the praise on the other hand for having done it and the positive reinforcement for doing it . . . Another thing was the insistence that I will not answer this kind of question. You really know who you can go to for help, you know. I feel that, that, (p) I was working in two directions. I was saying on the one hand: Do it. On the other hand, I continued to answer the questions and be irked and think to myself: Why don't you? But rather than insisting on, you know, and saying: I won't answer this question. You can go to Corinne or Sue.

Would she have allowed the list to: "Somehow it disappeared. I think it got covered up."?

So she'd already answered my question. I *knew* the answer. I was suggesting that she knew that I knew. I only wanted her to see how obvious the answer was. Pausing, and thus creating an opportunity for her to answer, or asking her the kind of question you suggest, would have inflicted emotional pain on Dawn: It's as clear as the nose on your face, DH. How come you couldn't see it? You really *don't* want Junior Xerox copies of Dawn, do you?

What I hoped I was doing was deepening DH's insight. Just how much I accomplished I'll probably never know, unless Dawn invites me to do more POC's with her.

* * *

ZA, before we conclude our discourse, I need to insert a parenthetical comment: Each teacher whose exact words we've discussed read both the transcription of her/his lessons/POC's *plus* the discussion you and I had about them. And each teacher gave me written permission to quote the material.

Teacher AC needed additional elucidation on why I had singled out a particular "major obstacle" in one of her POC's, though she and I never dealt with it. Only you and I, ZA, did in the discourse. Teacher DH, with whom I did not raise "planning meeting" as a POC issue, told me that her reference to it by that title was her error: planning was on an individual basis by that time of the school year and she should have referred to it as the "morning meeting," whose purpose was *not* planning.

The implication of both items is: Had AC and DH known what was on my mind, AC could have contested my reservations on that "major obstacle" and DH could have straightened me out on "planning meeting." Obviously, neither event could have occurred had they not read their portions of the manuscript. In real-life supervision, a second visit to DH could well have yielded "morning meeting," which would have caused me to ask how that contrasted with "planning meeting," and the issue would have been clarified. By analogy you can project a similar resolution in AC's case.

XVI.

Coda

I've paused once again, NS, since your last words on the conference with Dawn, paused to bring together a question I've been formulating for some time. It goes like this:

- If *I* am AC's real supervisor, will she tell *me,* as she told *you* that she's unclear about her role in the classroom?
- Would your music teacher admit to *her* department chairman that she was generally guilty of doing what comes naturally to her?
- Would a DH admit to her *principal* her problems with Gene and Karl?
- And would that principal assume, as you did, that the fault might lie in the very class organization he, no doubt, created or at least allowed to come into being?

In other words, if *you* NS, were a "real" supervisor, would you be able to elicit from your teachers the kind of precious and personal material JG, AC, and DH gave you in these five POC's?

You're raising a very large issue, ZA, to which I know no answer—an issue which some of my students and I have wrestled with from time to time. And it goes like this:

All schools are headed by some kind of administrative officer. Whereas the title may not always be "principal," the person who functions under that title generally does no classroom teaching, except in very small schools with teaching-principals. Larger institutions will have one or more assistant principals, while secondary institutions will also have some number of department chairmen. As you and I both know, these officers devote their non-teaching time to a variety of administrative matters which I need hardly enumerate. Suffice it to say, they give over but a small portion of their time to the combination of Cogan's "clinical" and "general" supervision. They don't devote even one hour per week to each teacher, let alone the three to four hours Cogan suggests for clinical supervision alone.

And yet the very reason schools exist is to provide education for students, using teachers as the delivery system. But that very delivery system, those teachers, come to their positions only partially prepared for their manifold responsibilities, having had no more than a semester or a year (and only the minority have a full year) of student teaching, where they were rarely, if ever, totally and absolutely responsible for a class of learners. So their first year or two are spent "learning on the kids" what they didn't know in the first place.

Furthermore, even advanced performers (in music, the theatre, athletics, etc.) either have or can hire coaches, managers, teachers, etc., or use audio and/or video recordings to get feedback on their performances. Teachers, on the other hand, are alone with students over 90 percent of the time, and rarely get even audio or video feedback.

The problem is complicated, as your questions suggest, even for that administrator who manages to divide his non-teaching time equally between administration and supervision. Within his power is the authority to assess, rate, or evaluate staff, and to recommend reappointment and/or tenure. He can also get you a better room, a more convenient schedule, a less troublesome group of students, a leg up to an administrative appointment, etc. Is it realistic to expect such functionaries to become clinical supervisors whom teachers will trust with precious and personal material, especially if there is a tight job market and the teacher doesn't have tenure?

Cogan's solution is to have available the services of *collateral personnel* in addition to titular administrators/supervisors. Aside from the factor of cost, that solution raises a new problem. If you separate those who do clinical supervision (who may be expected to establish open relationships with teachers) from administrators (who retain the authority to hire and fire), what data will the latter have for effective decision-making if they don't personally observe teachers in their classrooms?

So let them observe, you say. Let them make unannounced 5-10 minute "quickies" plus 2-3 "formal observations" each year. Well, you know how that works as well as I do, ZA. The word goes around the school very fast that the boss is on the prowl, doing "quickies." And, in "formal observations," teachers "put on a show" because so much is at stake.

Well then, if there are clinical supervisors, let them tell the principals what they've learned from that precious and personal material they're so good at eliciting.—And, again, you know what the consequences would be: teachers would clam up as soon as what they had confided as a weakness became the basis for a principal's rating.

Then why this long discourse about a seemingly insoluble problem? you ask.

For the simple reason that teaching needs improvement, that we have the knowledge and skills for doing so, and that learners and teachers alike will benefit from such efforts.

At the very beginning, in chapter II, I derived a series of five questions. I responded to the first three as a prelude to the last two.

The material on the "analysis strand" is my response to: *IV. Is it possible to define manners of teaching which result in movement towards goals and in an "increase in value . . ."?*

The "supervisory strand" material addressed itself to the first part of: *V. By means of what techniques does one oversee, direct, guide, etc., the teachers?*

In this Coda we've just been wrestling with: *Who uses these techniques? Why?*

I would like to see all functionaries with supervisory responsibilities use my techniques, because none of them can provide as much as 10 percent supervision for the classroom teacher. But I'd like, most of all, to have teachers master principles of learning, EG, PAT, and RAD, so that they would be able to *supervise themselves* and, perhaps, each other.

> You leave yourself open, NS, to one final question. Does your experience indicate that teachers can master both of your strands?

I can answer, without hesitation, that PoL's (Principles of Learning), EG (Empirical Grid), and PAT (Primitive Assessment Tool) are no problem. Most of my ZA's are still teachers when they come to me, so I speak from experience. They also get a conceptual grasp of RAD (Retelling-Agenda-Discussion), but two or three practice POC's (Post-Observation Conference) yield truly positive results only for those students with relevant backgrounds. What I must confess I don't yet know is whether teachers can apply RAD to themselves. Logically, I see no problem. Experientially, I was led into this whole business by those student teachers who wanted to analyze their own videotaped performances. What I lack is an accumulation of data to support my convictions.

Maybe you can help me acquire those data, ZA.

Index to Empirical Grid: Principles of Learning

Index